A History of Television News Parody in America

A History of Television News Parody in America

Nothing but the Truthiness

Curt Hersey

LEXINGTON BOOKS
Lanham • Boulder • New York • London

Published by Lexington Books
An imprint of The Rowman & Littlefield Publishing Group, Inc.
4501 Forbes Boulevard, Suite 200, Lanham, Maryland 20706
www.rowman.com

86-90 Paul Street, London EC2A 4NE, United Kingdom

Copyright © 2022 by The Rowman & Littlefield Publishing Group, Inc.

Parts of Chapter 2 previously appeared as "NBC's *That Was The Week That Was* as Proto-News Parody in the Network Era," *Historical Journal of Film, Radio and Television*, 38, no. 3 (2018), 603-621. © IAMHIST, reprinted by permission of Informa UK Limited, trading as Taylor & Francis Group, www.tandfonline.com on behalf of IAMHIST.

All rights reserved. No part of this book may be reproduced in any form or by any electronic or mechanical means, including information storage and retrieval systems, without written permission from the publisher, except by a reviewer who may quote passages in a review.

British Library Cataloguing in Publication Information Available

Library of Congress Cataloging-in-Publication Data Available

ISBN 9781793637789 (cloth) | ISBN 9781793637802 (paper) | ISBN 9781793637796 (electronic)

To Karen and Griffin
for laughing with (and sometimes at) me

Contents

Acknowledgments		ix
1	Tell Me Again about the Rabbit, John	1
2	That Was the Decade That Was: The 1960s and the Limits of Network News Parody	13
3	"Weekend Update": Moving News Parody to Late Night	47
4	News Parody in the Multichannel Era: HBO's *Not Necessarily the News*	89
5	*The Daily Show* in the 1990s: From Kilborn to Stewart	125
6	Stewart and Colbert in the Post-Network Era	157
7	Passing the Torch in the 2010s: A New Generation of News Parody Anchors	199
8	News Parody Moving Forward	251
Bibliography		261
Index		273
About the Author		285

Acknowledgments

Over the years I spent working on this book, I was assisted and supported by many friends and colleagues. Some directly impacted this book through feedback and conversations; others enriched my life when I was not writing. All of them helped me complete this project.

This book is an outgrowth of dissertation work begun when I was a graduate student at Georgia State University. I am indebted to my committee chair, Ted Friedman, for his guidance, encouragement, and quite a bit of patience during the process. Thanks also to the rest of my committee for their help and support: To Kathy Fuller-Seeley for her invaluable expertise in media historiography, as well as her unfailing positivity and humor, to Jason Mittell for challenging me to think through genre, to Alisa Perren for providing much-needed perspective on the media industry, and to Leonard Teel for sharing his vast knowledge of journalism history.

I received financial support to travel and research at various libraries and archives thanks to grants from Berry College, as well as funding from my former department chair, Bob Frank, and dean, Tom Kennedy. While at those archives, I was assisted by incredibly helpful professionals. Richard Holbrook and Richard Weigle at Paley Center for Media facilitated the viewing of several shows from the collection. Julie Graham at the UCLA Performing Arts Special Collection helped me access their HBO scripts. The staff at the UCLA Instructional Media Laboratory transferred old programs from their video archives for me to view. The New York Library for the Performing Arts staff assisted me in accessing the scripts, communication, and production materials in the Leland Hayward papers. Lastly, thanks to my friend Jen Nydick for housing me in New York City while I was visiting different archives.

Heartfelt gratitude to my Berry College Communication Department family: my colleagues and students, past and present. You could not ask for a more supportive, collegial group. Special thanks to Brian Carroll for his sage publishing advice and frequent feedback, as well as Kevin Kleine for his help in editing photos, and Haley Richards for assisting me in indexing the book.

In addition to watching many of these shows with me while growing up, my brother, Scott, also proofread the entire manuscript and frequently challenged me on some of my viewpoints—asserting an older brother's privilege. Jessie Tepper with Lexington Books offered fantastic assistance and feedback throughout the process. Thanks to my good friend and former newsroom colleague Dan Bevels for regularly arguing about and discussing partisanship in the media with me and generally offering a wonderful sounding board. I also want to recognize and thank my undergraduate advisor, Daniel A. Panici, for igniting a passion for television studies and showing me you can actually make a living at it.

Completing this project would not have been possible without the love and support of my family. My wife, intellectual partner, and fellow educator Karen helped in ways too numerous to count: talking through ideas, encouraging, inspiring, and challenging me, and helping me find time to write. My son, Griffin, has spent his life with his father watching lots of television, writing, and telling lame jokes—it finally all comes together. Thanks for humoring your dad and bringing me so much joy. Lastly, I have to honor my parents, who are no longer with us. They instilled a love of knowledge and indulged my love of television—probably not foreseeing how the two would meet.

Chapter 1

Tell Me Again about the Rabbit, John

In 2018, the family of Vice President Mike Pence published a children's book about their family bunny, Marlon Bundo, with proceeds going to charity. The impending release of *Marlon Bundo's a Day in the Life of the Vice President* seemed to predict a typical publicity tour and, with it, the positive buzz for Pence and his family. But, not so fast! The day before publication, the HBO news parody program *Last Week Tonight with John Oliver* (*Last Night*) devoted a 20-minute segment to Pence's dismissively conservative views about gender and his anti-LGBTQ+ rhetoric and policy stances. The show used video clips and quotes to highlight Pence's opposition to antidiscrimination laws, including when he called "homosexuality incompatible with military service." Toward the end of the segment, Oliver called out Pence for visiting the conservative group Focus on the Family on his book tour, sarcastically saying, "Now none of us can enjoy a book about your rabbit! Or, can we?"[1] Oliver then announced that the show was releasing its own book that night: *A Day in the Life of Marlon Bundo*, in which the titular bunny falls in love with another boy rabbit, Wesley. Proceeds were to go to LGBTQ+ charities, Oliver announced. The show was able to subvert the publicity for Pence, and its satirical book even outsold Pence's, becoming number one on Amazon the following day. Dueling books was a somewhat silly stunt by *Last Week* to generate publicity and online views, but a stunt linked to highlighting Pence's socially conservative viewpoints for the show's audience.

The case of the battling bunnies provides an example of how contemporary news parody often serves similar functions as traditional journalism, such as reporting facts and providing context, while also adding humor and a sense of activism. Oliver's report depended upon extensive research and reporting. The story was especially important because it called into question some of the news media's characterization of the vice president as more conventional and reasonable than then-president Donald Trump. *Last Week* is one of the many news parody programs recognized for contributing to American journalism. As early as 2004, young viewers reported getting more news from late-night comedy programs than traditional journalism outlets, igniting spirited debate about and a wave of research on late-night comedy, especially news parody.[2] Editorial pages featured hand-wringing about the ignorance of youth and repeated Neil Postman's admonitions that television could only trivialize the significant.[3] A counter-narrative emerged, celebrating programs like *The Daily Show with Jon Stewart* (*TDS*), claiming they offered more direct criticism of politicians than some traditional news outlets. Overlooked in the debate was the recognition that television news parody and satire had been around for decades, functioning throughout television history as a critique of journalism that both entertained and informed.

This project provides the first book-length history of news parody on American television. Since the 2004 Pew poll, there has been growing interest in the study of contemporary news parody and its political and cultural roles. Several early books and articles made a case for understanding programs like *TDS* as legitimate critiques of news and potential information sources.[4] Recent studies continue to find that viewers can sometimes learn as much about news and politics from these shows as traditional television news.[5] Experiments also continue to confirm an increase in political concern or participation from viewers of these programs.[6] Dannagal Goldthwaite Young has published multiple studies about viewership and learning from late-night comedy and news parody. Her book *Irony and Outrage* directly engages issues of audience partisanship and why viewers of the genre tend to lean more toward the political left. Young makes the fascinating case that political satire such as news parody naturally appeals to more liberal viewers because of their psychological traits. Conservative political opinion shows are a kind of corollary to political satire, engaging the persuasive strategies most appealing to conservatives.[7]

Much of the research about news parody programs like *TDS* has highlighted their positive contributions and potential civic benefits; however, some studies provide more cautionary and critical findings. A primary objection against news parody is that it might make audience members more cynical. Multiple studies from Jody Baumgartner and Jonathan S. Morris connect viewership of the genre with a general cynicism about the political process, more negative views about politicians, confusion over the meaning of ironic presentation, and little difference in political knowledge when compared to viewers of other news sources.[8] Their work warns against framing news parody as some solution to problems of journalism and democracy. Another study found young viewers were more cynical about television news when watching with *TDS*.[9] Extending the accusation of cynicism, other writers have accused programs like *TDS* of tearing down any sense of positive political outcome and reinforcing power structures by joking about them instead of encouraging positive action.[10] Additional research has also questioned the impact of knowledge gained by news parody viewers, finding a negative effect on less-educated and older viewers, as well as more effective learning from traditional journalism.[11]

While engaging such studies of news parody throughout, this book focuses on the genre's rich history that remains underexplored. Three main arguments form the foundation of this history:

1) As parodies, these programs critique the limitations of traditional television newscasts at the time of their production, as well as more general journalism norms and practices.
2) Television news parody constitutes a genre, with past shows influencing current programs.
3) Changes in television news parody correspond to the shifting industrial eras of American television, beginning on networks, branching out to cable, and then utilizing the multiple distribution opportunities of the post-network era.

This study is grounded in the belief that news parody programs are not *just* comedy, somehow removed from journalism and existing merely as entertainment, but also function as a needed corrective and watchdog of journalism. As news parody inhabits the format, presentational style, wording, and news values of television news, the genre critiques these elements. Aspects of the journalistic routine, such as neutral wording, the importance of video, and a reliance on official voices, are called into question by these parody programs. Whether it is *That Was the Week That Was* (*TW3*) in the 1960s inserting a graphic of a literal "dark horse" when talking about presidential candidates or *TDS* creating ridiculous official titles for its reporters, such as Jordan Klepper as the "New Senior Caucasian Correspondent," these programs lampoon the highly structured, mundane aspects of television news.

Pierre Bourdieu's conceptualization of "the journalistic field" offers a helpful structure for understanding the role of news parody within culture. The journalistic field encompasses the routines, practices, and norms of journalism but in a contested space where individuals struggle for position and participation.[12] Through their mimicry of presentational styles and practices and incorporation into the contemporary discourse on journalism, these shows have begun to operate as legitimate contributors within this field. According to Bourdieu, the journalistic field overlaps with the political field as members of both professions interact and sometimes vie for power. As a result, news parody hosts have gained standing to speak on political issues. In discussing each program, I focus on presidential politics to compare political coverage between shows.

Parody in these programs ridicules not only the conventional routines of newsgathering but also the foundation of American twentieth and twenty-first-century journalism: objectivity. The media ecosystem is awash with online outlets generating listicles, aggregating stories from hardworking reporters, and presenting celebrity intrigue for clicks, while professional journalists work against the tide to provide quality reporting without bias. However, some media outlets, especially cable and local television, have incorporated a kind of "vulgar objectivity" that seeks merely to provide two opposing points of view, regardless of the validity of those views. One example would be discussions of vaccines, with reporters inviting vaccine deniers on air and treating their views with as much legitimacy as those of infectious disease scientists. This approach to objectivity has been a frequent target for news parody programs. During the Trump presidency, news outlets questioned whether an "untruth" by a president could be called a "lie" in their coverage, providing fertile ground for humor anchors like Samantha Bee and Trevor Noah to question exactly what journalists *would* call demonstrable lies or willful misinformation.

The second major theme of the book focuses on genre, which continues to be an important lens through which to interrogate and understand media. The shows included in this book mimic the semantics and syntax of television news as part of their presentational style—thus, my use of the term *news parody*. Genre is not only approached through a structuralist lens of similarities between groups of texts but also conceived discursively. Imagining genre through discourse recognizes how culture links texts together by how shows are written about and discussed.[13] The programs included in this book have frequently been compared in popular and scholarly writing, even though they may only share certain elements of news parody. There are also interesting creative overlaps among some of the shows, with writers and personalities on one program later working on another, directly influencing shifts in and evolution of the genre.

Some writers have grouped late-night talk shows with news parody; however, focusing purely on news parody allows for a depth of comparison not only among historic examples of the genre but also with the primary source of their parody: television newscasts. As a referential genre, news parody offers an intriguing example of creators self-consciously attempting to define the elements of a genre in order to play with those features. As a result, news parody programs incorporate the technology and style of newscasts at the time of their production. The network presentation of the 1960s became the local news teams of the 1970s and 1980s, which, in turn, gave way to cable news formats in the 1990s and 2000s.

The last major thread of the book tracks news parody within the shifting eras of American television. NBC struggled with its news parody program *TW3* during the 1960s when advertisers still had major input into programming and an interest in avoiding controversy. Placing *Saturday Night Live* (*SNL*) and its "Weekend Update" segment on late night in the 1970s helped insulate the program against some of these pressures. With the rise of cable and the transition to the multichannel era, HBO was able to create a program free from the pressures of advertisers. The launch of Comedy Central in the 1990s provided an expanded space for news parody, with comedy and controversy included as important promises of the brand. The post-network era has allowed news parody programs to extend their reach beyond television by distributing clips online—segments easily embedded in news articles and shared via social media.

HUMOR AS CRITIQUE

News parody, especially in the twenty-first century, has been discussed primarily as media and political criticism. Humor on these shows is used as a weapon to, among other things, attack the ignorance of politicians, skewer the double-standards of gender expectations, or confront entrenched racism. Sometimes, though, jokes are simply about the absurdity of life or ridiculous advertising strategies. Humor is put to various uses depending on individual shows, different episodes of the same program, or even specific news stories.

In her analysis of twentieth-century humor, Jan Hokenson discusses the "dominant archetypal" and "populist" views of humor.[14] The dominant-archetypal perspective assumes comedy is rooted in social norms and upholds them. We laugh at people who fall outside the norms, feeling superior and reinforcing the status quo. The original 1990s *The Daily Show* with Craig Kilborn took this approach, featuring stories that made fun of odd people and their beliefs, holding them up to ridicule. The populist view utilizes comedy as a tool for social change. James Feibleman, writing about humor as part of a revolutionary principle, claimed "the corrosive effect of humor eats away the solemnity of accepted evaluation," forcing us to reevaluate society.[15] This type of humor, one that questions authority, reflects the dominant perspective of the shows analyzed in this work.

As discussed earlier, some critics have suggested that contemporary news parody fosters cynicism in its viewers or only gives the illusion of critique. Lance Olsen wrote about the rise of postmodern humor in the late twentieth century and its potential for radicalism, an approach certainly embraced by news parody since 2000. While humor can either reinforce social norms or question them, Olsen argues that postmodern humor exists to "disarm pomposity and power" and that its creator "becomes [an] aesthetic and metaphysical terrorist."[16] Postmodern humor is defined by its textual openness. Olsen sees positive and negative aspects of this humor, rather than nihilism, there is an emptiness that, once revealed, can be filled: "While [absences] may signal the possibility of *de*struction, they also signal the possibility for *con*struction, a radical freedom, a renewed sense of potential."[17] Instead of being grounded in an unquestioned Truth, postmodern humor reflects both negative and positive perspectives. Stephen Colbert's use of irony in *The Colbert Report* partakes in this approach, creating multiple layers of humor open to individual audience interpretation.

In evaluating critical uses of humor, Murray Davis offers a compelling approach linking humor to its social and cultural uses.[18] Davis divides humor into four levels of increasing potential for disruption of larger systems. The first level is linguistic humor that occurs due to ambiguous language or word play. Puns, for example, question language systems. The second level is logical humor that links terms through an irrational relationship, causing an audience to question relationships on a higher level. Anthropological humor destabilizes metanarratives by questioning their underlying logic. In one example, Davis discusses how a decrease in religious faith early in the twentieth century resulted in increased jokes about God and angels.[19]

His final level is humor and society, which is the main focus of his writings. Jokes that operate on this level undermine the competency, authority, and compatibility of economics, politics, culture, and other social units. Through this humor, the incongruence of units is revealed, and aspects of society are called to question. News parody operates on all four levels outlined by Davis. One of the major shifts in contemporary news parody is its production of more material on the final, higher level of humor and society.

PARODY, SATIRE, AND IRONY

News parody reflects the sensibility of the populist view of humor through its critique of politics and news events. It also integrates two specific strategies of humor into its format: parody and satire. Satire is humor used to critique in order to illuminate and motivate change. The humor of satire is intimately linked with its purpose. Paul Simpson argues that rather than a genre, satire is best understood as "a discursive practice that does things *to* and *with* genres of discourse."[20] In other words, satire operates across genres as a discursive mode, requiring the audience to connect the work to the external world and general discourse about the satirized subject. For instance, "Weekend Update" reports that then president Gerald Ford created his campaign slogan: "If he's so dumb, how comes he's president?" Viewers access specific knowledge about Ford and his public image as well as knowledge of the norms of campaign advertising to decode the satire. Satire is usually understood as being negative in its intent.

While satire comments *upon* a subject, parody is defined as *imitating* a subject by borrowing from an existing sign system. Margaret Rose, writing on the history of parody, defines it as "the comic refunctioning of preformed linguistic or artistic material."[21] Parody is identified by the style and content of a work and its reception by an audience. Parody creates at least three levels of meaning: signification borrowed from the original parodied source, the creation of its own parodic context, and new meaning forged from a union of the two. The parody of *TDS* is its form and content, altered by the audience connecting it to traditional newscasts.

Rather than viewing parody and satire as discrete categories, many writers have advocated treating the two as overlapping terms.[22] Linda Hutcheon utilizes a Venn diagram to show how parody, irony, and satire are each distinct forms that stand on their own but that often overlap and combine, as well.[23] According to Hutcheon, a parody can be satiric and/or ironic, but it does not *have* to be. Oftentimes news parody engages in these different modes of address. This book uses the term *parody* exclusively to describe texts that imitate other sources and also critically question those texts' norms and construction *through* satire.

One of the most influential contemporary frameworks for discussing the liberatory effects of humor in society is Mikhail Bahktin's concept of the carnival. In medieval Europe, the carnival referred to a specific time of the year when authorities allowed aspects of society to become temporarily inverted; the low were allowed to laugh at the powerful, and even religion was subject to ridiculing humor. Carnival provided an outlet for humor and pleasure during a time of rigid class structure and somber observance. During the carnival, including festivals of misrule and the likes, laws and traditions were subject not only to questioning but also to mockery. The imagination was freed, if only temporarily, to envision alternative social arrangements, and its participants were liberated through role play.

Bahktin identified this same dialogic spirit of carnival in what he calls the carnivalized literary genres, including parody.[24] Just as carnival opened up communication among peoples, "parody is an intentional dialogized hybrid. Within it, languages and styles actively and mutually illuminate one another."[25] Bahktin refers to parody as a "double-voiced discourse," meaning the parody is directed back not only at the original referent but also toward an additional extra-textual discourse. These discourses clash and create openings.[26] Although Bahktin was dismissive of contemporary parody, claiming it possesses a "solely negative character and is deprived of regenerating ambivalence," it should be noted that he was writing in Russia during World War II.[27] Shows like *Full Frontal* and *TDS* partake in the same kind of mocking renewal as that of carnival. Far from nihilistic, news parody suggests an advocacy for journalistic and political renewal and a vigorous and insightful coverage of public policy.

OVERVIEW OF CHAPTERS

This book outlines the history of television news parody in America, moving forward chronologically by decade. Each chapter features an analysis of one primary case study, although additional programs are also discussed.

Chapter 2 focuses on the 1960s and the NBC program *TW3*, which aired from 1963 to 1965. The program foregrounded news parody in its style by utilizing anchors at a desk and imitating the visual production look of network news. Brief news segments would transition to topical sketches or satiric songs and then return to the anchor desk throughout the show. Although debuting with positive reviews and solid viewership, the program quickly bumped up against the limits of political humor in the 1960s. Advertisers complained to the network about skits that outraged certain groups, pressuring producers to tone down the sarcasm, which then brought complaints from viewers wanting a more critical edginess. *TW3* became trapped between a viewership ready for its groundbreaking brand of television humor and an industrial system worried about offending sponsors and politicians.

The launch of *SNL* in 1975 created a successful and enduring space for news parody through its "Weekend Update" segment. Sectioned off by commercial breaks, "Weekend Update" became its own self-contained news parody within the show, innovating on the model of *TW3*. Both a loosening of cultural mores and the shift to late night provided greater latitude for the writers and cast to tackle hot-button political issues. Chapter 3 focuses on the show's first five seasons with the original cast, writing team, and producer. Emerging after the Watergate scandal, "Weekend Update" frequently focused on presidential politics. Its humor reflected the liberal sensibilities of the show's creators and target audience. Caustic coverage of President Gerald Ford from *SNL* helped define his image in American culture before shifting to a more light-hearted satire with the election of Jimmy Carter. As the longest-running example of news parody on American television, subsequent chapters discuss changes in the segment and its fluctuating influence on politics and culture.

The most disruptive force in television moving into the 1980s was the ascent of cable and the dozens of large and small stations created in the early part of the decade. HBO, one of the earliest and most successful cable channels, also became the first to launch a news parody program. Chapter 4 covers *Not Necessarily the News* (*NNTN*), which appeared as part of HBO's first wave of original programming in 1983 and ran until 1990. Like *TW3* before it, *NNTN* used an anchor desk and news parody as a central linking device to connect its skits and commercial parodies; however, its defining feature was the incorporation of readily available satellite newsfeed footage that allowed it to more closely replicate the look of newly emerging cable newscasts. Although *NNTN* was characterized as edgy satire by contemporary media, the program was mostly timid and inoffensive in its humor. The availability of news footage encouraged writers to create visual puns and limited more critical outlooks, despite having carte blanche from HBO to push boundaries. Rather than news parody, the show is better described as news pastiche, playing with the form of television but without much of a critical bite.

Comedy Central launched in the early 1990s as *the* channel for humor series and stand-up comedy. After losing several popular programs, executives launched *The Daily Show* in 1996 with host Craig Kilborn as a new programming centerpiece. Chapter 5 analyzes *The Daily Show*, which offered an expanded structure for news parody, with the majority of time devoted to an anchor desk and spot reporting packages, more closely imitating traditional newscasts. The program quickly established itself and garnered conflicting reviews, with some writers finding it a fun entertainment program and others condemning it as shallow and for being the perfect reflection of cable mediocrity. After three seasons, Kilborn was poached for a network late-night program, opening the door for Jon Stewart to take the anchor desk. There was no guarantee that Stewart would succeed. After some positive reviews on niche programs, an attempted syndicated talk show with Stewart only lasted a year. The 1999 season of *TDS* was unsteady at first, but the show hit its stride as it shifted to more political coverage going into the 2000 election.

Political coverage continued to grow as *TDS* entered the 2000s. Stewart's poignant response to the 9/11 attacks continued a trend of positive reviews and increased ratings. Chapter 6 chronicles how Stewart evolved over the 2000s from funny late-night host to, by some rankings, America's most trusted newscaster. In just one decade, *TDS* shifted from witty entertainment to must-watch media and political criticism. While previous news parody had remained on the fringes of the journalistic field, *TDS* became a participant—recognized by its viewers and other media, even while some of the latter shook their heads in dismay or embarrassment.

Halfway through the decade, *TDS* spun off its tongue-in-cheek foil, *The Colbert Report*. While Stewart played the even-tempered, compassionate liberal, Stephen Colbert parodied right-wing conservative pundits, such as Bill O'Reilly, a ratings leader for Fox News. Stewart often flirted with irony, but Colbert *embodied* it. The show quickly became as influential and discussed as *TDS*, with its own mode of criticism. What sets the two shows apart from their predecessors is not only the sustained news parody they enacted, anchoring multiple segments and shifting to interviews with mostly newsworthy guests, but also how frequently their humor moved beyond puns and personality to regularly deconstruct the ideology of conventional "wisdom" and the power structures of society. Each program's style of complex humor allowed them to claim legitimacy within the political and journalistic fields and struggle for hegemonic reconfiguration.

Stewart and Colbert continued their successful Comedy Central programs into the 2010s, also expanding their political satire into real-life interventions, such as The Rally to Restore Sanity/Fear in Washington, DC. Both hosts stepped down from their shows in the mid-2010s, opening the door for a wave of new programs and hosts discussed in chapter 7. These shows diversified the genre and innovated news parody's style and focus. In 2014, HBO launched *Last Week* after Oliver successfully filled in as anchor of *TDS*. An analysis of *Last Week* and its newsmagazine-style parody is the major case study for the chapter. The show devotes around 20 minutes of in-depth coverage to one story each episode, providing as much actual news and analysis as humor. Oliver often incorporates a kind of satiric activism into his program; for instance, while investigating the lax requirements for setting up a religious nonprofit, he dramatized the problem by legally creating his own church and soliciting donations.

"Weekend Update" returned to cultural relevance in the first decade of the new millennium after struggling in the 1990s, adding female writers and anchors and more political focus. In 2014, the segment cast its first black anchor, Michael Che. Che incorporates his background into his reporting, emphasizing race and inequality in "Weekend Update's" coverage. Che and co-host Colin Jost are the segment's longest-running anchor team. The following year Trevor Noah took over the anchor desk of *TDS*, becoming the first person of color to solo anchor a news parody program. While keeping the same show structure, Noah carved out his own style as host, emphasizing international issues and race. Samantha Bee, another *TDS* alum, launched *Full Frontal with Samantha Bee* on TBS in 2016 as a more advocacy-oriented, feminist approach to news parody. The election of Donald Trump in 2016 caught news-parody programs by surprise, forcing each to craft its own strategies for dealing with an administration that often made satire seem redundant.

NOTES

1. *Last Week Tonight with John Oliver*, March 18, 2018.
2. "Cable and Internet Loom Large in Fragmented Political News Universe," Pew Research Center, updated January 11, 2004, https://www.pewresearch.org/politics/2004/01/11/cable-and-internet-loom-large-in-fragmented-political-news-universe/.

3. Melanie McFarland, "Is This a Joke? Young People Turning Comedy Shows into Serious News Source," *Seattle Post-Intelligencer*, January 22, 2004, C, 1; David Shaw, "News as Entertainment Is Sadly Becoming the Norm," *Los Angeles Times*, July 11, 2004, E, 20; Neil Postman, *Amusing Ourselves to Death: Public Discourse in the Age of Show Business* (New York: Penguin Books, 1985).

4. Geoffrey Baym, "*The Daily Show*: Discursive Integration and the Reinvention of Political Journalism," *Political Communication* 22, no. 3 (2005); Jeffrey P. Jones, *Entertaining Politics: New Political Television and Civic Culture* (Lanham, MD: Rowman & Littlefield Publishers, Inc., 2005); Aaron McKain, "Not Necessarily Not the News: Gatekeeping, Remediation, and *The Daily Show*," *Journal of American Culture* 28 (2005).

5. Amy B. Becker and Leticia Bode, "Satire as a Source for Learning? The Differential Impact of News Versus Satire Exposure on Net Neutrality Knowledge Gain," *Information, Communication & Society* 21, no. 4 (2018); Lauren Feldman and Caty Borum Chattoo, "Comedy as a Route to Social Change: The Effects of Satire and News on Persuasion About Syrian Refugees," *Mass Communication and Society* 22 (2019); Julia R. Fox, "Journalist or Jokester? An Analysis of *Last Week Tonight with John Oliver*," in *Political Humor in a Changing Media Landscape: A New Generation of Research*, ed. Jody C. Baumgartner and Amy B. Becker (Lanham, MD: Lexington Books, 2018).

6. Jody C. Baumgartner and Brad Lockerbie, "Maybe It *Is* More Than a Joke: Satire, Mobilization, and Political Participation," *Social Science Quarterly* 99, no. 3 (2018); Amy B. Becker, "What About Those Interviews? The Impact of Exposure to Political Comedy and Cable News on Factual Recall and Anticipated Political Expression" *International Journal of Public Opinion Research* 25, no. 3 (2013); Hoon Lee and Nojin Kwak, "The Affect Effect of Political Satire: Sarcastic Humor, Negative Emotions, and Political Participation," *Mass Communication and Society* 17 (2014).

7. Dannagal Goldthwaite Young, *Irony and Outrage: The Polarized Landscape of Rage, Fear, and Laughter in the United States* (New York: Oxford University Press, 2020).

8. Baumgartner, Jody. "Humor on the Next Frontier: Youth, Online Political Humor, and the 'Jib-Jab' Effect." *Social Science Computer Review* 25 (2007); Jody C. Baumgartner and Jonathan S. Morris, "*The Daily Show* Effect: Candidate Evaluations, Efficacy, and the American Youth," *American Politics Research* 34 (2006); Baumgartner, Jody C., and Jonathan S. Morris. "One 'Nation' under Stephen? The Effects of *The Colbert Report* on American Youth." *Journal of Broadcasting & Electronic Media* 52, no. 4 (2008); Jody C. Baumgartner and Jonathan S. Morris, "Stoned Slackers or Super Citizens? *The Daily Show* Viewing and Political Engagement of Young Adults," in *The Stewart/Colbert Effect: Essays on the Real Impact of Fake News*, ed. Amarnath Amarasingam (Jefferson, NC: McFarland & Company, Inc., 2011). Baumgartner, Jody C., Jonathan S. Morris, and Natasha L. Walth. "The Fey Effect: Young Adults, Political Humor, and Perceptions of Sarah Palin in the 2008 Presidential Election Campaign." *Public Opinion Quarterly* 76, no. 1 (2012).

9. Holbert, R. Lance, Jennifer L. Lambe, Anthony D. Dudo, and Kristin A. Carlton. "Primacy Effects of *The Daily Show* and National TV News Viewing:

Young Viewers, Political Gratification, and Internal Political Self-Efficacy." *Journal of Broadcasting & Electronic Media* 51 (2007).

10. Hart, Roderick P., and Johanna Hartelius. "The Political Sins of Jon Stewart." *Critical Studies in Media Communication* 24, no. 3 (2007); Colletta, Lisa. "Political Satire and Postmodern Irony in the Age of Stephen Colbert and Jon Stewart." *Journal of Popular Culture* 42, no. 5 (2009).

11. Cao, Xiaoxia. "Political Comedy Shows and Knowledge About Primary Campaigns: The Moderating Effects of Age and Education." *Mass Communication and Society* 11 (2008); Kim, Young Mie, and John Vishak. "Just Laugh! You Don't Need to Remember: The Effects of Entertainment Media on Political Information Acquisition and Information Processing in Political Judgement." *Journal of Communication* 58 (2008).

12. Pierre Bourdieu, "The Political Field, the Social Science Field, and the Journalistic Field," in *Bourdieu and the Journalistic Field*, ed. Rodney Benson and Erik Neveu (Cambridge, UK: Polity Press, 2005).

13. Jason Mittell, *Genre and Television: From Cop Shows to Cartoons in American Culture* (New York: Routledge, 2004), 16–18.

14. Jan Hokenson, *The Idea of Comedy: History, Theory, Critique* (Cranbury, NJ: Associated University Presses, 2006), 85.

15. James Kern Feibleman, *In Praise of Comedy (Reissue)* (New York: Russell & Russell, 1962), 182.

16. Lance Olsen, *Circus of the Mind in Motion: Postmodernism and the Comic Vision* (Detroit, MI: Wayne State University Press, 1990), 18.

17. Ibid., 19.

18. Murray Davis, *What's So Funny?: The Comic Conception of Culture and Society* (Chicago, IL: The University of Chicago Press, 1993).

19. Ibid., 109.

20. Paul Simpson, *On the Discourse of Satire: Toward a Stylistic Model of Satirical Humor* (Philadelphia, PN: John Benjamins Publishing Co., 2003), 8.

21. Margaret Rose, *Parody: Ancient, Modern, and Post-Modern* (New York: Cambridge University Press, 1993), 52.

22. Linda Hutcheon, *A Theory of Parody: The Teachings of Twentieth-Century Art Forms* (Urbana: University of Illinois Press, 2000); Roger J. Kreuz and Richard M. Roberts, "On Satire and Parody: The Importance of Being Ironic," *Metaphor and Symbolic Activity* 8, no. 2 (1993).

23. Hutcheon, *A Theory of Parody*, 56.

24. Mikhail Bakhtin, *Problems of Dostoevsky's Poetics*, trans. Carl Emerson (Minneapolis, MN: University of Minnesota Press, 1985), 127.

25. Mikhail Bakhtin, *The Dialogic Imagination: Four Essays*, trans. Caryl Emerson & Michael Holquist (Austin, TX: University of Texas Press, 1981), 76.

26. Bakhtin, *Problems of Dostoevsky's Poetics*, 185–86.

27. Mikhail Bakhtin, *Rabelais and His World*, trans. Helene Iswolsky (Bloomington, IN: Indiana University Press, 1984), 21.

Chapter 2

That Was the Decade That Was

The 1960s and the Limits of Network News Parody

In 1967, musing over the past two decades of American television, CBS program chief Perry Lafferty proclaimed that viewers "don't want to be intellectually stimulated and they don't want to be educated; they want to bury their problems in the 23-inch screen."[1] To back his claim, Lafferty pointed to previous failed attempts by networks to target sophisticated viewers, including NBC's 1963–1965 topical satire show *That Was the Week That Was* (*TW3*). Lafferty's claim is one of many rationales the television industry developed to account for the program's cancellation, which debuted to critical praise and enthusiastic audience reception, only to be canceled in the middle of its second season. Other postmortems of the show pointed to ratings, political pressure, and network apathy. All of these factors undoubtedly contributed to the demise of *TW3*, but its primary difficulties were more cultural and stylistic. *TW3* attempted to parody newscasts as a part-time premise, mixing multiple forms of topical humor, creating a lack of structural consistency that failed to resonate with audiences. Although tame by today's standards, the humor of the program seemed overly acerbic and confrontational for an entertainment show at the time, polarizing audiences.[2] Less than ten years after *TW3*'s demise, far harder-hitting news parody emerged on the same network but into a changed cultural landscape eager to make fun of the powerful.

Following a well-received pilot, *TW3* debuted on NBC in January 1964 as a midseason replacement and ran for fifty episodes before its cancellation. The show is America's first and only regular prime-time network series to heavily feature news parody. Its short lifespan yielded a surplus of drama and controversy, yet the show is mostly forgotten in popular and scholarly works about 1960s television. This chapter demonstrates how *TW3* struggled to develop a vision of news-parody style, while also navigating the conflicting pressures of producing cutting-edge television satire on a conservative, commercial medium. The program was highly innovative in attempting to imitate newscasts of its day by incorporating moving and still images into stories and borrowing the concept of a central news desk. Although aspects of the program proved influential on future writers and producers of news satire, its genre-blending structure was rejected by subsequent news-parody shows.

TW3 was an American import of a BBC program by the same name. Appearing in the middle of the British satire boom of the late 1950s and 1960s, the program became one of the most talked-about programs in the BBC's history.[3] Producer Ned Sherrin and writer/actor David Frost headed up the program, which aired during 1962 and 1963. *TW3* offered satiric evaluations of politics and society that were more sustained, fearless, and occasionally vicious than any previous BBC program.[4] The usually stone-faced state television system developed the program both to tap into the success of satire in Britain and to attempt to take back some of the entertainment-oriented audience from ITV, its commercial competitor. Because ITV primarily re-broadcast American network programs, *TW3* provided hip satire with a local flavor the BBC hoped would pull in audiences. The show proved a hit, with a respectable 10–12 million regular weekly viewers.[5] However, *TW3*'s success brought as much controversy as accolades to the broadcaster. Television comedy about the Royal Family, Parliament, and the Pope proved equally as shocking as funny, resulting in organized complaints and parliamentary arguments. A victim of its own success, *TW3* was canceled by the BBC, who claimed it would be too difficult for the show to be impartial during the upcoming 1964 general elections. There was little doubt, however, that the network looked forward to silencing the storm of controversy the show had fueled. The last episode of the British *TW3* appeared just two weeks before the American version of the show started regularly airing in a nation with a drastically different cultural context.

While Britain was experiencing its satire boom, American popular culture continued an uneasy dance with social humor. The 1950s have often been characterized as an almost mirthless period in America, with McCarthyism and Cold War rhetoric assumed to be dominant discourses. Scholars like Ethan Thompson and Stephen E. Kercher, however, make compelling cases that parody and satire were quite successful with subcultures in America during the 1950s and even extended into mainstream media on occasion.[6] Comedians performing "sick humor," like Lenny Bruce, Mort Sahl, and Tom Lehrer, became club regulars making jokes about religion, sex, and other taboo topics. A number of these comics were able to spin their routines into successful record albums and television talk-show appearances.[7] The emergence and success of *Mad* magazine offers another example of satiric humor during this seeming decade of consensus. While young readers and college students often delighted in *Mad*'s critical humor, Thompson describes how some readers sent letters to the FBI, asking if the humor magazine was un-American.[8] Even if there was no "boom," satire in America certainly existed as an alternative practice that sometimes erupted within more traditional texts. Thompson argues that the rise of parody and other satiric humor during the 1950s was a reaction to the popularity and increasing commercialism of American media. Humor critical of middle-class media tastes helped to articulate the audience's dissatisfaction with media and create the illusion of a cultural hierarchy within popular culture, with satire and parody being treated as the high culture of devalued forms.[9]

In the 1960s, television seemed to be the medium most out of touch with changes in American culture. Sitcoms and family-oriented shows dominated the dial, creating a bizarre juxtaposition between network programming and network news. Coverage of racial violence, the expanding war in Vietnam, riots, and assassinations depicted a nation in social upheaval, while also debunking the myth of national consensus. Prime time on the three television networks continued to depict a mythic America of small towns free of crime, nuclear patriarchal families, and bright futures ahead, ignoring real-life events in the world. The network lineup for 1963 provided more of the same with returning Nielsen favorites *The Beverly Hillbillies* and *Bonanza* and the new series *The Patty Duke Show* and *Petticoat Junction*. In a September 1963 speech, FCC Chair E. William Henry chided the industry for avoiding controversial issues and thus producing mostly bland programming, observing that networks "have the advertiser to satisfy" and thus choose "not to deal realistically and in depth with the host of complex controversial issues that surround us."[10] Only months later, NBC took up the gauntlet laid down by Henry, adapting *TW3* for American audiences.

AUDIENCE AND CRITICAL RECEPTION

The British success of *TW3* spawned a number of imitators and spin-offs before and during the run of the American version of the show. The Canadian *This Hour Has Seven Days* (1964–1966) and the Australian *The Mavis Bramston Show* (1964–1968) were each popular series inspired by the BBC program. Adapting British satire for American audiences proved more difficult in a commercial environment. Local stations WNEW in New York and WTTG in Washington were among the first to attempt a *TW3*-style program for American television with the program *What's Going On Here*, featuring the British "Beyond the Fringe" comedy troupe. The initial May 1963 broadcast received positive reception, and *Variety* claimed that if the show was signed for a series, "it could justifiably be hailed as the most outrageous, audacious and sacrilegious entry on American TV." In the same *Variety* review, however, the writer predicted the program was just as likely to be a one-time "gesture of bravado whose consequences frightened its creators and patrons."[11] That fear proved prescient, as WNEW was unable to find sponsors for subsequent episodes and abandoned the concept.[12]

In the summer of 1963, press stories began reporting that the BBC had sold the American rights for *TW3* to Leland Hayward Production and that NBC was negotiating to carry the program. Critics familiar with the BBC program voiced surprise and doubt that American networks and advertisers would support the no-holds-barred satire characteristic of the British program. *New York Times* writer Val Adams, for instance, assumed the networks would automatically reject a program with such specialized content and audience appeal.[13] Producer Leland Hayward, who had made his name in Broadway and film production, attempted to prime audiences and also tamp down expectations in press interviews, saying, "Of course we won't be able to go as far [in humor] as they do in London."[14] Yet, in other reports, Hayward describes the show as groundbreaking for American television. These conflicting statements demonstrate that from the earliest press coverage the creative team of the American *TW3* engaged in an uneasy dance of attempting to capitalize on the cutting-edge humor of the BBC show, while also reassuring prospective networks and advertisers that the humor would still be within the bounds of American taste.

The one-hour pilot episode of NBC's *TW3* debuted on November 10, 1963, to high critical expectations.[15] The program was scheduled on a Sunday at 10:00 p.m. and topped the ratings for its timeslot against CBS's voyeuristic powerhouse *Candid Camera* and the ABC show *Laughs For Sale*. Reviews for the pilot were generally positive; however, most writers seemed to be reviewing the *potential future* of the program more than the content of the pilot. While *Variety* gushed that "sacred cows are milked for laughs," *New York Times* critic Jack Gould was more cautionary.[16] Gould welcomed the appearance of topical humor on American television but reported *TW3*'s "general level of wit was never particularly inspired."[17] *Washington Post* critic Rick Du Brow was likewise hopeful that a satire program could add to the quality of television and endorsed making the program a series but complained that *TW3*'s actors were too playful in their presentation. Despite the use of humor, Du Brow reminds his readers that "satire is basically serious business, and at its heart is not kidding . . . what we need now is not the tickling of tweezers but the swinging of hatchets."[18] These reviews reflect a discourse that runs throughout subsequent coverage of *TW3*, where writers want to celebrate smart comedy on television and want to see the show succeed. However, critics became increasingly disillusioned with *TW3*'s ability to deliver on its promise of cutting-edge humor.

Viewer reaction to the pilot was overwhelmingly positive and engaged. NBC received the largest mail response to any special program it had ever produced, receiving 10,516 letters from viewers, with a 15 to 1 favorable view of the show. A network analysis of the mail further noted that letters were "unusually articulate and literate" and that a number of them came from professionals, implying that the show attracted a more educated and financially well-off audience.[19] The positive mail was mirrored in viewer telephone calls. The New York City affiliate reported an overwhelmingly positive response with 639 calls the night of the broadcast, when most shows would elicit 20–30 calls.[20] One viewer compared the program to the satire of Jonathan Swift and Voltaire, while another seemed to summarize the general positive praise by saying, "your program has provided the greatest justification for the existence of television that I have yet seen."[21]

NBC picked up *TW3* as a midseason replacement series for the failed show *Harry's Girls*. The first regular season of the American *TW3* aired on January 10, 1964, only two weeks after the final episode of the BBC program. NBC scheduled the show in the 9:30 Friday night slot, leading into the highly rated *Jack Paar Show*. Despite high hopes, the first regular episode of *TW3* was almost unanimously a critical letdown. Jack Gould pronounced the overall show "pretty thin and trite," and *Variety* reviewers said that despite some high points, the episode was "as humdrum and pedestrian as [the pilot] was delightfully impudent."[22] Viewer mail ran positive, but only a smattering of letters in comparison to the pilot and nowhere near as effusive. Throughout the first season, idea submissions and requests for transcripts of songs or skits began to outnumber fan mail or complaints, demonstrating waning interest. The next several episodes in January received more favorable coverage by critics and emphasized the influence of British *TW3* cast member David Frost, who was signed for a handful of episodes of the American program, eventually becoming a regular. Critics gave special recognition to a sequence in the January 24 episode that paired the song *Smoke Gets in Your Eyes* with images of cigarettes, X-rays, and cancerous lungs.[23] After the first month, reviewers continued to sour on the program, wishing *TW3* would take more risks. For most of the 25 episodes of the first season, *TW3* ranked second in the ratings to the last season of CBS's *Twilight Zone*.

Waning reviews and ratings led to several changes for the program before it returned to the air in the 1964–1965 television season. With the exception of Phyllis Newman and "*TW3* girl" Nancy Ames, the entire cast was replaced, and David Frost was hired as a regular cast member. The content of the show was also revised, with the intention of seeming more politically even-handed and minimizing offense. Producer Marshall Jamison resigned from the program in protest over the proposed changes and was replaced by Herb Sargent. NBC signed the program for another season, but the network moved *TW3* to Tuesday night at 9:30, placing it against the popular *Petticoat Junction* on CBS and the highly anticipated *Peyton Place* on ABC. Although network executives still publicly supported the show, the scheduling decision was an unspoken sign that *TW3* was unlikely to last long.

The 1964 season began with three of the first four episodes preempted by advertising buys from the Republican National Committee. Despite some outrage over the preemptions, including a large number of fan letters, critics immediately began panning the new season. Jack Gould writes that the season premiere was "neither witty nor funny, only embarrassing in its persistent clumsiness and poor taste."[24] Viewer mail that came in during the preemptions and the first two episodes signaled further challenges for the show, with 430 supportive letters and 483 negative ones, half of which called *TW3* politically biased.[25] The program finally began airing regularly in mid-November, after the presidential election. Viewer mail shifted mostly positive but was tempered by pleas for better content. A number of letters in support of the program arrived in January, suggesting that a potential cancellation was public knowledge. One letter even starts off, "I have heard that you need fan mail."[26] In response to criticism, *TW3* writer Gerald Gardner lamented that sophisticated viewers want satire but have unrealistic expectations and claimed the program at least offered an alternative to mainstream television.[27] His defense was unsuccessful. In February, NBC informed Hayward that the show would not be renewed, and the program ended its run on May 4. Coverage of the show's demise tried to analyze why it was unsuccessful, while also offering some positive comments for a show that many critics wanted to like. Ultimately, postmortems failed to vindicate the show against the complaints of critics disappointed in *TW3*'s inability to live up to its own promise.

TW3 AS PROTO-NEWS PARODY

In comparison to more recent programs like *The Daily Show* and *Last Week Tonight*, *TW3* retrospectively seems less news parody than a hybrid between satiric news and a variety show. Rather than extended sequences mimicking network newscasts, *TW3* offered quick vignettes of news parody that linked satirical sketches, songs, and other variety-show material. The show opening exemplifies this approach: each episode opened with a voice-over announcement "live from New York," followed by a musical summary of the week's news sung by Nancy Ames, interspersed with faux newsreaders presenting satirical news reports.

In the first regular-season episode, Ames sings, "On Sunday Goldwater met the press, to make his own State of the Union address. Monday the GOP struck back." Cut to Henry Morgan as anchor, reading a news story about the activities of Republican presidential candidates. The beginning of the report sounds serious and sets up viewer expectation for a conventional news item, but then finishes with the laugh line, "there's a strong underground movement for Richard Nixon," as the visual cuts to a photo of Nixon standing in a mine, wearing a miner's helmet. The spoken and visual pun of "struck back/ miner helmet/underground" typifies how the show frequently played at the linguistic level of humor; Nixon becomes the butt of a joke, but one without any critical message behind it. The news item lasts for less than 20 seconds before cutting back to Ames for several repeats of song verse/news report/ song verse, before she finishes the musical number around three minutes into the program, singing the show title, "that was the week that was!"[28]

A defining aspect of *TW3*'s style was its consistent focus on topical news subjects, differentiating it from other variety-style programs at the time. Whether actors were parodying a news report or performing a skit, both were ultimately connected to contemporary issues. Each episode opened with newsreaders giving top headlines before settling into a blend of news reports, extended skits, and musical commentary that often became indistinguishable from each other. In one episode, for example, Elliott Reid stands at a news desk where he begins a story about Democrats looking for a running mate for President Lyndon B. Johnson. Reid continues the story as he walks from the desk to a backdrop of the White House, suddenly shifting character and becoming a Democratic campaign planner in a comedy sketch. Reid begins to discuss strategy with Henry Morgan, who ultimately recommends that Johnson needs a "Northern, liberal, isolationist who is an unmarried, atheist, alcoholic" as a running mate to fill in his weaknesses. Reid responds by deadpanning, "Which one?"[29] The joke satirizes both the American public's irreconcilable demands for candidates and the political parties' use of polling to appeal to voters. It also illustrates how *TW3* utilized news parody as a fulcrum to transition between its disparate presentational styles. The newly developing norms of television news became incorporated into the program, creating a prototype for subsequent television shows incorporating news parody.

TW3 debuted on American television just over a year after CBS launched the first nightly, half-hour network news program.[30] Although the *CBS Evening News* was the first to expand its coverage, news had been a part of television since the early days of broadcasting. NBC debuted *The Esso Newsreel*, a 10–15 minute news segment, in 1947, and CBS followed suit with *The CBS-TV News* the next year. By the early 1960s, television had incorporated a vocabulary, structure, and aesthetic for broadcast news. Organizations such as the Radio Television News Directors' Association (RTNDA) published materials to set journalistic practices, as well as technical specifications for newscasts.[31] In 1964, the RTNDA held a Newsfilm Standards Conference in New York City to attempt to codify prevailing knowledge and practices of broadcast-news organizations; this was followed by additional regional conferences. The resulting written reports provide an overview of news practices and cover a wide range of topics, from technical questions about what cameras to use and when sound and color film should be shot to the structure and staffing of newsrooms.[32]

The prevalence and acceptance of norms for television reports allowed *TW3* to parody newscasts with the assumption that the audience would instantly recognize references to common news conventions. Single anchors that both read stories and appeared in prepackaged reports or interview segments were the norm for most stations, with occasional on-screen appearances by other reporters. The news desk, where the central anchor either stood or sat, provided the visual focus of news programs and was surrounded by iconic representations of reporting like typewriters, clocks, phones, and sometimes television technology. George Corrin, the scenic staff designer for ABC, argued that news sets should make the reader aware that the station has all the devices for reporting news.[33] The on-set journalistic trappings were ultimately a visual claim to legitimacy by the news agency.

While the anchor behind the desk was an ever-present feature of 1960s newscasts, the centerpiece of every show was newsfilm. Location footage of a news event provided differentiation from newspapers and radio programs. Network newscasts mixed color and black-and-white film, as well as silent and sound. News value was an important consideration in ordering the rundown for a newscast, but the apportionment of available newsfilm also influenced what stories would be covered and their priority in the sequencing.[34] Along with footage, newscasts incorporated a variety of other visuals to supplement their coverage, including photos and graphics of charts and logos. By borrowing common visual and structural conventions, *TW3* encouraged comparison with television news, despite its satiric presentational mode and variety-show format.

Opening with Ames singing in front of a *TW3* logo set design, the show immediately foregrounds its link to television journalism by repeatedly cutting away to actors at a desk, delivering their short broadcast-news updates. Like newscasts, *TW3* structured its entire program around the desk as a space for both the reading of news and a link between the varied visual and narrative styles of the rest of the show. Unlike later parody programs, *TW3* did not attempt to totally copy the contemporary visual mise-en-scène of television news, with its claims to authority through clocks, typewriters, and other professional signifiers. Instead, the parody show established a simple, open news space situated on a large sound stage; the news desk had no accompanying false walls or props to define its boundaries, nor anything but microphones and scripts sitting on top of the desk (figure 2.1).

During transitions, the show occasionally cut to long shots revealing multiple sets together on the stage, including the news desk.[35] Sets used for other skits would either be rolled in or simply left for the remainder of the show. Based on available episodes, most sets merely suggested a setting, such as having books on a desk for an office or a screened backdrop of the White House to represent Washington. In the same way, the news desk provided a visual constant for the show as a whole, with minimal detail. Emphasis was on the writing and presentation.

Just as *TW3* mimicked the visual structure of broadcast news, it also borrowed story-presentation formats. During the news segments, and even during some of the topical skits, the show incorporated news footage and images in ways that seem commonplace now, especially in the age of YouTube and mashups; however, as workers on the first network news-parody program, the show's creative team was *innovating* visual humor. *TW3* used both sound and silent newsfilm readily available from syndicators,

Figure 2.1 ***TW3* Often Used a Very Simple Desk as Its Anchor Centerpiece, Sometimes with Multiple Cast Members.** Pictured from left: Elliot Reid, Henry Morgan, David Frost, Nancy Ames. *Source: Courtesy NBC/Photofest.*

using United Press International for footage and pictures at the launch of the program.

Silent footage allowed anchors to read over visuals, providing commentary on the images. One sketch features newsreel footage of the New York Mets stadium. *TW3* announcers describe the improvements to the ball field and then wrap with the lament, "now if [the stadium] only had a ball team." The baseball story is followed by a pointed political critique using footage of the Senate debate on civil rights legislation. Reading over the footage, the announcer observes, "In seventeen days of civil rights marathon, our Senators have racked up 1,676,000 words. Abraham Lincoln said it the right way in only 616 words—the Emancipation Proclamation."[36] In these examples, the moving images help to justify the written story. In reality, the footage is not essential; it is barely supplementary. Just as with newscasts at the time, *TW3* used footage as both an impetus for a story and as an integral aesthetic for televisual presentation.

The recontextualization of sound newsfilm was another popular strategy of *TW3* for their news-parody segments. Existing interviews or public statements were reordered, edited with other sound footage, or interspersed with new material to satirize public figures—usually politicians. The pilot episode features a press conference with newsfilm of President John F. Kennedy walking to a podium and answering questions, edited with footage of *TW3* cast members posing as reporters and asking fake questions. The results, of course, recontextualize Kennedy's original answers by creating humorous set-ups by the cast. This particular segment seemed enthusiastically received by the audience based on thunderous applause, perhaps indicating its novelty in structure, if not content.[37] As will be mentioned in the later section on presidential coverage, though, the bit did receive some pushback. The faux press conference touches more on incongruity than on satirizing government policy, but interspersing original footage with newsfilm allowed *TW3* actors to participate in a simulated debate with politicians, a method more elaborately and viciously employed by later news-parody programs.[38]

In addition to adding new footage, *TW3* also edited newsfilm to recontextualize and juxtapose multiple sound clips. In one of the final episodes, Nancy Ames reads a story about Republicans trying to change their image and then suggests the party could host a topical humor show on television. Cut to an introduction for "That Was the Party That Was," followed by footage of GOP stalwarts such as Barry Goldwater and Richard Nixon telling tepid jokes with an edited laugh track.[39] By linking together dire attempts at humor by two prominent Republicans, the show positioned the GOP as out of step with *TW3*'s audience and also took one of many parting shots at Republicans after the show's announced cancellation.

TW3, like network newscasts at the time, had limited access to immediate newsfilm due to the processing time and distribution methods of syndicators. Network-news operations had to either create their own development facilities or make prearranged deals for securing footage. Most news operations in the 1960s were still heavily supplementing their visuals with photos. The cheapest method was to shoot still images on an easel in studio but for better quality stations would use a teloptican. The "telop" was a device that allowed for the loading of several photos that could be flipped from picture to picture and then directly imported into the video system without a camera.[40] *TW3* utilized this process, incorporating many still images during production.

Photos were employed for varying purposes by *TW3*. Sometimes they were the source of humor, while other times they played a merely supporting role, adorning a story that could have been delivered purely with words. A favorite method of the show was to use a picture as a visual pun, setting up expectations with a word or phrase that opens multiple meanings and then subverting audience expectations through the accompanying photo. In the pilot, when discussing the potential for a dark-horse presidential candidate, a picture of a literal dark horse pops up.[41] The writers of the show would also use photos of politicians as if they were reacting to stories. Later in the show, a report that former-president Eisenhower will support whomever Republicans nominate in 1964 is followed by an anchor reading potential candidate names with accompanying images of Eisenhower looking sad, ashamed, facing backward, and so on, as if reacting to each GOP hopeful. Criticism and humor are created through the juxtapositioning of visuals with the actor's delivery of the story.

At other times, still images simply create visual variety. Frost reports that the state of Virginia is running two African-American candidates in elections, incorporating a *New York Times* story and headline directly from a newspaper sitting on an easel.[42] There is no direct reference to the newspaper clipping; the image only serves to create a new visual and correlate the *TW3* story with actual news being reported by the media. Similarly, a story about Malcolm X is accompanied by a close-up photo of his face, providing no additional information other than an image to connect with the name.[43] Approaching pictures as a mere *addition* to a story rather than as *part of* the story mimicked the practice of network newscasts, which used images to prevent long stretches of anchors from appearing on-screen.

Structurally, *TW3* presents itself as a genre blend, incorporating aspects of variety shows and their vaudevillian predecessors but mixing this structure with extended sequences of news parody. The use of newsreaders to "anchor" stories was an integral part of this process and further encouraged viewer comparison with contemporary newscasts. Discussion of the program, both in the popular press and in promotional materials from the producer and network, constantly highlighted *TW3*'s connection with news, privileging its interpretation as mainly a parody. The program was innovating a new format for American television, the first to foreground news parody.

OVERCROWDING AT THE ANCHOR DESK

To mimic the style of television news, it was essential that *TW3* replicate the central feature of the network newscast: the anchor. From the time Douglas Edwards began hosting the CBS nightly news in 1948, the networks labored to build their premier journalism shows around individual personalities. On the one hand, anchors were considered public figures who should embody the essence of watchdog journalism and function on behalf of the citizens. Yet, at the same time, the television corporations carefully watched ratings to determine whether their anchors were attracting enough viewers. Margaret Morse argues that the news anchor represents a complex web of news, industry, and public interest, wielding the ability to publicly speak and nominate topics in a way usually reserved for national leaders.[44] This power was already evident by the time *TW3* took to the airwaves, with all three networks vying for ratings and the cultural legitimacy those ratings reflected.

Network news in the 1960s was dominated by CBS and NBC. The team of Chet Huntley and David Brinkley were the ratings leaders throughout most of the decade with NBC's *The Huntley-Brinkley Report*. At one point, the program actually commanded an 84% audience share.[45] CBS offered strong competition after placing Walter Cronkite on the anchor desk in 1963. By the end of the decade, Cronkite had leaped to the top of the ratings.[46] These anchors were contemporary examples of the most exalted post in television news, and their style and presentations became the touchstone for news-parody satire.

With the exception of Huntley and Brinkley, the networks built their programs around a sole *man* being the visual gatekeeper. *TW3* drastically departed from this expectation by matching up rotating pairs and trios of actors at the news desk, giving almost every on-screen personality a turn as an anchor.[47] This formatting decision became a major regret for producer Leland Hayward, who considered the use of multiple anchors a stylistic mistake. Hayward's original program pitch to NBC references his intention to use a solo anchor, suggesting either Jonathan Winters or Bob Newhart as the main newsreader.[48] Only months into the first season, Hayward worried about the lack of breakout talent and insisted the show's staff must develop a primary anchor for the next season to carry the show.[49] Shortly after the start of the second season, Hayward shot off a withering memo to producer Herb Sargent complaining about the quality of the show and again singling out the use of multiple anchors as a key problem. Partially blaming himself, Hayward writes, "Using all the people to say news-casts is the oldest trap we ever fell into."[50] Based on Hayward's archives, one reason the show continually reverted to multiple anchors was the lack of a strong, central figure on the news desk. Various names are mentioned as potential choices in memos from Hayward and NBC executives but never materialize on screen. Another reason may have been the cross-genre nature of the program itself. News parody was sprinkled throughout *TW3*, rather than clearly sectioned off. *Saturday Night Live (SNL)* would successfully adopt the latter structure with "Weekend Update." *TW3*'s ensemble cast participated in every part of the program, making the format much more like a variety program. As a result, writers seemed to lean more on the interaction between talent for humor, encouraging the use of multiple anchors and lessening the direct parody of news structure.

The presentation by the *TW3* cast likewise veered away from network news style. A posture of high seriousness defined Cronkite and his contemporaries and created a sense of gravitas. Networks extolled the professionalism of their anchors; a CBS book from the period calls the anchor a "master reporter" whose "hours off the air are spent thinking, reading, and doing."[51] Geoffrey Baym contrasts the professional journalists of that era with later network anchors like Brian Williams, who seem less respected as a journalist and more regarded as a confluence of advertising desires and hybrid news formats.[52] The most successful anchors of the 1960s read the news with a commanding voice and limited distracting body language, while projecting a simultaneous air of authority and intimacy. News anchoring is a type of non-naturalistic acting, where performance is built around disavowing a role, removing emotion, and disconnecting from the audience. *TW3*'s actors seemed unable or unwilling to limit themselves to the tightly controlled emotions and body movements connected with broadcast news. Perhaps the cast of comedians, used to pushing boundaries and accentuating odd behaviors for laughs, found the complete earnestness of anchor style too constraining for their comedic intent.

Henry Fonda served as the central anchor in the pilot episode and came closest to assuming a traditional anchor persona. Fonda was an established Hollywood actor known more for dramatic roles in films such as *The Grapes of Wrath* (1940) and *12 Angry Men* (1957); however, he also proved his comedic chops in a smattering of comedies, such as the screwball *The Lady Eve* (1941). As an established actor, Fonda provided abundant gravitas for the American pilot. His delivery is authoritative but subdued, although vocal inflections are more pronounced than the ideal anchor delivery. This variation in tone is especially evident during transitions between stories. For instance, between a fake interview with a Senate cleaning woman and a skit on great political speeches, Fonda delivers the line, "Mrs. Fletcher may be looking ahead, but others are looking back." Rather than keeping an even tone, Fonda incorporates an optimistic lilt in the second half of the sentence.[53] There are also moments of faint smiles and acknowledgment of the studio audience. Fonda's performance brought accolades from reviewers, though, and his delivery was certainly the closest traditional parody of news presentation on *TW3*.

The regular season, absent Fonda, featured cast members noticeably departing from anchor norms by playing to the audience through multiple presentational strategies. Sometimes the actors create a kind of confessional delivery, as if in dialogue with the television viewer. In the first regular-season episode, Henry Morgan shares anchoring duties but provides most of the delivery. After the musical opening, Morgan announces the show is back as a regular-season program and warns, "to those who wrote in to say they hated our pilot show [*pauses, removes glasses and starts to chuckle*], wait'll you see this one."[54] Morgan's performance displays a willingness to drop pretense—not the kind of postmodern awareness common in contemporary parody, but more the cast's unwillingness to distinguish between news parody and comedy performance. Network anchors interpolate their audience by creating a one-sided dialogue; however, their presentation is tightly controlled to limit audience ownership of the conversation.[55] On *TW3*, the same actors who read the news instantly morph into characters in skits trying to get audience laughs, resulting in noncommittal performances where the cast members never truly embody their temporary roles on the news desk.

In surviving episodes of *TW3*, actors further eschew anchor norms by playing to their studio audience. In a guest appearance, Larry Storch reports that Malcolm X is calling for a Maoist movement in America. He concludes with great enthusiasm and anger, "no Malcolm X, what this country needs is an ex-Malcolm," followed quickly by an extended nod of his head, seemingly both as an affirmative gesture and almost as a bow to the applauding audience.[56] In addition to violating anchor norms, the content of the joke reflects how the politics of *TW3*, although progressive for the time, were still safely within the mainstream. Like stand-up comedians and vaudevillians before them, the actors on the program instantly responded to their live audience, delivering smiles, pointing and gesturing toward them, and visually scanning across the studio space. Such nonverbal cues are strenuously discouraged on the anchor desk. At the time, CBS recommended keeping eyes forward, sitting straight, and utilizing "an interested and serious noncommittal expression."[57] *TW3*'s actors chose not to keep "in character" while presenting the news, an issue that subsequent news-parody programs found various ways of negotiating.

News presentation during the second season of *TW3* seemed to make more attempts at stoicism and replication of the anchor role—with limited success.

A smaller cast led to greater consistency, as did the presence of David Frost in the role of lead anchor. Frost, a primary writer and actor on the BBC version of *TW3*, brought a more reserved British style of delivery, speaking quickly and with little fluctuation in tone. However, Frost was also more verbose, launching into lengthy criticisms with few supporting visuals. On one show, sounding more like a commentator than an anchor, Frost delivers a four-minute on-air diatribe about population explosion, with barely any laughs, leaving the audience seemingly unsure whether the story is meant to be humorous or merely didactic.[58] Nancy Ames and Buck Henry regularly joined Frost and presented a more subdued style behind the anchor desk. Stylistically, the cast in the second season more closely imitated the delivery and carefully controlled actions of network anchors; however, Frost's British accent played against the "nowhere USA" diction of national anchors who were partially chosen for their lack of regional dialect. In fact, some viewer mail complained about Frost being a "foreigner" and making fun of American culture and political leaders. Several letters called the show unpatriotic for casting Frost, and one particularly angry viewer wrote, "Send the stinking British home to their socialism. We don't want them or it here."[59]

The genre-blending format of *TW3* created tension between reserved news delivery and comedic performance, producing an inconsistent presentational style as actors tried to merge the two diverging traditions. The most jarring aspect of *TW3*'s news presentation was the rejection of an anchor's most valuable commodity: sincerity. The most crucial emotion for an anchor to convey is sincere concern for the viewers and the news that involves them. However, the whole point of news parody is to make fun of expectations, often through irony. So the overtly humorous anchor specifically says something sardonic or ironic—the antithesis of sincerity. As discussed in chapter 5, the greatest success of Jon Stewart may be his ability to successfully negotiate this tension between sincerity and satire. While Stewart and his contemporaries are able to conscript their audiences and make them feel in on the joke, the American *TW3* never seemed to achieve viewer rapport in the same way.

POKING FUN AT THE PRESIDENCY

Journalism's place as the Fourth Estate in American society emphasizes government and public policy coverage, so it seems almost a foregone conclusion that news parody would devote substantial time to the White House. As America's first network foray into the genre, *TW3* tread lightly on the presidency, poking fun and criticizing, but always with a defensive sense of "this is just for laughs." The satiric humor, however, often clashed with the desires of the network and advertiser to play it safe and not offend.

TW3's pilot episode appeared only 12 days before the assassination of John F. Kennedy, creating a potential dilemma for the show when it started as a regular-season series: was the country ready for political comedy in the wake of the national tragedy? A similar situation would face *The Daily Show* and other comedy outlets after the September 11, 2001, attacks. However, with a month and a half distance from the assassination, *TW3* simply chose not to address JFK's death and showed no signs of altering their style of presidential humor between the pilot and the regular season. Audiences in the United States got their only taste of the BBC *TW3* several weeks after the America pilot, when NBC aired a special episode of the British program eulogizing Kennedy following his assassination. The BBC program broke its satiric format to celebrate the president and grieve for the loss of his progressive politics. The tape was flown to America and aired on November 24, 1963.[60]

From the beginning, *TW3* revealed its liberal ideological leanings. Its satiric targets were most frequently and viciously conservative Republicans. The pilot episode featured Kennedy in only two stories, and neither presented him in a critical light. Fonda leads one story by saying that Kennedy has finally expressed his opinion about GOP presidential hopeful Barry Goldwater. The video then cuts to a photo of the president holding his nose as he speaks with Goldwater. The humor in this piece is squarely focused on the conservative Goldwater, with no satiric implications for Kennedy. As the Republican frontrunner and eventual nominee, Goldwater received steady attacks throughout the run of the program. The aforementioned Kennedy press conference sketch, with cast members asking fake questions, also appeared on the pilot.[61] The writers created inoffensive non sequiturs in the sketch, maligning neither the president nor his policies. However, even this innocuous humor generated complaints from viewers, with over two-thirds of critical phone calls taking offense at making fun of the president and clergy.[62] Hayward actually cut a joke from the press conference skit, where a reporter asks about whether magazines like *Playboy* should be banned from the mail because they "arouse in the reader a feeling of passion and a feeling of lust." Kennedy would have responded with, "I don't know where that feeling would arise." Hayward simply wrote "disgusting" on the original script, and the exchange was cut.[63] Whether the producer objected to the innuendo outright or especially in regards to the president is unclear. Kennedy's popularity among liberals and the optimism he represented seemed to discourage writers from treating him harshly, a consideration not extended to his replacement.

Hayward reportedly warned his staff to go easy on President Johnson since he had to step up to the presidency and also because of uncertainty about how the audience might react in the wake of the assassination.[64] The writers and cast of the program were not nearly as accommodating, providing a consistent diet of personal and policy jabs at the new president. The humor was not as dismissive or scathing as the satire pointed at Republicans, but *TW3* found a balance in its first season of tossing jokes down both sides of the political aisle, allowing them to claim nonpartisanship, whether true or not.

The first regular-season episode featured multiple stories and skits poking fun at Johnson. The humor never seems mean-spirited or pointed though, leading a *Variety* reviewer to complain that simply making political jokes does not equal performing political satire.[65] The most critical jab attacks Johnson for his seeming lack of ideological consistency and unwillingness to define himself to the public. Elliott Reid reports on Johnson's State of the Union Address, where he "promised to buy more security and fight more poverty with less money than ever before." The story leads into an Audrey Meadows song in front of a White House backdrop, lampooning LBJ's tendency to promise something to everyone. She croons that everyone likes Johnson: "People for segregation like Lyndon, people for miscegenation like Lyndon . . . nobody's mad at LBJ [*pause*] today!"[66]

Although the presidential humor was cautious at first, *TW3* soon extended its range to overtly satirizing American policy and the president personally. A news report that Johnson's family has over nine million dollars in its holdings leads David Frost to comment, "Nice going, sir. After all, if you're going to launch a war on poverty, there's nothing like setting a good example."[67] Criticism of Johnson included American involvement in Vietnam and his inconsistent Latin American policy. A story about Brazilian elections segues to Larry Storch providing a slideshow lecture explaining Johnson's policy of sending money both to suppressive anti-communist regimes and also to communist regimes in hopes of encouraging them to reject communism: "In short, everyone in Latin America gets US money except him [*a picture of Fidel Castro fills the screen*]."[68] By the end of the first season, *TW3* began a regular segment on the 1964 election hopefuls called "the presidential non-preference polls," covering the least popular presidential candidates. Johnson, of course, was included.

Although the start of the second season focused on the presidential election, the overall season featured less political news, following Hayward's desire for the show to appeal to a broader range of viewers through more varied topical humor and shorter segments.[69] As a result, less time is devoted to LBJ and more to celebrities and popular culture. The shift in focus brought the ire of fans and critics alike; *Variety* complained that the new season was "more like topical gags than biting satire" and accused the writers of seeming routine instead of "angry or slightly crazed young men."[70]

The most vicious political humor in the second season was directed at Republicans—presumably a combination of the writers' politics and the GOP's repeated preemptions of the program. The GOP purchased *TW3*'s airtime on September 22, October 6, and October 27, while NBC preempted the show on October 20 for a network special following the death of former president Herbert Hoover and then for election coverage on November 3. The committee to reelect Johnson purchased regular ad time on the September 28th episode, which prevented Republicans from buying the full-time slot and preempting *TW3* yet again. In place of *TW3*, Republicans ran features about their nominee, Barry Goldwater. Several *TW3* fans sent in sarcastic fan mail for the GOP programs, acting as if the advertisements were brilliant comedies; a number of other letters were complaints about the Republicans attempting to silence *TW3*'s political voice.

The beginning of the second season brought the most viewer mail since the pilot. Although some fans accused NBC of being pro-Goldwater for allowing the preemptions, most letters came from right-leaning viewers outraged over Goldwater jokes and the relatively light humor applied to Johnson. The opening song from September 29 provides an example of the unequal approach to the candidates: "While Goldwater hollers of crime in the streets, his Southern supporters are still wearin' sheets! And though he goes fishin' in state after state, still Lyndon refuses to rise to debate."[71] Ostensibly, the two lines each criticize the candidates, but one for his racist supporters and the other for simply being unwilling to debate. Coverage of the battle over *TW3*'s repeated preemptions took on political overtones, cast as a fight between the Republicans and Democrats.[72] Going through the *TW3* viewer mail, there are hundreds of confrontational, if not outright, belligerent letters leading up to the election, providing a striking parallel to today's conservative complaints about media. Some accused the show of being anti-American: "Try knocking the U.S.S.R., Red China and the Communist Party of America for a change. They're giving us a bad enough time without you chiming in." Others revealed their own biases, with one letter calling *TW3* a "Pro-Democratic, Pro-Jewish, Pro-Negro . . . Anti-Republican, Anti-Catholic TV show." A letter from a Connecticut viewer seems to sum up the criticism of many Republicans: "You are no longer satirists, you're political prostitutes."[73]

Although the show remained topical after the election, highly partisan presidential-related humor declined. A fairly long sketch, for instance, set up the premise of a news reporter watching LBJ, played by Bob Dishy, getting dressed for the inauguration and trying to interview him; however, the humor is singularly focused on the situation, such as the reporter offering to help him dress, with no satiric voice.[74] David Frost delivered one of the show's final political quips in the last episode, announcing, "Try to remember that after tonight, any TV news about President Johnson or the Congress that sounds perfectly ridiculous to you is not meant as a joke."[75] *TW3* emerged into its first season with moments of serious presidential satire that tackled some of the more controversial issues of its time. During its shorter second season, the show hit hard prior to the 1964 election but retreated away from politics as the producer and the network focused on their failed attempt to reformat the show and increase ratings.

CRITICAL USES AND TARGETS OF *TW3*'S HUMOR

TW3's extensive use of topical humor was unique when it appeared on television, tackling some of the most controversial issues of the day, including civil rights, nuclear weapons, and Vietnam. Although the jokes were tame compared to "sick humor" performers like Lenny Bruce, the term "sick" appears in a number of viewer letters, especially during and following the presidential election. Merely commenting and taking stances on political issues at the time was apparently enough for some audience members to perceive the show as inappropriate.

Following Murray Davis's typology of cultural and social humor, *TW3* most frequently utilized jokes within the lower, first two levels of humor: linguistic and logical. Linguistic jokes utilize the semiotic uncertainty of language to play with words and phrases, such as puns, with *TW3* adding photographic and video uncertainty to the humor mix.[76] Writers also play extensively with logical humor, where two ideas or terms are irrationally linked to force audience reevaluation. Logical humor allows for a more critical perspective that, through comparison, can question underlying logic.[77] In one news report, anchors Buck Henry and Pat Englund cover relatively minor laws passed by Congress, juxtaposing much more important national problems lawmakers failed to address during their session: "Another piece of legislation amends the Missing Persons Act to cover certain people detained against their will in foreign countries. This will come as a great relief to Civil Rights workers in Mississippi."[78] The joke forces a comparison of Congress taking action against countries detaining Americans, while civil rights workers were being murdered in Southern states.[79]

While primarily focused on linguistic and logical humor, there are also many moments where the show participates in comedy on the level of humor and society. In Murray's typology, this kind of humor is the most disruptive to systems, calling into question the authority of ideological structures that form the basic social units of society, such as government, family, and religion. The pilot episode includes an excellent example of such humor: Henry Fonda reads headlines about a return to morality in America, followed by an "on the street" interview about the strides of American churches, with Gene Hackman playing a reverend. While the interview ostensibly discusses a renewal in faith, the dialogue drips with irony as Hackman tells the reporter his church "is on the verge of becoming a real part of the community" (figure 2.2).

Figure 2.2 A *TW3* Skit about the Role of Religion in Small-Town America Featuring Pat Englund and Guest Gene Hackman. *Source: Courtesy NBC/Photofest.*

The skit dramatizes the estrangement between American society and its institutions, further reinforced when the imaginary town's mayor shows up and encourages citizens to bribe police for better services. The story, presented in the style of a news headline and live interview, highlights the inconsistencies embodied in ideologies of trust in government and religion. Hackman delivers the edgiest line of the skit when he reports that small sins are on the increase, such as stealing Bibles from hotel rooms. He pauses and then continues, "I can't imagine why?"[80] The line delivered few audience laughs and seems especially transgressive—suggesting that Bibles have so little value in modern society that they are not even worth stealing. The line is one of several jokes during the show's run critiquing the role and significance of religion. A number of viewers complained about the show's making fun of clergy, signaling the comedy was subversive for its time.

Race and civil rights were also major topics addressed by *TW3* that were largely ignored by entertainment programs on television at the time. From the very start of the show, race was used in a satiric way, with a Black actor answering the phone at the White House. Soviet Premier Nikita Khrushchev calls and asks, unsuccessfully, first for JFK, then Lyndon Johnson, and then Bobby Kennedy, before finally asking, "Well, who is running the country?"

The actor, to raucous studio laughter, replies, "We are!"[81] The short bit reportedly spawned several letters of protest from offended white viewers.[82] Despite some complaints, one study found a majority of Southern viewers enjoyed the pilot.[83] During the regular season, Roscoe Lee Brown appeared in a number of episodes and seemed to be the only recurring actor of color, although Hayward was apparently not a fan, referring to him in one memo as "a mediocre colored boy."[84] In one skit, he comes in for a job interview with Henry Morgan, who falls all over himself to assure Brown that he is a civil rights supporter and not racist until it turns out that Brown has put down a deposit on a house in Morgan's neighborhood, causing Morgan to instantly change his tune and offer a tepid assurance that he's in Brown's corner. Brown responds: "Oh, I can see that. And may I say—it's mighty white of you."[85] The sketch is one of several examples of the program extending its criticism beyond outright racism and including the bigotry and hypocrisy of liberals who advocated legal but not social integration. The job interview sketch led to a song about National Brotherhood Week that described different groups that hate each other but will somehow, suddenly get along: "Be nice to people who are inferior to you, it's only for a week so have no fear. Be grateful that it doesn't last all year!"

Coverage of racial violence and Southern segregation became more frequent as the first season progressed and into the second season, especially stories around the Mississippi killings. The song "Philadelphia, Mississippi" (where the murders took place) criticized the sheriff and includes lines like "I will always love the magic of Mint-juleps and all-white juries!"[86] Letters complaining about the song appear to be part of a planned effort, given the similarities in the framing of their arguments. Multiple letters used "whataboutisms" common in contemporary conservative news and claimed that people in New York City are killed by Black criminals and that the show should cover those crimes too.[87] In a second-season episode, David Frost reports on the first African-American candidates for offices in Virginia by wryly noting, "Negroes have been run there before: run out of town, run up hill, run into the ground."[88] The line of dialogue recognizes how small reports of racial progress did not suture over historic and contemporary abuse of African-Americans. As the show progressed and criticisms of segregation continued, some Southern affiliates began removing *TW3* from their lineups.[89]

Opponents of civil rights were regularly presented as buffoons, as in a sketch featuring Alan Alda, Stanley Grover, and Sandy Baron as segregationist plumbers singing about the hiring of minority workers: "If your sewer ever fell in he'd be eatin' watermelon. How can some Spik from San Juan know enough to turn the hot water on?"[90] *Variety* complained that the skit "had the kind of vituperation that backfires" and was simply too mean, a frequent criticism of the show and a recognition that television still had strict boundaries of decorum at the time.[91] As with much of *TW3*'s content, the staff's support for civil rights is very much in line with the liberal ideology of the era and political views found in other media outlets beyond television. The growth of liberal humor may be one reason critics were hesitant to fully embrace *TW3*, as the show's brand of satire was less daring and confrontational than "sick humor" stand-up comedians or even alternative publications such as *Mad*. As a result, *TW3* was rarely recognized by the press for the risks it took in bringing satire to the nation's most mainstream medium and pushing the boundaries of acceptable topics for television.

Military strategy, such as the domino theory, and even the Vietnam War itself were also criticized; however, jokes about the armed forces and military actions were always directed at politicians and top commanders such as Secretary of Defense Robert McNamara, rather than everyday soldiers. For example, on the final show, David Frost predicts the news for the rest of the year, reporting that the only remaining troops in America will be sent to Bolivia.[92] Rather than questioning specific *military actions*, such as the increased bombing in Vietnam, the joke revolves around the *political decision* to constantly deploy troops worldwide to support American interests. Similarly, an extended commentary on Vietnam delivered by Frost is mostly critical of South Vietnamese officers and troops, though lauding the American soldiers and their ability to fight with insufficient equipment.[93]

Like most comedy, *TW3* engages in varying levels of humor, from simple wordplay to more complex social critique. Although the extent and effectiveness of its satire can be argued, *TW3* displayed a willingness to occasionally question the role of traditional institutions in American society. As previous examples show, a great deal of humor revolved around the political system and America's inability to elect forward-thinking candidates, as well as the bickering of Democrats and Republicans. While political jokes could be superficial, directed at personality traits or appearance, *TW3* took politicians to task for being ineffectual and representing their own interests, suggesting the problems were endemic to the system rather than isolated incidents. In that regard, *TW3* can be seen as a direct ancestor of shows like *The Daily Show* and *Last Week Tonight*.

THE PROBLEMS OF NEWS PARODY IN THE NETWORK ERA

TW3 was truly an anomaly for American prime-time networks in the early 1960s. Television programs would occasionally weave social commentary into storylines, such as an episode of *Bonanza* tackling racism, and there were attempts to schedule programs with a progressive agenda, like the CBS drama *East Side/West Side*; however, network support of socially conscious content was infrequent at best.[94] NBC's decision to pick up *TW3* still seems surprising, given the potential risk of the material and the controversies that swirled around the BBC program.

This era of American television, from the 1950s to the rise of cable in the 1980s, has been referred to by Amanda Lotz as the "network era," due to the immense industry power of ABC, CBS, and NBC.[95] If a producer wanted the content to reach a national audience, there were only three options; as a result, the networks could negotiate favorable terms, causing production companies to shoulder the initial cost of making a program. In addition to the networks, advertisers also wielded enormous power, with producers like Hayward beholden to both. Press coverage and archive materials demonstrate the difficulty of producing *TW3* during the heyday of the network era.

Advertisers were a constant worry for Hayward from the start. When NBC negotiated to carry *TW3* after the strength of the pilot, it was picked as a mid-season replacement for the failed *Harry's Girl*, which was presented by Colgate toothpaste. Viewers were obviously aware of the risk for advertisers in sponsoring topical satire, as several letters following the pilot mentioned they would support the show's advertisers. One claimed to have switched from Crest to Colgate, and another said sponsors should be "awarded purple hearts" for their courage. Producers likely used such letters in courting advertisers since positive lines about the sponsors in viewer mail had been underlined in red ink. Colgate passed on *TW3* as "too controversial."[96] Despite some open advertising gaps on *TW3*, the network scheduled the show's debut in January, thereby regaining control over the time slot. Advertising executives warned that the very qualities that made the show successful in Britain would keep American advertisers from signing up, but watchband maker Speidel, Clairol, and several other companies booked two-thirds of the spots on the program's season debut.[97] Despite *TW3*'s consistent third-place showing during its first season, the program eventually sold out all of its spots due to the relatively low cost of its advertising rates. Halfway through the first season, though, Speidel was the only one willing to commit to sponsoring a second season.[98] By the beginning of the summer, Speidel and other advertisers were pressuring NBC and threatening to pull out.[99]

Advertisers would directly contact Hayward, as well as NBC, with concerns and ideas about the direction of the show. For instance, a letter from Speidel says the company is not so much worried about the topics covered by *TW3* as they are about the focus on intellectual viewers and how everyday audience members might find "nothing on the show they feel is related to them."[100] Only two major dust-ups between the show and its advertisers made their way to the press. During the second episode, a previously mentioned news report on the links between smoking and cancer transitions into images of X-rays, people smoking, and hospital patients, combined with the song *Smoke Gets in Your Eyes*. The Brown and Williamson Tobacco Company threatened to pull its 60-second ad if the network did not cancel the segment. NBC surprisingly allowed the program to keep the sketch, and the advertiser made good on its threat.[101] Brown and Williamson pulled ads from two additional shows during the first season over jokes about smoking.[102]

Another controversy erupted over a news story in the premiere of the second season when Alan Alda reported the Catholic Church was creating a group for married men and that although priests still could not marry, the Vatican "said nothing about going steady."[103] Speidel executives received complaints from Catholic customers and quickly demanded Hayward issue an apology. The producer responded with the public statement: "I can understand why some may have found the reference inappropriate and we are sorry to have offended them."[104] While the BBC program was free from the economic pressures of advertising, the American *TW3* was attempting marketable satire to a broad audience while striving to avoid offending corporate interests. To make matters worse, the program fell victim to a proxy advertising war between the Democrats and Republicans leading up to the 1964 presidential elections.

Throughout its run, the show also had to contend with the power of the network to censor and cajole. NBC made it clear from the beginning that *TW3*'s news parody should operate under the same code of non-bias as the network's newscasts, and Hayward attempted to oblige, despite the progressive politics of the show's cast and writers. Alasdair Milne, the executive producer of the British *TW3*, insisted his staff regarded their show *as journalism* and complained that the American version was just show business.[105] Milne seemed to be genuinely outraged that the NBC show focused more on creating comedy than editorializing on the news.[106] Objectivity in journalism was coming under increased scrutiny at the time, following the press's timid responses to the McCarthy hearings and segregation in the 1950s.[107] Still, objectivity continued to be the defining characteristic of American journalism and structured the routines of reporting, leading to common approaches for gathering and reporting news. Both NBC and Hayward likely appealed to objectivity for some of the same reasons as journalists—including to insulate the show and network from accusations of bias and the financial repercussions that could accompany such a perception.

From the start, rumors of interference circulated in the press. Hayward wrote a defensive letter after a *TV Guide* article reported that advertisers and the network were pressuring the show: "NBC has given us the fullest possible freedom to do our show as we want to as have the agencies and advertisers involved."[108] The reality did not seem to live up to the rhetoric, though. As the first season leaned more and more heavily on Republican targets, Hayward made special efforts to enforce an image of impartiality. The producer gave *TW3* writers reminders to switch out the victims of its humor, so if jokes were made about Goldwater one week, Hayward expected writers to look elsewhere the following week.[109] In a *Variety* interview, Nancy Ames claimed that NBC approved every word of scripts and forbade ad-libbing, reporting that the cast wanted to perform edgier material but was constantly told it might offend different groups and they should "mind their own business."[110] Shortly after the start of the second season, the network tightened the reins and flatly laid out that "all matters involving taste will be under the final and exclusive jurisdiction of NBC," and that *TW3* would have to abide by the Fairness Doctrine, the FCC policy requiring networks to provide equal time to conflicting political viewpoints.[111] Applying objectivity to comedy seemed an odd combination for some reviewers. One critic wrote that some politicians make themselves targets of humor by their stances and that "good satire doesn't pick its marks by any foolish concept of balance."[112] However, Hayward became so concerned about potential political controversies that he told reporters the show would increase the number of jokes about foreign countries in the second season because "domestic topics are touchier."[113]

Although both Hayward and NBC advertised the network's hands-off approach to *TW3*, reports from network and program staff reveal Hayward was under constant pressure to tone down content and avoid some controversial topics. During the second-season preemptions, Hayward reportedly threatened to send letters to newspapers accusing the Republicans of trying to block jokes about Goldwater, bringing a swift response from NBC that it "advised strongly against the tirade."[114] The network specifically claimed that such an action would compromise the show's objectivity. Network representatives attended show rehearsals and closely oversaw the production of the program, and NBC executive Ed Friendly coaxed Hayward into making decisions amenable to the network.[115]

By the time *TW3* entered its second season, the network had all but given up on its prospects of success. Producer Marshall Jamison objected to plans by NBC and Hayward to soften the program's satire and appeal to broader audiences and was forced off the program. The cast and crew were narrowed down to a smaller core group, and Herb Sargent replaced Jamison as producer.[116] NBC signaled its indifference to the show when the network gave in to Jack Paar, who wanted to extend his own program to 90 minutes, and switched *TW3* from Friday to Tuesday nights. Although *TW3* lagged behind its competitors in ratings, its audience was loyal, and as Jeffrey S. Miller points out, rescheduling a show called *TW3* early in the week seems especially illogical—yet another sign of the lack of network support.[117] One critic dubbed Tuesday at 9:30 the "least enviable timeslot," and another writer suggested the switch was the equivalent of placing *TW3* "on the sacrificial block."[118] As expected, *TW3* stayed at third in the ratings, with tepid numbers, and after only nine episodes of the new season, NBC formally announced it was canceling the show as of April.

The power of advertisers and NBC during the network era forced *TW3* to play its satire safer than future news-parody programs. Another byproduct of the limited distribution options for television programs was the necessity for any network show to target a national, homogenous audience. Despite a small, dedicated viewership, *TW3*'s numbers could not sustain a prime-time network program in the 1960s. After the cancellation was announced, an NBC source told *The Washington Post* that the network expected the program to appeal to a limited audience, but the share of even that smaller segment was insufficient to keep *TW3* on the air.[119]

TW3: AHEAD OF ITS TIME?

The actors and staff of the show made a concerted effort to bring satire and news parody to American television, but *TW3* was a poor fit for commercial prime time, both in content and appeal. Audiences and critics seeking savvy satire found themselves frustrated by its milquetoast approach, and interference from network executives and advertisers pushed the show to be as hesitant and inoffensive in its humor as possible. Had NBC, Hayward, and the era's advertising and economic conditions allowed the program to pursue the same humor as the BBC program, *TW3* might well have found the "limited audience" NBC was supposedly targeting. The cancellation of the British *TW3* and its Canadian spinoff *This Hour Has Seven Days* brought swift condemnations from audiences and some politicians. In comparison, press coverage of NBC's decision to cancel the program approached the story as if *TW3* were already dead and the network had just found a burial plot.

The show was attempting to break new ground at a time when television may have been *the* most conservative medium in the United States. By the beginning of the 1970s, the networks began to program shows more reflective of America's changing culture, but when *TW3* was being produced, entertainment programming was still largely stuck in a rarified 1950s concept of the nation. Despite its uneven humor, the program was one of the few to critique mainstream values and conventional wisdom at a time when television executives saw little to gain from controversy except angry advertisers.

If contemporary news parody has achieved success as a critic of journalism and culture, *TW3* can best be described as a milestone along that path. The program suffered from all of the shortcomings that inherently plague the news-parody genre, such as its reliance on already-existing press accounts and the agenda-setting abilities of traditional journalism. However, *TW3* emerged into a media environment where television journalists were still fighting their own battle for legitimacy. Publications by the RTNDA and CBS defensively argued that television reporters *are* journalists—not just technicians or actors, an assumption that reflects a bias against television reporters in the profession.[120] Television news lacked cultural capital in the journalistic field because of its youth and its connection to the visual over the written. Coverage of the Kennedy assassination showed the importance of the format, but it would be later in the decade, covering civil rights and Vietnam, when network news became an indispensable part of the journalistic milieu. Clearly, if the network newscasts themselves were still considered suspect, no one would consider whether a *parody* of those newscasts might raise legitimate critiques about politics and society. By the mid-1970s, when *SNL* went on air, news agencies could not help but recognize how the show's constant portrayal of a bumbling Gerald Ford helped shape public perception of the president. Had *TW3* debuted a decade later, especially in a post-Watergate culture, the show might have had an opportunity to influence culture and engage in more media critique.

Despite its struggles and ultimate cancellation, the greatest success of *TW3* was its influence on subsequent satire and news-parody programs and the lessons learned. The program seemed to show that the pressures of a prime-time network program are at odds with the appeal of the news-parody genre. Whether this is true or not, with few exceptions, the networks have stayed away from prime-time shows emphasizing news parody. Later programs moved to late-night and eventually cable outlets to find a more specialized audience, making *TW3*'s two shortened seasons the nation's longest run of prime-time network news parody.

Several people involved with *TW3* continued to pursue the genre, furthering the influence of the program. Herb Sargent, who produced the second season of *TW3*, went on to write for *SNL*, specifically helping to create the "Weekend Update" segment of the program. Sargent made a failed 1976 attempt to revive *TW3* after *SNL*'s successful debut and again tried to create a prime-time news-parody program with the short-lived *The News Is the News* in 1983. David Frost also participated in an attempt to remake *TW3*, this time in the 1980s, starring opposite Anne Bancroft. Actor Buck Henry went on to host and make guest appearances on *SNL* multiple times in the early days of the program.

Subsequent news-parody shows seemed to learn from *TW3*'s jumbled mix of variety-show formats, which was faulted by some critics. The constant digressions of sketch comedy worked against *TW3* constructing a consistent parody since broadcast news utilized one of the most highly structured television formats. The repeated shifting of actors back and forth between playing anchors and characters in other skits and songs also interrupted the immersion required for effective parody. By interspersing skits, the news parody was limited in its scope. The syntax of individual news *stories* could still be copied, but the overall look and sobriety of the news *programs* could only be suggested.

Although *TW3* was considered a failed experiment by both critics and the network itself, the program suggested an American appetite for news satire and parody—even if the time was not right. NBC executive vice president Walter Scott wrote a report on the show shortly before the network decided not to renew *TW3*. Scott said he was glad they tried the show but acknowledged that the pressures and unique format of topical satire were simply too much for television at the time:

> On the matter of quality, there is a strong feeling that the show is impossible to do on a regular basis. The task of being topical, original and funny every week is a heavy one for the producer, director and writers. No other show in television faces such a task.[121]

NOTES

1. Dave Kaufman, "Lafferty: Public Demands TV Dream World; Cites Drop in Show Presentations," *Daily Variety*, July 27, 1967, 1, 10.

2. Hal Erickson, *"From Beautiful Downtown Burbank": A Critical History of Rowan and Martin's Laugh in, 1968-1973* (Jefferson, NC: McFarland & Company, Inc., 2000), 37.

3. For more on the satire boom and the British *TW3*, see Humphrey Carpenter, *A Great Big Silly Grin: The British Satire Boom of the 1960s* (New York: Public Affairs, 2002); Matt Crowder, "A Space and Time for Entertainment: *That Was The Week That Was* and Viewers' Utopian Expectations," *Historical Journal of Film, Radio and Television* 34, no. 3 (2014); Jeffrey S. Miller, *Something Completely Different: British Television and American Culture* (Minneapolis, MN: University of Minnesota Press, 2000); Jerry Palmer, *The Logic of the Absurd: On Film and Television* (London: British Film Institute, 1987); Keith Suter, "The British Satirical Revolution," *Contemporary Review* 285, no. 1664 (2004); Stephen Wagg, "Comedy, Politics and Permissiveness: The 'Satire Boom' and Its Inheritance," *Contemporary Politics* 8, no. 4 (2002).

4. A *New York Times* article, for instance, called the program "the most controversial show in British television history." Sydney Gruson, "B.B.C. Satire Show to Take Breather," *New York Times*, May 2, 1963, 5.

5. Clive Barnes, "Britain's 'TWTWTW'," *New York Times*, September 22, 1963, 133.

6. Stephen Kercher, *Revel with a Cause: Liberal Satire in Postwar America* (Chicago, IL: The University of Chicago Press, 2006); Ethan Thompson, *Parody and Taste in Postwar American Television Culture* (New York: Routledge, 2011).

7. For more on sick humor, see Tony Hendra, *Going Too Far* (New York: Dolphin Book, 1987); Vwadek P. Marciniak, *Politics, Humor and the Counterculture: Laughter in the Age of Decay* (New York: Peter Lang, 2008), Chapter 2.

8. Thompson, *Parody and Taste*, 45.

9. Ibid., 146.

10. "FCC's Henry: 'If Dig You Must (on Controversy) We'll Back You'," *Weekly Variety*, September 25, 1963, 27, 44.

11. Herm, "What's Going on Here," *Weekly Variety*, May 15, 1963, 39.

12. Another attempt at topical satire on WNEW, *The Establishment*, likewise failed later the same year.

13. Val Adams, "News of TV and Radio," *New York Times*, June 16, 1963, 103.

14. Jack Hellman, "Light and Airy," *Daily Variety*, September 25, 1963, 27, 44.

15. *That Was the Week That Was*, Pilot, Paley Center for Media - Catalog ID T78:0228. November 10, 1963.

16. Helm, "That Was the Week That Was," *Daily Variety*, November 12, 1963, 6.

17. Jack Gould, "'That Was The Week That Was'," *New York Times*, November 11, 1963, 63.

18. Rick Du Brow, "3TW Experiment Should Be a Series," *Washington Post*, November 13, 1963, C8.

19. Report on the Mail Response to *That Was the Week That Was*, November 10, 1963, Leland Hayward Papers (LHP), Box 154, Folder 8, New York Public Library for the Performing Arts (NYPL).

20. Telephone Transcript: Leland Hayes and Katherine Cole, November 13, 1963, LHP, Box 120, Folder 10, NYPL.

21. *That Was the Week That Was* Viewer Mail, LHP, Box 117, Folder 1, NYPL.

22. Jack Gould, "TV: 'That Was Week That Was' Returns to N.B.C.," *New York Times*, January 11, 1964, 53; Helm, "That Was the Week That Was," *Daily Variety*, January 13, 1964, 6; Rose, "'That Was the Week That Was'," *Weekly Variety*, January 15, 1964, 35.

23. Jack Gould, "TV: Finding the Target," *New York Times*, January 25, 1964, 49.

24. Jack Gould, "TV: Tasteless Satire," *New York Times*, September 30, 1964, 87.

25. "*Fan Mail Report for Sept. 29-Nov. 9, 1964*" 1964, LHP, Box 154, Folder 8, NYPL.

26. *That Was the Week That Was* Viewer Mail, LHP, Box 119, Folders 1–3, NYPL.

27. "Lament of 'TW3' Writer; 'Save Us from Friends'," *Weekly Variety*, December 13, 1964, 20, 36.

28. *That Was the Week That Was*, Episode 1, Paley Center for Media - Catalog ID T78:0257. January 10, 1964.

29. *That Was the Week That Was*, Pilot.

30. The *CBS Evening News* became the first nighttime half hour network news program on September 2, 1963, expanding from its previous 15-minute format, but retaining Walter Cronkite at the anchor desk.

31. See, for instance, CBS News, *Television News Reporting* (New York: McGraw-Hill Book Company, Inc., 1958); Leo Willette, *So You're Gonna Shoot Newsfilm* (Detroit, MI: Inland Press, 1960).

32. The Radio Television News Director Association and Time-Life Broadcast Inc., ed., *Television Newsfilm Standards Manual* (New York: Time-Life Broadcast, 1964).

33. George Corrin, "Make News Come Alive by Visual Means," in *The Newsroom and the Newscast*, ed. The Radio Television News Director Association and Time-Life Broadcast Inc. (New York: Time-Life Broadcast, 1966).

34. CBS News, for example, encouraged stretching out footage over the course of the newscast to retain viewer interest. CBS News, *Television News Reporting*, 109–10.

35. The technique of revealing sets is a shared device of both newscasts and variety programs. Revealing nondiegetic space or laying bare the artifice, while violating traditional film and television aesthetics, is commonly incorporated into both of these television formats, creating a point of visual overlap.

36. *That Was the Week That Was*, Episode 13, Paley Center for Media - Catalog ID T78:0256. April 17, 1964.

37. *That Was the Week That Was*, Pilot.

38. Matt Fotis describes how the public was very familiar with Kennedy's press conferences. As a result, comedians like The Second City and Vaughn Meader also used mock Kennedy press conferences in their routines. Matt Fotis, *Satire & the State: Sketch Comedy and the Presidency* (New York: Routledge, 2020), 90.

39. *That Was the Week That Was*, Episode 48, Paley Center for Media - Catalog ID T78:0262. April 20, 1965.

40. For more on the use of pictures and graphics in news production during the late-1950s and early 1960s, see Ted Siller, Ted White, and Hal Trekel, *Television and Radio News* (New York: The Macmillan Company, 1960), 116–18.

41. *That Was the Week That Was*, Pilot.

42. *That Was the Week That Was*, Episode 48.

43. *That Was the Week That Was*, Episode 13.

44. Margaret Morse, "News as Performance: The Image as an Event," in *The Television Studies Reader*, ed. Robert C. Allen and Annette Hill (London: Routledge, 2004), 213.

45. Jeff Alan and James M. Lane, *Anchoring America: The Changing Face of Network News* (Chicago, IL: Bonus Books, 2003), 90.

46. Ibid., 117.

47. As a result, *TW3* featured female news anchors a decade before network newscasts, producing another, perhaps unintended, critique.

48. *That Was the Week That Was* Presentation 1963, LHP, Box 122, Folder 1, NYPL.

49. Leland Hayward to Marshall Jamison, March 13, 1964, LHP, Box 121, Folder 11, NYPL.

50. Leland Hayward to Herb Sargent, December 9, 1964, LHP, Box 121, Folder 20, NYPL.

51. CBS News, *Television News Reporting*, 132.

52. Geoffrey Baym, *From Cronkite to Colbert: The Evolution of Broadcast News* (Boulder, CO: Paradigm Publishers, 2010), 9–15.
53. *That Was the Week That Was*, Pilot.
54. *That Was the Week That Was*, Episode 1.
55. For more on the role of the news anchor in constructing the audience, see Stuart Allan, *News Culture*, 3rd ed. (Berkshire, UK: Open University Press, 2010), 115–17.
56. *That Was the Week That Was*, Episode 13.
57. CBS News, *Television News Reporting*, 161–63.
58. *That Was the Week That Was*, Episode 48.
59. *That Was the Week That Was* Viewer Mail, LHP, Box 117, Folder 3, NYPL.
60. For discussion of the BBC special episode and the response by American audiences see Aniko Bodroghkozy, "Political Satire, *That Was The Week That Was*, and the Assassination of John F. Kennedy," *Television & New Media* 22, no. 8 (2021).
61. *That Was the Week That Was*, Pilot.
62. Telephone Transcript: Leland Hayes and Katherine Cole, November 13, 1963.
63. *That Was the Week That Was*, Pilot Draft Script, 1963, LHP, Box 122, Folder 13, NYPL.
64. Interview with writer Robert Emmett, reported in Kercher, *Revel with a Cause*, 376–77.
65. Rose, "'That Was the Week That Was.'"
66. *That Was the Week That Was*, Episode 1.
67. *That Was the Week That Was* As Broadcast Script, June 12, 1964, LHP, Box 131, Folder 5, NYPL.
68. *That Was the Week That Was*, Episode 13.
69. Bill Greeley, "'Gotta Be More Witty Than Mean' Keys Hayward Revamp for 'TW3'," *Weekly Variety*, July 8, 1964, 19, 42.
70. Les, "That Was the Week That Was," *Weekly Variety*, October 7, 1964, 26.
71. *That Was the Week That Was* As Broadcast Script, September 29, 1964, LHP, Box 133, Folder 12, NYPL.
72. The controversy led David Frost to tell reporters the show would be a better ad buy for Democrats because of all the *former* Republicans in *TW3*'s audience. "Behind-the-Scene TV Confrontation for Demos & GOP," *Weekly Variety*, September 23, 1964, 35.
73. *That Was the Week That Was* Viewer Mail, LHP, Box 117, Folders 3-6, Box 118, Folder 1, NYPL.
74. *That Was the Week That Was* As Broadcast Script, January 26, 1965, LHP, Box 139, Folder 5, NYPL.
75. *That Was the Week That Was*, Episode 50, Paley Center for Media - Catalog ID T78:0131. May 4, 1965.
76. Murray Davis, *What's So Funny?: The Comic Conception of Culture and Society* (Chicago, IL: The University of Chicago Press, 1993), 36–44.
77. Ibid., 66–71.
78. *That Was the Week That Was* As Broadcast Script, December 29, 1964, LHP, Box 137, Folder 15, NYPL.

79. The line is a specific reference to the murder of three civil rights workers in Mississippi in 1964 by white supremacists, including law enforcement, and the refusal of authorities to prosecute the killers. *TW3* had addressed the story on several previous episodes as details emerged. Perhaps unfairly, the joke ignores the important passage of the Civil Rights Bill of 1964 following the murders, although racial violence was obviously not brought to an end by the legislation.

80. *That Was the Week That Was*, Pilot.

81. Ibid.; Telephone Transcript: Conversation with Hedda Hopper, November 13, 1963, LHP, Box 120, Folder 10, NYPL. The line was originally the grammatically incorrect "We is," but Hayes reported in his conversation with Hedda Hopper that he tried the joke on the show's band leader and an actor, both of whom were Black, and they suggested the change.

82. Reported in Kercher, *Revel with a Cause*, 368.

83. "Southern Conservatives Don't Mind Being Ribbed; a Survey to Prove It," *Weekly Variety*, November 20, 1963, 37.

84. Leland Hayward to Marshall Jamison, March 13, 1964. Given the date and the lack of other Black actors, I am inferring this was a reference to Brown.

85. *That Was the Week That Was* As Broadcast Script, February 21, 1964, LHP, Box 125, Folder 4, NYPL.

86. *That Was the Week That Was* As Broadcast Script, December 8, 1964, LHP, Box 136, Folder 6, NYPL.

87. *That Was the Week That Was* Viewer Mail, LHP, Box 119, Folder 1-2, NYPL. One inventive viewer even sent in a song parody about violence in Northern towns called "Oh Manhattan," calling it the "Equal Time Song."

88. *That Was the Week That Was*, Episode 48.

89. Dave Kaufman, "TV 'Chicken', Beefs Henry; Silliphant Changes Mind," *Daily Variety*, May 25, 1966, 13.

90. *That Was the Week That Was* As Broadcast Script, May 8, 1964, LHP, Box 128, Folder 16, NYPL. The sketch, 'Plumb Line,' was about an actual work stoppage in New York City, following the hiring of four non-union minority plumbers by a contractor.

91. Bill, "That Was the Week That Was," *Weekly Variety*, May 13, 1964, 39.

92. *That Was the Week That Was*, Episode 50.

93. *That Was the Week That Was* As Broadcast Script, December 29, 1964, LHP, Box 137, Folder 15, NYPL.

94. For more discussion of American television and social commentary during the 1960s, see Aniko Bodroghkozy, *Groove Tube: Sixties Television and the Youth Rebellion* (Durham, NC: Duke University Press, 2001); LeRoy Ashby, *With Amusement for All: A History of American Popular Culture since 1830* (Lexington, KY: The University Press of Kentucky, 2006), 357–65.

95. Amanda Lotz, *The Television Will Be Revolutionized* (New York: New York University, 2007), 9–12.

96. "Colgate Brushes Timeslot as NBC-TV Replaces 'Girls' with 'The Week That Was'," *Daily Variety*, December 4, 1963, 1; "'TW3' Too Hot, Colgate Sez No," *Weekly Variety*, November 27, 1963, 21.

97. George Rosen, "Kintner: 'We'll Take Charge'," *Weekly Variety*, December 11, 1963, 21, 36.

98. Bill Greeley, "'That Was the Cast That Was' as NBC Plans Fresh Show for Fall," *Weekly Variety*, April 22, 1964, 105, 20.

99. Thomas Ryan to Leland Hayward, June 2, 1964, LHP, Box 121, Folder 14, NYPL.

100. Charles Spitzer to Leland Hayward, March 2, 1964, LHP, Box 121, Folder 11, NYPL.

101. "'T.W.3' Smoking Spoof Gets in Sponsor's Eye," *New York Times*, January 24, 1964, 57. The segment was an audience favorite and was repeated on the last episode of the program.

102. Greeley, "Gotta Be More Witty."

103. *That Was the Week That Was* As Broadcast Script, September 29, 1964, LHP, Box 133, Folder 12, NYPL.

104. Val Adams, "N.B.C. Apologizes to 'T.W.3' Sponsor," *New York Times*, October 3, 1964, 59.

105. "British Producer Laments: TV News Needs Bit of Wit," *Weekly Variety*, December 4, 1963, 38.

106. Jeffrey S. Miller provides an excellent comparison between the two versions of *TW3* and the inability of the NBC show to translate the British sensibility of the original. Miller, *Something Completely Different: British Television and American Culture*, 113–23.

107. See David R. Davies, "The Challenges of Civil Rights and Joseph Mccarthy," in *Fair & Balanced: A History of Journalistic Objectivity* ed. Steven R. Knowlton and Karen L. Freeman (Northport, AL: Vision Press, 2005).

108. Leland Hayward Letter to TV Guide, January 22, 1964, LHP, Box 121, Folder 9, NYPL.

109. Greeley, "'Gotta Be More Witty.'"

110. Dave Kaufman, "Report Sponsor Sensitivity Weakens 'Week That Was'," *Daily Variety*, April 1, 1964, 8.

111. Thomas Ryan to Leland Hayward, October 14, 1964, LHP, Box 121, Folder 18, NYPL.

112. Bill, "That Was the Week That Was."

113. Paul Gardner, "'Week That Was' Won't Stay as Is Next Season," *New York Times*, July 10, 1964, 59.

114. Bill Greeley, "TV's 'Undesirable' Ad Clients: Demos & GOP Pose Headaches," *Weekly Variety*, September 30, 1964, 31, 48.

115. Ed Friendly to Leland Hayward, April 13, 1964, LHP, Box 121, Folder 11, NYPL.

116. "Jamison Exits 'TW3' in Hassle," *Weekly Variety*, June 17, 1964, 26, 42.

117. Jeffrey S. Miller, "What Closes on Saturday Night," in *NBC: America's Network*, ed. Michele Hilmes (Berkeley, CA: University of California Press, 2007).

118. Les, "That Was the Week That Was."; Greeley, "TV's 'Undesirable' Ad."

119. "The Week That Wasn't," *Washington Post*, May 8, 1965, A, 14.

120. The Radio Television News Director Association and Time-Life Broadcast Inc., *Television Newsfilm Standards Manual*.

121. Report on *That Was the Week That Was*, February 9, 1965, LHP, Box 122, Folder 2, NYPL.

Chapter 3

"Weekend Update"
Moving News Parody to Late Night

A decade after *That Was the Week That Was* (*TW3*) exploded onto American airwaves and quickly fizzled out, the longest-running news parody segment in television history debuted again on NBC. *Saturday Night Live* (*SNL*) and its "Weekend Update" segment proved immensely popular with both audiences and critics. Although only ten years had passed from 1965 to 1975, the landscape of popular culture had shifted in favor of edgy comedy, looking to cut national leaders down to size. The remnants of television's "golden age" were long absent from the dial, replaced with programs attempting to tackle contemporary issues, like *All in the Family* and *Maude*. Assassinations, Vietnam, Watergate, and other national traumas combined with movements demanding greater equality, forcing ideological shifts reflected in changing popular tastes. *SNL* emerged into a very different culture than *TW3* left; one dramatic indicator of this shift is how conservative politicians attempted to preempt *TW3*, while in contrast, Gerald Ford, the sitting Republican president, made a cameo appearance on *SNL* during its first season.

Changes in the cultural milieu can only account for so much of the success of *SNL* and "Weekend Update" during their first five seasons. This chapter examines how "Weekend Update" effectively created a separate generic space for news parody to flourish and how the segment went beyond simple mimicry of news formatting to critique not only newsmakers but also broadcast journalists and their methods, participating in the larger journalistic field. Discourses surrounding "Weekend Update" accelerated comparisons to traditional journalism in the twenty-first century, often grouping the segment with *The Daily Show with John Stewart* (*TDS*) and *The Colbert Report* (*Colbert*) as a type of entertainment-oriented news or media critic. However, even in its infancy, "Weekend Update" generated some concerns about potential confusion with traditional news, as its satire became watercooler talk for politicians and journalists.[1] Its inroads into the journalistic field began during these formative seasons.

From the time *TW3* left the air to the creation of *SNL*, political humor gained momentum and more acceptance in mainstream culture. On television, several shows attempted to keep political humor alive, while navigating the murky waters of network control. Running from 1967 to 1969, *The Smothers Brothers Comedy Hour* ran afoul of the same type of network fears that sank *TW3*. Through sketch comedy directed at politicians, race relations, and Vietnam, as well as their choice of musical acts connected to the counterculture, Tom and Dick Smothers consistently squared off with CBS executives and censors, which resulted in cancellation after only three seasons.[2] When Dan Rowan and Dick Martin developed *Rowan and Martin's Laugh-In* for NBC in 1968, the sketch comedy pushed the limits but never ended up in the kind of bitter network feud the Smothers Brothers experienced and lasted until 1973. *Laugh-In* even regularly featured a news segment called both "The Rowan and Martin Report" and "*Laugh-In* Looks at the News." The segment was purely stand-up comedy and sketches about the news, though, not a parody of network newscasts. When *SNL* began, some critics linked the program's tendency to push the limits of network television with *Laugh-In* and *TW3*.[3]

Political satire was likewise on the rise in other media.[4] In theaters, films like *Blazing Saddles* (1974) and *M*A*S*H* (1970) found success marrying humor and politics. In 1970 *National Lampoon* magazine began publishing its own brand of satire, finding success among college students and expanding its humor brand to include radio programs and films. A number of *SNL* writers and cast members worked for *National Lampoon* media, including Michael O'Donoghue, Bill Murray, John Belushi, and Gilda Radner. Comedians like George Carlin and Richard Pryor brought their stand-up routines of cultural criticism to record stores and concert halls and became involved with *SNL* as hosts. The program benefited from the cross-pollination of humor during the 1970s, picking up performers and writers from other successful media. When *SNL* debuted, the program was almost a compendium of contemporary directions in comedy and seemed groundbreaking mostly for appearing on television, perhaps the tamest medium at the time.

THE ORIGINS OF "WEEKEND UPDATE"

In 1974, NBC hired Dick Ebersol to create weekend late-night programming. Ebersol sought out Lorne Michaels, who had written for *Laugh-In* and Lily Tomlin specials, to develop a late-night program. The network was especially interested in targeting young people, and early promotions for *SNL* played up the show's potential for edgy comedy. A month before the program debuted, Ebersol told reporters the late-night time spot would make *SNL* "free of primetime restraints, [they] can experiment with new forms as well as new fades [*sic*]."[5] From its first episode, *SNL* became the talk of the entertainment industry and of the young crowd NBC was hoping to attract.[6] Writers aligned the program with a young, hip demographic through drug and sex references and its consistent bashing of conservative politics. *SNL* was a major success, and the program was frequently referred to as NBC's biggest hit of the 1975 season—a particularly dismal one for prime-time shows, with one reviewer calling *SNL* "the most significant and welcome TV development of the year."[7] With the network in last place for ratings, the program represented a bright spot executives hoped to capitalize on, wanting "to capture the contemporary appeal of the show during primetime."[8]

From the earliest incarnations of *SNL*, Michaels planned to include a news-parody segment. His 1970 Canadian program *The Hart and Lorne Terrific Hour* featured a recurring news-parody sketch. He adapted the idea when pitching *SNL* to the network. After Watergate and the hours of television time devoted to coverage of the scandal, Michaels said audiences "were very familiar with news and news anchors and how the news was presented."[9] For Michaels, the entire show would be a meta-reference to television conventions and would at least satirize those conventions, if not outright parody them. He reportedly told Ebersol in their first meeting, "I want to do a show for the generation that grew up on television."[10] Michaels tapped former *TW3* and *Tonight Show* writer Herb Sargent and newcomer Alan Zweibel as the main writers for "Weekend Update," although others would regularly submit jokes for the segment. The coverage of late 1960s and early 1970s riots, assassinations, marches, and government scandals made television news one of the most familiar genres on the small screen and ripe for parody.

Earlier programs like *TW3* and *Laugh-In* provided inspiration for *SNL* creators, but "Weekend Update" represented a total revamp of news parody. *SNL* crafted a cohesive, self-contained news segment, where the structure and presentation were as much a part of the humor as the scripted lines. True parody is based on an imitation of style. In *Reading Television*, John Fiske and John Hartley describe the aesthetic codes of television and how they work on both denotative and connotative levels to create audience expectation and meaning.[11] So, on a formal level, we know we are watching a soap opera because of its mise-en-scène and method of production, and we as an audience adjust our expectations based on those codes. The more elaborate mimicry of news style in "Weekend Update" set it apart from the variety show structure of *SNL*, tied closer to its source material of news than the surrounding skits.[12] By carving out a special segment dedicated to news, *SNL* provided a familiar, recurring format and time for the audience to immerse themselves weekly in sustained television news parody divorced from sketch comedy.

The segment was a catalog of the visual and spoken grammar and syntax of television news in the 1970s. As the decade moved along, "Weekend Update" introduced small changes to further replicate newscasts. As Jeremy Butler has written, television style encompasses a broad range of elements, including editing, camera placement, and even methods of persuasion.[13] One obvious aspect of visual style is set design, and the ever-evolving news set of "Weekend Update" offers a highly salient example of how the segment shifted to replicate different approaches to news.

CHANGING STYLE OVER THE FIRST FIVE SEASONS

Before the show's debut, Michaels reportedly planned to anchor the segment himself but grew concerned about potential conflicts from having to act as both producer and talent.[14] Instead, Michaels assigned former *Smothers Brothers* writer Chevy Chase to the anchor desk following a screen test.[15] Chase acted as the sole anchor for the first season of "Weekend Update," although other talent regularly appeared as supporting cast: Laraine Newman portrayed a roving reporter who would conduct faux-live shots from a separate set; Jane Curtin appeared to deliver editorial statements, usually as Chase silently mocked her; and Gilda Radner debuted her Emily Latella character, known for confusing words and inadvertently delivering commentary on "presidential erections" and "the deaf penalty." There was no doubt, however, that Chase was considered to be the embodiment of "Weekend Update" in the inaugural season of the show. Thanks to the news-parody segment and his frequent pratfalls in character as Gerald Ford, Chase quickly became the biggest star on *SNL*.[16] The first season established the structure for "Weekend Update," including its placement within the lineup around midnight (partially to keep viewers watching) and the initial inclusion of a fake commercial spot, which broke the segment into two parts. The segment doubled in length over the course of the first season, eventually taking up almost nine minutes of the program.

When Chase began anchoring in 1975, the "Weekend Update" set was minimalist—a sketch of an actual newsroom. He was seated at a simple anchor desk with a black phone on top in front of a gray wall with a sign reading "Weekend Update." When graphics were called for, an angled shot of the desk revealed a crude cutout meant to look like a monitor. However, unlike *TW3*, which jumped from set to set, "Weekend Update" limited the segment to that simple news space. Even when "live reports" were taking place on another set, the cameras never reveal the artifice. This was a major innovation of "Weekend Update," creating a tightly controlled diegetic space separated from the rest of the studio to further the parody (figure 3.1).

In episode eight of the first season, the set gets a slight revamp. A lighter gray, marbled look for both the wall and entire anchor desk gives a brighter, more contemporary feel. Even the sign on the wall is repainted with the same color scheme. The original, small desk is replaced with an L-shaped desk with Chase positioned at the bend and the "Weekend Update" logo in cut letters moves from the wall to across the middle of the desk. The changes resulted in a more modern, professional appearance for the remainder of the season. The segment included an audio track of a teletype machine playing underneath the main audio to reinforce the trappings of journalistic authority.

This set remained in place during season two as Chase continued to anchor "Weekend Update." Jane Curtin filled in for the second and third episode of season two after Chase reportedly injured himself in the season opener. Curtin permanently took over the "Weekend Update" desk on episode seven, after Chase's departure from the show. The structure of the segment did not change, with Newman continuing her occasional remote reports and Radner reprising her Emily Latella character. New cast member Bill Murray provided infrequent commentaries, but, overall, fewer cast members appeared on "Weekend Update" in its second season.

In 1977, the premiere of the third season of *SNL* inaugurated a redesigned look and structure for "Weekend Update." Copying a format increasingly favored by local news, the segment adopted an "eyewitness" news-team

Figure 3.1 Chevy Chase on "Weekend Update," Season 1. *Source*: Screenshot by the author.

approach. The eyewitness style emphasized the concept of a news "family," with male and female anchors, weather and sports coverage, and reporters appearing on set. Curtin and Dan Aykroyd acted as coanchors, with Murray as an entertainment critic. In the first episode, Garrett Morris provided sports, and John Belushi appeared on the desk as a special correspondent, while Newman reprised her roving-reporter role.[17] The redesign drew praise from a *Variety* reviewer, who singled out "Weekend Update" as one of the best changes for the new season.[18] However, the segment seems rushed and disjointed, and by the second episode of the season the cast was trimmed, with only Curtin, Aykroyd, and Murray remaining as regulars on the news desk. Other talent continued to appear in special roles for the segment, including Newman's live reports and a new editorial character from Radner, Roseanne Roseannadanna.

The set also hewed more closely to local news style. The fake ad break was removed, creating one longer, sustained segment. The simple, more neutral grays of the set were replaced with warm blues and high-energy visuals. An open V-shaped desk reinforced the news-team feel, allowing reporters to sit right next to Curtin and Aykroyd to create a sense of intimacy. The set was much more dynamic, with "Weekend Update" running across the length of the wall in multiple columns, populating the entire background with letters. This visual emphasis on the program name was in line with local news, which increasingly used their newscast show title to market journalism as a product. The black telephone remained on the desk, providing a visual constant between shots. The overall design was one of slick professionalism.

The set originally lacked a monitor area to key visuals; instead, images were chroma-keyed directly behind the anchors. This approach to news graphic presentation looks odd in retrospect, with the wall reading "Weekend Update" appearing or disappearing from behind the anchor based on graphics; however, chroma-keying anchors into newsfilm was actually in vogue with some stations at the time.[19] *SNL* producers apparently rejected the look and added a fake monitor for graphics by the seventh episode. The changes in season three visually shifted the segment's parody to local "action" news teams.

The news-team concept continued during seasons four and five, but with Murray replacing Aykroyd as coanchor with Curtin. Two recurring characters were introduced: Garrett Morris played the highly stereotyped Hispanic ex-baseball player/sportscaster Chico Escuela, and comedian Don Novello appeared as the fictional priest Father Guido Sarducci, credited as the gossip columnist and music critic for *The Vatican Enquirer*. Radner's Roseanne Roseannadanna also continued as a regular commentator.

The set changed from the former sleek, blue, modern look to a more traditional wood-veneer design in seasons four and five. The desk became boxier, and the walls were scattered with icons of journalistic authority, including a map of the Earth and three clocks on each side of the map. The clocks add both a look of professionalism, as many news sets had clocks showing times around the world, and understated humor, with every clock set to the same time. Over the monitor in the center of the set, a plain "Weekend Update" logo overlaps a cutout of a globe, further invoking common visual tropes of television news. This redesigned set remained in use until the mass departure of the original cast members at the end of season five (figure 3.2).

The fifth season of "Weekend Update" introduced some new personas, as several writers were added as irregular cast members following the departure of Belushi and Aykroyd from *SNL*. Writer Al Franken, who only had minor appearances on the show previously, became a recurring character on "Weekend Update"—first as a science editor and then as a commentator, advocating for the 1980s to be the "Al Franken Decade." Harry Shearer, who was hired for the 1979 season as a writer and cast member, attempted to create a new sports-reporter persona named The Vicker but only appeared twice.

Changes in casting and set design are specific decisions on the part of show producers, and such moves had to be motivated by changes in format or other practical reasons. In the case of "Weekend Update," set changes seem as if they were meant to copy specific visual styles of television news. Drastic redesigns

Figure 3.2 Jane Curtin and Bill Murray on "Weekend Update," Season 5. *Source*: Screenshot by the author.

were accompanied by alterations in the segment's format and, occasionally, casting. The first season connected its news parody with the solo anchor and look of network newscasts. By season three, the set began to replicate the more modern, sleek, and extravagant appearance of top-market local news and the eyewitness style, leading to a revision in the last two seasons toward a more professional, subdued interpretation of the news-team concept.

PARODYING JOURNALISM STYLE AND VISUALS

As discussed in the previous chapter, the incorporation of still images and footage has been an essential aspect of newscast style since the late 1950s; as a result, news-parody shows have attempted to mimic those conventions as best they could. By the 1970s, newscasts were dominated by moving images, partially thanks to the continued development of videotape. The video format offered cost savings, much lighter camera gear, and, most importantly, the fastest turnaround from shooting to broadcast. In 1972, news organizations learned their lesson when Henry Kissinger's premature proclamation that "peace is at hand" in Vietnam made it onto CBS in 25 minutes because the crew was using videotape; this beat the other networks by hours, who had to wait to develop their film.[20] The dominance of moving images on newscasts makes it seem especially strange that "Weekend Update" contained very few stories accompanied by external video. Over the course of five seasons, only 15 stories featured pre-shot video. When video was included, the stories often made extensive use of the footage, which tended to dominate the length of the segment. For instance, the only use of footage in season one is a mock basketball game between diminutive singer Paul Simon and NBA player Connie Hawkins, heavily edited to make it appear that Simon beats Hawkins. The story lasts almost seven minutes—well over half of the total segment. Other video stories were spread about equally over the next four seasons.

Story length was one reason writers might have chosen to shy away from incorporating video. Cost might have been another. The show had the ability to borrow footage from NBC News, but writers reportedly worried that using the news division's video in a controversial way might prevent future use by *SNL*.[21] The other option would have been video wire services, but the video was much more expensive than services for photo and copy.

One way around such barriers was to use old, less expensive video. Several stories utilized canned and licensed film with anchors providing conflicting narration for the images, such as a medical story about the development of the blood-clot medication hemomycin. Garrett Morris, the show's "science editor," looks through a microscope to see the effects of the drug. Cut to video of an old Mighty Mouse cartoon meant to represent cells in the body, as Morris provides details on how the drug works.[22] This type of joke usually depended on films in the public domain. The only timely news footage used by "Weekend Update" was in season three. In 1977 demonstrators at a press conference hit an outspoken opponent of gay rights, Anita Bryant, with a pie, and the show played footage from the incident. Bryant and her anti-equality activities were a favorite punching bag for the show, so the footage must have been especially gratifying for the staff and justified going to the trouble of procuring the footage. Following the video, Curtin reports, "Fortunately, Ms. Bryant, who was not injured, enjoyed a good laugh, and said it was okay if the assailant dated her husband!"[23]

Although video footage was used sparingly, photos were a constant source of humor in the segment. "Weekend Update" used the Associated Press and United Press International wire services both as inspiration and to add to the humor of a story.[24] The use of photos was remarkably similar to *TW3*'s, often parodying the way mainstream newscasts used photos that added little context to stories. Some pictures were used simply to have a visual. For instance, a story about the possible exhumation of Lee Harvey Oswald's body leads to a fake quote from potential presidential candidate Ted Kennedy: "If it's not Oswald, I'm not running."[25] A picture of Oswald is shown over Curtin's shoulder, followed by a picture of Kennedy.

Awkward photos of politicians or celebrities became building blocks for entire reports. A story about Patty Hearst's being released on bail while she appealed her conviction is accompanied by the famous photo of the heiress wielding a machine gun in front of a Symbionese Liberation Army symbol. Curtin reports that Hearst moved back into her parents' apartment, redecorated her room, and is "shown here ordering some new wallpaper at a department store."[26] The story recontextualizes the familiar photo and brought laughs from the audience—one of many stories about Hearst on "Weekend Update" during this era. In a less inspired story, Federal Reserve Chair Paul Volcker is shown propping his head on his hand while holding a cigar, prompting a story about his ability to smoke through his forehead.[27] A year after Jimmy Carter took office, a story is inspired by a photo of his mother, Miss Lillian, seemingly with her hand over the president's crotch. Curtin describes Carter's struggles since taking office and concludes with the pun that Miss Lillian feels like "he's still growing in his job."[28] In these stories, the photos themselves became the actual subject of the joke, and the verbal structure is built around the visual.

Some of the hardest-hitting jokes came from stories covering actual news events that were punctuated by photos. Often the image is unrelated to the actual story. For example, a picture of a Klansman dressed in white robes accompanies a story about Vice President Spiro Agnew attending a masquerade party. Chase adds that Agnew is "shown here before he picked a costume."[29] Following the Three Mile Island nuclear accident, a photo of three blindfolded men tied to posts with Arabic writing is identified as the executives most responsible for the nuclear meltdown. They were supposedly tried and executed. Curtin ends the story by saying officials "would've electrocuted the men, but they couldn't afford the electricity."[30] After Ted Kennedy decided to run in the 1980 presidential election, an image of a car going off a bridge with a throng of onlookers ran with a story saying Kennedy decided to recreate the Chappaquiddick accident to finally clear himself, "unfortunately new doubts were raised when the press had to wait nearly ten hours for the senator to appear and answer questions."[31] In these examples, the photos are the linchpins of the joke—the visual is integral both to the humor and successfully parodying television news.

In another nod to the visual style of 1970s news, "Weekend Update" made extensive use of graphics and the technology available to them as a network program. Guest interviews and reporters, especially Newman, were placed in front of chroma-key screens to make it look as if they were on live remotes, a tactic that has continued to be used by later news-parody shows. In one report, Newman is supposedly at Cape Canaveral reporting on efforts to send nuclear waste into outer space as footage plays of a missile launching and blowing up behind her.[32] Graphics were fairly simple and crude in the early seasons of the show, but they began using more professional titling equipment and art. During the third season, for example, they cover a murder trial where the defense attorney argued that the teen defendant learned to be violent from watching the television show *Kojak*. The story is accompanied by a color over-the-shoulder graphic of a gavel banging on a television, with a split down the middle of the television and text underneath that reads "T.V. on Trial."[33] The graphic looks very similar to those being used on network newscasts of the day.

Beyond the visual elements, "Weekend Update" parodied a range of other news tropes. Like *TW3*, the live performance of *SNL* reinforced "Weekend Update's" similarity to television news. The program was the first live entertainment show produced by NBC in a decade. Michele Hilmes points out that the live aspect of *SNL* "returned sketch comedy to its roots in live stage and broadcast performance."[34] The show's immediacy and imperfections only helped the parody of "Weekend Update." By contrast, when *Not Necessarily the News* appeared on HBO in the 1980s, the show was heavily edited and pre-taped, which worked against the immediacy and liveness so integral to news style.

One aspect of being live that was increasingly used in news-team environments was "happy talk," the innocuous (and often vapid) conversations anchors have when transitioning between segments or stories. "Weekend Update's" happy talk humorously featured bizarrely inappropriate reactions and non sequiturs. After a medical story where hospitals recommend being more aggressive with fevers, Aykroyd turns to Curtin and says, "You know, my grandma used to say swallow a cold and take a chainsaw to a fever." Curtin responds with "So did mine," and then returns to reading the news.[35] In the same newscast, after a story about the anniversary of Galileo's death, Aykroyd comments, "Smart man, that Galileo!" "Indeed, he was Dan," follows Curtin. The inane comments of "Weekend Update's" anchors perfectly captured the forced and awkward conversations played out at news desks across America, where happy talk is sometimes even planned within scripts.

The repetition of certain broadcast-news tropes, such as the peculiar use of headlines, datelines, and bulletins, likewise reinforced the segment's connection to the news. During the first year of "Weekend Update," Chase would often copy this structure, starting a story with "Tragedy this week" or "Dateline: New York!" Despite the emphasis on conversational language in writing, many news organizations still clung to this kind of vernacular from the early days of radio broadcasting. Television news also inherited the use of bulletins from radio, where breaking stories were handed live to anchors. Like newscasts, the "Weekend Update" writers were so concerned with referencing the latest news that they would watch 11 O'Clock newscasts and literally write until the last minute, occasionally finishing stories while under the "Weekend Update" desk and handing them up to the anchors to read while on the air.[36] "Weekend Update" took the bulletin to a new level in season three, with Gilda Radner dancing onto the set wearing an NBC logo, with only her legs exposed.[37] The "dancing N" appeared several times during the season with a bulletin taped to its side, requiring Aykroyd and Curtin to lunge over the news desk, trying to grab the bulletin as she danced by. The joke worked on at least two levels, poking fun at the news-bulletin idea and NBC's recently redesigned $1 million logo.[38]

The on-air correction was another trope borrowed from newscasts of the day. When broadcast organizations made a significant mistake, they would read corrections on air (a rarity in today's news culture). "Weekend Update" followed suit, using common television transitions such as "a correction to a story from last week." However, the anchor would then apologize for something "Weekend Update" never reported, often adding ridiculous clarifications. For instance, Curtin apologizes for a story that Supreme Court Justice Warren Burger won the 1958 Kentucky Derby (which they never reported) and follows with, "what we meant to say was that Tom Snyder is one of a pair of Siamese twins."[39] The fake corrections parody an established stylistic element of newscasts but usually offered little in the way of satire.

The multiple methods of simulating television news style through set design, use of visuals, and recurring tropes helped to establish a cohesive news parody segment. Amber Day and Ethan Thompson downplay the segment's parody of news style over the years, arguing that at its creation "Weekend Update's" humor was more about being anti-establishment than critical of journalism.[40] In evaluating the segment since its inception, it would be fair to say "Weekend Update" does not remain consistently engaged with a critique of journalism itself; however, during its formative years, writers and the cast certainly take strides not only to mimic news style but also to critique assumptions of that style. Whether that was from a deep-seated desire to call out journalists or simply a reaction to the mainstream does not necessarily change the message. As with most parody, the audience is left to connect the humor in the segment to newscasts and read the parody as critique.

I'M A NEWS PARODY ANCHOR—AND YOU'RE NOT

Like traditional network newscasts, "Weekend Update" was originally built around the anchor. On "Weekend Update," they are the public voice and personality of the segment and, in return, have often received disproportionate attention from the press and public compared to other *SNL* talent. Day and Thompson even argue that the segment evolved "primarily as a vehicle for comic personalities" more than a platform for news parody.[41] The publicity boost for anchors might partially be attributed to the show's producer. Before *SNL* ever aired, Michaels insisted that Chase use his own name for the segment. Rather than a feeble "Walter Crankcase" copy of an iconic anchor, Michaels planned for "the news" itself to be the subject of the humor and insisted that anchors play themselves.[42] Of course, each person who takes the desk enacts their own concept of an anchor, but Michaels encouraged the cast not to use fake voices or go beyond minimal artifice.

Chevy Chase Defines the Role

For many viewers who grew up on *SNL* in the 1970s, Chevy Chase is remembered as *the* anchor of "Weekend Update." In reality, his tenure on the segment was among the shortest, barely outlasting the disastrous early 1980s cast members Charles Rocket (1980–1981) and Brian Doyle-Murray (1981–1982). The major difference, of course, is that Chase defined the role on "Weekend Update" and then left the show voluntarily on his own terms.

The first several episodes of *SNL* saw Chase attempting to become comfortable with his anchor persona. His inexperience in front of the camera led to a breakdown in the carefully orchestrated dance that usually exists as a newscaster deftly turns from one camera to another. Instead, Chase frequently became confused during camera changes on the first several episodes, fumbled lines, and generally appeared fidgety, unsure of what to do with his hands. "Weekend Update" began with announcer Don Pardo introducing the segment, while Chase talked on the phone in media res, caught in sexually suggestive conversations that often slipped past network censors. As the comedian quickly hung up the phone, the actual reading of the news commenced.

Although the phone shtick remained part of the opening while Chase was on the desk, the tendency on "Weekend Update" over the first season was toward replicating news conventions. Rather than basking in laughter, Chase began arranging scripts on the desk during times of audience applause and otherwise attempted to stay in character as the stoic newsman. By the fourth episode, he adapted a network persona and also debuted what would become his signature opening, "I'm Chevy Chase, and you're not."[43] The pompous phrase was adapted from New York WABC anchor Roger Grimsby, who would open the local news with, "I'm Roger Grimsby, and here now the news."[44] The phrase seemed to fit perfectly, copying the exalted position of anchors who deliver news as if from on high. Chase would later tire of the repetitive opening and create other nonsensical extensions to the tagline, such as "I'm Chevy Chase and you, you're merely a statistic" or "I'm Chevy Chase and you can't."[45] At the start of the season, Chase's style leaned toward a comic delivery similar to the *TW3* cast. However, he quickly began reining in his tendency to overemphasize his voice and body movements, developing a solemn vocal delivery that he would sometimes use just to deliver nonsense. After one news story, he turns to the camera and fervently intones a traditional spiritual: "Joshua fit the battle of Jericho, Jericho, Jericho. Joshua fit the battle of Jericho & the walls came tumbling down. More on that later."[46] Chase grew in the same way as traditional anchors, learning to adapt to the position.

Staying true to Michael's instructions, Chase never totally lost himself in the anchor role. He retained a slightly self-satisfied manner, slyly smiling, and sometimes calling attention to mistakes or jokes that were falling flat by crumpling up and tossing scripts. As Nick Marx writes, Chase "was ultimately consumed with the maintenance of his own laid-back image" on *SNL*, including "his cool detachment from the news" when anchoring.[47] His presentation always seemed good-natured, though, reacting in an almost childlike fashion. In their history of the early era of *SNL*, Doug Hill and Jeff Weingrad describe how "even if a joke wasn't working, [Chase] had a way of looking knowingly at viewers with an eyebrow raised that was utterly disarming."[48] Logically, such behavior should have called attention to the constructed parody, but Chase's cocksure serenity in the face of stumbling blocks actually worked to smooth over and retain the façade. He loved the role, and as a writer Chase enjoyed working with both the short form of the news stories and the immediacy of the jokes, saying, "You can't dawdle with parody."[49] Even when mocking others, his taunts were behind their backs, like a child. Critics have written (both positively and negatively) about Chase's self-confidence, but his unflappability on-screen counterintuitively mirrors the expected authority of a network anchor. The odd combination of innocence and authority exuded by his persona on the desk has definite similarities to Jon Stewart and John Oliver and may help to explain the popularity of all three. The combination also helped to make Chase a convincing parody of the role played by John Chancellor and Walter Cronkite, who both sought trust and intimacy from audiences.

Jane Curtin, the Professional Fake Anchor

For the five years spanning the original Not Ready for Prime Time Players, Jane Curtin was the most consistent face of "Weekend Update," anchoring all but four episodes of seasons two through five. After filling in for an injured Chase, she took over duties with the November 13, 1976, episode. The transition was awkward; Curtin was known for specializing in "straight" roles on the comedy show and largely adopted the same approach to "Weekend Update." She presented herself as a professional, no-nonsense journalist, serious about the content, and emotionally neutral, as objective anchors are encouraged to be. Once she settled into the role, it worked. Her faux seriousness made her the straight person for the joke embedded in the script, much like Stephen Colbert, who would take the formula to a whole new level. However, Curtin's early days on the anchor desk were reportedly difficult. Unlike Chase, who wrote much of the segment himself, Curtin was unhappy with a lot of the scripts being written for her, especially their constant sexism.[50]

Curtin barely missed out on becoming the first female news anchor on a network, even if it was a comedy program. A month before Curtin took over "Weekend Update" Barbara Walters broke that barrier, sharing the desk with Harry Reasoner on the *ABC Evening News*. Like Walters, Curtin was faced with the sexism and patriarchy of the television industry. When Chase returned to temporarily take back the anchor position following his injury, he thanked Curtin for filling in and announced she would be a regular contributor to "Weekend Update," saying, "Much has been said about the pros and cons of a woman anchoring the national news. There's certainly no question in my mind about the validity of women in any so-called traditional male roles." Curtin thanks Chase and then delivers a hard-hitting report on fluorocarbons as Chase leans behind her and begins making faces and taunting her.[51] Demonstrating that *SNL*'s satire was not always progressive, the joke mocks women's demands for equal rights in the workplace. The segment was an opening salvo against Curtin, who would continue to struggle to be taken seriously as Chase's replacement.

For the first several newscasts she anchored, the writers kept the break between Pardo's introduction and the headlines. At first, Curtin continued to answer phone calls for Chase, retaining the gag. This shifted to Curtin engaging in gender-stereotyped behavior, such as putting on perfume, taking birth control, or filling out a magazine sex quiz, acting as if she was unaware that she was live on camera. The break was eliminated when Curtin finally began using her own authoritative introduction, "I'm Jane Curtin, here now the news."

After almost two months at the desk, Curtin finally addressed the specter of Chase, saying viewers' letters had been coming in complaining that "Weekend Update" had gone downhill and that the network was pressuring to have someone else take over the anchor desk. Curtin counters with,

> I just assumed it was responsible journalism you wanted, not sex. I gave you more credit than that [*pause*] but I was wrong. What can I say besides try these on for size, Connie Chung! [*ripping open her blouse to reveal her bra underneath*] If it's raw thrills you want, it's raw thrills you'll get!

The audience breaks into applause as Curtin begins reading the news with her shirt halfway open.[52] She reportedly regretted doing the bit, but the writers continued to push her sexuality as a source of humor for the rest of the season.[53] Only weeks later, she starts the newscast by saying that she's wearing black mesh stockings and leather boots, "but let's talk about my panties for one second, shall we? They're mesh—black mesh string bikini. I love them. You would too. I wish I had them on right now. They're in my laundry basket—at home."[54] A number of critics have pointed out how men have traditionally been in control of the program, and the bits written for Curtin certainly reflect what Caryn Murphy calls the show's "comedy taste culture that excluded and marginalized women."[55] At times, the writing seemed to conflict with the character Curtin was developing on screen. As a result, she fell victim to other types of stereotyped writing but seemed to push back at times, calling attention to jokes that failed by commenting on them or giving over-enthusiastic laughs.[56]

In playing the role of straight professional, Curtin could come off as cold and unfeeling. Her scripted interactions with correspondents like Radner's Emily Latella leaned into this aspect, presenting Curtin as a humorless, mean authoritarian. Whereas Chase would calmly and kindly correct Latella's mistakes, Curtin would warn the character to get it right, leading to the gentle Latella calmly calling Curtin a "bitch." In season three, when Aykroyd and Curtin mimic a point-counterpoint segment, Aykroyd finally gives voice to the other aspect of Curtin the writers were creating by addressing her as "Jane, you ignorant slut." These dueling accusations, embedded within the larger cultural context of sexual control through labeling women with such terms as "bitch" or "slut," made it very difficult for Curtin to emerge as either a likable or strong character within the second season of "Weekend Update."

In the following years, writers toned down some of these aspects of Curtin's anchor. The sex jokes became less frequent and less demeaning. She not only maintained her professional demeanor but also could have lighter moments. Having additional actors at the anchor desk undoubtedly helped, as humor could be drawn from their interactions, rather than Curtin carrying the segment alone. She was still the straight person for many jokes, and that meant sometimes having to play the heavy, such as when Murray questions why news is so different from entertainment coverage or reeling in Roseanne Roseannadanna's discussion of eye crust. Curtin also acted as the progressive voice in the point-counterpoint segment to Aykroyd's conservative commentator, advocating positions more in line with the show's audience. During seasons three through five, she established a compelling persona, reading the news with authority while also furthering the comedy of others through her role. Unlike most of the cast, Curtin had very few signature sketch characters, so her anchoring on "Weekend Update" may be the most defining aspect of her time on *SNL*.

Aykroyd and Murray—Anchoring Makes Me Feel Good

Aykroyd and Murray rounded out the main anchoring team from the original cast. Aykroyd coanchored with Curtin in season three, and Murray took over that role in seasons four and five. Aykroyd began playing his role very straight, imitating the limited movements of network anchors and even graying his temples to look more seasoned. He seemed uncomfortable on the desk at first, pausing and making mistakes, but became more at ease in the role as the season progressed. When the point-counterpoint feature debuted toward the end of the season, Aykroyd would take extreme positions on topics. Aykroyd's ironic commentary damned his viewpoint through calculatedly self-parodying praise, a style later expanded by Stephen Colbert. Aykroyd was reportedly never truly happy playing himself on screen and was relieved when Murray took over anchor duties.[57] Season four opened with an explanation that Aykroyd was now the station manager, so he frequently returned to "Weekend Update" to reprise his conservative role, delivering commentaries in a segment called "Strictly Speaking" or opposite Curtin in point-counterpoint.

When Murray took over anchoring duties for season four, he had already made frequent appearances on "Weekend Update" as an entertainment correspondent. Murray played on the stereotype of Hollywood gossip reporters, addressing the audience and coworkers informally, casually telling them in an overly familiar way, "I love you guys, no, get out of here, I mean it," and referring to celebrities by nicknames. Since Murray's character already existed in the world of "Weekend Update," the writers transitioned him into a news-anchor role when the fourth season began. This serial aspect of "Weekend Update" sets it apart from the rest of *SNL*, which mostly embraced the discrete, continuity-free nature of sketch comedy. Instead, writers took care to create internal consistency for repeat characters. When Murray began season four, he portrayed an entertainment reporter befuddled by the complexities of actual news, but within a couple of episodes he tamped down the over-the-top persona and played it straighter.

The varied representations of anchors in these first seasons of "Weekend Update" mirrored tensions in journalism at the time, as the "old guard" of news anchors, many of whom had cut their teeth in radio, were retiring and being replaced by young, attractive newsreaders meant to bring in ratings. Curtin and Aykroyd played their roles mostly straight, acting as seasoned journalists presenting information with the same attempt at professionalism exhibited by the network anchors, while Chase and Murray appeared to have less knowledge of the news and to exist more as entertaining presenters, amiable local newscasters having fun while reading the day's events. Writing in the late 1960s, one observer bemoaned that an anchor often was chosen "by virtue of his stage presence, his authoritative voice, his delivery skills or his looks."[58] With the growth of the eyewitness format and advertising consultants, local news began to resemble the entertainment world. Ron Powers, in his scathing critique of news in the 1970s, accused anchors of ignorance regarding their role in democracy and of merely being celebrities: "There is very little feeling of real partnership with the viewer, only a vague condescension."[59] The different actors on "Weekend Update," through their roles, entered into this debate about news presentation at the same time they were parodying the authority, substance, and style of television anchors. Their criticism of journalists was often indirect, and, between the lines, much more subtle than the humor pointed at politicians.

COMEDIC PRESIDENTIAL COVERAGE IN THE POST-WATERGATE ERA

In his overview of *SNL*'s satire of presidents, John Matviko notes that it was relatively rare to find television making fun of the president during the 1970s.[60] Late-night comedians like Johnny Carson would lob softball jokes, but actual confrontational humor, much less presidential satire, on the networks was virtually nonexistent. In its first season, *SNL* focused most of its humor on sex, drugs, and politics, and the "Weekend Update" segment followed suit. Jeffrey Jones makes the case that political satire is an integral part of *SNL*'s brand, providing an accessible outlet for political humor for the mass audience (especially during presidential campaigns), as well as helping to keep the show continually relevant by engaging current politics.[61] Thanks to the collaborative nature of the program's writing, the political sketch comedy of the show in its formative years informed and reinforced the political humor of "Weekend Update." Taken as a whole, *SNL* constructed a fairly cohesive progressive political discourse in its comedy, with the majority of its attacks on conservative politicians and viewpoints.

Throughout *SNL*'s more than three decades on the air, its political satire has ridiculed politicians mostly on a personal level rather than focusing on policies. A number of studies have shown that topical comedy shows and other soft news programs emphasize political personalities.[62] Joseph Boskin, repeating a common criticism that includes such shows, condemns the way political humor tends to obscure power by focusing on individual politicians at the expense of actual political structures and actions.[63] "Weekend Update" falls victim to this tendency even more than the rest of *SNL*. Mimicking the news briefs of broadcast television, jokes on the segment are short and move between wildly divergent topics, making sustained topical satire difficult—a problem later programs solved through their singular focus on news. My analysis of "Weekend Update's" presidential humor confirms that writers mostly shied away from critiquing specific policies, possibly because audiences were less likely to get the humor or perhaps because other types of jokes were simply easier to write.

Although Boskin's point is important, that humor about individual politicians is less politically useful than humor aimed at social structures, not all such jokes of the former type are the same. Humor about political players *can* be more or less destabilizing, based on whether the critique is purely personal or reflective of commonly held political views and strategies. For instance, the first season of "Weekend Update" featured a number of jokes about whether Ronald Reagan colored his hair. By contrast, following the death of the brutal Spanish dictator Francisco Franco, the show repeated an actual quote from Richard Nixon, who called Franco a loyal ally of the United States and said he "earned worldwide respect for Spain through firmness and fairness." Juxtaposed against the quote is a picture of Franco and Adolf Hitler giving a fascist salute together, undercutting the substance of Nixon's statement.[64] Ridiculing the dishonesty and historical revisionism of Nixon's eulogy of Franco differs substantially from merely making fun of Reagan's appearance. Both jokes are ultimately about individual action, but "Weekend Update's" satire covered a broad range, veering from the substantive to the facile.

Gerald Ford's Accidental Presidency

A comedic television show could have hardly asked for an audience more primed for political humor than 1975 America. The show appeared on television just over a year after Nixon resigned the presidency in shame. His successor Gerald Ford became president without a vote and the large base of support that comes with running for election, then he alienated many voters by pardoning Nixon.[65] With a generation of reporters that had come of age during Vietnam and Watergate, Ford was already under attack; the negative coverage became criticism *SNL* could bounce off and reinforce.[66] The young audience targeted by the show was especially predisposed to view conservative politicians with a mix of disdain and irreverence, so the program's satire of politicians, specifically Ford, proved quite popular.

In its first season on the air, *SNL* helped define the presidency of Ford for its viewers. Despite Ford's past as a college athlete and multi-term representative (including eight years as Republican Minority Leader), the show portrayed the president as clumsy and dimwitted—a caricature that stuck in popular culture. The writers were obviously inspired by Ford's visit to Austria in June 1975, just prior to *SNL*'s debut, where Ford fell down a wet staircase departing Air Force One and then tripped twice more during the European visit. Throughout Chase's time at *SNL*, he regularly portrayed Ford in skits, falling off podiums and committing other physical gaffes such as holding a full glass of water up to his ear, mistaking it for a phone. This caricature from the skits "intertextually reinforced" similar coverage on "Weekend Update" of Ford as unintelligent and clumsy.[67]

In the first season of the show, every "Weekend Update" but one featured jokes about Ford, and subsequent seasons kept the president as a favorite punch line, even after his 1976 electoral defeat. The majority of the laughs in season one came from the show's already-established depiction of Ford's clumsiness. One common joke structure in early episodes had Ford accidentally hurting himself, only to have "alert Secret Service agents" wrestle an object or person to the ground. Variously, agents were reported to have subdued a little girl with flowers, a fork, a handkerchief, a car, and even Ford's own thumb. This depiction dovetailed perfectly with *SNL*'s general treatment of the president.

"Weekend Update" writers especially enjoyed combining fake quotes from the president with actual news items, making Ford appear ignorant and confused. Following a report that the CIA was involved in assassination plots of nine foreign leaders, Ford reportedly says, "Boy, I'm sure glad I'm not foreign!"[68] In a story about the upcoming presidential primaries, Ford is reported as saying that in addition to winning the primaries, he will also win the "secondaries."[69] Heading into the 1976 election, polls showed Jimmy

Carter tied with Ford. Coverage of the poll includes a real quote from Carter, dismissing the importance of polls, followed by a fictitious quote from Ford: "The Poles are an independent and autonomous people and I don't believe they consider themselves to be under Soviet domination."[70] This joke is one of several used on the segment making fun of Ford's gaffe during a debate, where he misspoke and claimed, "There is no Soviet domination of Eastern Europe." The show's depiction stuck in the public mind and is often discussed as part of Ford's legacy and a potential factor in his losing run for the White House in 1976.[71]

Perhaps the most discussed episode of season one featured Ford press secretary Ron Nessen as guest host. After Ford's decision to seek reelection, his team knew they would have to rehabilitate the president's image in the press and slowly became willing to consider entertainment shows as part of their strategy.[72] Chase appeared at the 1975 Radio and Television Correspondents dinner opposite Ford, with the president laughing at the comedian's over-the-top, clumsy imitation. Nessen, a former NBC News correspondent, was convinced to accept an invitation to host *SNL*, thinking that playing along with the show might mitigate some of its criticism of the president—a major mistake on Nessen's part, as he was savaged by the press following the episode.[73] Knowing the president would be watching, the writers took advantage of Nessen's appearance to push the limits of the show, writing a fake ad for douches and setting one skit in a men's bathroom.

The evening Nessen hosted, "Weekend Update" began with Chase's normal tagline, "I'm Chevy Chase and you're not," only to be followed by pre-shot film of Ford saying, "I'm Gerald Ford and *you're* not." Ford's stiff attempt to play along with the gag became co-opted by *SNL*, as Chase continued "that late-breaking story just out of Washington. Doctors say the president is almost completely over his identity crisis, but should continue the therapy daily."[74] Throughout the show, Nessen's attempts to use *SNL* for political gain backfired and made him and Ford the butt of jokes. Later in the newscast, Chase tosses to a "live shot" with Newman, who introduces Nessen as press secretary for the late Generalissimo Francisco Franco (playing off a recurring joke about the deceased Spanish dictator). In the interview, Nessen downplays Franco's death and emphasizes that the former leader's condition is stable. The skit is almost painful to watch, as Nessen merely reinforces what many in the country already believed—that the job of the press secretary is to lie for a president. A number of reporters took Nessen and the White House to task for their involvement with the show. *Variety* called the appearance "politically unwise" and said "sober political observers will have to question [White House] judgment."[75] Most of the mail received by the White House was reportedly critical of the administration's involvement with the program, describing *SNL* as objectionable.[76] The show's writers used the controversy as a springboard for jokes on the next episode, reporting Ford as under fire from conservatives for appearing on *SNL*. In the story, Ford is reportedly asked whether his involvement made him look stupid, replying, "nonsense, pass the soup to my face please."[77] In reflections about his guest-host stint, Nessen says he underestimated how vicious the humor might get, mistakenly thinking the show's comedy would be more in line with Bob Hope or Johnny Carson's playful teasing. Talking about Chase's portrayal of Ford, Nessen writes, "there was no gentle ribbing, no well-intended satire, no good-natured spoofing. A lot of it was nasty, and all of it was designed to denigrate Ford."[78] Nessen thought he could use the show for Ford's gain but ultimately regretted trying to tame satire for political purposes.

Criticism of Nessen's appearance was also directed at the show itself. Some writers accused *SNL* of selling out and becoming too cozy with the political establishment. John O'Connor of the *New York Times* complained that having Ford and Nessen on the show reduced the satire to "a symbiotic routine between the Establishment and its court jesters. Far from being outrageous, it is reassuring. Far from being naughty, it is a resounding endorsement."[79] Other politicians seemed to learn a lesson from Nessen's experience and stayed away from the show for the rest of the 1970s.

In the last episode before the 1976 election, the show spent considerable time focused on the presidential vote, with Ford as the butt of most jokes. One of the most memorable moments from that night's show was a "Weekend Update" story about two supposedly unreleased campaign ads from the candidates. A fake commercial from the Ford campaign had Aykroyd imitating Carter and talking about how he lusts in his heart, juxtaposed with images of women in bathing suits. Following the Ford ad, a fake Carter commercial, rather than delivering a funny retort, simply featured Ford's full speech pardoning Nixon, with images of Ford and Nixon walking together, laughing together, and so on.[80] Writers reportedly wanted to be sure the public remembered the pardon going into the election, feeling the press had underplayed Ford's actions.[81] Playing the audio of the pardon was a particularly vivid intervention into politics. The former president remained a favorite punch line for the next four years.

Jimmy Carter and Half-Hearted Satire

While "Weekend Update" seemed to relish personal attacks on Ford, Jimmy Carter was often cast as a well-intentioned lightweight with a lovable, dysfunctional family. Despite raging inflation, oil shortages, and economic instability, the first three years of Carter's presidency featured less stinging satire by writers and more goofy wisecracks. In their analysis of *SNL* during the 1976 campaign, William T. Horner and M. Heather Carver argue that the show tended to characterize Carter as "supremely confident to the point of arrogance" and light on policy details; however, *SNL*'s image of Carter was nowhere near as critical as that of Ford.[82]

During the campaign, a number of stories ostensibly about Carter morphed into jokes about Ford; a report about Carter and *Playboy* magazine provides one excellent example. With only months before the election, Carter's interview with the "men's magazine" that featured nude pictures of women faced immediate criticism from the emerging evangelical Christian movement, and the interview seemed to have the potential for serious political damage. In two stories about the *Playboy* interview, however, "Weekend Update" flipped the focus from Carter to Ford. The part of the *Playboy* interview that became the most widely quoted was when Carter admitted that he had "lusted in his heart" for women. In their reporting, "Weekend Update" said Ford also admitted that "in his heart, he committed celibacy."[83] In a follow-up story, Ford criticized Carter for the *Playboy* interview. The story ends with Chevy Chase reporting that Washington was, thus, surprised that a Ford interview would be appearing in the hardcore pornographic magazine *Hustler*. In his defense, "Ford said he thought the magazine was for aggressive athletes."[84]

Visual puns were a frequent format for jokes about Carter early in his term, using photos that seemed awkward or suggestive and providing an outrageous backstory. For instance, a photo of Carter and a young girl, with Carter's hand reaching around her upper torso, accompanies a story about the president visiting the Bronx, where "he got a feel for that neighborhood."[85] In another story about the cost of the campaign, an image of Carter holding up a coffee cup is paired with the line: "The president-elect is shown here begging on the streets of Plains for money to make up his campaign debt."[86] Along with jokes about his prominent teeth, this kind of innocuous humor provided little actual satiric news with depth.

The writers seemed to enjoy making fun of the Carter clan more than the president during his first two years in office. Opportunistic brother Billy, perhaps best remembered for marketing his own brand of beer, received frequent mentions, as in a story where he bought shares in the Carter hometown newspaper *The Plains Stateman*. Billy reportedly "celebrated in the typical fashion, by drinking a keg of beer and then throwing up into the agreement."[87] A "Weekend Update" report about Carter's first year in office read by Curtin perfectly illustrates how the show mined some of the bizarre aspects of the First Family:

> His best friend, Bert Lance, has been accused of questionable banking practices. His son, Chip, is having marital problems. His brother, Billy, is a beer-drinking clown. His mother, Lillian, is a wrestling groupie. His White House Staff Chief, Hamilton Jordan, is getting a divorce. His sister, Ruth Carter Stapleton, is

associating with Larry Flynt, a known pornographer; but to be fair, let's look at the brighter side. His daughter Amy's nurse is a convicted murderer. It restores one's faith, doesn't it?[88]

What Carter lacked in easily mocked traits, his family gave in abundance. As a result, the president shared the satiric stage on "Weekend Update," and writers never seemed to develop the same kind of defining caricature of Carter as they did with Ford.

Carter's lack of guile was the most often-mocked aspect of the president during his first several years in office. *National Lampoon* writer Tony Hendra, in discussing Dan Aykroyd's presidential portrayal, wrote that *SNL* perfectly caught Carter's "gluey sanctimoniousness."[89] Both sketches and "Weekend Update" mocked the president's sincerity, which seemed too good to be true. In a rare instance of a guest host appearing during "Weekend Update," actress Ruth Gordon plays Carter's mother, Miss Lillian, giving a live interview to Newman after the inauguration. Miss Lillian recalls how Jimmy told her as a child that he would never tell a lie, continuing, "It was at that very moment, I said to myself, 'Lily, if he can sell that crap to his own mother, he can make anybody believe it.'"[90] This final line from Gordon is almost drowned out by audience laughter—suggesting *SNL* writers were tapping into existing doubt about the president's squeaky-clean image.

Although Carter jokes tended to be softballs during the show's first four years, by the end of the fifth season, leading up to the 1980 election, the show started to focus more on Carter's weakness as a leader, especially in light of the 1979 Iranian revolution and the Soviet invasion of Afghanistan. Despite *SNL* writers' obvious disdain for Republican nominee Ronald Reagan, Carter's ineffectual responses to growing unrest in the world resulted in more pointed sarcasm and satire from "Weekend Update." Carter's announcement that the United States would boycott the 1980 Olympics in Moscow in response to the Afghan conflict was derided as a merely symbolic gesture toward actual war. One story reports that the Soviet Olympic Committee, shamed by Carter's speech, has decided to boycott its own games.[91] In another report, Carter warns that if the Soviets attempt to take the Iranian oil fields, "the US will also be forced to boycott the 1980 Miss Universe pageant this June."[92]

The Iranian hostage situation received similar treatment, especially after the administration's failed rescue attempt in April 1980. A week before the botched rescue, a story about the opening of America's first embassy in Zimbabwe describes how Carter included a gym, kitchen, and beds "for the comfort of employees held hostage for any length of time."[93] The next episode reports that Secretary of State Edmund Muskie is resigning over another surprise rescue attempt, but Carter is asking him to postpone his resignation "until next week's attempt fails."[94] Sadly, the *Not Ready for*

Primetime Players and many of the show's writers left at the end of season five, leaving the actual election to be covered by a less experienced, less satire-oriented, and less funny cast in season six.

"Weekend Update's" coverage of presidents Ford and Carter reflects the dominant politics of the show. Horner and Carver, in comparing *SNL*'s treatment of the two presidents during the 1976 election, contrast two events to dramatize those different standards. On the one hand, the show featured several jokes about Ford's misstatement that the Soviets did not dominate Eastern Europe (which they obviously did). However, a much more serious error by Carter, when he said he saw no problem with neighborhoods maintaining "ethnic purity," received very little attention.[95] The unequal coverage, especially given the different severities of the statement, demonstrate how each president was treated. The conservative Ford received often-vicious personal attacks and a more pointed critique of his actions and policies (such as his pardoning of Nixon). In comparison, stories about Carter were often told with a wink. As the country grew increasingly disillusioned with Carter, writers began to focus more on his policy failings, at least as they related to contemporary events.

NEWS COMMENTARY ON "WEEKEND UPDATE"

Contemporary reviews of *SNL* either applauded or condemned the show for its brand of humor and choice of topics. Typifying the negative response, *The New York Times*' Richard Whelan lambasted writers and actors for being emblematic of a new era of comedians—middle-class, sophomoric, and self-indulgent. He accused the crew of placing themselves above the subjects of their humor and opined about feeling "unclean" after watching, "let down, guilty, depressed at having enjoyed the shallowness of the humor."[96] His reaction reflects how *SNL* was outpacing other humor programs in the 1970s in its willingness to address taboo topics and poke fun at even the most exalted public figures. In terms of news parody, "Weekend Update" represented a break from *TW3*'s much more sedate, observational approach.

Humor also shifted onto journalists themselves with "Weekend Update," participating more in the journalistic field than its predecessor and wielding some limited standing to engage in political and journalistic discourse. At the time, the boundaries of official news were much less permeable than today; however, the show's creators viewed *SNL* as an intervention into politics. Michaels wanted "Weekend Update" to have an actual political voice and educate in its satire.[97] For *SNL*'s target audience, the program likely would have influenced their opinions on news and potentially played an agenda-setting role. Michaels is very clear that in the early years of the program, messages were specifically geared for hip, young audiences, saying, "If viewers are in the least square, dense or inattentive, fuck 'em."[98]

By trying to craft such a highly specialized audience, one not catered to by traditional news outlets, "Weekend Update" positioned itself as an educational and political voice relevant to its viewers. Day and Thompson seem to dispute this interpretation of the segment as politically satiric, claiming that during this era "Weekend Update" "made no explicit critical statements about the media or the political landscape as a whole."[99] However, it seems clear that the aggregate of the segment, the discourse created about politics and the media episode after episode, speaks much more powerfully as a critique than any particular individual joke.

"Weekend Update's" most valuable critical contribution was its willingness to deconstruct official voices. The segment frequently reported findings and statements from government sources, only to use satirical methods to expose their implications or flaws. The earlier example of Nixon's praise of Franco is one example. In season four, Bill Murray reports General William Westmoreland's claims that medical advances made during the war in Vietnam have saved more lives than those killed in the conflict. To illuminate the ridiculous reasoning of the military leader, Murray ends the story by saying, "The Pentagon has recommended that the United States immediately begin World War III in the hope of wiping out all disease."[100] During the controversy over South Africa's investigation into the killing of anti-apartheid activist Steven Biko, who died in police custody, "Weekend Update" aired several reports highlighting the lies and misdirection the South African government was feeding the press. Officials claimed Biko died of a hunger strike, despite massive injuries to his head. Curtin reports that the CIA appealed to South Africa for help reinvestigating the death of John F. Kennedy: "Their findings? John Kennedy died of natural causes. His head wounds were self-inflicted. Thank God, now we have the answers, Dan!"[101] The ridiculous premise of Kennedy's killing himself, combined with the anchor's faux seriousness and then relief, mocks the fraud of South African officials and displays a needed skepticism of official voices.

"Weekend Update" took special delight in destabilizing social structures around identity politics, although Curtin's treatment at the anchor desk reflects the program's own hypocrisy at times. Regressive concepts of gender, race, religion, and class were all frequently attacked through the segment's satire. During season two, Garrett Morris, who was the only Black cast member, is sent to report live from the "Black Governor Conference," finding only an empty ballroom. Morris reports there are no Black governors in America, with Curtin responding, "We were all wondering when you'd catch on to our little joke. Have fun next week when we send you to the conference on Black popes."[102] In another example, writers heaped scorn upon California

Senator S. I. Hayakawa, who advocated raising gas prices, after he claimed in an actual quote, "the poor don't need gas, because they're not working."[103] The following week, after Hayakawa was caught napping during a treaty briefing, Curtin presents a fictitious quote from the Senator: "I need my sleep. Poor people don't need sleep because they aren't working and they don't get tired."[104] By not only highlighting dismissive and offensive statements of those in power but extending and analyzing their logic, "Weekend Update" engaged in political criticism.

Another tactic of "Weekend Update" writers was to juxtapose different contemporary topics, creating a deeper level of critique. For instance, abortion and the unequal treatment of the poor are combined in a story highlighting the Supreme Court's ruling to uphold a ban on Medicaid money being used for abortions. Curtin reports, "The Court ruled that a fetus becomes a human being at three months if the parents earn $15,000 or more a year, and at one month if the parents earn less."[105] The audience begins clapping, forcing Curtin to pause before her next story. By placing the ruling within the context of economics, the story extracts how access to abortion, while a right, is still inaccessible for some based on economics.

The show often received complaints because of its frequent attacks on religion, especially Catholicism. After *SNL* was named one of the 15 worst programs by the Catholic Archdiocese, Murray reports that the Catholic Church turned up fifth on *SNL*'s list of worst religions.[106] In seasons four and five, the character of Father Guido Sarducci, the Vatican gossip columnist, became a pretext for jabs at Church policies and the sitting pope. Writers tackled the issues of religion and gender in a single story after a Vatican report proclaimed that women do not look like Christ and, therefore, cannot be priests. The story spins off to a sidebar that claims, "Colonel Sanders reports he won't employee anyone who doesn't look like a chicken."[107] According to humor theorist Murray Davis, conflating the sacred world with the ordinary is a specific humor strategy that acts to destabilize social units by either elevating the mundane or, in this instance, bringing the exalted (Catholicism) down to the level of the mundane (fast food).[108] This strategy of logical extension was a favorite *SNL* method of creating humor, especially when it came to inequality.

Writers' relationships with social topics were often complicated and conflicting; they might damn politicians for offensive statements, only to fall into their own stereotyping through representations on the show. "Weekend Update" regularly hit politicians hard for racist or racially insensitive comments. Democratic presidential candidate George Wallace was consistently derided for his support of segregation. Most of the Wallace jokes either alluded to his earlier blatant racism or mocked his use of a wheelchair (the former Alabama governor was severely injured in a 1972 assassination attempt). One news story that combines both subjects reports that Wallace will "roll ahead" in his quest for the presidency and claims "his physical disabilities have never and will never prevent him from continuing a determined policy of bigotry and right-wing extremism at home and unflagging ignorance on the foreign front."[109]

In 1976, Republican Secretary of Agriculture Earl Butz created a firestorm when he was informally asked on a flight why his party was not attracting Black voters. His response led to his resignation, multiple news stories, and a recurring joke on "Weekend Update" when he was quoted as saying: "I'll tell you what the coloreds want. It's three things: first, a tight pussy; second, loose shoes; and third, a warm place to shit." Like most news organizations, *SNL* paraphrased to remove the profanity but conveyed the shocking racism. In their first story about Butz, they added that the Secretary apologized to Senator Edward Brook, who is Black, by sending him a bale of cotton and hair straightener. Later in the newscast, a story on Muhammad Ali's announced retirement attributed a fictitious quote to the boxer, saying, "He looks forward to a future of good sex, comfortable shoes, and a warm place to go to the bathroom."[110] Although the show continued to extend criticism of Butz, the condemnation remained isolated to the politician, rather than condemning a society and political class that freely shares such racist statements in private. As in this example, criticism of racism was often woven into coverage on the segment but usually remained on the level of the individual rather than institutional.

Stereotyping and dismissive jokes about identity *within* "Weekend Update" sometimes undercut attempts to use satire for progressive politics. One popular recurring character from the original *SNL* cast was Garrett Morris's baseball player-turned-sportscaster Chico Escuela. Appearing in seasons four and five, Escuela was a stereotype of Latino athletes. Supposedly hailing from the Dominican Republic, he spoke broken English, often responded with his catchphrase, "baseball been berry, berry good to me," and called Jane Curtin "Hane." While humor sometimes extends stereotypes to critique them, Escuela operated purely as the butt of the joke, with no broader message. The same can be said for multiple other instances of racial and gender humor, such as a story featuring a picture of a Black man holding a large radio up to his head. Murray claims the man had found the fallen satellite SATCOM 3 and quotes him as saying: "I ain't giving this sucker back to nobody!"[111] *SNL*, both in its sketch humor and "Weekend Update," found itself walking a line between advocating for liberal issues on the one hand and still wanting to tap into stereotypes merely to generate laughs on the other.

Sexual and gender identity were issues writers of "Weekend Update" never bothered to question through their humor, instead opting to denigrate and minimize LGBTQ+ concerns. In the most egregious example, the segment covered the 1978 assassination of San Francisco Alderman Harvey Milk, the first openly gay man to be elected in California. Supposedly reporting live from San Francisco's Chinatown, Newman narrates over real footage of a Chinese communist rally, saying, "Milk, a homosexual, was especially popular here in predominately gay Chinatown." Showing images from the massive communist gathering, Newman reports that 300,000 homosexuals from the community marched. The coverage belittles Milk's death and, as if to leave no question whether they are playing gay rights for laughs, Newman finishes the story saying, "next week Chinatown will be celebrating the Chinese New Year, ushering in, ironically enough, the year of the fist."[112] NBC later issued an apology for the story after San Francisco affiliate KRON-TV was picketed and received letters of complaint about the story.[113] Other public figures who crossed binary concepts of sexuality also received mocking treatment from "Weekend Update" for stepping outside established boundaries. Two episodes before the coverage of Milk's assassination, the show reported that Elton John was in the hospital: "John, an admitted bisexual, had been complaining of an aching prostate gland and menstrual cramps."[114] This story was one of many aimed at the singer after he publicly acknowledged his sexuality. Enduring similar treatment, Dr. Renée Richards, who underwent sex-reassignment surgery, was mocked for wanting to play tennis in the US Open. The show reported that a book about her life would be called "Tennis Without Balls," eliciting uproarious laughter and applause from the audience.[115] Perhaps unsurprisingly, given the largely male writing pool for the segment, virtually all of the antigay humor was directed toward people society identified as men. The Othering of gay men in the 1970s, even among politically progressive writers, reflects the conservative tendency of humor to continue to ridicule groups outside of power.

Despite its offensive jokes about queer issues and instances of condescending humor directed at other groups, "Weekend Update" still offered a bold, sarcastic voice for overall liberal politics on prime time, and attempted (with varying success) to use its humor to critique dominant ideology and oppressive social structures. Its constant engagement with items in the news rearticulated those stories, questioning the official voices attempting to shape news items and sometimes the underlying premise of the questions they raised. Like *TW3*, "Weekend Update" used satire to comment, but by creating a self-contained news segment closely modeled on newscast structure (and perhaps through simple longevity), the segment ended up both commenting on journalism and having its coverage becoming the subject of news. One of "Weekend Update's" biggest contributions to the news-parody genre was extending its critique to the journalistic enterprise.

MAKING FUN OF THE NEWS

In 1977, a giant of broadcast journalism was unceremoniously forced into retirement. Eric Sevareid, who started his career with Edward R. Murrow at CBS during World War II, left due to the network's mandatory age-65 retirement policy. "Weekend Update" took Sevareid's last broadcast as an opportunity to criticize broadcast journalism in general and parody news anchors specifically. Curtin introduced Bill Murray, playing the CBS veteran, made up with graying hair and doing his best Sevareid imitation. Murray, with the reserve and officiousness of the real Sevareid, complains about television viewers' lack of literacy and inability to follow the awkward speech patterns of veteran broadcast journalists steeped in radio delivery. Summing up the conflicting styles of old and new broadcasters, Murray says:

> What is at question is my relative viability as a television journalist. Some argue that I often make perfect sense, illuminating subtle nuances of conjecture upon the great problems of the day. Others would argue the opposite, that my use of tired syntax and sentence structure, coupled with a staccato & often sing-song delivery, make these editorials incomprehensible and an exercise in futility, like so many grains of sand against the tides of the oceans. I have no strong argument with either proposition.[116]

Murray's brilliantly delivered commentary makes fun of both the over-literary writing of golden-age broadcasters and the elementary-level style of contemporary journalists. By the mid-1970s, Sevareid's delivery was increasingly anachronistic. One training book reminds aspiring broadcast journalists to "save your convoluted sentences and erudite works for term papers."[117] While news agencies were rejecting the practices of the old guard, there was equal criticism of the dumbing-down of journalism. "Weekend Update" waded into such debates by going beyond the stories covered in the news to the actual newsmakers and methods of journalism.

Playing on the exalted status of anchors like Walter Cronkite, the segment used humor to knock self-important news personalities off their perches. Curtin frequently made suggestive comments about Cronkite, treating him as a sex symbol. In a story about Egyptian president Anwar Sadat's visit to Israel, the writers invoke the CBS anchor by mentioning that on the plane are "some of the most prestigious journalists, including NBC's John Chancellor, CBS's Walter Cronkite, and *Screw* magazine's Al Goldstein."[118] The joke encourages audiences to compare esteemed reporters with a publisher of pornography, destabilizing objects of different cultural worth. *TW3* had largely left the press alone, but "Weekend Update" regularly commented on television reporters, both through the content of stories and the segment's recurring characters.

The growing use of correspondents and on-set specialty anchors was increasingly satirized beginning in the third season, as the segment adopted the "eyewitness news" style. John Belushi's sometimes-drug crazed, sometimes-enraged correspondent repeatedly appears—originally as a weather forecaster, but later providing commentary that quickly degenerates into personal stories and abusive attacks on Curtin. Radner's Roseanne Roseannadanna is a science correspondent who digresses into tales of disgusting bodily behaviors. Radner envisioned the character as a reaction to the male-dominated profession, a newswoman who is comfortable and sure of herself—even when talking about eye crust. Roseanne was the opposite of women on newscasts who always seemed under pressure to be perfect or risk losing their jobs, such as Curtin's anchor persona.[119] Along with the main anchors, the news personalities populating "Weekend Update" mocked television journalists and satirized trends both past and present.

Bill Murray offered an especially trenchant criticism of the growing shift toward infotainment in the news industry with his Hollywood insider reporter, who first appeared in season three. Only the year before, ABC News President William Sheehan had warned broadcasters about mixing entertainment and journalism, saying, "The line between show-biz flair and making the news interesting must not be crossed."[120] Ironically, Sheehan's network debuted the infotainment powerhouse *Good Morning America* the previous year. A commentary on the trend, Murray's character oozed ignorance and false sincerity. The entertainment reporter Murray created was rooted in his hatred of critics and their fabricated intimacy with their subjects.[121] Murray spent season three conducting interviews with fake celebrities and reviewing new movies. The satire became much more pointed in season four when he replaced Aykroyd on the anchor desk. After Curtin introduces Murray as her new coanchor, saying he will "report the news with credibility and dignity," Murray begins a story on Beirut only to begin talking with the audience like a six-year-old trying to understand global politics: "The Jews and Egyptians are trying to be good, but the Syrians won't let 'em. We have nothing like this in show business. . . . You do the hard news and you learn a lot about people, wow!" Moving to the next story about Congress sustaining a veto over President Carter, Murray suddenly stops and incredulously implores, "Who cares? There are people being killed in Lebanon!"[122] The joke worked on multiple levels—as a critique of infotainment and, on a deeper level, questioning the erratic content of newscasts and the importance placed on political stories in comparison to the violence and suffering across the world. Within a couple of episodes, Murray begins to play it straighter when anchoring and saves his over-the-top persona for celebrity interviews. By initially feigning ignorance about news and events, Murray's character created some stinging moments of commentary on news practice, reinforcing the segment's already acerbic attitude about television news.

Through its satire, "Weekend Update" questioned journalistic practices and also mocked reporters' claims to professionalism. In her time at the anchor desk, Curtin repeatedly invokes objectivity and journalistic ethics, damning both with intentionally self-revealing praise. In browbeating Radner's Emily Latella character, who forever transposed editorial topics, Curtin complains, "You're ruining Update's credibility as responsible journalists!"[123] Curtin ironically voices concern about ethics and journalism's high calling, while, at the same time, the subtext of "Weekend Update" ridicules the profession.

Like jokes aimed at objectivity, "Weekend Update" satirizes a host of broadcast-news idiosyncrasies and journalistic assumptions. Media critics often discuss the narrow scope and insider politics of news organizations. Pierre Bourdieu writes about this aspect of the journalistic field as "an egoistic closing-in" that results from a field's becoming too autonomous from other fields.[124] As the news became more standardized and insular, this tendency increased. Michael Schudson, also addressing this limitation, argues that unlike other disciplines such as science, journalism has no means "for policing its own intellectual narrowness," no external peer-review or testable findings.[125] Even ombudsmen, who exist to provide an independent voice (and who are becoming increasingly rare), focus more on fact-checking and bias and generally hail from the same pool as other journalists, with the same basic assumptions and perspectives about news. On "Weekend Update," anchors comment on the narrowly accepted scope of news, such as when Jane Curtin reported about a rabbi's suggestion that Jewishness should extend to children of Jewish fathers, not just mothers. Following the story, Curtin says, "Well, this story represents the most frequent use of the word Jewish in any one story in the history of TV news; another first for Weekend Update!"[126] Although played for laughs, the joke provides an unsubtle critique of journalism's dedication to dominant ideological topics—in this case, religion, where stories are predominantly about Christianity and the concerns of other faiths are considered too specialized for coverage.

The segment also satirizes broadcast news' relationship with its audience—its dependency upon viewers on the one hand and its condescending stance toward them on the other. Combining commentary on audiences and polls, multiple stories during season four compared the public's knowledge about useless trivia with actual world events. For instance, Murray reports that a new NBC poll finds that 41% of Americans know you can set flatulence alight, while only 23% can name the new religious leader of Iran. The story is accompanied by an over-the-shoulder graphic: "Flatulence—41%,

Khomeini—23%."¹²⁷ The ignorance of the potential audience satirized in this story is a constant concern for real journalists, who must try to attract viewers. Anchors, especially Curtin, frequently mention ratings in "ad-libbed" commentary after stories. In one example, after "the dancing N" news bulletin taps through the set, Curtin asks Aykroyd to dance, eliciting the response, "What about our credibility?" Curtin answers, "What about our ratings? People want to be entertained!" Aykroyd concedes, "Well, that's true. If people don't watch us, we're out of work. OK, let's dance!" The two then don straw hats, pull out canes, and tap with "the dancing N."¹²⁸ The uneasy dance between the two becomes a metaphor for the journalist's awkward attempts to balance entertaining and educating the audience.

Probably the most consistent source of humor about journalism on the show also tapped into one of the more recent trends in news. Long considered a prestige program for local television stations, as well as partial fulfillment of its public-services requirements, local news was changing in the early days of *SNL*. Television broadcasters once expected to lose money on journalism, but during the 1970s local stations turned to popularized formats, consultants, and advertising departments to reinvigorate their newscasts and turn them into moneymakers—one of the few growth areas for broadcasters.¹²⁹ "Weekend Update" played with this trend toward the commercialization of news, although often in a subdued way. Throughout season one and most of season two, "Weekend Update" was divided into two blocks with a commercial-parody break between. The formatting worked especially well because it parodied the actual structure of television news, contorting itself around the most important content—advertisements. About a third of the way through season three, the segment again included jokes about the intersection of news and commerce. Beginning with a tease of a story, announcer Don Pardo introduces "Weekend Update" and says the show is sponsored by a specific company, changing the business name each week. The actual content of the sponsor announcement is always a verbal pun, such as the show being brought to viewers by "Pussywhip, the first dessert topping for cats." However, the recurring sponsorship joke highlights the constant intrusion of commercialization into journalism, especially in contemporary local news.

By mocking journalists themselves, "Weekend Update" added a missing facet to news parody and also deepened its roots as a critic of television news practice. The segment commented not only on newsmakers but also the reporters and anchors encouraging a dialogue with the audience about the process of news. The segment was self-reflexive, calling attention to its own construction but also to the unnatural construction of all broadcast news and the artificial selection and prioritization of what counts as news. Later news-parody shows like *TDS* and *Colbert* borrowed heavily from "Weekend Update's" mix of topical humor and journalism satire.

LATE NIGHT IN THE NETWORK ERA

SNL emerged in a television environment where networks still dominated the airwaves. Cable television slowly increased in viability from the middle to late 1970s, but its influence was still weak, with only 15 million subscribers and cable penetration under 20%.[130] In the next decade, cable subscriptions surged, but at the moment the networks were in control, despite efforts by the Federal Communication Commission (FCC) to curtail their power. In 1970, the FCC deployed two policies to encourage new voices in television and to break up the dominance of the Big Three. The Financial Interest and Syndication Rules (Fin-Syn as they were called) barred the networks from owning their own prime-time shows and also limited their interest in the syndicated programming they aired. Along with the Prime Time Access Rule, which decreased prime time to three hours a night, Fin-Syn was the FCC's attempt to jump-start local and nonnetwork syndicated shows. After initially fighting the new policies, NBC finally agreed to settle a Justice Department antitrust lawsuit in 1976, allowing the network to produce 2.5 hours of prime-time content each week, 8 hours of daytime, and 11 hours of fringe, with those fringe hours including the NBC-produced *SNL*.[131]

Despite the uneven power relationship between *SNL* and network executives, the success of the show led to considerable latitude for Michaels and his writers. NBC fell into a ratings slump in the mid-1970s, but *SNL* represented a rare bright spot in its programming schedule. The network trailed CBS and ABC every year from 1975 to 1979, but episodes of the late-night program were reaping financial rewards. NBC made around $8 million in profits from the show just in 1979.[132] An hour-long "Best of *Saturday Night Live*" entered the prime-time lineup the same year, with estimated profits of $134,000 per episode.[133] *SNL* was considered such a success that NBC utilized a closed-circuit "Weekend Update" newscast in 1978 to preview its next season's shows for network affiliates.[134] Unlike *TW3*, which received regular interference from the network and advertisers, *SNL* was allowed to play to its audience, even if executives might not get the joke.

The edgy humor of the television show not only promised advertising executives access to a highly sought-after young, hip, and culturally influential audience but also opened the agencies' clients up to potential scandal from the show's humor. Advertisers mostly understood the nature of the show, so rather than pulling commercials from episodes as with *TW3*, advertising executives focused on policing the placement of ads *within* the show, alert to possibly unfortunate juxtapositions with *SNL* skits. Advertising representatives attended dress rehearsals to scout for such problems. To accommodate them, NBC placed commercials on multiple reels, rather than the normal single reel, enabling last-minute movements in ad placement.[135]

Hyping the show before its debut, Dick Ebersol claimed the program would be "free of primetime restraints," meaning that greater latitude would be given to writers because of its late-night time slot and intended target audience.[136] However, as an NBC-produced program, *SNL* still had to deal with the network's Broadcast Standards department, otherwise known as the censors. Unlike *TW3*, political pressure was minimal; the show's writers say that sex and religion were much bigger concerns for NBC, including the stories on "Weekend Update."[137] Michaels became legendary among his staff for doggedly fighting censors, finding new and inventive ways of pushing the already-expanded limits given by the network. One tactic was to convince the censor to see sketches in dress rehearsal, trying to show that the material was less offensive or funnier than it seemed in the script. He was persistent in his appeals as well, going up the chain of command as far as possible to get the go-ahead. If all else failed, Michaels might take advantage of *SNL*'s live format, instructing actors to change lines during dress rehearsal only to have them revert back to the original script once on the air.[138] He was not above extortion either, quitting the show on more than one occasion until he got what he wanted.[139] Still, there were times the network would not relent. For instance, Standards warned the show not to mention the Jonestown massacre after the story became public in November 1978. Tom Davis went ahead and wrote a "Weekend Update" story in defiance, even pulling an AP photo to use; however, the censors tossed the story.[140] The fact that NBC put up with the power plays by Michaels and others on the show illustrates both the success of *SNL* and the uncertainty of the network, trailing its competitors and increasingly watched by the FCC and Justice Department for potential monopoly activity.

The limits of comedy during the waning network era quickly became delineated when "Weekend Update" satirized the head of NBC. Fred Silverman took over as president of the network in 1978, leaving a successful stint at ABC that included signing off on a number of popular shows. By contrast, his tenure at NBC was marred by just as many high-profile failures, resulting in several jokes from "Weekend Update." In one episode, Curtin reported Silverman had tragically collapsed after watching the premiere of *Hello Larry*, a show now legendary for being among the worst failures on television.[141] Later during the same network season, the show announced that President Carter, fresh from his Middle East peace conference, would be trying to create an NBC programming strategy.[142] Such jabs at the network were tolerated until they became personal. In one of his "Al Franken Decade" editorials during season five, Franken grouses about having to ride in taxis, going on to complain that Silverman gets a limousine, saying, "here's a guy who's a total and unequivocal failure! The guy's been here two years, and he hasn't done diddly squat, and he gets a limo." His rant continues with charts of the top television shows, none of which are NBC programs, and eventually instructs the audience to send postcards to Silverman demanding a limo for Franken. The comedian insists the ploy will work because Silverman is "timid, indecisive and easily pressured—he's weak!"[143] Silverman reportedly called the control room only a minute after the piece ended. The network president took it as a personal attack, essentially ending the then-ongoing negotiations to try to keep Michaels involved with the show for another season. In addition, Franken (who wrote Silverman a palpably insincere apology) was no longer considered a potential producer for *SNL*'s next season. The flare-up amounted to a largely mutual breaking point between the network and the original *SNL* cast and writers.[144] The next fall, Michaels was approached by NBC to produce a live, one-hour "Weekend Update" special to air the week before the 1980 presidential election. Most of the original *SNL* cast had signed on, but Silverman—perhaps out of fear of offending the politicians or perhaps as a final parting shot—canceled the show in favor of a Bob Hope and Smothers Brothers special.[145]

As Michaels and company departed *SNL*, the television industry itself was on the precipice of radical change. Newly introduced videocassette recorders, cable expansion, and soon a new competitor in the form of the Fox Network would change the business and content of television during the 1980s, and herald the transition to the multichannel era of television. *SNL* would also change, moving into the most troubled period in its history with a new executive producer, cast, and writers and a mandate to somehow recreate the original while making it different.

In just over a decade, television news parody had made the jump from its troubled beginnings on *TW3* to the creation of the longest-running sketch comedy show on television. Expanding boundaries in the culture had undoubtedly created a more fertile reception for "Weekend Update," as had changes with the network and advertisers. Perhaps the most important difference, though, was the time slot. Moved out of prime time and into the late night-fringe, where affiliates had more choices about whether to carry the show and financial expectations were lower, news parody thrived as an essential and consistent part of *SNL*.

NOTES

1. Les Brown, "Notes: Is the Zany Newscast a Threat to the Real Thing?," *New York Times*, June 20, 1976, 83. Aaron Reincheld, "'Saturday Night Live' and Weekend Update: The Formative Years of Comedy News Dissemination," *Journalism History* 31, no. 4 (2006): 192.

2. For more on the *Smothers Brothers* and their conflict with CBS, see David Bianculli, *Dangerously Funny: The Uncensored Story of The Smothers Brothers Comedy Hour* (New York: Touchstone, 2009).

3. Peter Andrews, "'Saturday Night' Never Plays It Safe," *New York Times*, February 29, 1976, 55.

4. For more on counter-culture humor at the time, see Tony Hendra, *Going Too Far* (New York: Dolphin Book, 1987).

5. "NBC Late-Night 'Saturday' to Showcase New Talent," *Daily Variety*, September 15, 1975, 10.

6. The show debuted with the title *Saturday Night*, because Howard Cosell was already hosting an ABC variety program called *Saturday Night Live*. Cosell's program only lasted five months, so NBC renamed their show in 1977.

7. John O'Connor, "The '75 Season - a Few Nuggets Amid the Dross," *New York Times*, Dec. 28, 1975, 1975.

8. Dave Kaufman, "NBC Set Sept. 27 Start Date for '76-77 Season to Give Producers More Time," *Daily Variety*, December 11, 1975, 1, 23.

9. Reincheld, "'Saturday Night Live' and Weekend Update," 192.

10. Doug Hill and Jeff Weingrad, *Saturday Night: A Backstage History of Saturday Night Live* (New York: Vintage Books, 1987), 18.

11. John Fiske and John Hartley, *Reading Television*, 2nd ed. (New York: Routledge, 2005), 43–44.

12. For more on the show's variety format and the history of the variety show genre, see Michele Hilmes, "The Evolution of Saturday Night," in *Saturday Night Live and American TV*, ed. Nick Marx, Matt Sienkiewicz, and Ron Becker (Bloomington, IN: Indiana University Press, 2013).

13. Jeremy Butler, *Television Style* (New York: Routledge, 2010).

14. Reincheld, "'Saturday Night Live' and Weekend Update," 191.

15. Tom Burke, "Saturday Night," *Rolling Stone*, July 15, 72.

16. Beyond *SNL*, Chase became one of the most talked-about stars in all of television during his first year on the show, even being named the funniest man in America by *New York Magazine*. Jeff Greenfield, "He's Chevy Chase and You're Not, and He's TV's Hot New Comedy Star," *New York Magazine*, December 22, 1975, http://nymag.com/arts/tv/profiles/48252/. His popularity and his negotiation of a one-year contract allowed him to set off on his own during the second season of *SNL*, with NBC giving him his own short-lived prime-time variety show in 1977.

17. *Saturday Night Live*, December 10, 1977.

18. "Saturday Night Live," *Weekly Variety*, September 28, 1977.

19. Vernon Stone and Bruce Hinson, *Television Newsfilm Techniques* (New York: Communication Arts Books, 1974), 91–92.

20. C. Robert Paulson, *Eng/Field Production Handbook* (New York: Broadcast Management/Engineering, 1976).
21. Hill and Weingrad, *Saturday Night: A Backstage History*, 280.
22. *Saturday Night Live*, March 11, 1978.
23. *Saturday Night Live*, October 15, 1977.
24. Reincheld, "'Saturday Night Live' and Weekend Update," 193.
25. *Saturday Night Live*, October 20, 1979.
26. *Saturday Night Live*, November 27, 1976.
27. *Saturday Night Live*, November 10, 1979.
28. *Saturday Night Live*, October 29, 1977.
29. *Saturday Night Live*, May 29, 1976.
30. *Saturday Night Live*, April 14, 1979.
31. *Saturday Night Live*, November 17, 1979.
32. *Saturday Night Live*, December 20, 1975.
33. *Saturday Night Live*, October 8, 1977.
34. Hilmes, "The Evolution of Saturday Night," 36.
35. *Saturday Night Live*, October 8, 1977.
36. Tom Shales and James Andrew Miller, *Live from New York: An Uncensored History of Saturday Night Live* (Boston, MA: Little, Brown and Company, 2002), 61.
37. *Saturday Night Live*, October 8, 1977.
38. The show had made fun of the redesigned NBC logo on its January 10, 1976 episode also.
39. *Saturday Night Live*, February 26, 1977.
40. Amber Day and Ethan Thompson, "Live from New York, It's the Fake News! Saturday Night Live and the (Non)Politics of Parody," *Popular Communication* 10, no. 1–2 (2012): 172.
41. Ibid., 171.
42. Hill and Weingrad, *Saturday Night: A Backstage History*, 132.
43. *Saturday Night Live*, November 8, 1975.
44. Hill and Weingrad, *Saturday Night: A Backstage History*, 132.
45. *Saturday Night Live*, February 21, 1976; *Saturday Night Live*, April 24, 1976.
46. *Saturday Night Live*, October 16, 1976.
47. Nick Marx, *Sketch Comedy: Identity, Reflexivity, and American Television* (Bloomington, IN: Indiana University Press, 2019), 66.
48. Hill and Weingrad, *Saturday Night: A Backstage History*, 132.
49. Rowland Barber, "Is Chevy Chase Immune to Phenomenitis?," *New York Times*, May 1, 1977, D, 25.
50. Hill and Weingrad, *Saturday Night: A Backstage History*, 247–48.
51. *Saturday Night Live*, October 23, 1976.
52. *Saturday Night Live*, January 29, 1977.
53. Hill and Weingrad, *Saturday Night: A Backstage History*, 248.
54. *Saturday Night Live*, March 19, 1977.
55. Caryn Murphy, "'Is This the Era of the Woman?': *SNL*'s Gender Politics in the New Millennium," in *Saturday Night Live and American TV*, ed. Nick Marx, Matt Sienkiewicz, and Ron Becker (Bloomington, IN: Indiana University Press, 2013), 174.

56. In addressing sexism in the writing, it should also be pointed out that Curtin certainly had agency. There are repeated accounts of actors rejecting or requesting changes to scripts on *SNL*. In addition, some report that Curtin was considered the strongest negotiator in the cast and, as a result, was sent to represent the talent for contract terms. Hill and Weingrad, *Saturday Night: A Backstage History*, 247.

57. Ibid., 234.

58. I. E. Fang, *Television News: Writing, Editing, Filming, Broadcasting* (New York: Communication Arts Books, 1968), 30.

59. Ron Powers, *The Newscasters* (New York: St. Martin's Press, 1977), 13.

60. John Matviko, "Television Satire and the Presidency: The Case of *Saturday Night Live*," in *Hollywood's White House: The American Presidency in Film and History*, ed. Peter Rollins and John O'Connor (Lexington: The University Press of Kentucky, 2003), 336.

61. Jeffrey Jones, "Politics and the Brand: *Saturday Night Live*'s Campaign Season Humor," in *Saturday Night Live and American TV*, ed. Nick Marx, Matt Sienkiewicz, and Ron Becker (Bloomington, IN: Indiana University Press, 2013), 78.

62. See for instance, Matthew Baum, "Talking the Vote: Why Presidential Candidates Hit the Talk Show Circuit," *American Journal of Political Science* 49, no. 2 (2005); Patricia Moy, Michael Xenos, and Verena Hess, "Priming Effects of Late-Night Comedy" (Annual Meeting of the International Communication Association, New Orleans, LA, May 2004).

63. Joseph Boskin, "American Political Humor: Touchables and Taboos," *International Political Science Review* 11, no. 4 (1990): 475.

64. *Saturday Night Live*, November 22, 1975.

65. Ford's approval rating dipped from 71% to 50% following the pardon and hovered around that mark for the remainder of his presidency. Charles Franklin, "Gerald R. Ford and Presidential Approval," Political Arithmetik, updated December 27, 2006, http://politicalarithmetik.blogspot.com/2006/12/gerald-r-ford-and-presidential-approval.html.

66. William T. Horner and M. Heather Carver, *Saturday Night Live and the 1976 Presidential Election: A New Voice Enters Campaign Politics* (Jefferson, NC: McFarland & Company, 2018), 20–27.

67. Day and Thompson, "Live from New York, It's the Fake News!," 173.

68. *Saturday Night Live*, November 22, 1975.

69. *Saturday Night Live*, February 21, 1976.

70. *Saturday Night Live*, October 23, 1976.

71. Horner and Carver, *Saturday Night Live and the 1976 Presidential Election*. Horner and Carver offer an excellent in-depth analysis of *SNL* and the election in their book, which also covers the popular assumption of the show's impact on Ford. See also, Yanek Mieczkowski, *Gerald Ford and the Challenges of the 1970s* (Lexington, KY: The University Press of Kentucky 2005), 52–53.

72. Kathryn Cramer Brownell, "The Historical Presidency: Gerald Ford, *Saturday Night Live*, and the Development of the Entertainer in Chief," *Presidential Studies Quarterly* 46, no. 4 (2016): 934–35.

73. Hill and Weingrad, *Saturday Night: A Backstage History*, 178–89. Horner and Carver, *Saturday Night Live and the 1976 Presidential Election*, 80–94.
74. *Saturday Night Live*, April 17, 1976.
75. Mick, "Saturday Night," *Weekly Variety*, April 21, 1976, 82.
76. Peter M. Robinson, *The Dance of the Comedians: The People, the President, and the Performance of Political Standup Comedy in America* (Amherst, MA: University of Massachusetts Press, 2010), 200.
77. *Saturday Night Live*, April 24, 1976.
78. Ron Nessen, *Making the News, Taking the News: From NBC to the Ford White House* (Middletown, CT: Wesleyan University Press, 2011), 197–98.
79. John O'Connor, "TV Review; NBC 'Saturday Night' Meets Ford People," *New York Times*, April 19, 1976.
80. *Saturday Night Live*, October 30, 1976.
81. Hill and Weingrad, *Saturday Night: A Backstage History*, 183.
82. Horner and Carver, *Saturday Night Live and the 1976 Presidential Election*, 96.
83. *Saturday Night Live*, September 25, 1976.
84. *Saturday Night Live*, October 16, 1976.
85. *Saturday Night Live*, October 8, 1977.
86. *Saturday Night Live*, November 20, 1976.
87. *Saturday Night Live*, February 18, 1978.
88. *Saturday Night Live*, January 21, 1978.
89. Hendra, *Going Too Far*, 443.
90. *Saturday Night Live*, January 22, 1977.
91. *Saturday Night Live*, May 10, 1980.
92. *Saturday Night Live*, April 12, 1980.
93. *Saturday Night Live*, April 19, 1980.
94. *Saturday Night Live*, May 10, 1980.
95. Horner and Carver, *Saturday Night Live and the 1976 Presidential Election*, 103–104.
96. Richard Whelan, "Cruelty vs. Compassion among the Comics," *New York Times*, Oct. 7, 1977, D.
97. Reincheld, "'Saturday Night Live' and Weekend Update," 191.
98. Burke, "Saturday Night," 34.
99. Day and Thompson, "Live from New York, It's the Fake News!," 174.
100. *Saturday Night Live*, December 9, 1978.
101. *Saturday Night Live*, December 10, 1977.
102. *Saturday Night Live*, March 19, 1977.
103. *Saturday Night Live*, May 19, 1979.
104. *Saturday Night Live*, May 26, 1979.
105. *Saturday Night Live*, October 15, 1977.
106. *Saturday Night Live*, November 17, 1979.
107. *Saturday Night Live*, January 29, 1977.
108. Murray Davis, *What's So Funny?: The Comic Conception of Culture and Society* (Chicago, IL: The University of Chicago Press, 1993), 207.

109. *Saturday Night Live*, November 15, 1975.
110. *Saturday Night Live*, October 2, 1976.
111. *Saturday Night Live*, December 15, 1979.
112. *Saturday Night Live*, December 2, 1978.
113. "'*Saturday Night Live*' Irks San Franciscans," *Broadcasting*, December 11, 1978.
114. *Saturday Night Live*, November 11, 1978.
115. *Saturday Night Live*, September 18, 1976.
116. *Saturday Night Live*, December 10, 1977.
117. Stone and Hinson, *Television Newsfilm Techniques*, 143.
118. *Saturday Night Live*, November 19, 1977.
119. Roy Blount Jr., "The Many Faces of Gilda," *Rolling Stone*, April 20, 1978, 46, 48.
120. "All Candidates but Mr. Ford Say They'll Participate in TV Debate," *Broadcasting*, July 7, 1976.
121. David Felton, "Bill Murray: Maniac for All Seasons," *Rolling Stone*, April 20, 1978, 29.
122. *Saturday Night Live*, October 7, 1978.
123. *Saturday Night Live*, March 12, 1977.
124. Pierre Bourdieu, "The Political Field, the Social Science Field, and the Journalistic Field," in *Bourdieu and the Journalistic Field*, ed. Rodney Benson and Erik Neveu (Cambridge, UK: Polity Press, 2005), 45.
125. Michael Schudson, "Autonomy from What?," in *Bourdieu and the Journalistic Field*, ed. Rodney Benson and Erik Neveu (Cambridge, UK: Polity Press, 2005), 219.
126. *Saturday Night Live*, December 8, 1979.
127. *Saturday Night Live*, February 24, 1979.
128. *Saturday Night Live*, November 12, 1977.
129. Powers, *The Newscasters*, 29–32.
130. Patrick R. Parsons, *Blue Skies: A History of Cable Television* (Philadelphia, PA: Temple University Press, 2008), 366.
131. "NBC Breaks Rank on Suit, Settles with Justice," *Broadcasting*, November 22, 1976.
132. Jack Loftus, "NBC's Day-Night Profits: The $$ from the Shows," *Weekly Variety*, May 14, 1980.
133. Jack Loftus, "NBC Primetime Profits: The $$ from the Shows," *Weekly Variety*, April 30, 1980. The "Best of" program was originally planned for syndication, but syndicators refused to abide by NBC's caveat that the program not run after 11:00 p.m.
134. "NBC Yuks It up with Affils," *Weekly Variety*, December 13, 1978. Interestingly, the network had used *TW3* in a similar way, having cast members perform a mock newscast for affiliates at the National Association of Broadcasters convention in 1964.
135. Hill and Weingrad, *Saturday Night: A Backstage History*, 167–68.
136. "NBC Late-Night 'Saturday' to Showcase New Talent."
137. Reincheld, "'Saturday Night Live' and Weekend Update," 194.

138. Hill and Weingrad, *Saturday Night: A Backstage History*. Chapter 15 recounts the show's battle with network censors.

139. Shales and Miller, *Live from New York: An Uncensored History of Saturday Night Live*, 62, 65.

140. Tom Davis, *Thirty-Nine Years of Short-Term Memory Loss* (New York: Grove Press, 2009), 149.

141. *Saturday Night Live*, January 27, 1979.

142. *Saturday Night Live*, March 17, 1979.

143. *Saturday Night Live*, May 10, 1980.

144. Hill and Weingrad, *Saturday Night: A Backstage History*, 371–76.

145. Ibid., 379–80.

Chapter 4

News Parody in the Multichannel Era
HBO's Not Necessarily the News

The year 1980 was the final season for the original Saturday Night Live (*SNL*) cast and creative personnel. *SNL*'s immediate plummet in quality and laughs for the next several seasons of the new decade mirrored television's own struggle to adapt to a changing industrial landscape. NBC's revamped program faced challenges to its dominance of late-night comedy, including the network's own *SCTV*, imported from Canada, and ABC's *Fridays*; however, the real competitor for both *SNL* and network programming, in general, was the rapid expansion of cable.

The explosion of cable channels in the 1980s, new technologies such as the VCR and remote control, and the industrial changes of media conglomeration brought on by deregulation resulted in upheaval within an industry that the three networks had dominated virtually from television's beginning. Amanda Lotz refers to this shift moving into the 1980s as the beginning of the "multichannel era" of television, typified by greater choices for audiences and more control over viewing technology.[1] There was no instantaneous unshackling of the power of the three networks, but over the course of the 1980s, an ever-expanding channel lineup and growing subscription base created viable cable alternatives for program creators and audiences. Offering alternative financing arrangements, potentially looser censorship, and an opening of the programming bottleneck of the network era, cable channels slowly became another viable outlet for program creators.

The longest-running cable news-parody program of the multichannel era appeared on one of the industry's earliest and most successful cable channels, HBO. The station began operations in the early 1970s and had become cable's top pay-channel by the 1980s. Although movies accounted for the channel's primary programming strategy, films were heavily mixed with sports and comedy specials. In 1983, HBO expanded its comedy offerings with the regularly scheduled news-parody program *Not Necessarily the News* (*NNTN*). The show ran until 1990, making it one of HBO's most consistent offerings during that era. An ensemble cast mixed satiric reports from a newsroom with advertisement parodies and sketch comedy within a rapid-pace format. *NNTN* aired regular, short seasons in its first couple of years before shifting to infrequent specials and an eventual reboot in 1989, with a new cast and format change.

Despite running seven seasons, *NNTN* exists as a virtual footnote in television history, with only brief mentions of the show in mainstream and scholarly writing. A chapter in *The Essential HBO Reader* about the network's contributions to comedy offers a paragraph about *NNTN*, summarizing its cultural contribution with the "sniglet" feature.[2] The paragraph is emblematic of the show's forgotten status in television studies. However, by its final season, *NNTN* had won more cable ACE awards than any other show and was the first scripted, recurring program on pay cable. The lack of attention paid to its success undoubtedly reflects more on the overall low quality of original cable programming during the 1980s.[3] The program was uneven, but *NNTN* still occasionally receives kind mention by critics. Its humor, like its format, is sometimes awkward and unfocused, its satire somewhat toothless. Like cable programming itself in the 1980s, *NNTN* offered an alternative to network fare but without consistency.

HBO AND THE TRANSITION TO THE MULTICHANNEL ERA

Cable television took a long time to reach its eventual form before the heady days of growth in the 1980s. In its earliest incarnations, cable existed as an alternative distribution method for television, offering a form of shared antenna for communities without broadcast reception. From the 1950s through the late 1970s, cable was a service no one usually *wanted* but was sometimes necessary to get over-the-air content. Some legislators and media critics saw the potential for cable to offer an actual alternative to traditional broadcasters. 1968–1974 has been called the "blue sky" era of cable, partially because of optimistic attitudes that the industry might begin producing a larger array of programming that could serve specialized and minority audiences.[4] Favorable outcomes in several court cases and improved political support resulted in rapid growth, but although the cable industry flourished during the 1980s, the dream of a programming renaissance never fully developed. Most of the content produced by cable during the multichannel era was simply retreads of existing network fare and meant to target the largest possible audience. Megan Mullen points out that cable stations were essentially "nothing more than independent broadcast stations whose signals had been uplinked to satellite"—perhaps with a slightly more narrow focus, but with little to differentiate its programming from that of traditional broadcasters.[5]

It was during the blue sky era that the first successful pay-television channel was launched. HBO was a joint effort between Sterling Manhattan Cable and Time, Inc., and began operations in 1971 with a programming lineup of local sports and other events combined with a smattering of films. HBO's beginning years were precarious, losing subscribers during its first full year of operations. George Mair wrote an early history of HBO and referred to it as "the almost accidental company . . . facing stiff competition in the marketplace, it was beleaguered by its competitors, overregulated by the government, and unloved by its own parent, Time Inc.," who actually considered folding the channel's operations.[6] Perhaps the biggest factor in HBO's success in the latter part of the 1970s was its early adoption of satellites for signal distribution. The company's competitors mostly used hardwired cable or physical media to get content to cable providers, but HBO distributed its signal via microwave. As a result, when RCA launched Satcom I in 1974, HBO was poised to easily move its operations from microwave to satellite. The channel paid dearly to license satellite time, but it would be years before its competitors were able to follow suit. The live cablecast of the Muhammed Ali-Joe Frazier "Thrilla in Manila" boxing match in October 1975 became the channel's showcase for its new delivery system and proved a major success. By the end of 1975, HBO subscriptions increased 500%, from 30,000 to 287,199—largely credited to the satellite system.[7]

HBO's programming strategy evolved partially in reaction to its uneasy relationship with the Hollywood studios. From the early days of the channel, movies formed the core identity of HBO, but executives consistently used sports, concerts, and, later, stand-up comedy specials to differentiate its content. HBO also began ramping up its own original programming. One example was the series *Flashback*, a low-budget show based on real historical events. In the early 1980s, HBO's original programs were in no danger of competing with the networks—but that was never the point. Rather than attracting subscribers, these programs were more supplementary—taking the place of the "B movies" Hollywood wanted to license to HBO. The channel made a conscious effort in 1983 to cut back on its film dependence, as the studios were increasingly playing hardball with their best offerings.[8] In this light, original programming like *NNTN* was less about branding or increasing subscribers than programming diversification, and it had the added benefit of being relatively cheap. In his extensive history of the cable industry, Patrick R. Parsons describes how the economics of programming was an essential question for the health of early cable channels. For instance, CBS Cable overinvested in its programming and lost to more frugal channels like CNN.[9]

HBO smartly used its economic assets to invest in film production, pressure the studios, and create its own alternative offerings, with *NNTN* as part of this initial wave of programs.[10]

In 1983, both HBO and its chief pay-cable competitor Showtime made a push to produce recurring shows. HBO planned to spend $60 million over two years to expand its programming, prompting one entertainment reporter to label the strategy "a quiet revolution within the television entertainment industry."[11] Besides *NNTN*, over 1983–1984, the channel also launched the children's show *Fraggle Rock*, mystery anthology *The Hitchhiker*, prison drama *Maximum Security*, and the comedy *The Investigators*. Michael Fuchs, who led the company through much of the 1980s, tried to emphasize the difference between their shows and the broadcast networks, calling network programs "artificial": "What we're doing is trying to provide a little more of an edge, with subject matter that is a little more authentic."[12] Fuchs's pronouncement was perfectly in line with Christopher Anderson's evaluation of HBO's branding techniques during this period. Unlike the 1990s and 2000s, when HBO was attempting to develop a relationship with subscribers based on must-watch serial content like *Oz*, *The Sopranos*, and *Six Feet Under*, HBO during the 1980s and early 1990s positioned itself as a luxury brand within the low culture of television, a channel-wide alternative.[13] Throughout the 1980s, Fuchs positioned the channel against both the networks and Hollywood, playing up the questionable claim that HBO's films and recurring programs more consistently delved into controversial topics. Even if much of the content barely deviated from traditional television, simply playing up the difference was important for the channel. Tony Kelso argues that because the channel relies on subscribers rather than advertisers, HBO *must* take more risks simply to attract new customers.[14] However, throughout the 1980s, those risks were carefully managed, barely suggesting the kind of innovative programming that would emerge in the 1990s when their strategy moved from luxury to sophistication. As a result, when Fuchs said in the 1980s that HBO "dig[s] more deeply into more mature, more intelligent programming," such statements can be retrospectively interpreted as more marketing than reality.[15]

THE DEVELOPMENT OF *NNTN*

When *NNTN* debuted on HBO, its visual style certainly *seemed* fresh and even innovative. The heavily edited program broke with many of the traditions established by earlier network news parody shows. Producer John Moffitt had developed an *SNL* competitor for ABC called *Fridays*, which also included a news-parody segment. Moffitt was having difficulty finding news footage he could use on the show and went to the Cannes Television Festival looking for a source. What he found was the BBC-produced topical sketch series *Not the Nine O'Clock News* (1979–1982). The BBC program was cutting-edge comedy in Britain at the time, prompting comparisons to the original British *That Was the Week That Was* (*TW3*). *Not the Nine O'Clock News* was essentially a sketch-comedy program like *SNL*; however, the program borrowed *TW3*'s concept of continually returning to a "metashow"—as if once a sketch or prerecorded sequence ended, the viewer was returned to a show in progress, such as a news broadcast or talk show. *Not the Nine O'Clock News* made infrequent use of news parody, sometimes incorporating an anchor and other times eschewing news-style presentation for entire episodes. The program focused more on satirizing television as a whole rather than limiting its scope to a single genre. One of the British show's major innovations was its consistent mixing of news footage with produced material, such as juxtaposing a shot of Margaret Thatcher looking down during a news conference with a shot of a female cast member's nails being painted. The edited result made it appear that the Prime Minister was primping while fielding press questions. *Not the Nine O'Clock News* made this type of visual joke a hallmark of its format and often strung recontextualized footage together into extended montages.

Moffitt and coproducer Pat Tourk Lee snapped up the American rights for *Not the Nine O'Clock News* but were leery of developing the show for the broadcast networks. Moffitt had grown tired of dealing with ABC's continual interference with *Fridays*, and the network seemed uninterested in the idea. Moffitt decided to pitch his new show to HBO, which wanted to expand its original offerings.[16] The network ordered six episodes as a tryout, and *NNTN* debuted in January of 1983 in a half-hour format. The show ran for four years before moving to sporadic one-hour specials. Unlike the British version, Moffitt homed in on news as the primary visual style and incorporated *Not the Nine O'Clock News*'s fast-paced use of news footage.

Both the audience and critical receptions for *NNTN* were inconsistent. The program was consistently hailed by the cable industry, winning the most ACE Awards of any program during the 1980s. In reality, viewership was reportedly never very high. For example, in January 1984, *NNTN* ranked fourth in terms of audience for original HBO programming, behind the top-rated *Fraggle Rock*, *All the Rivers Run* (a licensed miniseries), and a *Best of Consumer Reports* special.[17] Because many television critics at that time declined to even write about cable programming, reviews were infrequent and usually indifferent. *The New York Times*' John O'Connor delivers a typical response, saying the humor is "inevitably uneven, but there are enough on-target routines to merit further encouragement."[18] One of the biggest challenges for the show was HBO's haphazard scheduling, frequently changing time slots and days. As the decade wore on, *NNTN* continued to recycle its central concept with few shifts in form or content. By the time O'Connor wrote another review of the show four years later, his optimism had turned to weariness, saying the show "can claim far fewer hits than misses. Halfway through the hour, the pileup of jokes begins to take on the queasy aspects of a fatal auto pileup on some busy highway going nowhere."[19]

It took another two years before HBO executives agreed with O'Connor's diagnosis, dictating that Moffitt recast and reformat *NNTN*. An interview with Michael Fuchs clarifies that the relaunch was one final attempt to generate renewed interest in the show before cancellation.[20] There is an uncanny parallel between the framing of *NNTN*'s revamp by its producers and the discourse surrounding NBC's decision to shift direction between *TW3*'s first and second seasons in 1964. In both cases, executives assured audiences their reworked shows would be edgier and funnier, with neither living up to the hype. *NNTN* finally received a regular time slot, and the program began taping on the same day it aired, allowing for the most up-to-date content. However, the 1989 relaunch received even worse reviews than the original version. *Newsday* writer David Friedman summarized the response, pointing out that with political satire "some things don't get better. They just get older."[21] The attempted reboot became *NNTN*'s last season, marking the end of a program that spanned the formative programming years of HBO and the cable industry.

FORMATTING POST-PRODUCTION NEWS PARODY

Previous chapters discussed the strange relationship between politicians and earlier news parody programs, the latter often eliciting a mix of fascination and fear as political figures contemplated being the target of satire or, worst of all, being ignored completely. *TW3* was the talk of the capital for days after it aired—who got skewered? Who got airtime? Likewise, *SNL* was a must-see comedy that amused and infuriated the political elite. By contrast, no one really seemed to care about *NNTN*.

The story of its official launch could be taken as a portent. George Mair, HBO's newly hired chief public relations counsel at the time, tells the story of how network executives set up a special screening of *NNTN* for members of Congress before its official debut. Mair told HBO that the location of the event was too far away from Capitol Hill and scheduling on a Monday was a poor choice because most politicians would be out of town. Then, to top it off, the day before the special screening a US Marine barracks was bombed in Beirut, killing 231 soldiers. HBO went ahead with the event anyway, with no members of Congress in attendance.[22] From its beginning, the program seemed to exist in a different universe from Washington politics, barely scratching the surface and only incorporating the most obvious of political puns and players. The lack of depth in its political humor likely limited the potential for *NNTN* to cross over and engage in the journalistic or political field, unlike its NBC predecessors.

The show's smaller footprint undoubtedly also limited its reach. Despite HBO's success, pay-cable penetration was still small compared to network television. HBO ruled the pay-channel universe entering the 1980s, with 70% of pay-channel subscribers, and by the time *NNTN* went on the air, they had a total potential audience of 13.5 million households.[23] That was still less than a third of all cable subscribers, though, and many times fewer than the over-the-air audience. Although the show's pay-channel origins decreased its potential influence, the creators' formatting decisions and lack of consistent political satire also limited *NNTN*'s ability to create consistent news parody.

Postmodern Television Style

Out of all the shows discussed in this book, *NNTN* veers the farthest from a vision of news parody as political and media criticism engaging in debates within those fields. The show's opening immediately contextualizes it more as a comedy with a news parody shell than a sustained effort to replicate and satirize broadcast journalism. The opening combines news footage with shots of the six original cast members, creating the illusion that they are interacting with the footage. For example, Anne Bloom fires a slingshot, followed by footage of a rocket crashing to the ground. These individual vignettes are linked together with audio of Eric Clapton's fast-paced, fret-spanning slide guitar from the song "Motherless Children" and a laugh track, creating an upbeat and energetic pace. Because television openings help create audience expectations and frames of interpretation, *NNTN* producers primed viewers to expect comedy but not "necessarily" news. As previously discussed, "Weekend Update" utilized a traditional news opening to play against expectations, and *TW3* incorporated a weekly song referring to contemporary politics and events to connect its presentational style to news content. *NNTN*, instead, offered decontextualized and generic footage with traditional slapstick comedy and puns, foregrounding its primary identity as a sketch/variety show. Although the opening would change in subsequent years to make the actors appear more "newsy," fast-paced rock music and canned laughter continued to set the pace.

One of the most effective innovations of "Weekend Update" was sectioning off its news parody into a self-contained segment, couching the entire sequence in news style, removed from sketches. Moffitt followed that segment's lead in developing "Friday Edition" for *Fridays*, but then decided to intermingle news parody with other comedy segments in formatting *NNTN*.

Perhaps the change was an opportunity to start fresh after trying to compete at late night with *SNL* or to hew closer to *Not the Nine O'Clock News*, but *NNTN*'s awkward mélange of news, contemporary subject sketches, and commercial parodies actually hearken back more to the structure of *TW3*. In another similarity to *TW3*, *NNTN* also utilized its numerous cast members in all types of productions, meaning that an actor would appear in an advertisement for "Normal K" cereal and then immediately reappear at an anchor desk. During the next newsbreak, another person would be reporting. As a result, many of the problems *TW3* contended with because of its blended format are replicated in *NNTN*.

The most defining and innovative stylistic quality of the HBO show and the one that most sets it apart from other news parody programs both before and after, is its pre-produced, highly edited presentation. *TW3* and *SNL* made liveness an essential aspect of their style. Even *The Daily Show* (*TDS*) and *Full Frontal with Samantha Bee* seem to strive to have as much live-to-tape content as possible. Instead, *NNTN* assembled mostly pre-shot content with talent linking that content together in front of a studio audience. For example, a brief sports report by Rich Hall shot on a desk in the studio cuts to an edited sight gag where a baby stroller has its wheels stolen; this then cuts to a fake commercial, followed by a string of edited news footage, and then finally returns to an anchor desk before going back to pre-taped content. Besides altering the live dynamic of previous news parodies, the format leaves much less time at the anchor desk for news reports. The pace is rapid-fire, making constant use of newsfeed, licensed reels, and original, pre-shot footage. The frenetic style is reminiscent of playing with tape-to-tape edit controllers in the 1980s, flipping the shuttle control back and forth, amused by changes in tape direction and speed. One sports segment actually does play a tape backward for humor, first making it look as if a dog is going in reverse and then as if water is coming off a runner and back into a garden hose.[24] In these moments, *NNTN* seems to devolve into a kind of "videotape of attractions," with the creators taking delight in the Méliès-esque fun the technology allowed.[25] As a viewer of the show myself during the 1980s, I recall its delight in using video as a defining aspect of *NNTN*. Much of its appeal and humor simply came from editing serious and comical content together.

NNTN creators obviously attempted to frame the show as news parody, given its title, but the frequent use of the anchor desk is what most links the program to other news-parody shows. The news set of *NNTN* inherently evokes network news. One of the benefits of having pre-taped segments was the creation of a roomier, working newsroom environment for the set. A somewhat nondescript, angular anchor desk with an overlapping top sits in front of multiple office desks in the middle ground and a wall of monitors in the background, giving the set more depth than "Weekend Update." In the early years of *NNTN*, a false wall stuck out behind the desk, with a filing cabinet extending out from behind the wall slightly. The organization and business-like atmosphere created by the file cabinet is reinforced by the multiple desks angled in the middle, sometimes with "reporters" working behind the anchor, writing and shuffling their papers—signifying that the quest of the journalist never ends, even during the newscast. The monitors on the back wall are all tuned to different images, suggesting a newsroom connected to the world via satellite and microwave, displaying multiple sources of "first-hand" footage.

The set design and graphics match the aesthetics of network news during the 1980s. A pastel, muted yellow and pink color scheme is replaced mid-decade by light blues and grays, and by the incorporation of the *NNTN* logo into the set design. During extended sequences, an official title graphic appears on-screen at the beginning of news segments, with the anchor shifted to one side and a title such as "The Nightly News with Bob Charles" sharing the screen with the anchor. The title font is typewriter-style with long serifs, very similar in appearance to the font used by CBS News in the 1980s. The obligatory audio of a teletype machine was an ever-present feature of the news segments, further linking it to traditional news.

News reporters on *NNTN* included virtually every cast member of the show, appearing with their own fake reporter names and personas. Stuart Pankin appeared most often on the desk and might be referred to as the show's lead anchor. Often, Pankin shared the desk to create a "news team" look. A wall-mounted monitor that was usually off-screen could be framed in the shot to talk with reporters who were supposed to be on location. The visual look of the news set offered a perfect location for parody, but that potential was stymied by the brief and haphazard integration of its use (figure 4.1).

NNTN weaved news-oriented content with other types of skits and puns, its accelerated pace creating a bewildering mix. The show diverged so much in its topics that it was more of a commentary on television culture in general. Moffitt acknowledged this expansive perspective of the show's humor: "It's about what people are talking about. . . . It's what's on people's minds. Changes in the way people dress, what's the popular music, whatever's hot."[26] As a result, the more news-oriented content is mixed with entertainment parody and visual jokes via montage. An advertisement for the fake television show "Still the Cleavers" portrays Beaver and Wally coming downstairs to eat breakfast with Black Panther leader Eldridge Cleaver, dressed in sunglasses and a beret. Later in the show, a skit where a man tries to rob a diner turns into a commercial for Bounty paper towels, and in a montage of news items a hearse door closes to reveal a bumper sticker that says, "My Other Car is an Ambulance." All of the content seamlessly moves from joke to joke, linked purely through editing.

Figure 4.1 *NNTN* **Original Cast.** Pictured from left: Lucy Webb, Danny Breen, Stuart Pankin, Anne Bloom, Mitchell Laurance. 1982. *Source: Courtesy HBO/Photofest.*

Stylistically, *NNTN* shares similarities with 1980s television content labeled postmodern. The rapid pace, self-awareness, and fascination with technology find affinities with *Max Headroom* and MTV music videos. The format seems especially well suited for maximizing the largest number of jokes per episode, which was an obvious consideration for the show. Montage allowed for the compression of material into just the gag, with no need to set up or transition between bits, creating strings of quick visual jokes. The sheer number of discernible segments is dramatized when looking over *NNTN* scripts, where each bit is separated so that associated talent, audio, and video sources can be noted. Episode 1 includes 33 discrete segments, not including slates, titles, and the show opening.[27] Episode 2 includes 40 such segments.[28] The majority of these items are very short; in Episode 1, there are 19 under 30 seconds and 27 in Episode 2. Most early episodes only had one or two segments that lasted more than two minutes, and those were usually either sniglets or an extended movie trailer. Critics frequently mentioned the pace of jokes, although not always as a positive. John O'Connor accused the show of striving for quantity over quality, saying, "In the craft of hit-or-miss comedy, the kind that flings dozens of jokes at you in the expectation that a few may actually connect, few series have been more energetically determined than Not Necessarily the News."[29] Volume was a definite strategy for the show's writers. Original cast member Anne Bloom told a reporter, "The good thing about our show is that nothing is very long—so if it stinks it's over real fast."[30] By trying to throw as many jokes out as fast as possible, the humor tended to run together, conflating moments of news parody with its other modes of comedy.

Mimicking Cable News

Like the program's other content, the short length of news elements is a unique aspect of *NNTN*'s parody of journalism. Rather than extended segments of anchor/story/anchor, most of the time spent on the desk is framed around "news bulletins" or "updates." This fragmented presentation of news mimicked local news' strategy of "breaking in" to regular programming to provide information about immediate events or promote their newscasts. The practice was rare for the networks and usually only reserved for major news. Even with the creation of CNN in 1980 and its sibling station Headline News in 1982, television journalism still commonly structured itself around 30-minute runtimes, delivered in blocks with commercial breaks. *NNTN*'s stop/start, break-in, update method of news delivery is much more in line with contemporary 24-hour news networks and their constant emphasis on the *next* big event.

Another way the cable show broke with previous news-parody norms was its extensive dependence on footage. Moffitt had originally been looking for a news-video source for *Fridays* when he happened upon the format that would be adapted into *NNTN*. The program reflected the increasing availability of footage in an age of stock videotape and news-agency satellite distribution. Scripts show that *NNTN* used multiple sources for video and suggest they also had an internal library, perhaps of previously used footage. Jokes often originated from timely newsfilm, such as footage of Soviet tanks leaving Afghanistan, followed by a fake video of a sign welcoming people to the

USSR and reminding them to "buckle up."[31] Other times, writers would craft jokes and then request footage. Episode 8 includes a sketch about the United States sending comedy advisors to El Salvador to help write jokes. The script for the episode notes that "footage of paratroopers landing in Central American Type Terrain" will have to be ordered.[32] The program sometimes found it difficult to convince traditional news organizations to make footage available, since the video would inevitably be recontextualized. At one time, CNN licensed video to the show, but the relationship was severed after *NNTN* redubbed an interview between Jane Fonda and CNN founder Ted Turner to make it sound as if they were discussing their sex life.[33] The dust-up probably had more to do with Turner's notoriously thin skin than making any stand for journalistic integrity. Still, as a show structured around borrowed footage, *NNTN* had to be mindful of maintaining its relationship with video sources.

One of *NNTN*'s most common techniques for turning video into a joke was to combine it with other images to create an imaginary interchange between footage. Sometimes video is added to newsfilm, such as when Nancy Reagan is on the White House lawn receiving birthday balloons from well-wishers. The clip is followed by *NNTN*-shot footage of red shoes being lifted off the ground to make it look as if Reagan has become airborne.[34] In a segment very similar to *TW3*'s fake news conference with Kennedy, a press briefing with Ronald Reagan is interspliced with video of *NNTN* reporters asking questions, making the president's answers sound nonsensical.[35]

Other times, unrelated news footage is edited back-to-back to create humor simply through the juxtaposition of incongruent material. For example, a video of Senator Jesse Helms saying "the opera isn't over 'til the fat lady sings" is followed by footage of the heavyset Speaker of the House Tip O'Neill, with opera audio dubbed in.[36] *NNTN* kicked off its very first program with this kind of humor, showing the funeral procession of Soviet Premier Leonid Brezhnev. Cast members Danny Breen, Audrie Neenan, and Stuart Pankin narrate in hushed, reverent tones as if they are covering the funeral live, until Pankin, with rising excitement, reports,

> Wait . . . now all eyes are on something else in the distance. Yes, yes, here he comes. [*Funeral images suddenly change to footage of a large Thanksgiving Day parade as giant balloons drift down the street*] Here comes Bullwinkle![37]

All of the bits are short and very linear—in other words, there is no intricate editing to create a sustained interplay between footage, such as modern news-parody programs might feature. The joke comes from the immediate incongruence and then quickly moves on.

Footage would also be recontextualized by adding new audio. In one episode, the sound of a drowning Pankin desperately calling for help is edited over footage of Nancy Reagan milling about on a beach, looking untroubled.[38] The program enjoyed taking advantage of having an ex-movie star in the White House by occasionally using clips of Ronald Reagan's films and adding original audio dubs. One episode begins with the audio "from the Western White House" as if going live to a press conference and then cuts to a black-and-white movie clip of Reagan entering an old west saloon. A man looks up from a card table and Breen's edited audio asks, "Mr. President, I'm poor and unemployed, what am I going to do?" Reagan lunges and hits the man while saying "shut up!"[39] The same strategy worked on the anchor desk when Pankin reads a fake story about the 5000th anniversary of the biblical battle of David and Goliath, reporting that in a recent reenactment the Palestinians played David and the Israelis were Goliath. The report is accompanied by images of Palestinians hurling rocks and the Israeli military clubbing protesters.[40] The presentational style of news items was heavily dependent on editing and remained mostly consistent throughout the first six seasons of the program.

The 1989 reboot of *NNTN* resulted in both a stylistic and substantive change, utilizing a structure more similar to "Weekend Update" or even *TDS*. Each episode was shot live to tape on the day it aired, moving away from the highly edited format that had defined the program. As a result, the production style more closely mimicked standard newscasts, including keying over-the-shoulder graphics and using camera zooms to isolate anchors. The first reformatted episode reflects the difficulty the technical staff had shifting to a live environment; several technical slipups appear, such as allowing tapes to freeze on screen before switching back to anchors.[41] *NNTN* also scaled down its large rotating cast to two main anchors, with several supporting cast members providing special reports and commentary. Only Lucy Webb remained on air from the previous cast, and only as a featured player. Like "Weekend Update," the opening of the program mirrors a traditional broadcast-news trope of keying the show title over a wide shot of the news desk, revealing some of the surrounding studio space. The opening was one of many changes spurred by the live production style.

Although the format of the program changed, humor strategies remained mostly consistent with *NNTN*'s previous incarnation. Just like the Reagan press conference, the reboot used footage from an interview with Vice President Dan Quayle and his wife to create a faux live interview with anchor Tom Parks on the desk. Predictably, the segment portrayed Quayle as an intellectual lightweight.[42] Presaging a dominant aspect of *TDS*'s style, the reboot incorporated pre-edited special reports from a small team of reporters. One recurring feature was "The Rosen Report," in which Richard Rosen gives extended coverage to news items with a twist, such as the problem of New York City housing. Rosen reports on residents being "overhoused," showing footage of opulent dwellings in the city and discussing the terrible burden of large homes.[43] Creators structured the rebooted *NNTN* like a newscast, with definable blocks, commercial parodies, and other gags to provide "breaks" between blocks, very similar to "Weekend Update" in its early days. The reboot of *NNTN* attempted to create a sustained 30-minute news-parody program, but it was too late for HBO, who canceled the show the following year.

Actors Acting Like Anchors

In one of his final interviews before the cancellation of *NNTN*, Moffitt reflected on the show's overall lack of success. One particular problem he identified, with some regret, was the decision to cast talent in multiple roles rather than having actors specifically portray anchors or other parts.[44] Moffitt lamented that, as a result, "there was no audience identification with our people. [*NNTN*] never achieved an audience following."[45] Just as with *TW3*, this approach to casting may have hurt not only ratings but also *NNTN*'s ability to create a credible anchor persona as everyone appeared both as journalists and part of the repertory cast for comedy segments. Once or twice during an episode, there might be news segments running several minutes, but more often anchor appearances lasted only seconds and were limited to quick news updates or introductions of other material, which exacerbated the problem of not connecting actors to their roles as anchors. Jane Curtin and Bill Murray appeared in other skits for *SNL*, but their sustained time at the "Weekend Update" anchor desk solidified those newscast characters—an opportunity severely limited for *NNTN*'s cast by the manic structure of the show.

Stuart Pankin was the favorite go-to for news anchor. In most of the extended (2 to 3 minute) news parody sequences, Pankin at least made an appearance on the desk. His role is even more central on special episodes; for instance, in the 1984 Year in Review, Pankin is explicitly given the central anchor role, with Lucy Webb covering entertainment and Mitchell Laurance as a sports anchor. Pankin harkens back to *TW3* by depending more on the set design and news content to clue the audience into the parody than his own portrayal of a news anchor. Pankin presents his anchor persona, Bob Charles, as over-the-top and arrogant. In an almost direct rejection of traditional newscast style, he overemphasizes movements, overenunciates words, condescendingly laughs at others, amuses himself in overt moments of self-awareness, and presents a kind of Ron Burgundy figure. Pankin's presentational style is pure comedy, eschewing the distanced, limited reactions that were long the hallmark of television news anchors and most news satirists.[46] The same year *NNTN* debuted, Peter Jennings took over the anchor desk for ABC News. Jennings had fulfilled various roles for the network-news division since the

1960s and embodied the anchor persona of the era, described as being "celebrated for a cool, intellectual style. He avoids the pitfalls of overt emotion and its evil twin, cynicism."[47] Bob Charles could scarcely be more different than Jennings and his network contemporaries. *NNTN* seemed to be increasingly imitating the 24-hour news channel CNN, which debuted in 1980. However, even CNN's anchors at the time, such as Lou Waters, adopted the dispassionate and physically reserved dominant style of anchoring. Pankin's approach on the desk constantly foregrounded a comedy of excess over mimicking news style, which aligned with the show's broader focus on television culture.

Perhaps replicating the broadcast journalism world too well, *NNTN* had very little racial diversity in its talent. Occasional guest stars, such as *Night Court*'s Marsha Warfield, made one-shot appearances, and the hour-long special *Not Necessarily the Media* included Claudette Wells as part of the anchor team, but the lack of diversity in the recurring main cast and featured players is glaring. Especially at a time when broadcast networks were at least attempting to address a visual lack of diversity, *NNTN* missed an opportunity to create a critical dialogue with its source material (figure 4.2).

The program moved to a more traditional news-anchor approach with the 1989 restructuring and the addition of coanchors Annabelle Gurwitch and Tom Parks. Taking a page from "Weekend Update," the two used their real names, rejecting the fake on-air personas created in previous seasons. Gurwitch and Parks replicate the presentational style of traditional news much more closely

Figure 4.2 *Not Necessarily the Media* **Was One of Several Hour-Long Specials Produced for HBO in the Late 1980s as Regular Seasons Became More Sporadic.** Pictured from left: Claudette Wells, Stuart Pankin, Lucy Webb, Anne Bloom, Danny Breen. 1987. *Source: Courtesy HBO/Photofest.*

than previous *NNTN* talent. They each play up the emotionless and slightly vapid stereotypes of newsreaders, leading *Newsday* critic David Friedman to lash out at Gurwitch's stereotyped portrayal of women in the news, saying she "reeks of misogyny and does a grave disservice to the truth." He offhandedly dismisses Parks as a rip-off of *SNL*'s Dennis Miller, without the charm.[48] Friedman ignores the irony, taking issue with their satiric enactment of the anchor role. In reality, the pair fell squarely within a presentational mode established by "Weekend Update": mirror the dominant news style, while occasionally overemphasizing the norms and letting the material generate the comedy. *NNTN*'s cancellation cut short the possibility that the new format and anchors might eventually connect with audiences.

NEWS PARODY OR NEWS PASTICHE?

This chapter has approached *NNTN* as a news parody up to this point, even though producers were not focused primarily on satirizing journalism and politics. Genre in media studies has traditionally been approached from a structuralist viewpoint, identifying groups of texts based on commonalities. Rick Altman's use of semantic and syntactic elements in constructing genre is one well-known process.[49] There are certainly some genre elements *NNTN* shares with other news parody programs based on visual and stylistic references to television news, but there may be just as many differences due to its eclectic format. From this perspective, it could be legitimately argued whether *NNTN* is a news parody. However, genre can also be defined discursively. Jason Mittell describes how interpretive communities discursively construct definitions of genres by the way audiences, critics, creators, and the popular press discuss groups of television shows.[50] When *NNTN* first appeared, critics often compared it to its precursors, *TW3* and "Weekend Update." With the appearance and success of the original *The Daily Show* and the Stewart-led *TDS*, the HBO program continued to be grouped by the press and audiences as part of this developing genre. When *NNTN* is discussed in culture, which is admittedly rare, the show circulates within the same discursive realm as other news-parody programs. Despite my own fond teenage memories of watching the program and the vague moments of hilarity that circulated in my hazy recollections of the program, my reading of scripts and archival viewing of *NNTN* forced a reevaluation that the HBO show offers very little satire of either news or newsmakers, and instead creates more of an homage to emerging television style.

As previously established, *NNTN*'s approach borrows heavily from the production practices of postmodern television. John Fiske, writing about MTV, describes how the combination of images within the often-loosely structured narratives of music videos partakes of this style, calling it "a recycling of images that wrenches them out of the original context that enabled them to make sense and reduces them to free-floating signifiers whose only signification is that they are free."[51] In a similar way, *NNTN* presents its viewers with a mélange of references ripped from their original popular-culture context (advertisements, logos, catchphrases, etc.) and combined into a flow of signifiers. Fiske connects this television style to Mikhail Bahktin's liberating concept of "carnival," offering a hopeful, although perhaps dated, perspective. Focusing on humor in postmodern media, Lance Olsen likewise celebrates the way radical comedy destroys concepts under postmodernity, thereby allowing renewal.[52] However, in evaluating the use of *NNTN*'s postmodern style and humor, there is little radical or destructive to be found. Instead, the show creates a celebration of form that rarely questions journalism, politics, or society with a satiric spirit and certainly offers no alternative "better" solution. Fredric Jameson's theory of "pastiche" seems more applicable than Bahktin or Olsen. Writing in the 1990s, Jameson claimed postmodern parody had become largely stripped of its critical roots, instead participating in a play of signification without purpose. Pastiche is "amputated of the satiric impulse, devoid of laughter . . . blank parody."[53] It exists as an endless circulation of borrowed sign systems, and although humor may be attached, the critical spirit is absent. While discursively grouped within the news parody genre, the show rarely participates in true satiric parody. Instead, pastiche perfectly describes *NNTN*'s delight in the play of visual and structural newscast similarity and its lack of deeper criticism of method or substance.

The bar for *NNTN*'s humor remained consistently low. Coproducer Pat Tourk Lee once told a reporter, "as long as we can find some message, anything is up for grabs."[54] His statement reflects the lack of cohesive comic vision that both previous and later news-parody programs would display. Using Murray Davis's concept of progressively destabilizing humor, the HBO program generally operates at the lowest two levels: the linguistic and the logical. Rarely does it use humor to question either fundamental categories or social structures.[55] Puns and incongruence dominate.

In the late 1980s, media critics coined the term "infotainment" to describe a shifting news landscape.[56] Driven by ratings and the swing from the news as station prestige to news as an advertising commodity, infotainment described a journalism less concerned with traditional Fourth Estate topics like politics and civics and more focused on celebrities, features, and conflict. Some news programs even attempted to incorporate modified aspects of the postmodern style. *NNTN* seems to be primarily a pastiche of the trend toward infotainment, although incorporating more satiric perspectives on occasion. While the show most consistently mimicked the style of network newscasts or CNN, it would often include short skits structured like various soft-news programs, such as *Good Morning America* or *Entertainment Tonight*. In one example, a group of insipid reporters discusses international politics on "The Morning Edition," displaying no actual knowledge of the issues: "More advisors in El Salvador? Boy, they sure need a lot of advice down there!"[57] In another segment called "The Random Report," Pankin begins sentences and then consults items of chance to complete each thought. Introducing himself with "I'm Bob Charles with [*he pauses to spin a wheel with multiple words, landing on news*] with the news." He continues: "Congress approved a new [*pulls ball out of jar*] budget appropriation bill."[58] Such skits foreground the blending of entertainment with news occurring during the 1980s, although without an identifiably critical edge.

Infotainment's emphasis on self-promotion and spot news stories also became topics for the show's humor. The rapidly accelerated news cycle that came with the quest for ratings and 24-hour news networks resulted in excessive coverage, with *NNTN* often poking fun at this obsession with timeliness. Special report "break-ins" frequently popped up with immense fanfare, only to offer minor bits of information. In the first episode, a sports report is interrupted by the sounds of a teletype, a "special report" graphic, and a voice-over, "we interrupt this program for a special bulletin. Here's Rich Hall at the news desk." Hall appears on-screen looking confused and verbally stumbles before saying, "No, I'm sorry. Nothing to report. Sorry." The announcer then tosses back to the sports program.[59] In the first episode of the 1989 reboot, the news show continually cuts to reporter Joe Guppy, reporting live from Hawaii on the deathwatch for former Philippine president Ferdinand Marcos. Every time the show cuts to Guppy, he enthusiastically encourages viewers to stay tuned because Marcos is "still near death!"[60] The media emphasis on death and crime over larger social issues is keenly satirized when Pankin interrupts a report by Danny Breen about the nation's poor, saying, "like the rest of the nation, we've lost interest."[61] The ceaseless barrage of jokes thrown at the screen overshadows such moments of true critique, though, quickly slipping back into pastiche as *NNTN* recreates television style without commentary.

The topic of sexism in journalism offers an interesting point of comparison between the pastiche incorporated into *NNTN* as opposed to the parody of "Weekend Update." As outlined in the previous chapter, Jane Curtin's anchor character often was belittled and sexualized by male newscasters but had agency and a voice. While sometimes playing into stereotypes, Curtin also retaliated and fought back, creating a conflicted persona. *NNTN*, by contrast, presents hyperbolic instances of casual sexism, but without any follow-up to contextualize the jokes as satire. In the 1984 Year in Review episode, Pankin introduces Anne Bloom's character in his most condescending voice:

And now, with a brief report, [*speaking as an aside with the audience*] that I hope won't take too much time away from more important matters, [*chuckling*] we go to cute, perky Frosty Kimmelman, with a piece of fluff on women in 1984, and I'd like to add my personal thanks to the little lady—the coffee's been great all year long!

She thanks him for the introduction, and Pankin pats her hand, saying, "No problem sweetheart, just keep it short." Bloom begins a report on the state of women in society, but after less than a minute Pankin suddenly puts his arm around her and asks in a sing-songy voice, "honey, is this over yet? I've got a major story."[62] Obviously, Pankin is ironically overplaying the part, creating humor through exaggeration, but whereas Jane Curtin would have delivered a withering retort, Bloom meekly finishes so Pankin can read his story. The bit reflects how *NNTN* most commonly addressed sexism in journalism by raising the topic and letting it drop without suggesting a particular stance. This ambiguous approach to journalistic humor was also extended to its treatment of presidents and politicians.

NOT NECESSARILY POLITICAL

Even before *NNTN* went on air, executives played up the show as a cutting-edge comedy, unafraid to step on toes and tackle newsmakers. The reality did not live up to the hype. Writers and producers seemed conflicted over whether to be a news-comedy show touching on politics or a news-parody show satirizing newsmakers from a consistent ideological position. In a 1985 interview, HBO Chairman Michael Fuchs claimed the program was "the only political satire on American TV today," reflecting the network's desire to at least present the show as oppositional.[63] Co-executive producer Pat Tourk Lee claimed Fuchs was enthusiastic about Ronald Reagan jokes and never told the producers they had to practice any objectivity in their political humor.[64] Yet, only a couple of years later, Moffitt cautiously softened that image by claiming *NNTN* is doing "responsible satire," highlighting ridiculous topics in society, and trying to entertain, because "you can't preach."[65] Framing the show's reboot less than a year after that interview, Moffitt then claims their "live-to-tape" format will "really help us to be more biting, to really get in there and be sharp with all our barbs."[66] Fuchs's and Moffitt's comments reflect the clashing pressures on the program. Network and show executives seemed caught in a noncommittal dance between wanting the show to function as true political satire and a desire to avoid the kind of audience backlash that satire can create. By trying to occupy a middle ground, the show ultimately failed to strongly connect with audiences.

Both satire and parody function to "comment upon," existing as a reaction to events, stances, and even people. Past and future news-parody programs mostly lean toward liberal politics, although shifting along the political continuum. *NNTN*'s most damning problem was its lack of a core, consistent ideological stance from which satire could emerge. Instead, like its commentary on journalism, its politics produces a pastiche of observational humor about politics, rather than an oppositional concept of "better" politics. One example that stands out occurred during the reboot of the program after the 1989 killing of Chinese students in Tiananmen Square. Tom Parks begins the show with a traditional anchor intro and says the news has been hard to get from Beijing; however, their correspondent was able to send a report. He then reaches under the desk and pulls out a fortune cookie, breaks it open, and reads, "you are greatly admired by those around you." The camera then zooms in to frame him with an over-the-shoulder graphic of student demonstrators in China.[67] In the story, Parks reports, "China has issued the most severe crackdown yet on student demonstrators—all dorm privileges have been canceled, and the student pub has been closed indefinitely." Annabelle Gurwitch takes the next story, a sidebar reporting Hollywood already has a musical underway about the protests called "Can't Stop the People," accompanied by a video of troops marching to MGM-style music.[68] The strident and cynical tone of the segment is remarkable, essentially treating the story as if Chinese officials just gave a slap on the wrist to misbehaving students, rather than deploying heavy weapons of war to massacre civilians protesting for political change. Rather than moral outrage, the program responds with the same smug attitude applied to politicians caught in a sexual affair. Such a response would be unimaginable by other news parody programs, which might have underplayed the event's importance, but would inevitably have directed their attacks at Chinese officials.[69] The coverage is emblematic of *NNTN*'s pastiche approach, applying humor indiscriminately, with no critical core or deeper message—a method constantly utilized in covering presidential politics in the 1980s.

Almost the entire run of *NNTN* took place with Ronald Reagan in the White House, a time when despite heated political differences, popular culture seemed to reflect consensus politics with Reagan at its core. In her book on 1980s television, Jane Feuer contends that programming was more ideologically complex than critics suggested at the time; however, even when shows attempted to take on aspects of Reaganism, they often extended the underlying ideologies of the era.[70] *NNTN* constantly covered Reagan, but usually in a good-natured, poking fun way, rather than attacking his policies or positions, consistent with a pastiche approach. While the humor may be weak, the HBO show was still one of the rare programs willing to joke about the president. *Late Night with David Letterman* writer Steve O'Donnell suggests that audiences had become jaded after the "orgy of political humor about Watergate and Gerald Ford," and television responded by largely avoiding presidential humor during the Reagan Era.[71] Network executives may have also feared a political backlash. The year before *NNTN* debuted, many believed Reagan had won a major symbolic battle over his detractors in the entertainment industry with the cancellation of the program *Lou Grant*. The show's star, Ed Asner, questioned Reagan's policies and spoke out for progressive politics at a time of rising conservative power, resulting in a firestorm of controversy and CBS's cancellation of the show.[72] The public-relations victory reinforced Reagan's fighting male image, especially on the heels of recovering from his 1981 assassination attempt. Susan Jeffords writes of how Reagan became connected to the male hard-bodied action film heroes of the 1980s; his defeat of the soft-bodied, liberal Ed Asner on television fit perfectly with this emerging discourse surrounding the president.[73]

As the 1980s and Reagan presidency continued, the boundaries of discourse on popular television seemed to narrow, yet not discussing the president on a program dedicated to making fun of the news was simply impossible. Every episode featured video of Reagan, making it at least *seem* that *NNTN* regularly made fun of him. Actress Anne Bloom even reports that show personnel called Reagan their "sixth cast member."[74] Many reviews of *NNTN* mention that the president gets played for laughs, and one writer notes that the political right is more often the focus of jokes on the program.[75] Of course, Reagan *was* the president. His appointments, overwhelmingly conservative, ran the executive branch, and Republicans controlled the Senate for most of the decade. Republican presidents had even appointed most of the Supreme Court too. Although Democrats controlled the House, *NNTN* wrote jokes about a government mostly controlled by the GOP; as a result, the volume of jokes about conservatives says much less about the program's politics than the substance and type of humor they employed in those jokes.

Like many comedy programs, *NNTN* played primarily upon Reagan's personality rather than addressing specific policies. Jokes often playfully made him look forgetful or oblivious, dovetailing with mainstream discussions about his age. These were usually rendered by adding audio or juxtaposing clips. For instance, Nancy Reagan is shown with headphones and asks if everyone got "the things for their ears." Cut to a shot of the president with headphones sitting on his face, saying, "What?"[76] On another show, Reagan is throwing a ball to his dog Lucky. Cut to footage of Soviet leader Mikhail Gorbachev sitting and waiting, as if the president has forgotten their meeting.[77] Moffitt claimed at one time, "We feel there are no holds barred when it comes to the Administration or any big names in the news."[78] This sentiment seems drastically overblown, though, given the show's lack of satiric impulse. In general, *NNTN* played into Reagan's own "aw shucks" style of wit. In his book on humor and the presidency, Peter Robinson discusses how Reagan used humor to silence and disarm his detractors and how the president "simultaneously embodied the showman president and the comic-heroic everyman."[79] *NNTN*'s pastiche often reinforced a strategy that set up opponents to underestimate Reagan. The show's copious use of Reagan footage probably would have delighted the administration. Reagan's press team was reportedly pleased when newscasts used video of the president, even if the story was negative, because they realized that audiences would mostly remember the president looking strong and forget the context.[80] At the end of *NNTN*'s first episode, after the credits, a graphic reads: "The producers of 'Not Necessarily the News' would like to thank Milton Friedman, David Stockman, Congressman Jack Kemp, and President Reagan for their help in keeping people at home, out of work, and in need of laughter. Stay the course."[81] Had he been aware of the program, Reagan may have been just as grateful to the show's producers for their coverage and for keeping him in the minds of HBO subscribers.

While the show, by and large, kept a playful attitude toward the president, in line with its pastiche style, there are some moments of more genuine satire, many of which are significantly subtler than the show's normal humor. In a promotion for an upcoming special report on hospital overcrowding, Rich Hall walks into a bathroom where doctors are performing surgeries. Cutaways show an EKG printing onto toilet paper and a patient whose head is bandaged with a towel still attached to the wall roller. Reporting from the bathroom, Hall says,

> Reaganomics has acted like a rusty scalpel and cut services back, to cause chronic understaffing. The answer to the problem? [*Hall opens a stall door to find Pankin operating on a patient*] Sorry. [*Hall turns back to camera*] Find out on an upcoming special report.[82]

The skit stands out from *NNTN*'s normal fare by including some actual critique, although brief, of Reagan's economic policies, included within the broader visual joke on hospital overcrowding. In another example, video of Reagan is preceded by a pointed condemnation of his Teflon presidency. Lucy Webb reports that "one of the big stories was how the president was able to emerge untarnished by the failures of his administration." Cut to cast members dressed as military personnel with Webb asking, "Who is responsible for American military failures?" Each point to another until the camera cuts to footage of Reagan, who then points his finger at someone off camera.[83]

In the same episode, *NNTN* incorporates a humor strategy later employed by *TDS* and *The Colbert Report* (*Colbert*) of letting individuals damn themselves with their own words, using Reagan's ridiculous public statements about the

U.S. invasion of Grenada. After showing footage of the press conference, the video cuts to Anne Bloom as a reporter asking why, other than producing nutmeg, Grenada is important. The show rolls Reagan's famous comments linking the island with a communist plot to steal Christmas:

> Number one, Grenada does produce more nutmeg than any other place on Earth. Number two, the Soviets and the Cubans are trying to take Grenada. Number three, you can't have Christmas, or you can't make eggnog without nutmeg. Number four, you can't have Christmas without eggnog. Number five, the Soviets and the Cubans were trying to steal Christmas.

Cut to Bloom and other reporters looking confused, and then to Pankin on the anchor desk similarly tilting his head, trying to understand Reagan's logic.[84] To be fair, the president's comments were actually paraphrasing a letter he reportedly received from an army pilot who was attempting to humorously link nutmeg with the island's political significance.[85] The nonsensical logic of the quote, however, seemed to perfectly fit with Reagan's ability to project consistent conviction regardless of the content of his words. Often called "the Great Communicator," the president tended to connect with audience emotions, even when the stories were actually lifted from his old movie plots.

From the relatively small pool of critical presidential jokes on *NNTN*, perhaps the most sustained topic was the xenophobic rhetoric of the Reagan administration. The president's constitutive speeches often attempted to reclaim the greatness of Americans by separating off groups who wanted to "keep America weak." Communists topped the list, but most of the major social moments of the 1960s and 1970s, such as feminism, gay rights, and civil rights, were also treated as misguided, if not unpatriotic. As with most of the show, *NNTN*'s critique of Reagan's statements usually incorporated video. In one example, footage of repairs to the Statue of Liberty cuts away to a sign reading, "No Tired. No Poor. No Huddled Masses. President Ronald Reagan."[86] In an even more pointed instance, the new racism of 1980s conservatism comes under fire with an NNTN News Bulletin. A still image of a Ku Klux Klan cross-burning is accompanied by a voice-over: "The new members of the president's revamped commission on civil rights gave interviews to the press last night at a White House barbeque."[87] The administration's refusal to stand up against apartheid is addressed by using one of Reagan's old western films. As a man approaches Reagan in the movie, an audio dub plays: "Mr. President, I just can't support South Africa." Reagan grabs the cowboy and punches him several times. "I'm sorry, but it's a racist government." Reagan starts to hit him again until the cowboy falls to his knees, saying, "Okay. Maybe you're right." Reagan kicks him, and the scene ends.[88] Although these examples reflect a fairly pointed criticism of Reagan, they also illustrate how *NNTN* depended on video to question the presidency. For the most part, on-screen talent rarely critiqued Reagan or took stances on his policies through their own voices, instead using footage as a buffer or merely staying at the level of pastiche. As a result, the politics of these brief visual moments of satire are disconnected from *NNTN*'s cast, whereas David Frost, Jane Curtin, and more recent news-parody hosts are strongly connected with particular political outlooks.

The show's discourse on Reagan diverged into conflicting accounts of the president, usually depicting him as an amiable, somewhat clueless old man and less frequently presenting him in a more critical frame as a heartless, crafty politician. These seemingly dichotomous images of Reagan could also be found within the broader culture, where the president deftly navigated news coverage to present a strong, nationalistic image softened by homespun wisdom and self-deprecating humor. He was the first to use television as a primary tool of the presidency to both cajole and connect, becoming, in the words of Robert Denton, "a much better actor as president on television than he ever was in Hollywood."[89] As a result, *NNTN*'s coverage resonated with existing presentational frames for Reagan.

By contrast, *SNL* provided a brilliant commentary on the subject in the 1986 skit "President Reagan: Mastermind." Finishing an interview with a reporter, Reagan (played by Phil Hartman) claims total ignorance about the Iran-Contra affair. As soon as the journalist leaves the room, Reagan's entire demeanor changes, calling in his cabinet and issuing rapid-fire orders in fine detail to supply arms, launder money, bribe agencies, and drug opponents. He suddenly returns to his singsong delivery and simplistic speech pattern for a photo-op with a Girl Scout and then quickly returns to issuing orders once the child is out of the room.[90] Hartman's instantaneous transformation between the two extremes engaged one frequent criticism of Reagan during his presidency: that his public persona was simply a continuation of his acting career and Reagan was duplicitous with the American people and not the public face he tried to present. However, *NNTN* never attempted to connect the two Reagan personas, remaining content with its dominant mode of political pastiche and only occasionally sneaking in jokes with more substance.

For the brief period of time it was on the air during the George H. W. Bush presidency, *NNTN*'s coverage was even less insightful and biting than during Reagan's two terms. Perhaps Bush's own lack of a strong public image made it difficult for joke-writers to emphasize particular qualities. The rebooted 1989–1990 season mostly treated the Bush administration as ineffectual, the president himself as lacking a personality, and—along with every other comedian in America—Vice President Dan Quayle as an idiot.

Beyond simple personality-based humor, though, there was little content about the administration. A commentary from Will Durst on the first 100 days of the Bush administration offers the simple: "So far, he's done nothing!"[91] In another episode, Tom Parks promises the news team will break in with special coverage if the Bush administration does *anything*.[92] Overall, presidential humor during the last season was unremarkable. Although the show occasionally delivered on-target, critical hits at Reagan and other politicians in previous years, the sheer barrage of jokes about inconsequential matters dwarfed those moments of actual satire.

PROBLEMS AND POSSIBILITIES OF NEWS PARODY IN THE EARLY MULTICHANNEL ERA

Despite its lengthy run of seven seasons and multiple cable awards, *NNTN* occupied a precarious space of being a little-watched pay-channel program without a dedicated audience. The show would have undoubtedly been canceled had it appeared on a broadcast channel or even later in HBO's programming development. However, as one of the first programs on the network, *NNTN* benefited from initial name recognition, low relative cost, and HBO's need for programming it could control. In many ways, *NNTN* ran afoul of the same comedy problems as *TW3*: content that was too satirically safe and formatting that never committed to a presentational mode.

NNTN's cautious approach to political humor reflected a core problem for the show. On the one hand, the format was topical comedy. Yet, on the other hand, executives clearly placed limits, taking few political chances and minimizing the risk of offending audiences. The two directives seem irreconcilable. While continuing to emphasize HBO's lack of censorship, Moffitt seemed hesitant to create controversy. His concept of "responsible satire" structured the program, and he makes it clear in interviews that *NNTN* held back on more touchy issues. In one example, he claims they were "more delicate" in their coverage of Tiananmen Square, but what he actually discusses is their coverage of Bush's *reaction* to the massacre—not the actual event.[93] Rather than blasting Bush for his tepid response that he had "deep regret" over the killings, writers made a joke that deep regret falls just short of "total regret." Interestingly, in the same article, the reporter mentions that *NNTN* rarely makes fun of its corporate owners, barely mentioning the Time-Warner merger or a failed attempt by Paramount to take over Time. This hesitance to step on toes and push the limits hurt *NNTN*'s attempt to provide compelling news parody and ultimately moved the program more toward pastiche.

As one of the network's earliest shows, *NNTN* was designed to demonstrate what programming in the multichannel era could be, especially on a pay-channel. From the beginning of the show, both Moffitt and Fuchs emphasized a lack of restraint. Moffitt even reports that when he was producing *Fridays*, he was "warned by ABC not to go that heavy on Reagan. We had to be careful not to overdo it."[94] By contrast, he claimed there were no censorship problems with HBO, saying they can use profanity on the show and even suggesting that the network is open to nudity. That much is true, with the program occasionally weaving in "shit" and "fuck." However, transgressive language did not produce transgressive satire. *NNTN*'s writers utilized their freedom from network indecency standards but seemed more hesitant to address divisive political and social issues. By contrast, some of HBO's other programs really were pushing the boundaries of content in comparison to network programming, tackling AIDS and other topics the Big Three broadcast networks avoided.

The fate of *NNTN* likely reflects the timing of the program. In the 1980s and early 1990s, HBO fashioned itself as a luxury brand, attempting to appeal to Reagan Era yuppies as a signifier of status. Only half a decade after the cancellation of *NNTN*, HBO adopted its new slogan, "It's Not TV. It's HBO," suggesting the quality was in the content, not just the appearance of the brand. The network began developing its image as the primary purveyor of risky "quality" programming, fostering serial content to elicit habitual viewing.[95] The rise of a more liberal and accepting professional-managerial class and the educated elite in the 1990s became a larger demographic for HBO and its programming. Had the show appeared a decade later, the network likely would have pushed Moffitt to take more risks. Ironically, after being canceled from ABC for making controversial remarks about 9/11, Bill Maher moved to HBO, the same channel that had produced such cautious political discourse in the 1980s.

Another problem *NNTN* shared with *TW3* was its erratic formatting. Despite the incorporation of postmodern visual aesthetics at the time, the drastic shift in focus and style, from presidential politics to popular advertisements to non-topical sight gags, allowed no breathing room and no opportunity to orient. The lack of commercial breaks due to its pay-cable exhibition only exacerbated the problem. In the 1970s, Raymond Williams redefined the form of television content for media studies with his concept of "flow." Williams describes how the actual experience of television viewing involves not discrete programs, but continually interrupted sequences of program, ad, news break, program, ad, and so on—a *flow* of information.[96] The rapid stream of images *NNTN* presents to viewers ends up constituting its own flow, but without discrete blocks or sequences, missing essential orienting aspects of programming that viewers had learned to expect. As a result, the nonstandard stylistics and conflicted content work against the cohesiveness of the program. Instead of isolating its news parody, as *SNL* had successfully tried, it went back to *TW3*'s method of mixing content. In one of the final reviews of the show, the 30-minute format is singled out as a major problem for *NNTN* and contrasted with "Weekend Update," saying, "the big risk about doing a 30-minute show satirizing a newscast is that it might end up just as dull and silly as the newscast it wants to satirize."[97] The statement is a kind of epitaph for *NNTN* and a reminder that the program was both discursively grouped with "Weekend Update" and forever in its shadow, or at least the shadow of the segment's heyday.

NETWORK NEWS PARODY LIMPS INTO THE 1980S

SNL greeted the 1980s with a new cast and executive producer and dismal ratings. The writers, actors, and creative personnel who launched the show and kept it one of the most relevant programs on television for five seasons were gone. The sixth season introduced a new cast, writers, and executive producer Jean Doumanian, who ended up shouldering most of the blame for the show's drop in esteem and viewership. After a respectable opening to the season, every subsequent episode lost viewers. Critics excoriated the show, leading to a siege mentality and constant rumors the network might change the cast or leadership. One writer told *Variety*, "Now I know what Hitler's bunker must've felt like during the last days of the Third Reich."[98] Joe Piscopo, the only breakout cast member of the season, felt trapped: "You just knew that this was America's favorite television show, and yet here we were, taking it right into the toilet."[99]

As bad as the skits were, "Weekend Update" seemed even worse. Cast member Charles Rocket took over the anchor desk, bringing a smug, self-obsessed style that either ignored or rejected the efforts of previous *SNL* actors who tried to emulate newsreaders when hosting the segment. Perhaps surprisingly, Rocket had actually worked in journalism both as a reporter and anchor for several small-town television stations. He was one of the first cast members picked by Doumanian, who expected Rocket to be a star. Rocket self-consciously mugged for the camera, blowing kisses, raising his eyebrows, and generally acting incredibly pleased with himself, even if the audience was not. Doug Hill and Jeff Weingrad, in their book on the early days of *SNL*, discuss how audiences barely responded to Rocket and how long studio silences "made Update truly chilling to watch."[100] For the most part, jokes on the segment tended to be more juvenile and satiric than shocking. Writers regularly complained that Doumanian shifted the show's overall humor toward puns and visuals and away from dark or edgy humor,[101]

"Weekend Update" largely fell in line with this perspective, although there were moments of more subversive material, such as a story on the 1980 Republican election landslide. Rocket reports citizens should all expect a turn to the right, outlining how

> six Klansmen were acquitted of murder last week. Ten gays were machine-gunned in the streets of New York, and when a Michigan high-school girl wore this slit skirt in a homecoming parade [*cut to image*], eggs were thrown at her house and funeral wreaths were scattered on her parents' lawn. Looks like a nationwide return to traditional American values and morality![102]

Such jokes were rare; in fact, writers groused that advocating progressive politics often resulted in jokes or entire sketches being pulled and that Doumanian objected to liberal bits she thought were "propagandistic and preachy."[103] The dismal season was mercifully cut short by a writer's strike, but not before Doumanian and Rocket were both fired after Rocket, live on the air, muttered the word "fuck" during a closing "Who Shot J.R.?" sketch.

Dick Ebersol, who hired Lorne Michaels to create *SNL*, took over as executive producer between 1981 and 1985 and decided to break with the past, twice renaming the "Weekend Update" segment, and frequently switching out talent at the anchor desk. Brian Doyle-Murray, sometimes accompanied by Mary Gross, hosted the newly named "SNL NewsBreak" during the seventh season. Doyle-Murray attempted to play a more traditional, bland anchor role, but the writing continued to lag. Commentaries by Eddie Murphy and appearances by Piscopo, as both Ted Koppel and a sportscaster, were the only real bright spots. Subsequent seasons saw the now-renamed "Saturday Night News" change hands from Brad Hall for part of a season to a rotating staff until Christopher Guest finished 1984–1985. *SNL* from 1980 to 1985 has largely been forgotten and treated as noncanonical.[104] Only recently, with the launch of the streaming service Peacock, have some selected segments of those years been made available.

For the next 11th season, Lorne Michaels returned as executive producer, bringing consistency to the news-parody segment for the first time since his departure. In general, Michael's returning season proved problematic, with a young cast unable to gel. But newcomer Dennis Miller's regular appearances on "Weekend Update" (the segment went back to its original name) proved one of the most popular features. As a result, despite other personnel changes, Miller remained both on the program and at the anchor desk until 1991, becoming the face of *SNL*'s fake news for a new generation of viewers. Like his contemporaries on *NNTN*, Miller seemed to be unconstrained by the need for verisimilitude, innovating a self-aware, postmodern style of news parody delivery. Whereas previous "Weekend Update" anchors mostly played their roles straight and allowed the jokes to be the focus, Miller was unapologetically "in" on the joke with the audience, but not in an ironic, *Colbert* way. After the 1986 refusal by France to allow the use of its airspace to bomb Libya, Miller begins an episode with

> welcome to all, unless you happen to be French and then you can just go to hell. [*audience applauds*] Time for a boycott folks. I'll never kiss with my tongue again [*laughter and pause*], unless of course the situation demands it.[105]

The delivery typifies Miller's lack of distance from the audience. In their article on "Weekend Update," Amber Day and Ethan Thompson also note this pattern, discussing Miller's odd positioning as both actor and viewer surrogate and how he "regularly commented on his own delivery and chided or congratulated the audience on their reactions to the jokes."[106] Miller was memorable, but divisive, transitioning the segment to a much more infotainment visual style and largely walking a mainstream political line.

Although Miller created the most memorable persona from the multichannel era of "Weekend Update," the single best piece of *SNL* news parody came from a sketch—not the usual fake-news segment. In 1983, two sequential episodes of *SNL* featured an extended segment on the fictional assassination of Eddie Murphy's recurring *Little Rascals* character Buckwheat. Both skits feature Joe Piscopo portraying ABC anchor and *Nightline* host Ted Koppel reporting the event, as if live from the anchor desk, in an obvious parody of network news' excessive coverage of Ronald Reagan's assassination attempt two years earlier. After "breaking in," Piscopo announces Buckwheat has been shot and rolls pre-recorded footage of Murphy's character exiting the 30 Rock building and suddenly being gunned down as he moves toward a limousine, mimicking footage networks aired of Reagan approaching the presidential motorcade as shots rang out. News outlets such as *Nightline* repeatedly aired footage of the attempted presidential assassination in their coverage, sometimes showing it in slow motion or narrating the images. Creating comedy through excess, the first *SNL* skit took every opportunity to reshow footage of Buckwheat's shooting, airing it five times during the almost six-minute skit. The segment also takes jabs at the increasing commercialization and branding of news by repeatedly sprinkling in mentions of imaginary sponsor Texxon (an obvious reference to oil companies Exxon and Texaco). At one point, the segment cuts to a still image of Buckwheat with the ABC news music and the text, "Buckwheat Dead: America Mourns." Crossfade to the Texxon logo and the voice-over, "Brought to you by Texxon; life goes on and Texxon is there."[107] The following week's program continued coverage with Buckwheat's killer (also played by Eddie Murphy) being apprehended and subsequently assassinated as police moved him after a court appearance, evoking Jack Ruby's killing of Lee Harvey Oswald on live television. Piscopo signs off from the last report saying, "We'll be here tomorrow night and every night as long as this senseless killing continues."[108] The segments are brilliant parodies of *Nightline* and other news agencies' fascination with violence, immediacy, and increasing entanglement with corporate sponsors, coming at a time when the "Weekend Update" segment itself was sliding toward irrelevance.

As *SNL* and "Weekend Update" stumbled through the early 1980s, NBC made several attempts to expand its news-parody programming. Canadian show *SCTV* aired from 1981 to 1983 on the network and incorporated a fake news report into its overall parody of television broadcasting.[109] The segment made fun of news formatting but created purely fictional stories without any connection to topical events, playing more with form than substance. NBC tried to move the program into prime time, but producers balked at the stricter decency standards and took *SCTV* to cable. Following the show's departure, NBC hired *SNL* and *TW3* alum Herb Sargent to produce a summer replacement prime-time news-parody program called *The News Is the News* (1983). The program disappeared shortly after its first show with *Variety* saying, the "mundane material made it mostly a primetime shambles."[110] NBC had earlier attempted to restart prime-time news parody by reviving *TW3* in 1976 with a pilot called *That Was the Year That Was*, but viewers and critics panned the show. It was even called "sort of a toothless Saturday Night Live," illustrating how even prime-time audiences expected more cutting-edge humor by that point.[111]

Television executives attempted to revive *TW3* once again, though, in 1985—this time on rival network ABC. Original *TW3* actor and writer David Frost and film star Anne Bancroft hosted the hour-long Sunday 8:00 p.m. broadcast, with Sargent producing. The show was a pilot for a planned regular series but was so dismal that no more episodes were ever shot. Sargent reworked the original format to transform *TW3* into a traditional variety program, with lots of sketch comedy and the feel of big-time network specials, with emphasis on audience accessibility, glitz, and musical cues. The stage design was borrowed from 1970s variety programs like *Donny and Marie*, with large movable platforms and lots of lights and color. Any visual link to broadcast news is almost entirely absent, except a brief segment imagining network news if Ted Turner succeeds in taking over CBS. Instead, the show emphasized set pieces for skits and stand-up comedy. Political humor stagnates at the level of crude, childish laughs. Rather than offer satiric jabs at Reagan and British Prime Minister Margaret Thatcher's policies, a skit with look-alike puppets merely devolves into the two marionettes kissing in the throes of passion. Perhaps tellingly, the most biting satire in the show is reserved for liberals, with Frost singing a song making fun of how liberals "forgive Jane Fonda for being in Hanoi, but not in *Barbarella*."[112] The show's laughs mostly came from the actors themselves, with cutaways revealing listlessly clapping audience members. The only real connection to the original *TW3*, besides the name, is the participation of Frost and Sargent—the humor and content of the reboot bear more relation to the awkward all-star variety programs favored by networks in the 1980s than to the original show. Reviews of the pilot were horrible, with one writer calling the program "a generally witless fiasco."[113] ABC mercifully canceled plans to produce a full season.

News parody in the first decade of the multichannel era struggled, with brief moments of innovation buried under bland, mainstream entertainment. The genre remained in the public consciousness both through the longevity of *NNTN* and "Weekend Update" and through network attempts to revive a prime-time version. However, the controversy of *TW3* and the influence and esteem of "Weekend Update" during the 1970s were absent. Programs struggled to define themselves in the era of Reagan, turning more toward depoliticized pastiche than parody, avoiding political controversy and audience offense. In 1990, the same year *NNTN* was canceled, a small cable channel devoted to humor launched, creating a new home for news parody in the 1990s and the reinvigoration of the genre moving into a new millennium.

NOTES

1. Amanda Lotz, *The Television Will Be Revolutionized* (New York: New York University, 2007), 12–15.

2. Bambi Haggins and Amanda D. Lotz, "At Home on the Cutting Edge," in *The Essential HBO Reader*, ed. Gary R. Edgerton and Jeffrey P. Jones (Lexington, KY: The University Press of Kentucky, 2008), 161. Sniglets was a popular feature of the show, where cast member Rich Hall presented imaginary words that should be in the dictionary. The segment led to a series of Sniglet books and to name recognition for Hall, who was briefly tapped for *SNL*'s 10th season.

3. Megan Mullen provides an excellent overview of the different programming strategies of cable channels during the multichannel era. Megan Mullen, *The Rise of Cable Programming in the United States: Revolution or Evolution?* (Austin, TX: University of Texas Press, 2003).

4. For more on the blue sky era, see Megan Mullen, *Television in the Multichannel Age: A Brief History of Cable Television* (Malden, MA: Blackwell Publishing, 2008), 85–87.

5. Mullen, *The Rise of Cable Programming*, 95.

6. George Mair, *Inside HBO* (New York: Dodd, Mead & Company, 1988), 21.

7. Ibid., 26.

8. Ibid., 72.

9. Patrick R. Parsons, *Blue Skies: A History of Cable Television* (Philadelphia, PA: Temple University Press, 2008), 523.

10. Examples of HBO's efforts to invest in film during this time include its partnership with Columbia Studios and CBS in forming Tri-Star, as well as its creation of Silver Screen Partners.

11. Sally Bedell, "Pay TV Challenges Networks," *New York Times*, April 3, 1983, A, 1.

12. Ibid.

13. Christopher Anderson, "Producing an Aristocracy of Culture in American Television," in *The Essential HBO Reader*, ed. Gary R. Edgerton and Jeffrey P. Jones (Lexington, KY: The University Press of Kentucky, 2008), 30.

14. Tony Kelso, "And Now No Word from Our Sponsor," in *It's Not TV: Watching HBO in the Post-Television Era*, ed. Marc Leverette, Brian L. Ott, and Cara Louise Buckley (New York: Routledge, 2008).

15. Ann Hodges, "HBO Pushes for Quality Programs," *Houston Chronicle*, October 15, 1985, 1.

16. Jerry Buck, "Satiric Show on HBO Ends Blues over News," *Houston Chronicle*, January 20, 1986, 4.

17. "HBO Dispenses Its Own Ratings Report," *Broadcasting*, March 12, 1984.

18. John J. O'Connor, "TV: News Spoof on HBO," *New York Times*, May 26, 1983, C, 27.

19. John O'Connor, "TV Views: 'Not Necessarily the Media' on HBO," *New York Times*, August 18, 1987, C, 18.

20. Steve Weinstein, "Ample Targets for the New 'Not Necessarily the News'," *Los Angeles Times*, May 24, 1989, 10.

21. David Friedman, "Satire Is What Closes on Saturday Night," *Newsday*, June 20, 1989, 9.

22. Mair, *Inside HBO*, 183–84.

23. Ibid., 47, 107.

24. *Not Necessarily the News*, 6th Annual Cable Ace Awards Entry, Paley Center for Media - Catalog ID B:32995. 1984.

25. Playing off Gunning's cinema of attractions. Tom Gunning, "The Cinema of Attraction: Early Film, Its Spectator and the Avant-Garde," *Wide Angle* 6, no. 2 (1986).

26. Buck, "Satiric Show on HBO Ends Blues over News."

27. *Not Necessarily the News*, Episode 1 Script, UCLA Performing Arts Archive Collection - Collection 79. January, 1983.

28. *Not Necessarily the News*, Episode 2 Script, UCLA Performing Arts Archive Collection - Collection 79. February, 1983.

29. O'Connor, "TV Views: 'Not Necessarily the Media' on HBO."

30. Steve Schneider, "Cable TV Notes; a Zany Troupe Parodies the Year," *New York Times*, December 22, 1985, 2, 30.

31. *Not Necessarily the News*, Episode 71, UCLA Film & Television Archive - Catalog ID T41297. May 24, 1989.

32. *Not Necessarily the News*, Episode 8 Script, UCLA Performing Arts Archive Collection - Collection 79. August, 1983.

33. John Moffitt, "Not Necessarily the News," *Electronic Media* 21, no. 43 (2002).

34. *Not Necessarily the News*, Episode 35, UCLA Film & Television Archive - Catalog ID T42098. 1985.

35. *Not Necessarily the Year in Review*, Paley Center for Media - Catalog ID T87:0052. December 15, 1984.

36. *Not Necessarily the News*, Episode 2, Paley Center for Media - Catalog ID B:13629. February, 1983.

37. *Not Necessarily the News*, Episode 1, Paley Center for Media - Catalog ID B:04681. January, 1983.

38. Ibid.

39. *Not Necessarily the News*, Episode 2, February, 1983.

40. *Not Necessarily the News*, Episode 68 Script, UCLA Performing Arts Archive Collection - Collection 79. April, 1989.

41. *Not Necessarily the News*, Episode 71, May 24, 1989.

42. Ibid.

43. Ibid.

44. Although Moffitt never mentions *Saturday Night Live*, the NBC show was adept at creating recurring roles that became closely identified with particular actors, including the "Weekend Update" anchors. Given his previous show, *Friday*, and its competition with *SNL*, it certainly seems possible Moffitt may have been comparing *NNTN* with its network competitor.

45. Jerry Buck, "'Not Necessarily the News'; Sending up the News; Its Satire Is Uncensored; Highly Honored," *Washington Post*, July 16, 1989, Y, 5.

46. As an example of this news anchor style, see Kimberly Meltzer, *TV News Anchors and Journalistic Traditions: How Journalists Adapt to Technology* (New York: Peter Lang, 2010), 82–87.

47. Jeff Alan and James M. Lane, *Anchoring America: The Changing Face of Network News* (Chicago, IL: Bonus Books, 2003), 243.

48. Friedman, "Satire Is What Closes on Saturday Night."

49. Rick Altman. *The American Film Musical* (Bloomington, IN: Indiana University Press, 1987).

50. Jason Mittell, *Genre and Television: From Cop Shows to Cartoons in American Culture* (New York: Routledge, 2004), 16–18.

51. John Fiske, *Television Culture*, 2nd ed. (New York: Routledge, 2011), 252.

52. Lance Olsen, *Circus of the Mind in Motion: Postmodernism and the Comic Vision* (Detroit, MI: Wayne State University Press, 1990), 19.

53. Fredric Jameson, *Postmodernism, or, the Cultural Logic of Late Capitalism*, 9th ed. (Durham, NC: Duke University Press, 2001), 17.

54. Weinstein, "Ample Targets."

55. Murray Davis, *What's So Funny?: The Comic Conception of Culture and Society* (Chicago, IL: The University of Chicago Press, 1993).

56. Daya Kishan Thussu, *News as Entertainment: The Rise of Global Infotainment* (London: Sage, 2007), 7–8.

57. *Not Necessarily the News*, Episode 71, May 24, 1989.

58. *Not Necessarily the News*, Episode 36, UCLA Film & Television Archive - Catalog ID T42098. 1985.
59. *Not Necessarily the News*, Episode 1, January, 1983.
60. *Not Necessarily the News*, Episode 71, May 24, 1989.
61. *Not Necessarily the Year in Review*, December 15, 1984.
62. Ibid.
63. Hodges, "HBO Pushes for Quality Programs."
64. James Andrew Miller, *Tinderbox: HBO's Ruthless Pursuit of New Frontiers* (New York: Henry Holt and Company, 2021), 56.
65. Eleanor Blau, "TV Notes: Culling 'Not News'," *New York Times*, June 16, 1988, C, 26.
66. Weinstein, "Ample Targets."
67. Over-the-shoulder graphics appeared with the reboot, copying traditional live newscast style. Earlier episodes rarely used them, perhaps because they were switching so fast between stories.
68. *Not Necessarily the News*, Episode 71, May 24, 1989.
69. Although it would be interesting to compare coverage, *Saturday Night Live* had just ended its season shortly before Tiananmen Square, so "Weekend Update" did not cover the tragedy.
70. Jane Feuer, *Seeing through the Eighties* (Durham, NC: Duke University Press, 1995), 150.
71. Steven D. Stark, "Once a TV Staple, Political Comedy Is in Short Supply," *New York Times*, March 1, 1987, H.
72. For more on the *Lou Grant* controversy, see Paul Kerr, "Drama at MTM: *Lou Grant* and *Hill Street Blues*," in *MTM 'Quality Television'*, ed. Jane Feuer, Paul Kerr, and Tise Vahimagi (London: BFI Publishing, 1984), 134–47; Todd Gitlin, *Inside Prime Time* (Berkeley, CA: University of California Press, 2000), 3–11.
73. Jeffords discusses how the assassination attempt played into Reagan's body image, Susan Jeffords, *Hard Bodies: Hollywood Masculinity in the Reagan Era* (New Brunswick, NJ: Rutgers University Press, 1993), 29–30.
74. Schneider, "Cable TV Notes."
75. Walter Goodman, "HBO's 'Not Necessarily the News'," *New York Times*, July 2, 1987, C, 26.
76. *Not Necessarily the News*, Episode 41, 1985.
77. *Not Necessarily the News*, Episode 71, May 24, 1989.
78. Schneider, "Cable TV Notes."
79. Peter M. Robinson, *The Dance of the Comedians: The People, the President, and the Performance of Political Standup Comedy in America* (Amherst, MA: University of Massachusetts Press, 2010), 206.
80. Hedrick Smith, *The Power Game: How Washington Works* (New York: Random House, 1988), 408–409.
81. *Not Necessarily the News*, Episode 71, May 24, 1989.
82. *Not Necessarily the News*, Episode 2, February, 1983.
83. *Not Necessarily the Year in Review*, December 15, 1984.
84. Ibid.

85. Michael Schaller, *Reckoning with Reagan: America and Its President in the 1980s* (New York: Oxford University Press, 1992), 144.

86. *Not Necessarily the News*, Episode 41, 1985.

87. *Not Necessarily the News*, 6th Annual Cable Ace Awards Entry, 1984.

88. *Not Necessarily the News*, Episode 2, February, 1983.

89. Robert E. Denton, Jr., *The Primetime Presidency of Ronald Reagan: The Era of the Television Presidency* (New York: Praeger Publishers, 1988), 71–72. Denton provides a compelling argument that Reagan was the first "true" television president.

90. *Saturday Night Live*, December 6, 1986.

91. *Not Necessarily the News*, Episode 71. May 24, 1989.

92. *Not Necessarily the News*, Episode 72, 1989.

93. Buck, "'Not Necessarily the News'; Sending Up."

94. Bedell, "Pay TV Challenges Networks."

95. Anderson, "Producing an Aristocracy of Culture in American Television," 30.

96. Raymond Williams, *Television: Technology and Cultural Form* (London: Routledge, 1974), 86–96.

97. Friedman, "Satire Is What Closes on Saturday Night."

98. John Dempsey, "NBC's 'Saturday Night Live' Just Ain't," *Daily Variety*, December 17, 1980, 41.

99. Tom Shales and James Andrew Miller, *Live from New York: An Uncensored History of Saturday Night Live* (Boston, MA: Little, Brown and Company, 2002), 198.

100. Doug Hill and Jeff Weingrad, *Saturday Night: A Backstage History of Saturday Night Live* (New York: Vintage Books, 1987), 420.

101. Ibid., 402.

102. *Saturday Night Live*, November 11, 1980.

103. Dempsey, "NBC's 'Saturday Night Live' Just Ain't."

104. Dan Amernick, "The 'Not Ready for Archive Players': The Lost Seasons of *Saturday Night Live*," *Journal of Popular Film and Television* 46, no. 2 (2018).

105. *Saturday Night Live*, April 19, 1986.

106. Amber Day and Ethan Thompson, "Live from New York, It's the Fake News! *Saturday Night Live* and the (Non)Politics of Parody," *Popular Communication* 10, no. 1–2 (2012).

107. *Saturday Night Live*, March 12, 1983.

108. *Saturday Night Live*, March 19, 1983.

109. The years NBC syndicated *SCTV* were the fourth and fifth seasons of the program.

110. Bok., "The News Is the News," *Weekly Variety*, June 22, 1983, 72.

111. Daku., "That Was the Year That Was," *Weekly Variety*, December 29, 1976, 34.

112. *That Was the Week That Was*, Pilot, UCLA Film & Television Archive - Catalog ID T74134. April 21, 1985.

113. Daku., "That Was the Week That Was," *Daily Variety*, April 23, 1985, 8.

Chapter 5

The Daily Show in the 1990s
From Kilborn to Stewart

The 1990s got off to an inauspicious start for news parody with the cancellation of *Not Necessarily the News* (*NNTN*) from pay cable. The potential for a show bound not to advertisers but to channel subscribers opened up a new venue, especially with no indication that broadcast networks were willing to risk a prime-time slot on the genre. "Weekend Update" continued throughout the decade, as will be discussed later, but more as a shell of its former self. In this new decade, innovation came from a highly unlikely source: expanded basic cable.

It feels safe to say that when *The Daily Show* debuted in 1996, no one expected that it would become one of the most politically influential shows on television, much less that it would last for over 25 years and introduce several prominent personalities who would host their own news-parody programs. The show was innovative and funny but was like a rowdy student in the back of the room throwing spitballs—it got laughs, but no one was going to take it seriously or confuse it with legitimate journalism. This chapter chronicles the journey from the birth of the upstart program, through the pivotal selection of new host Jon Stewart, and the program's coverage of the 2000 election, a year many critics and creative personnel with the show recognize as a turning point that would eventually lead to *The Daily Show* becoming a serious critic of contemporary media and politics and an active participant in the journalistic field.

The pre-Stewart years of *The Daily Show* have received scant discussion in either television studies literature or popular media. There are no books about the birth of the program or even individual chapters devoted to its development. *The Daily Show (The Book)*, by Chris Smith, is an oral history of the program's first 20 years but reduces 1996–1998 to a four-page introduction that precedes the official 400-plus pages chronicling the show under Stewart. The book is a microcosm of culture's treatment of the original run. Recordings of those early seasons are nowhere to be found on Comedy Central's website, while the complete Seasons 3–20 featuring Stewart are all online for streaming. The first two years of *The Daily Show* have been excised, like the early 1980s non-Lorne Michaels years of *Saturday Night Live*. Cocreator Madeleine Smithberg laments that those years "have been erased from consciousness" and the original creators and staff "built the foundation and the structure of the show that has gone on for 25 years, and it's just really depressing to me that that has been erased from the public record."[1]

The Daily Show was born in two roommates' mutual discontent with media in the 1990s. Cocreator Lizz Winstead sat in a bar and watched CNN's first night covering *Operation Desert Storm*. Unlike networks in the Vietnam era when reporters struck a sober tone, CNN was awash with graphics, a musical theme, and live video of missiles launching. In her memoir, Winstead wrote, "I felt like I was watching a video game . . . it felt like a trailer for a movie about war."[2] Her expressed disgust planted the seeds for what would become *The Daily Show*. Winstead's stand-up comedy grew more political in response, a shift neither her management nor audience seemed to appreciate.

Winstead was hired as a segment producer for *The Jon Stewart Show*, which ran on MTV from 1993 to 1995. Smithberg was already with the program, and, eventually, Winstead moved in with Smithberg. Perhaps presaging the future direction of the show, two other figures involved in creating *The Daily Show* also worked on *The Jon Stewart Show*. Doug Herzog was in charge of MTV original programming at the time and in 1995 was hired as president of Comedy Central with a mandate to expand original programming. Eileen Katz was hired as executive vice president of development for Comedy Central after having executive-produced Stewart's MTV program. The four would be integral to the birth of *The Daily Show*.

COMEDY CENTRAL EMERGES

The year after HBO decided to cancel *NNTN*, Comedy Central launched on expanded basic cable. The channel formed from the ashes of two failed all-humor outlets: HBO's The Comedy Channel and Viacom's HA! The two merged, forming a new channel in 1991 with eclectic humor programming that originally consisted of stand-up routines, syndicated content like the edited-down, one hour episodes of *Saturday Night Live* (*SNL*) from the 1980s, and low-cost films. Comedy Central quickly began developing its own programming, with early breakout hits *Politically Incorrect*, a topical talk show, and *Mystery Science Theater 3000*, which had originally appeared on a local Minnesota station. The two shows helped to make a name for Comedy Central but were so successful that both were poached by other networks in 1995. The departures left the channel with a hole to fill. Herzog and Katz needed new content. They asked Smithberg and Winstead to pitch a pilot, but what they really wanted was a new tentpole for their important late-night audience.

Politically Incorrect had aired Monday through Thursday night at 11:00 p.m., and Herzog wanted a replacement. Like ESPN's *SportsCenter*, the new show would be the flagship for Comedy Central. According to Smithberg, Herzog said he wanted "a show where if something happens in the world, everyone's going to need to tune in to Comedy Central to see how *The Daily Show*, and that was the working title, spins it."[3] Smithberg and Winstead accepted the challenge of creating a nightly weekday program with the unusual agreement from Herzog that they would not have to produce a pilot, the show would be guaranteed to air for its first year, and they would have a set production budget.[4]

Smithberg and Winstead charted the course for the show's humor and decided the program would be a commentary on contemporary media. The Gulf War had been followed by a full shift to infotainment on the television networks, with wall-to-wall television coverage of the Rodney King case, the O. J. Simpson trial, and salacious crime stories like the severing of John Wayne Bobbitt's penis. Journalism not only embraced celebrity culture; it was actually creating new celebrities. Everyone from the prosecutors to the judge of the Simpson trial became gossip fodder. NBC debuted its newsmagazine program *Dateline* in 1992 and quickly moved to airing it three nights a week, eventually expanding to four and then five nights by the end of the decade. *Dateline* embraced scandal journalism, and *The Daily Show* waded into mocking the trend. Winstead says critics accused their program of being too pop culture but points out that "when we launched the show, we were satirizing the news media that existed at the time."[5] Each of the broadcast networks, in addition to their traditional newscasts, created supplementary news programming to discuss and analyze the latest scandals.

The two creators hit on the idea of mimicking the news, but rather than simply mocking them "we were going to make fun of them by becoming them. We would operate as a news organization while acting like a comedy show. It simply had never been done before."[6] While acknowledging that programs such as *That Was the Week That Was* (*TW3*) and "Weekend Update" produced satire and criticism, Winstead says they "wanted the entire show to be *a character*."[7] Previous news parody had commented on existing coverage, making jokes and reediting footage, but *The Daily Show* would also *create* actual coverage, which would be every bit as inane as the journalism of 1990s television. They would copy news conventions and highlight the façade of gravitas hiding the infotainment core of broadcast journalism. Acting like an official news organization would produce its own irony. As Smithberg described, "once you're anchored in mock seriousness, you can be as silly as you want."[8]

Smithberg would focus on the logistics of running the show, while Winstead helped set the tone. Winstead described, "Madeleine was the brains and the structure. . . . She really knew how to run a show. And I was the person who knew a lot about politics and a lot about humor."[9] A call for writers attracted around 150 submissions, and they hired six with a mix of journalism and comedy experience. Speaking in retrospect, Winstead wistfully noted that all those hired were white men, but only two submissions had come from women.[10] With writers in place, the biggest question was who would be the host of the program and what role would the host take?

In the years since *The Daily Show* debuted, several names have emerged as the original frontrunners for the hosting job. Smithberg mentions Mike Rowe as their first pick, who would have been fresh off his stint with home shopping network QVC.[11] Winstead wrote that Jon Stewart was the first choice but he was already under contract.[12] Regardless, the consistent story is that Comedy Central president Doug Herzog had seen Craig Kilborn on ESPN and was convinced the blonde, six-foot-four sports bro was the person to fill the seat.

They auditioned a lot of comedians, but most brought their own respective personalities to the anchor chair. Winstead says that what they wanted was someone who could really act like a news anchor, "that you couldn't tell if they were in on [the satire] or they weren't in on it."[13] Kilborn fit the bill. For *The Daily Show* writers, he would be their voice: a vessel they could fill with satire, a tailor-made parody of vacuous news anchors picked primarily for their looks. Kilborn leaned into the stereotype in interviews after the show launched, telling one reporter, "I take it seriously, I get offended when people don't see past the blond hair and the piercing blue eyes and the supple lips and the—I'm not going to say perfect nose—but it's a decent nose, and they don't listen to what I'm saying. It's not fun and games. It's delivering the news."[14]

The final piece of the puzzle would be to hire correspondents to go out in the field and generate original news coverage. A. Whitney Brown, who wrote and performed for *SNL* in the late 1980s, was hired to focus on politics. Comedian Beth Littleford would do celebrity interviews. The final correspondent came from the legitimate news world. Brian Unger had been hired by Connie Chung to be a producer on *CBS News*, and he worked during the first O. J. Simpson trial. He found himself disillusioned by the state of journalism, saying he "felt kind of empty inside," and leapt at the chance to harness his anger to mock programs like *Dateline* in covering hard news for *The Daily Show*.[15]

The first episode of *The Daily Show* debuted on July 22, 1996, at 11:30 p.m. on Comedy Central. MSNBC launched the week before, and Fox News would begin later that year. Few would have guessed that all three would still be on the air today.

The Daily Show helped Comedy Central become the default home for youth-oriented, cutting edge comedy on cable, predating Cartoon Network's "Adult Swim" and other eventual competitors in the 2000s. The success of such programs as *Mystery Science Theater 3000*, *Politically Incorrect*, and *Win Ben Stein's Money* created a foundation on which the Kilborn version of *The Daily Show* was built; however, the station catapulted to controversy and cultural relevance with the debut of the animated series *South Park* in 1997. The cartoon's success increased demand for the channel, and the following year Comedy Central surpassed 50% market penetration, making it available on most expanded cable packages. By the end of the decade, Comedy Central had established its bona fides as *the* place for youth comedy.

The Daily Show would also benefit from Comedy Central's early incorporation of the Internet as a medium for extending its brand. At a time when few Americans were online, the station developed games and downloads related to its most popular shows. In the latter half of the 1990s, the percentage of adults using the Internet grew from 14% in 1995 to 46% by 2000.[16] A disproportionate number of those users were young adults, with 65% of ages 18–29 with Internet access in 2000.[17] College campuses offered some of the fastest access speeds at the time, and the original *South Park* featurette "The Spirit of Christmas" became a college download sensation before the actual show even debuted. Comedy Central took advantage of the technology available to its target audience, creating simple games for *South Park*, *Win Ben Stein's Money*, and even a "five questions" game for the Kilborn *Daily Show*. The station's extension of its content to other media, such as digital, is emblematic of the post-network era activities extending television beyond the confines of appointment viewing on a traditional television screen—developments integral to the growth of *The Daily Show*'s popularity.

STYLE AND FORMAT IN *THE DAILY SHOW'S* NEWS PARODY

In comparison with previous news-parody programs, *The Daily Show*'s most important formatting innovation was the blending of segmented news parody in the tradition of "Weekend Update" with the talk-show format. The show featured Kilborn kicking off the first block of "Headlines," usually followed by an additional block of "More News." The second and third block leaned heavily on extended correspondent news packages (discussed later in this chapter), followed by a fourth block with an on-set guest interview and then a brief closing segment. The format was highly successful in creating an extended, sustained news-parody show. Previous programs like *TW3* and *NNTN* diluted their attempts at parody by incorporating skits and fake commercials, while "Weekend Update" was effectively cordoned off into a short, dedicated segment. *The Daily Show* improved on these formats by creating a cohesive program dedicated to traditional news formats.

During the Kilborn era, *The Daily Show* drew its humor from imitating the celebrity and infotainment-obsessed major networks and their countless news-magazine programs. Getting the look right was an important part of the joke. The program kicked off with a spinning globe graphic that was repeated throughout the program as a transitional device—first with the show's logo and then with other titles as they cut to headlines and recurring features. The set was decorated with dozens of small monitor screens behind and to the side of the anchor desk. The screens displayed stills and footage, creating a sense that stories were constantly being monitored and prepared for coverage. An open blue area to the left of the desk replicated the graphics globe to create a background for over-the-shoulder graphics during the program. Kilborn's desk was extended to accommodate correspondents and included an attached, separate area for interviews. The desk, monitor wall, and accents mimicked the look of wood—the faux wood popular in ostentatious 1990s offices, seeming to look serious but also trying a bit too hard to impress (figure 5.1).

The interview segment during the last third of the program further solidified *The Daily Show*'s infotainment parody. Like morning news segments and late-night comedy programs, guests appeared on the program to shill for their latest projects; but while *Good Morning America* and *The Tonight Show* might receive a visit from sitting and former politicians and officials (especially if they had just released a book), guests on *The Daily Show* were strictly drawn from the world of film, television, and music. For entertainers, there was no downside to appearing opposite Kilborn, who chatted informally, joked with the guests, and wrapped up with his "Five Questions." This final bit was one of the few features created by Kilborn, where he asked five ridiculous questions unrelated to the guest (sometimes with actual, verifiable answers), such as "name the three *Happy Days* spin offs?" or "More artistic nudity: Botticelli's Venus or Guccione's August Pet of the Month?" Like infotainment programming itself, where a story about military deaths suddenly segues to a cohost baking a cake with a celebrity, the shift from news parody to celebrity interview on *The Daily Show* is abrupt. News pretense is dropped, and now the audience is watching something different—a congenial

Figure 5.1 Craig Kilborn on *The Daily Show* set. *Source: Courtesy Comedy Central/Photofest.*

conversation about the cool project the guest is hyping or insider entertainment gossip. The interview segment contrasted with the traditional news approach of the rest of the show.

In terms of look and format, *The Daily Show* became the first program to effectively replicate the presentational styles of newscasts. "Weekend Update" has always contended with time constraints that limited the use of footage and interviews, instead relying heavily on still images. By contrast, *The Daily Show* made extensive use of video resources from outlets like the Associated Press, Reuters, and satellite feeds with local stories.[18] These resources allowed the program to incorporate voiceovers, sound-on-tapes, and packages, which created a seamless news style. For instance, a story about the explosion of a Boeing rocket carrying a new communication satellite is accompanied by wire footage of the rocket taking off. Upon explosion, Kilborn remarks it "exploded into a million Florida lawn ornaments."[19] Other stories incorporate soundbites, allowing Kilborn to remark on official statements. In describing the show to a reporter, Winstead and Smithberg said, "if you had your TV muted you'd think you were watching 'legitimate media.'"[20] Their characterization was no overstatement, though. Aside from Kilborn's snarky delivery and the actual content of the stories, *The Daily Show* visually appeared to be just like any other news program of its period.

CRAIG KILBORN AS ANCHOR—STONE PHILLIPS MEETS CLUELESS FRAT BOY

As with network newscasts, the personality on the anchor desk became indistinguishable from the show itself. Kilborn solo-anchored the first three segments, occasionally sharing the desk with correspondents who were discussing stories they covered. He conducted the celebrity interviews. When journalists discussed the show, Kilborn was almost always central to their evaluation of the program, and their assessments tended to be negative.

After playing college basketball, Kilborn went to work in radio and then on small-market television as a sports reporter and anchor. His break came in 1993 when he was tapped by ESPN to anchor *SportsCenter* during its 2:00 a.m. block. He developed an on-screen persona on the sports network with several signature phrases before catching the eye of Comedy Central's new president.

From the beginning, Kilborn seemed to play against all the expectations of a traditional news anchor. He came up through the sports-broadcasting ranks, a pathway that usually limits a journalist to talking only about sports. Six feet and four inches tall, blond, and good looking, Kilborn played into stereotypes of anchors chosen for appearance over brains, perhaps one of the reasons he was cast. One reporter referred to his "eugenic looks" and said he "appears to have been extruded at a Mattel plant in Minnesota, designed to serve as Local Newscaster Ken at the side of Infotainment Barbie."[21] Anchors tend to emphasize their own expertise and seriousness, but Kilborn loved to present himself as an underachiever who wandered into a television career. He told a *Playboy* reporter, "I never applied myself in high school. I've coasted my whole life. I'm an inspiration to a lot of young people who aren't exerting themselves.... I make a decent living and I'm still not trying."[22] In an era where some in Generation X were embracing the label of "slacker," Kilborn had an odd yet appealing mix of being authentically apathetic.

Kilborn's anchor style mirrored his image, combining his more emotive sports delivery with a detached, "can't be bothered to care" attitude. The famous broadcaster David Brinkley, who anchored various network newscasts for more than 40 years, was quoted as saying, "The one function that TV news performs very well is that when there is no news, we give it to you with the same emphasis as if there were."[23] Kilborn countered this norm by treating every single story as equally unimportant, whether it was a former Mouseketeer going to jail for stock fraud or the bombing of Iraq.

The Daily Show writers and executives reveled in Kilborn's approach, seeing him as the perfect vehicle for critiquing American journalism's slide into sensationalism and infotainment. Smithberg compared Kilborn to Ted Baxter, the narcissistic nitwit anchor from *The Mary Tyler Moore Show*, "where he was not in on the joke, but just kind of sitting in front of the camera and reading the teleprompter."[24] Kilborn's seeming uninterest in the stories meant that the writers could make mean jokes without Kilborn's appearing to realize they were mean. A. Whitney Brown says the writers described the vacuous Kilborn delivering their jokes as "a plastic gun shooting cop-killer bullets."[25] The show's writers controlled the content, with Kilborn showing up later in the morning for the first rehearsals. Other than minor word changes, often written directly on the script, Kilborn provided limited input on the news-satire part of the program.[26]

In interviews, Kilborn cultivated a comedically sexist frat-boy persona, drawing mixed receptions. *Esquire* called the show Emmy-worthy and characterized Kilborn's performance as "an odd mix of arrogance and good-natured cluelessness."[27] On the opposite pole, *Rolling Stone* held Kilborn up as an icon of everything wrong with basic cable programming in the mid-1990s: "Craig Kilborn *is* cable. He's shallow, pretty, always winking and teasing—a dumb blond who fronts as though he's in on the joke, although he's even dumber than he pretends to be."[28] As the centerpiece for a parody about the state of television journalism, Kilborn seemed to exemplify the focus of the show's humor.

THAT'S INFOTAINMENT! PARODYING TABLOID JOURNALISM

Although later seasons of *The Daily Show* actively engaged politics and satirically held public officials to account, humor during the Kilborn era focused on making fun of journalists and the types of stories that media organizations were chasing in the 1990s. The show would attempt to cover politics, but there was little interest in *being* political—in fact, Comedy Central was not even available in Washington, DC, when the show launched.

The writers received around 40 newspapers each day, supplemented by the Associated Press wire and the Internet service LexisNexis. The production staff was divided into groups assigned to different regions of the country. Writers would work from 8:00 am to 1:45 pm, when they would do a readthrough with Kilborn, Smithberg, and Winstead. They would choose jokes and continue to refine the show and submit material to network executives for approval and feedback.[29]

The Daily Show adapted major news stories to find humor and bounce off of the premise, but a lot of screen time was devoted to weird or unusual news stories about everyday people. Brown says he would search LexisNexis for terms like "grisly find," "bad teacher," and weird stories from Florida.[30] By focusing on these types of infotainment stories, the program tended to display a mean-spirited humor aimed at everyday people, using interviews to mock people's ignorance or hold their beliefs up to ridicule. Rather than punching up at those in power, the focus ended up being on people on the fringes of society. This was especially true of packages created by the correspondents, who would travel for weeks putting together stories with a field crew. The original executives and correspondents appeared for a 25th anniversary vodcast, where they discussed several fondly remembered news segments. Because these stories were chosen as emblematic of their work and accessible episodes of the original run of the show are lacking, I discuss each package they chose as examples of the kind of humor and satiric strategy employed on the program.

Brian Unger carries the distinction of creating the first field-produced package to appear on *The Daily Show*. In the piece, Unger sets up the story with an on-screen stand-up, making it sound like a celebrity behind-the-scenes piece: "She had imitators, a fan club that adored her, and a press that likened her to Mary Tyler Moore." The actual subject is a cat named Princess Kitty, who played piano, performed tricks, and acted in movies. Unger keeps his role straight, incorporating footage and pictures of Kitty, while interviewing subjects with apparent sincerity. Princess Kitty's trainer Karen Payne is the primary interviewee and is obviously unaware that her fond remembrances and emotions are going to be played for laughs. The narrative creates a fall-from-grace twist when Unger, standing in a grimy alley littered with cardboard boxes, slowly approaches the camera, narrating, "It all started in an alley like this one. The princess ran with a fast crowd, living on the street day to day, mostly from handouts. And what the street lacked in sustenance, it made up for in danger. It's here she caught a BB in the back, an injury that would plague her for much of her career." We learn Kitty underwent surgery to remove the BB, but she died as a result. Interviews with the veterinarian transition to slow-motion video of Kitty as Payne describes how she will miss her cat. Unger leans in to hug Payne at the end.

On the one hand, the package is a brilliant parody of news pieces mourning minor celebrities who had little real impact on the world. Unger discusses how when he joined *The Daily Show* he was angry at news for what it had become and felt propelled by that anger.[31] In Winstead's memoir, she recalled the Princess Kitty story and how Unger had reported "in a tone that rivaled the way any news outfit would have covered the tragic loss of a child. It was perfect satire."[32] However, understanding the report as satiric depends on assessing and analyzing the goals of the humor. Satire requires the audience to connect the Princess Kitty package to the referenced work (emotional celebrity reports) and general discourse about the satirized subject (criticisms of the rise of infotainment and decline of serious journalism). The responsibility of drawing these connections is on the satirist. However, Unger plays his role straight, as expected of a reporter, so the incongruent feature is the subject of the humor: a cat who happened to find media success and a woman who adored her cat. *They* are the butt of the joke. As viewers, we are encouraged to laugh at the subjects of the report. Smithberg says they immediately began high-fiving each other after viewing the Princess Kitty story because "we knew we were on to something huge."[33]

Another package, created by A. Whitney Brown, focused on a man from Michigan who performed his own root canal. David Kruithoff, identified on-screen as "Farmhand," found stones similar in color to his teeth for replacement. In talking about how they were able to get people to appear on their reports, Brown describes, "People are so hypnotized when you put them on camera that you can get them to say about anything."[34] *The Daily Show* was not well-known in its early days, making it easier to schedule interviews; they would also provide vague information about who they were to avoid connecting themselves to Comedy Central. As a result, subjects often appear to think they are being interviewed by traditional journalists. In exploring his do-it-yourself dentistry, Kruithoff discusses the list of problems he encountered. Brown responds, "Other than the pain and the possibility of massive infection are there any real drawbacks to this?" Kruithoff responds, "No."

Again, the humor is focused both on Brown acting as if the report is a very normal subject to be covered by news and the oddity of this Midwestern man drilling into his own teeth. The more rural setting is also key to the humor: by constructing an image of Kruithoff as a bumpkin who decides to save some money, he can be laughed off. One obvious issue raised by the story is whether Kruithoff had insurance and healthcare options and what role that played in him taking up self-dentistry, but this line of inquiry is never raised in the story. Smithberg calls the package "a quintessential early *Daily Show* piece," which is likely one reason the program was ridiculed for being mean-spirited.

The last example I want to discuss is from Beth Littleford, who was the show's lifestyle correspondent. This often meant she would track down B-list celebrities—everyone from Kato Kaelin to David Duke. In a parody of celebrity-journalism aesthetics, Littleford would interview with ridiculous amounts of flowers behind her and in soft focus with a hazy filter, like a 1930s starlet. She also produced feature stories, such as one about a farm in Iowa. Littleford exclaims that this particular package "put us on the map."[35] On its face, the story is about a farm where they collect pig semen for breeding. The backstory is that the farmland was so expensive that the owners needed to expand their business to recoup costs. *The Daily Show* spin went beyond the obvious, sophomoric humor of masturbating a pig. This was the era when reporters regularly involved themselves in stories, and Smithberg says *The*

Daily Show became obsessed with the way "the reporter would go out and they would stomp the grapes or they would throw the frisbee or whatever it was."[36] Littleford walks through the entire collection process, with farm owner Genette Fox guiding her. As the correspondent puts on a glove and goes to work, video rolls of the pig thrusting with his mouth frothing in ecstasy, and eventually a bag of semen. Littleford prepares to depart and says, "I'm gonna take what I learned back with me to the city."

The story caused a stir at Comedy Central, going beyond even the channel's low bar of good taste. Smithberg argued with the network about where video would get digitized to remove pig privates and when audio would bleep. Littleford claims that some viewers were shocked: "people in the middle of the country were not scandalized by this, but both coasts, like, freaked out."[37] But, of course, shocking the coasts was the point. The idea that people actually would do this as part of their living was a major part of the humor, even more in this case than the satirization of the media. The show could have also delved into why farmland is so expensive that farmers can no longer make a living just from raising crops, but *The Daily Show* was not yet about satirizing the state of society or politics. The jokes were primarily about the people they encountered and interviewed, in a parody of news style.

PRESIDENTIAL COVERAGE—SAY YES TO THE DRESS

Bill Clinton may have been the perfect president for *The Daily Show*. The program went on air just a month before he was officially nominated to run for a second term. The show even received its own area at the 1996 presidential and vice presidential debates, giving them the opportunity to make fun of how journalists covered politics. Correspondents created some unexpected moments, such as when Brown asked Clinton press secretary Mike McCurry, "Would Bill Clinton support the death penalty if Kitty Dukakis were raped and murdered?" The rest of the press were reportedly "stunned."[38] The question was a call back to 1988 Democratic presidential nominee Michael Dukakis, who many believe ruined his chances when he was asked the same question about his wife during a presidential debate, and responded that he would not support the death penalty.

In their first year and a half, the program covered Clinton, but not in any sustained way. Writers made fun of his personal traits, Hillary Clinton, and breaking news about the administration that could be mined for humor. That changed in January 1998, when the scandal involving an affair between Clinton and former intern Monica Lewinsky exploded on to front pages and televisions. *The Daily Show* happened to be on break, but everyone came back early from vacation to get the show back on air. Smithberg told a reporter, "This is our reason for being," and that whether the rumors of the affair were true or not, "for us, it matters that the story is as big as it is. If it turns out to be fake, we cover that."[39] The Lewinsky scandal was tailor-made for *The Daily Show*: it had sexual details perfect for the program's sophomoric humor, it featured the most powerful person in America, and, with the rest of the media obsessed with the story, it created the perfect source material for the show's news parody. In one of the first episodes with coverage about the scandal, Kilborn summarized its effect by ending with "What have we learned? We learned the president's taste is improving." While news organizations scrambled to investigate every past associate and action of Lewinsky, *The Daily Show* went all in on satirizing shallow coverage by paying $20 for a high school production of *The Music Man* featuring Lewinsky, repeatedly using footage from the play on their show.[40]

Humor in covering the Clinton administration mostly focused on puns and incongruence, comparing actions to totally unrelated events. A story about a December 1998 missile launch against Iraq provides an example of these strategies. After a year dominated by coverage of the Lewinsky affair, Congress debated in December whether to impeach the president. The same month Clinton launched Operation Desert Fox, a four-day series of missile strikes and bombings against Iraq after the country failed to comply with United Nations inspectors. *The Daily Show* report begins with a graphic of the two nation's presidents and the text "Perversion Diversion '98." Kilborn reports that Clinton "successfully delayed his impeachment for a while by falling back on an old crowd pleaser, bombing the snot out of Iraq . . . how many times do we have to watch this man get off?"[41] The criticism of "wagging the dog" was a popular framing of the attacks across most media at the time, although *The Daily Show* added its own twist with the reference to Clinton's sexual appetite, a favorite target for writers. Coverage was short and in headline style, though, which prevented any in-depth critique of the president or the administration's actions.

At times, the show's humor does seem to take on more of a critical edge, but those moments are brief. Clinton ended the attack on Iraq only minutes before the start of the Islamic observance of Ramadan, a somewhat hollow gesture after four days of bombing. The end of *The Daily Show* story highlights this fact by reporting, "To prove he's not totally insensitive to Iraq's Muslim majority, Clinton ordered the missiles to spell out 'Happy Ramadan' in rubble."[42] Stories on the anchor desk were meant to have a headline feel and pass quickly, so Kilborn immediately moves along to the next story where he jokes about the United States only bombing when CNN is around to provide coverage. The one critical joke is subsumed within the larger stream of humor.

To be fair to the intention of the creators, *The Daily Show* was not meant to offer savvy political commentary, at least in its original iteration. As Winstead described, "We followed the trends of the news."⁴³ Journalists and popular culture were the actual targets of the writers, not necessarily those in power. News conventions were ripe for parody, such as the dramatic turn toward the camera reporters love to include in stories. Sending up this trope, Unger once included 35 camera turns in one package. The program highlighted the excess and shallowness of the infotainment media in the 1990s, even if its coverage ended up seeming mean-spirited and denigrating toward the everyday people they sometimes interviewed.

Shortly before the Lewinsky story broke, *The Daily Show* creators dealt with their own scandal. News of conflict between Winstead and Kilborn had appeared in the press before, but the feud went highly public in an *Esquire* report. The article revealed that Kilborn complained to Comedy Central executives about Winstead and the written material he had to deliver, arguing that it could affect his long-term image. The other writers sent a petition supporting Winstead. Herzog downplayed the feud and told the reporter it was mostly in the past. Kilborn, however, reignited the conflict with a stunningly sexist statement that he specifically told the *Esquire* reporter was on the record: "There are a lot of bitches on the staff, and, hey, they're emotional people. You can print that! You know how women are—They overreact. It's not really a big deal. And to be honest, Lizz does find me very attractive. If I wanted her to blow me, she would."⁴⁴ Kilborn attempted to write the statement off as a joke, but Comedy Central suspended him for a week, and he officially apologized. In a later promotional tour after leaving the show, Kilborn became very defensive when asked about the *Esquire* interview and, in response to questions about his style, said, "Well, it's much more than frat-boy humor. However, frat-boy humor is funny and it always will be."⁴⁵

At the beginning of May of 1998, only months later, CBS announced that Kilborn would be departing *The Daily Show* at the end of the year and replacing Tom Snyder as host of *The Late, Late Show*. The announcement apparently came during contract negotiations between Kilborn and Comedy Central over extending his time on the show, surprising and annoying network executives.⁴⁶ The host's contract with Comedy Central actually ran through August of 1999, so executives sued Kilborn for breach of contract and CBS for encouraging him to do so, although Herzog eventually relented. Kilborn's leaving the anchor chair was the catalyst for numerous changes in the program that would lead it to new heights and unexpected admiration.

ANCHORS AWAY—FROM PARODY TO SATIRE

Although Jon Stewart had connections with many people involved in the show and had been discussed as the original host, there was no guarantee he would get the now-empty anchor chair. After rising to prominence in the early 1990s, his career seemed to be on the decline before being tapped as Kilborn's replacement. Stewart's television work began at MTV with several programs connecting him to young viewers. Hosting chores for *Short Attention Span Theater* (1990–1992) and *You Wrote It, You Watch It* (1993) spun off into his own hip talk show, *The Jon Stewart Show* (1993–1995). The latter show's success on MTV led to Paramount Television picking the program up for syndication as a replacement for Arsenio Hall's talk show, but poor ratings doomed *The Jon Stewart Show* after its first year in syndication. Stewart developed a favorable celebrity persona from these programs that followed him to *The Daily Show with Jon Stewart* (*TDS*). Early press coverage uses adjectives like "hip," "cheeky," and "fresh" and plays up his approachability and likeability. After the cancellation of his talk show, Stewart was frequently mentioned as a potential replacement for Tom Snyder, Garry Shandling, Larry Sanders, and several other talkers, creating an "almost host, but never chosen" narrative. A 1997 article in a television trade publication even features Stewart as one of several "falling stars" in the industry.[47] Coinciding with the release of his book *Naked Pictures of Famous People*, Stewart's selection and four-year contract to take over *TDS* at the beginning of 1999 created a "comeback" storyline for Stewart in the press, helping to fuel interest in the show.

Stewart's ascent to the anchor chair led to consternation and departures from *The Daily Show* writer's room. Winstead, the head writer and cocreator of the show, left a couple of months before Stewart started, although she has never clearly stated why. Unger and Brown also departed, leaving Littleford and Stephen Colbert. Colbert had been hired from *Good Morning America*, where he was doing lifestyle segments. Both Unger and Brown, in *The Daily Show* 25th reunion vodcast, were dismissive of Stewart and the direction the show took under his watch. Brown says he left because "it was very obvious it was no longer going to be a writer-driven show. It was going to be a personality-driven show."[48] Brown's statement is key to understanding the early, turbulent behind-the-scenes of *TDS*. Writers controlled the show in the Kilborn era. Some were surprised by the choice of Stewart. Writer J. R. Havlan, who stayed with the show from its launch to 2014, originally thought of Stewart "as a sort of leather-jacket-wearing, hipster young dude," far from the anchor persona they had crafted for Kilborn.[49] When he began, Stewart says that he found a writing team that was "annoyed that I had an idea about where I wanted to go, who thought that I was going to MTV it up." The remaining staff quickly realized that Stewart had a definitive path he wanted the show to follow, and they could either join that vision or get replaced.

Under Stewart, the show slowly grew more substantive and political in its first few years. The number of stories covered in the headlines decreased, but they grew in depth. This allowed for additional research and more video. Stewart wanted to cut the focus on celebrity news and strive for relevance—in his words, "turning the machine in a direction more toward politics, media satire."[50] As opposed to Midwesterners making their own teeth, the targets of humor would be people in power, politicians, and journalists. Colbert described it as turning away from "the guy with a UFO in his yard" and, instead, actually following the day's major events, but "in a way no straight news organization would think of covering."[51]

Within months, writers rebelled as Stewart exerted more control and changed their jokes. In response, Stewart says, "I basically told them all to fuck off."[52] In April, Ben Karlin was hired from the satirical newspaper *The Onion* to be head writer. Under Karlin, most of the older recurring segments were cut. According to the show's staff, the hire felt like the moment that Stewart became firmly in control of *TDS*.[53] They quickly did away with the noon meeting where writers would read and advocate for their jokes. Instead, writers would turn in jokes, allowing Karlin and Stewart to make the pick.[54] Prior to Stewart, the show had been much looser and collaborative, but Smithberg says that changed: "Instead of things being in this big free-form orbit, *boom*, suddenly we had a sun, and Jon Stewart was the sun."[55] While increasing efficiency, the changes clearly signaled who was now making the decisions.

Changes in the show over the course of 1999 under Stewart were slow and uneven. After a month in the anchor seat, headlines still tended to focus on news of the weird, such as a potbelly pig that received an award for rescuing her owner who had suffered a heart attack in their mobile home.[56] The year ended with a shift toward more political stories, including coverage of the Supreme Court hearings on whether Miranda rights are required. Although the topic itself was more substantive, the humor still tended to be pretty surface level, joking about television cops reading rights as they shove suspects against walls.[57]

In December 1999, *TDS* booked its first political guest, and a major one at that. Long-time Senator and former Republican presidential candidate Bob Dole appeared for an interview split over two episodes. At the time Dole was raising money and awareness for a World War II memorial in the nation's capital, so he was obviously attempting to reach an untapped younger audience. Stewart took advantage of the chance to talk politics with a legitimate insider and asked Dole to explain the state of the upcoming 2000 election since "we do a lot of election coverage here, but none of us know how to read."[58] Stewart included more mundane bits about MTV viewers and Al Gore being dull, but he also seemed to relish discussing the political scene, asking about the influence of money in campaigns. In the second part of the interview, Dole says there will be a woman president or vice president someday, suggesting that perhaps she is watching even now. Stewart pauses and responds, "No, not on Comedy Central. I can almost assure you that that's not going to be happening tonight here." At points during the interview, Stewart momentarily drops being a comedian to engage in relevant questioning about the state of politics and media, foreshadowing the public image he would eventually solidify. As Dole talks about still believing in public service and voting, Stewart seems to want to agree, but adds, "I have to admit, when I sit at home and I watch and I see all the shows, *Crossfire* and all those kinds of things. It looks like, sometimes, kids that can't get along and are missing the issues, and winning for winning's sake and fighting for fighting's sake, and it's difficult to watch at times."[59] Both his critique of *Crossfire* and his disappointment in politics would be integral to the show's success in the new millennium.

FINDING ITS VOICE: INDECISION 2000

The year 2000 seemed to be the perfect time for a transition to Stewart's new vision for the show. With Clinton preparing to step down from the presidency, the race was on to secure the nomination in both parties. *TDS* launched its coverage of the presidential campaign, called "Indecision 2000," a moniker the show would continue to use for subsequent elections. The look of the show's political coverage was assisted by new director Chuck O'Neil, who started in the summer of 2000. O'Neil had worked on *Good Morning America* and wanted to change the set, pacing, and graphics to make the show look more like traditional newscasts.[60] This was the year *TDS* shed itself of the remaining holdover segments from the original *Daily Show* and truly became its own program.

TDS reporters needed the chance to make connections with politicians and got help from an unexpected source. Republican Senator John McCain had a bus he called "the Straight Talk Express," where journalists could ride with the presidential hopeful between campaign stops. New *TDS* correspondent Steve Carell was originally on McCain's press bus but was eventually invited onto the Straight Talk Express, offering a level of validation for the show. Carrell often asked joke questions but would unexpectedly mix in serious topics from time to time. McCain's wife Cindy says the candidate enjoyed having Carrell and the field staff: "They were a hoot to be around."[61] *TDS* suddenly found itself sharing time and space with traditional journalists.

The show stepped out of the studio and onto the larger political stage when the producers planned to cover both the Republican and Democratic political conventions. Coverage of the GOP convention in Philadelphia kicked off with a cold open of Stewart, flanked by Colbert, Carell, Nancy Walls, and Mo

Rocca outside the site of the convention. Stewart covers his eyes and instructs the correspondents to scatter throughout the convention.[62] As became the tradition for debates and similar political coverage, the program was shot in the host city, this time at the University of Pennsylvania. *TDS*'s turn toward politics and relevance became apparent by the guest list for the debates. In a major triumph for the program, Bob Dole appeared on the desk as a commentator with Stewart. Other officials, such as John McCain and former Secretary of Labor Robert Reich, also visited as guests on the program (figure 5.2).

Staff and talent would spend their days gathering interviews and footage from the convention, but actual coverage was presented by correspondents standing in front of green screens during the live program as if they were reporting from the convention floor. Colbert, with delegate footage behind him, reports that Republicans want to give working families $183 a month for health insurance. The show cuts from a one-shot to Colbert and Stewart in two different boxes and a background graphic as if they were in separate locations. Stewart responds, "Well, clearly Stephen $183 a month, that's not enough to cover a family of four." Colbert: "True Jon, but only if they get sick. Republicans think of this as an incentive program to stay healthy."[63] The structure allowed Stewart to play the role of the audience, following up with logical questions about the bizarre political logic presented by the

Figure 5.2 Jon Stewart in Philadelphia for an on location *The Daily Show with Jon Stewart* Covering the 2000 Republican Convention. *Source: Courtesy Comedy Central/Photofest.*

correspondents: political logic that was actually coming from the parties themselves. It was Smithberg who came up with the idea of shooting video at the convention to be used as green-screen background, but more as a time saver. Using the fake live shots allowed two correspondent reports in the first half of the show, rather than the usual single report.[64]

The four days of coverage of the GOP convention were considered a success; however, the shift to covering the Democratic convention later that month in Los Angeles proved more challenging. The comedy was less satiric and more observational. At various times Stewart looked dissatisfied with the jokes he was telling. Unlike the GOP convention, there were fewer policy-related segments and more focus on surrounding events, such as a package on how the police department was preparing for public safety. Some of the show's staff and writers seemed to find it more difficult to critique their own politics. Smithberg said, "The problem with the Democratic convention was there was no evil," because it "was teachers and the unions and legalized pot and no death penalty and increase the minimum wage."[65] The statement is telling and highlights one common critique of *TDS*, that the humor is partisan. Although the shows from Los Angeles were still largely successful, they furthered existing rifts within *TDS*.

As executive producer, Smithberg was ultimately in charge of the production of the Democratic convention coverage. Being on the West Coast meant that everything started later, resulting in what Smithberg called "a really fucked-up production schedule. It was a mess." Stewart called the coverage "a disaster," and Karlin referred to it as a "shitshow," with Smithberg receiving the blame. The fallout resulted in a tense meeting where Smithberg claims Stewart threw a newspaper at her, while Stewart says he only slammed a paper on a desk.[66] Regardless of what happened, tensions between Stewart and Smithberg continued beyond 2000 as the show grew past its origins.

The satiric coverage of the presidential election by *TDS* fit right in with the actual events of November 7, 2000. Throughout their live broadcast, Stewart checked in on the electoral-college vote and found out, along with the rest of America and the press, that the election would be closer than anyone could imagine. *TDS* again secured Bob Dole to provide live commentary, adding some political gravitas to their coverage. Major networks began to call Florida for Al Gore during the evening, only to reverse themselves and put it back in the toss-up column. Media then began to announce during the early morning of the next day that George W. Bush had taken Florida, only to reverse themselves again and report that a recount would be needed to decide the winner. In the days following the election, politics and media had become the joke as America waited to find out who had won, and *TDS* was the natural place for audiences to turn. As Smithberg said, "This is a dream for us . . . if you pitched this as a plot line for *The West Wing*, everyone would've said it's too far-fetched to be believable."[67]

The show's staff and writers covered the electoral uncertainty with glee, and *TDS* became must-see media satire. Suddenly, the program was the focus of serious discussion by other journalists. *The Chicago Sun-Times* reported laudingly that *TDS* "brilliantly savaged not only the news but the news media nightly with uncanny accuracy and zeal." In the same article, Smithberg even pointed out that, amidst the absurdity of the election, "Jon Stewart is now a kind of recognized, viable pundit."[68] Mainstream sources seemed to agree. *The New York Times* wrote of the *TDS*: "Once an obscure cable program with a cult following, 'The Daily Show' is emerging from the prolonged presidential campaign as an almost legitimate though farcical news outlet for young people."[69] In fact, the *Times* article mentioned that more 18- to 34-year-olds watched election coverage on *TDS* than on Fox News, identifying a trend that accelerated in subsequent years.

Coverage of the presidential campaign brought newfound public awareness and cultural capital for *TDS* and Stewart. Average audience size had increased 47% over 2000.[70] Stewart and the writers were receiving media attention as legitimate commentators, rather than the derisive sneers afforded the Kilborn years. Stewart noted that their political coverage really created a comparison with networks like Fox News: "We were serious people doing a very stupid thing, and they were unserious people doing a very serious thing, and that juxtaposition really landed."[71] The "Indecision 2000" coverage presaged Stewart's impact in the 2000s.

JON STEWART—THE MOST TRUSTED NAME IN NEWS

Over the course of his second year on the air, Stewart began adopting the persona that would make him one of the most influential media commentators on television during the show's run. Although this chapter focuses primarily on the 1990s, I want to jump slightly ahead to discuss how Stewart, through these early years and the first decade of the 2000s, created a unique and highly successful approach to anchoring news parody.

In 2009, Jon Stewart won a poll in which *Time* magazine asked Americans to choose their most trusted newscaster, taking 49% of the vote. NBC's Brian Williams was the runner-up with 29%. Two years earlier, Stewart tied for fourth place with Tom Brokaw, Brian Williams, and Anderson Cooper for the most admired news figures.[72] Although the value (and validity) of such popularity contests is limited, the polls reflect the positive public image Stewart developed during his time on *TDS*. Stewart's enactment of the anchor role dramatically diverged from previous news-parody personalities. In this section, I examine the image cultivated by Stewart and how he broke out of the traditional nonpartisan anchor role while minimizing backlash against his political and media critiques.

When Stewart replaced Kilborn on the anchor desk of *TDS*, a choice had to be made whether to extend Stewart's previous media persona adopted on programs like *The Jon Stewart Show* or conform to the role vacated by Kilborn as a snarky, elitist, and entertainment-oriented host. Stewart chose to build on his existing celebrity image as funny, satiric, and quick-witted, yet sincere and authentic. While films create stars, the everyday repeat-viewing characteristic of television generates the illusion of proximity with televisual celebrities.[73] As a result, audiences often perceive these actors as presenting their "real selves" rather than playing a role. Most viewers probably perceived Stewart the media interviewee, Stewart the host of *TDS*, Stewart the (mostly failed) film actor, and Stewart the actual person as one and the same. This seems to be a central aspect of his appeal—a lack of duplicity and image-making. Part of Stewart's authenticity springs from the belief that he is *not* playing a role and merely being himself.

As discussed in earlier chapters, news anchors commonly embody a dispassionate, removed style, presenting the facts without judgment as oracles of truth. Jane Curtin most closely paralleled this professional, no-nonsense approach from the previously discussed shows. Other anchors, like Chevy Chase and *NNTN*'s Stuart Pankin, played their role straight, but then suddenly veered out of character with stand-up comic style, exaggerated facial expressions, and goofy body language. The news parody ground to a halt, replaced by physical comedy. Stewart's defining quality as a comedic news anchor was his ability to navigate a narrow passage between authoritative news anchor and physically expressive comedy. Throughout the news blocks of each episode, Stewart seamlessly shifted from *presenting* the news with seriousness and reserve to *reacting* to the news, yelling and wildly flailing, and then transitioning back to the anchor, all without breaking the presentational flow. Stewart prevented a rupture in the diegetic news space by always keeping the humor in service to satire. His moments of emotion and reaction created a further commentary on the news and became part of the show's critique of events. After the 2008 presidential elections, *TDS* aired a sound bite from president-elect Barack Obama reminding everyone that Bush was still the president. The clip cuts back to Stewart, who mockingly repeats Obama's statement in a voice dripping with irony, punctuated by Stewart literally saying "wink, wink" as he offers the physical gesture.[74] As in this example, Stewart shifts from the role of unemotional news presenter to evaluating and commenting on the substance of content, smoothing over the disruption of moving from anchor to critic.

Stewart's frequent moments of physical comedy, when he breaks out of the reserved stasis expected from anchors, reinforce the host's persona while furthering the program's critical mode. Jonathan Gray suggests that satirists like Stewart remove themselves from expected limitations on political and media speech as a way of embodying genuine audience emotions: "They curse, they rant, they fume, and so forth . . . their mode of discourse is more mundane and everyday."[75] Stewart frequently used profanity for effect, content barred from traditional journalism and broadcast stations. After a conservative commentator claimed the 1990s assault-weapons ban failed, Stewart reacted, "You know what they say: if at first you don't succeed, fuck it."[76] The profanity is "bleeped," but still plainly discernible. In another example, covering a meeting of the United Nations, Stewart humorously claimed Obama quoted Gandhi as saying, "I came here to fast and kick ass and I'm all out of no food!"[77] In these moments, Stewart identifies with the audience by speaking in nonofficial language.

While reacting *for* the audience, Stewart also reinforced his image of sincerity when he would segue from the anchor role into respondent. A disingenuous political sound bite cuts back to Stewart rubbing his eyes in disbelief, exaggeratingly rotating both wrists. At other times he would wave his arms about in anger or dismissal. Despite the editorializing, Stewart maintained an air of sincerity, seeming truly surprised, shocked, or dismayed by statements or events—despite the obvious scripting of such moments. In one especially emotional example following the 2008 election, *TDS* presents its recurring feature highlighting the activities of Vice President Dick Cheney, "You Don't Know Dick." Covering a PBS interview with Cheney, *TDS* plays a clip of Jim Lehrer asking Cheney about the president's and vice president's role in foreseeing economic crises. Cheney curtly responds, "Did you see it coming, Jim? You're an expert." Cutting back, Stewart hunches over the desk in wide-eyed surprise and meekly whispers, "This whole thing has been Jim Lehrer's fault?" Clips of the PBS interview continue with Lehrer attempting to pin Cheney down for any responsibility over his eight years, finally asking Cheney if the miscalculation of the Iraqi people's response to the American invasion contributed to the chaos after the fall of Saddam Hussein. Cheney responds, "I can't say that. I can't link those two particular points." A quick cut-back and Stewart screams, while throwing his head back with both hands affixed. He then lunges toward the camera and rapidly, yet tersely, responds:

> You can't link those two? You linked Saddam Hussein and 9/11! You were the link master! You were Art Linkletter, Linky Tuscadero, Link from *The Mod Squad*, Abraham Linkage! [*audience breaks out into applause and cheers*] But that mystifies you? Well, I guess if we expect a man who's kept alive by IV

drips of panda tears and angel blood to understand cause and effect, we still *just don't know dick!*[78]

Stewart's outrage and anger seemed to be a genuine extension of the political beliefs and expectations advocated by years of TDS coverage. Beyond simple partisanship, Stewart tapped into a kind of political and media idealism, reacting to the failure of politicians to live up to the potential for representative democracy. In physically reacting to his outrage, Stewart invoked pathos, but also utilized an ethos established night after night on the program. Using Aristotelian concepts of *ethos*, Jonathan Barbur and Trischa Goodnow describe how TDS exhibits goodwill towards its audience and good temper, not allowing the humor to become overly acerbic.[79] While emerging from the various aspects of the show itself, this ethos comes primarily from Stewart's actions both on and off the program.

Stewart's complex image was built on an almost wide-eyed innocence and belief that politics and the media serve a useful function. The program's critique emerges from a utopian vision of political discourse often absent in the political and journalistic fields. Tapping into a Habermasian concept of the public sphere, Stewart's rhetoric envisioned the equality of all to speak (not just those in power) and to speak truthfully, as well as the media's responsibility to facilitate that process. Counterintuitively, his use of irony actually reinforced his authenticity. He often feigned ignorance and presumed ethical behavior from public leaders, only to have his utopian assumptions smashed by the reality of the news. In one repeated strategy, Stewart would utter something unbelievable with self-knowing exaggeration to illustrate that a situation could always be worse. So, in talking about the record profits of Goldman Sachs only a year after a government bailout, he says, "To pull that off, you'd think the Treasury Secretary who designed the bailout use to be Goldman's CEO," laughing to himself at the implausibility. Stewart then raises a hand to the IFB in his ear, as if receiving a message from an invisible producer, responding, "You, really, he was? Hank Paulson literally left Goldman Sachs to take the Treasury job?" Stewart then repeats the shtick several more times during the story, his hopes for accountability and ethics in the financial sector repeatedly dashed.[80]

The idealism and sincerity of Stewart's character were further developed by his interactions with the show's correspondents. On traditional news programs, reporters appear on set to provide further context for stories they cover, answering the news anchor's often pre-scripted questions. On TDS, correspondents usually took extreme and illogical positions, challenging the normal omnipotence of the anchor. The ensuing interactions established Stewart as a voice of reason next to the irrational comments from correspondents. Michael Gettings discusses how the dialogue between

Stewart and correspondents helps viewers discern the intended message of *TDS* from its ironic statements, with reporters presenting hyperbolic language obviously meant to be rejected.[81] As an example, media controversy followed after comedian Wanda Sykes's confrontational performance at the 2009 White House Correspondents Dinner where, among other statements, she suggested conservative talk show host Rush Limbaugh should be waterboarded as a terrorist. *TDS* used the manufactured outrage from conservatives to debate actual terrorism and torture. Stewart questioned whether Sykes went too far—could she have been less aggressive and still gotten her message across? Correspondent John Oliver defended her act with the same language advocates of torture use, saying her jokes must have been approved at the highest level and "although not pleasant, they are effective." Oliver argued that the situation called for her style of humor because "this was a pressure situation. The clock was ticking. She was responsible for the light entertainment of a thousand people eating dinner."[82] Oliver's transference of the logic of torture to defending Sykes' jokes called underlying assumptions about torture into question and made Stewart's cautious responses sound all the saner by comparison. An idealistic willingness to speak out often results in allegations of false piety and egocentrism; neither charge tended to be levied at Stewart from mainstream sources (although far-right media did sometimes use such accusations). Along with his sincerity, the host also effectively disarmed critics through his self-deprecation, a strategy often used when mentioning his Jewish identity.

Stewart as "Cool Jew"

In Lawrence Epstein's history of Jewish humor in America, he writes about the rise of new Jewish comedians during the 1970s and 1980s, artists like Al Franken, Andy Kaufman, and Richard Belzer, who mined satire and political humor.[83] Stewart came of age as an entertainer during this era, incorporating the same sensibility, and has said that, like most comedians, his early material revolved around his background, including being Jewish.[84] In his early years, the comedian changed his name from the more ethnic-sounding Jon Stuart Leibowitz. Several authors describe Stewart as emblematic of what Amy Becker calls the "New Jewish Revolution," a cultural shift early in the 2000s where Jewish identity was celebrated as cool, more hipster than outsider.[85] Stewart frequently invoked his Jewish identity on *TDS*, weaving his past and culture into his political commentary, creating what one writer calls a "'Borscht Belt Meets Ivy League' sensibility."[86] Jewish humor has a strong history of challenging authority, whether through the physical anarchy of the Marx Brothers or Lenny Bruce's cross-cultural taboos. Stewart taps into this tradition, reflecting "a Jewish sensibility in the way he blends optimism and hopefulness with a strong sense of irony and a certain cynicism about current events."[87] In his role as *TDS* host, he actively cultivated his Jewish identity.

Throughout the history of television, Jewish actors wove references to their heritage into their performances. Milton Berle frequently dropped Yiddish words into his dialogue, and other shows would mention foods, holidays, or rituals that would resonate with a Jewish audience. Stewart often made reference to Jewish culture, but also specifically mentioned his own identity both in the news segments and during interviews. Stewart sprinkled Yiddish words into reports, calling Israeli Prime Minister Benjamin Netanyahu "bubby" or hilariously questioning Michele Bachmann's use of the word "chutzpah" in reference to President Obama. He would mention Jewish holidays and America's general lack of knowledge about Jewish tradition. *TDS* writer Rob Kutner claimed Stewart is not an observant Jew, but he "feels comfortable relating openly to the fact he is Jewish. It gives him an idiom, a frame of reference."[88] The many nods to Jewish culture on the show continued to reconstitute this frame for Stewart and also connect him with some traditional Jewish humor strategies, such as self-deprecation.

Covering a 2010 controversy over plans to place a Muslim community center near ground zero in New York City, *TDS* presents a montage of conservative politicians and commentators discussing how far away the center should stay from the 9/11 ground zero. The final media personality suggests, "why not the Upper West Side in Woody Allen's building?" Stewart responds with a look of disbelief, incredulously restating, "Woody Allen? Woody Allen? That's your go-to out-of-touch, New York, liberal Jew reference? What, are they asking to build a mosque in 1976?" He continues in a sing-song voice, "New York, out-of touch, liberal Jew? Hello? I'm right here."[89] Equating himself with Woody Allen works for the joke, but unlike Allen's persona, commonly referred to as a "nebbish," Stewart is forceful and successful, strong qualities the satirist tries to mitigate. Like Jack Benny before him, Stewart embraces a tradition of self-deprecation, referencing his shortness, graying hair, and lack of sexual appeal. Previewing an interview with military expert Craig Milany, who wrote the book *The Unforgiving Minute*, Stewart comments that the book is "apparently about my wedding night."[90] These self-deprecating jokes softened the potential negatives of Stewart's strong opinions, mastery of facts, and partisan leanings. Emphasizing his own shortcomings helped to retain his positive connotations and sincerity. Due to this public persona, the host became an influential participant and commentator in the journalistic field while hosting the show, enabling him to operate as a kind of teller of truth. "Indecision 2000" started that journey and, as discussed in the next chapter, the 9/11 attacks and George W. Bush's policies and actions in response would reinforce Stewart's chosen role in the public's mind.

"WEEKEND UPDATE" STRUGGLES IN THE 1990S

With the cancellation of *Not Necessarily the News*, *SNL*'s "Weekend Update" was the only major competitor of *The Daily Show*. Creators of the Comedy Central program specifically wanted to differentiate their show from the long-running segment, because, for a large part of the public, "Weekend Update" was the essence of news parody. However, *The Daily Show* picked a good decade to compete with the venerable feature.

Over the 1990s, *SNL* struggled to find a consistent, appealing voice for the "Weekend Update" news desk. After his long run as an anchor, Dennis Miller left the show in 1991. The low-key Kevin Nealon took over duties from 1991 to 1994. Contrasting with Miller's narcissistic, over-the-top style, Nealon played it straight without much personality. Like a local news anchor running through the stories without a fuss, Nealon had a workmanlike style of delivery that emphasized the stories and jokes over his own role.

Norm Macdonald took over anchoring duties following the departure of writer Al Franken, who was known for his acute political comedy. Macdonald and writer Jim Downey refashioned the segment away from traditional news and politics and more toward celebrity. Macdonald attempted to keep Miller's self-awareness without letting the audience in on the joke. He usually began his newscasts with the wry "I'm Norm Macdonald, and now the fake news." Macdonald viewed "Weekend Update" as *his* segment and was not very interested in news. He was even less interested in whether the audience understood or got the humor, saying he would have preferred to have no dress rehearsal for testing jokes so that "I could just do the jokes that *I* thought were funny, because I have more faith in me and Jim than I did in any audience. I just like doing jokes I like, and if the audience doesn't like them, then they're wrong, not me."[91] As a result, audiences widely diverged on the quality of "Weekend Update" under Macdonald. He would often drop his anchor delivery and go off into asides. For instance, after a story about authorities looking for suspects in a suicide bombing in Israel, he looks confused and says, "Suspects in a suicide bombing? Well, here's a hint, look for the dead guys and, uh, you're probably on the right track."[92] After a joke about a Haitian general stepping down and holding a garage sale (backed by a picture of rows of skulls), the audience barely laughs. Macdonald reacts, "Big fans of the Haitian strongman, are you?"[93] He constantly seemed pleased with himself, whether the audience was following or not, which tended to be his approach to news parody.

During his first two years on the desk, the trial of O. J. Simpson dominated the news, and Macdonald went all in, making fun of Simpson and his guilt at every opportunity. In one story, he reports the jury is currently torn into two camps: "those who think he is guilty and those who are really, really stupid."[94]

After Simpson was found not guilty, Macdonald begins the segment with, "Well, it is finally official—murder is legal in the state of California." He then describes how the police have a new lead and are looking for three men observed fleeing the scene and have released a sketch. They are, of course, three sketches of O. J. Simpson. Later in the segment, Macdonald reports how the children of one juror are thrilled to have their mom home: "And no wonder, she lets them get away with murder."[95] The jokes continue long after the verdict, with Simpson remaining a favorite target.

Lore has it that Macdonald's harsh and ceaseless jokes about the now-exonerated Simpson cost him the anchor desk due to an executive's friendship with the ex-football player. Those reports have been denied, but the story regularly shows up in discussions of Macdonald's time on the show. He was removed from "Weekend Update" in 1997. While Macdonald has often been remembered as divisive on the anchor desk, his unexpected death from cancer in 2021 was met with columns showing many critics had reevaluated his work on "Weekend Update," retrospectively celebrating him for being ahead of his time in his ironic, self-aware presentation.

Macdonald was replaced by Colin Quinn, who had a short tenure, anchoring from 1998 to 2000. Quinn never seemed comfortable on the anchor desk, essentially playing himself instead of acting like a journalist. His reading and cadence were "regular guy from Brooklyn." In retrospect, Quinn says he was not suited for "Weekend Update," and when he was on the anchor desk "would self-destruct, as you can see if you watch it."[96]

MOVING TO THE 2000S

The 1990s began with optimism. The Soviet bloc began to crumble. Americans suddenly felt the lifting of the specter of impending nuclear annihilation and the Cold War that had dominated culture since the 1950s. The Gulf War seemed to be a return to the "ethical" intervention of American forces, washing away some of the ghosts of Vietnam. The decade was dominated by two terms of a Democratic president. By the end of the decade, the Internet and tech boom helped to raise stocks and the economic outlook for some in the middle and upper class. The Y2K bug and related concerns seemed to be America's biggest problem as it closed out the century. And news parody during the 1990s struggled to make fun of it.

There were plenty of actual problems festering in the country: economic inequality, incarceration, the so-called war on drugs, lack of mental health services, and so on; however, the news media turned toward celebrity and infotainment. News parody followed suit. The Kilborn era *Daily Show*, as well as the Macdonald- and Quinn-helmed "Weekend Update," parodied the shallowness of media at the time, but without much satire—without a critical edge that imagined a better path forward. It took Stewart almost two years before *TDS* left behind its entertainment-oriented focus and began to truly incorporate media and political satire within its parody.

The new millennium would prove to be a renaissance for news parody. The promise of *TDS*, expressed in its coverage of the 2000 election, would reach fruition and launch Stewart and the program's correspondents onto a national stage with their coverage of a new president, the aftermath of 9/11, and the war in Iraq. "Weekend Update" would hit upon a string of successful anchors and writing teams. And *TDS* would spin off the first of many successful news-parody programs helmed by a former correspondent, making Comedy Central the unofficial home for news parody in the 2000s.

NOTES

1. Lizz Winstead, "The Daily Show Turns 25," July 19, 2021, Livestream produced by RushTix, 87:51.
2. Lizz Winstead, *Lizz Free or Die: Essays* (New York: Riverhead Books, 2012), 98.
3. Winstead, "The Daily Show Turns 25."
4. Ibid.
5. Lucy Zhang, "Q & A: Daily Show Co-Creator Lizz Winstead," *University Wire*, Dec. 10, 2015, https://www.proquest.com/wire-feeds/q-daily-show-co-creator-lizz-winstead/docview/1747823969/se-2?accountid=8577.
6. Winstead, *Lizz Free or Die: Essays*, 167.
7. Ibid., 168.
8. Winstead, "The Daily Show Turns 25."
9. Chris Smith, *The Daily Show (The Book)* (New York: Grand Central Publishing, 2016), xvi.
10. Winstead, "The Daily Show Turns 25."
11. Ibid.
12. Winstead, *Lizz Free or Die: Essays*, 168.
13. Winstead, "The Daily Show Turns 25."
14. David Daley, "Who's the Blonde Taking Late-Night TV by Storm? It's Craig Kilborn of 'The Daily Show'," *The Hartford Courant*, August 21, 1997, 19.
15. Winstead, "The Daily Show Turns 25."
16. Kathryn Zickuhr and Aaron Smith, "Digital Differences," Pew Research Center, updated April 13, 2012, https://www.pewresearch.org/internet/2012/04/13/digital-differences/.
17. Amanda Lenhart, "Who's Not Online," Pew Research Center, updated September 21, 2000, https://www.pewresearch.org/internet/2000/09/21/whos-not-online/.
18. Brian Unger, "How the Press Fell in Love with *The Daily Show*," *Slate*, August 5, 2015, https://slate.com/culture/2015/08/the-daily-show-with-jon-stewart

-evolution-former-senior-correspondent-brian-unger-on-how-the-show-transformed-from-a-scrappy-underdog-to-a-media-institution.html.

19. *The Daily Show*, August 27, 1998.

20. Richard Leiby, "The Deadpan Zone; on Comedy Central's 'Daily Report,' Craig Kilborn Takes the News for a Spin," *The Washington Post*, May 31, 1997, C, 1–2.

21. Ibid.

22. "20 Questions: Craig Kilborn," *Playboy*, 1998, 95.

23. Donald A. Ritchie, *Reporting from Washington: The History of the Washington Press Corps* (New York: Oxford University Press, Inc., 2005), 192.

24. Winstead, "The Daily Show Turns 25."

25. Ibid.

26. Smith, *The Daily Show (The Book)*, 61.

27. Joe Bargmann, "Broadcast Bruise," *Esquire*, January 1, 1998, 41.

28. Rob Sheffield, "Scratching the Niche," *Rolling Stone*, November 17, 1998, 65.

29. Winstead, *Lizz Free or Die: Essays*, 175.

30. Winstead, "The Daily Show Turns 25."

31. Ibid.

32. Winstead, *Lizz Free or Die: Essays*, 181.

33. Winstead, "The Daily Show Turns 25."

34. Ibid.

35. Ibid.

36. Ibid.

37. Ibid.

38. Winstead, *Lizz Free or Die: Essays*, 178–79.

39. "Raw Humor Is Legal for Comics Lampooning Clinton," *The Salt Lake Tribune*, January 26, 1998, A, 6.

40. "20 Questions: Craig Kilborn."

41. *The Daily Show*, Dec. 16, 1998.

42. Ibid.

43. Winstead, "The Daily Show Turns 25."

44. Bargmann, "Broadcast Bruise."

45. Allan Johnson, "Role Reversal: Craig Kilborn Doesn't Answer All the Questions," *Chicago Tribune*, March 29, 1999, https://www.chicagotribune.com/news/ct-xpm-1999-03-29-9903290130-story.html.

46. Scott Williams, "Kilborn Wants out of 'Daily' Routine," *Austin American Statesman*, May 10, 1998.

47. Joe Schlosser, "Falling Stars," *Broadcasting & Cable*, August 4, 1997.

48. Winstead, "The Daily Show Turns 25."

49. Smith, *The Daily Show (The Book)*, 3.

50. Ibid., 7.

51. "'Daily Show' Celebrates America's Eccentricity," *Knight Ridder Tribune News Service*, March 5, 2002, https://www.proquest.com/wire-feeds/daily-show-celebrates-americas-eccentricity/docview/456673380/se-2?accountid=8577.

52. Smith, *The Daily Show (The Book)*, 9.

53. Ibid., 11.
54. Ibid., 36–37.
55. Ibid., 10.
56. *The Daily Show with Jon Stewart*, December 9, 1999.
57. *The Daily Show with Jon Stewart*, December 8, 1999.
58. Ibid.
59. *The Daily Show with Jon Stewart*, December 9, 1999.
60. Smith, *The Daily Show (The Book)*, 65.
61. Ibid., 29.
62. *The Daily Show with Jon Stewart*, August 1, 2000.
63. Ibid.
64. Smith, *The Daily Show (The Book)*, 41.
65. Ibid., 46.
66. Ibid., 46–47.
67. Kevin D. Thompson, "Botched Vote a Mother Lode to Gag Writers," *The Palm Beach Post*, November 15, 2000, D, 1.
68. Phil Rosenthal, "A Comic Koppel - No 'Indecision': Stewart Is TV's Funny, Neo-Pundit," *Chicago Sun-Times*, December 15, 2000, 2, 65.
69. Jim Rutenberg, "News Is the Comedy," *New York Times*, November 22, 2000, E, 17.
70. Smith, *The Daily Show (The Book)*, 54.
71. Ibid., 51.
72. "Today's Journalists Less Prominent: Fewer Widely Admired Than 20 Years Ago," Pew Research Center, updated March 8, 2007, https://www.pewresearch.org/politics/2007/03/08/todays-journalists-less-prominent/.
73. Graeme Turner, *Understanding Celebrity* (London: Sage Publications, 2004), 15.
74. *The Daily Show with Jon Stewart*, November 11, 2008.
75. Jonathan Gray, *Television Entertainment* (New York: Routledge, 2008), 148.
76. *The Daily Show with Jon Stewart*, January 8, 2013.
77. *The Daily Show with Jon Stewart*, September 27, 2012.
78. *The Daily Show with Jon Stewart*, January 19, 2009.
79. Jonathan E. Barbur and Trischa Goodnow, "The *Arete* of Amusement: An Aristotelian Perspective on the Ethos of *The Daily Show*," in *The Daily Show and Rhetoric: Arguments, Issues, and Strategies*, ed. Trischa Goodnow (Lanham, MD: Lexington Books, 2011).
80. *The Daily Show with Jon Stewart*, April 15, 2009.
81. Michael Gettings, "The Fake, the False, and the Fictional: *The Daily Show* as News Source," in *The Daily Show and Philosophy*, ed. Jason Holt (Malden, MA: Blackwell Publishing, 2007), 20–21.
82. *The Daily Show with Jon Stewart*, May 11, 2009.
83. Lawrence J. Epstein, *The Haunted Smile: The Story of Jewish Comedians in America* (New York: Public Affairs, 2001), 231–39.
84. *Jon Stewart: The Most Trusted Name in Fake News*, Fresh Air, October 4, 2010.

85. Simcha Weinstein, *Shtick Shift: Jewish Humor in the 21st Century* (Fort Lee, NJ: Barricade Books, 2008), Chapter 4; Amy B. Becker, "Riding the Wave of the New Jew Revolution: Watching The Daily Show with Jews for Jon Stewart" (International Communications Association, Chicago, IL May 20 2009).

86. Weinstein, *Shtick Shift: Jewish Humor in the 21st Century*, 86.

87. Becker, "Riding the Wave of the New Jew Revolution." 11–12.

88. Richard Rabkin, "The Daily Show with Rob Kutner," *Aish*, updated January 13, 2007, http://www.aish.com/j/f/48942146.html.

89. *The Daily Show with Jon Stewart*, August 10, 2010.

90. *The Daily Show with Jon Stewart*, March 10, 2009.

91. Tom Shales and James Andrew Miller, *Live from New York: An Uncensored History of Saturday Night Live* (Boston, MA: Little, Brown and Company, 2002), 430.

92. *Saturday Night Live*, April 15, 1995.

93. *Saturday Night Live*, September 24, 1994.

94. *Saturday Night Live*, April 15, 1995.

95. *Saturday Night Live*, October 7, 1995.

96. Matt Wilstein, *The Last Laugh*, podcast audio, Colin Quinn is 'Actually Glad' he got COVID, 54:002021.

Chapter 6

Stewart and Colbert in the Post-Network Era

The day after America's 2006 congressional midterm elections, President George W. Bush announced the resignation of Secretary of Defense Donald Rumsfeld. Despite widespread criticism of Rumsfeld, the move surprised the American press because, only a week earlier, Bush insisted Rumsfeld would remain in his cabinet until 2008. NBC and ABC news offered the strongest network criticism of Bush's duplicity, saying the president "misled" reporters. CBS labeled his previous statement a "fib." Neither CNN nor Fox News bothered to mention Bush's flip-flop. Jon Stewart, however, plainly labeled what had occurred: a lie. The night after Rumsfeld's resignation, *The Daily Show with Jon Stewart* (*TDS*) played a clip from a White House press conference where Bush explained that he told reporters Rumsfeld would stay to keep from politicizing the decision. Stewart, doing his oft-repeated Bush impersonation, followed the clip by explaining, "Don't you see? Don't you get it? I was only lying for my own good."[1] By the mid-2000s, the program's political commentary had moved beyond its beginnings and that of earlier news-parody shows. The pastiche and delight in playing with form and technology prominent during the 1980s and 1990s gave way to programs actively engaging both politicians and the media—calling them to task, holding them accountable, and commenting on substance; in short, news parody began to function as criticism and sometimes even as journalism.

TDS served as a focal point for conversations about the seeming cross-pollination between news and entertainment on television in the new millennium. Shortly after the reformatting of the program under Stewart, accolades began accumulating, but not merely for its humor. The program's coverage of the 2000 presidential election, discussed in the last chapter, won an Emmy and a Peabody Award for accomplishments in broadcast journalism.

The following year, Stewart's response to the September 11, 2001, terrorist attacks brought additional attention and praise.

Like most television entertainment, *TDS* chose to go on hiatus in the days immediately following 9/11, airing reruns. The press questioned when media entertainment should resume and whether comedy, much less satire, would be accepted by a grieving nation. *TDS* staff was uncertain of the future. Steve Carell recalled that "it all just seemed . . . so irrelevant and small," and Madeleine Smithberg reportedly said, "I don't even know if we have a show anymore."[2] On September 20, *TDS* went back on the air, opening not with music or graphics but with Stewart silently seated at the anchor desk. In this cold open, he tells the audience, "They said to get back to work. And there were no jobs available for a man in the fetal position, under his desk, crying, which I gladly would have taken."[3] He says the show's staff felt privileged to be able to entertain their audience and to exercise the freedom of satire. In a nine-minute monologue, Stewart, unsuccessfully holding back tears at times, wove together his personal reactions, thoughts about the role of comedy during times of tragedy, and hope for the future into a tribute to national resiliency: "That's why we've already won. It's light. It's democracy. We've already won. They can't shut that down." Stewart won praise from the media.

Politically Incorrect's Bill Maher, by comparison, tested and found the limits of political satire after 9/11 when, agreeing with a guest who said the perpetrators of the terrorist attacks were not cowards, Maher instead called America's use of cruise missiles "cowardly." Commentators immediately condemned the host for his remarks, and Maher quickly apologized; however, criticism only increased, with White House Press Secretary Ari Fleischer saying the incident is a "reminder to all Americans that they need to watch what they say, watch what they do, and that this is not a time for remarks like that. It never is."[4] ABC's cancellation of *Politically Incorrect* the following June was widely seen as a response to Maher's 9/11 comments.[5]

By comparison, Stewart's monologue struck an emotional yet conciliatory tone that resonated with the public's emotions. *Rolling Stone*'s coverage was emblematic of the reception, calling Stewart's opening "a four-hankie monologue that hit all the right notes."[6] In the months following 9/11, Stewart, along with outlets like *The Onion*, moved into a more critical mode, raising questions traditional broadcast media tended to ignore. Writing about comedy's post-9/11 response, Paul Achter commends these parodies as "a way of reflecting on what had happened and, perhaps more importantly, why."[7] Stewart began to be sought out by journalists for his views, appearing in 2002 on CNN's *Inside Politics* and ABC's *Nightline*.

TDS struggled with finding balance between satire after the attacks and still having a sense of decorum and even patriotism. Following 9/11, letters containing anthrax were mailed to some officials and media outlets. Having a new story to cover helped shift the show away from purely focusing on the terrorism. By 2002, the average audience size had more than doubled since the Kilborn era, and by the end of the year attention turned to the midterm elections as the show went live from Washington, DC, in the lead-up to the vote.[8] *Indecision 2002* continued the show's well-regarded political coverage, but it also seemed to mimic the stress of the live coverage of 2000. Once again, friction between Stewart and Smithberg simmered, but Stewart was now clearly in charge. At the end of the year, Smithberg announced her departure from the show she helped create. Reports diverge on exactly how the split came about. For 2003, Ben Karlin replaced Smithberg, and David Javerbaum moved up to head writer. The invasion of Iraq dominated coverage the following year, further increasing *TDS*'s profile in the media ecosystem.

Generally enthusiastic discussions of *TDS* continued to circulate in popular press discourse leading up to the release of a 2004 Pew Poll showing that young people were increasingly turning to late-night comedy shows for their news rather than traditional sources.[9] Controversy erupted, with journalists and critics raising concerns about uneducated and disconnected youth and the potential effects on democracy. A follow-up study from Pew quickly challenged dominant narratives by showing that viewers of *TDS* and its spin-off program, *The Colbert Report* (*Colbert*), were among the most knowledgeable news consumers.[10] Often lost at the time, both in press discussions and media-effects research, was the potential function of news parody not as a *replacement* for traditional journalism but as a supplement and a corrective. In this chapter, I explore how *TDS* and *Colbert* emerged in the post-network era of television, tapping into a shifting industrial landscape and popularizing a model of news parody for a new millennium.

MIMICKING FORMAL NEWS STYLE ON *THE DAILY SHOW*

TDS's look and format were still developing in the early 2000s. It quickly became more tied to parodying contemporary cable news. The firm hired for the show's 2007 set makeover had designed sets for *Good Morning America*, ABC's *World News Tonight*, and CNN's *Piers Morgan Tonight*, bringing a very contemporary newscast feel to *TDS* by the end of the decade. The set was dynamic, utilizing a 46-inch flat-screen to display motion graphics and images, virtual newsroom backgrounds, a world map, a four-foot globe with an integrated ticker hanging above the desk, and more than 560 color LED fixtures.[11] The anchor desk was the centerpiece, with correspondents appearing on set, allowing a dialogue with Stewart following a package or news story. Space to the left was reserved for the featured guest interview in the style of late-night talk shows. The new set was part of an overall visual redesign leaning even more heavily on graphics (figure 6.1).

During the 2000s, *TDS* was the first news-parody program to take full advantage of the lower cost and availability of digital designs, with Stewart surrounded by a dizzying array of graphic elements. As with traditional news anchors at the time, Stewart would be offset on camera, with the other side of the screen occupied by motion graphic beds, moving visuals that are then overlaid with pictures or composite images, themselves further overlaid by lower-third titles. The multiple layers of graphics replicated a cable-news look, with information crowding screen space. Not coincidentally, some members of the *TDS* graphics team had previously worked in the news for MSNBC and CNN. A team of four designers and a producer created all the graphics using industry-standard tools on deadline, sometimes adding new elements literally minutes before show taping. One night two new images were ordered to accompany stories 15 minutes before taping, one of Hillary Clinton wearing a pantsuit covered with NASCAR-style logos and another of Hillary morphing into Bill Clinton.[12] The dynamic graphics and images of the set established the centrality of visuals in the program, including the extensive use of video within news-parody segments.[13]

The use of news footage was an essential element of both *TDS* and the Kilborn version of the program, differentiating it from its "Weekend Update" contemporary. Amber Day sets *TDS* off from previous news-parody programs partially because of its use of news footage, incorporating real journalistic content into its mimicry of form.[14] While the program did not represent

Figure 6.1 Jon Stewart on the Set of *The Daily Show with Jon Stewart*. *Source*: Screenshot by the author.

a total break from the past, *TDS* undeniably reformulated the use of footage in news parody. Producers of *NNTN* essentially structured their entire show around newsfilm; however, the footage was always decontextualized, joined with unrelated footage, redubbed with audio, or with alterations to produce a joke about the clip itself, but rarely with any connection to broader political events. By contrast, *TDS* almost always kept the footage in context, focusing on the story or the substance of the video. Whereas *NNTN* subscribed to newsfeeds to generate fodder for its jokes, *TDS* benefited from a broad array of digital feeds, stock-footage sources, Internet clips, and the ability to capture live broadcasts for later use. In the early 2000s, researchers used multiple DVRs to record content, but by the end of the decade they had worked with a company to not only digitally record and store television content for later use but also convert audio into searchable text. This allowed them to pull instances of certain phrases or topics, reportedly decreasing search and production time by 60% to 70%.[15]

Rather than humor being the only factor in clip selection on *TDS*, video satisfied many of the basic newsworthy qualities journalists seek: prominence, conflict, impact, timeliness, and so on. On *NNTN*, an image would appear and be quickly replaced by another, moving rapidly from one joke to another. However, *TDS* often subjected a clip to analysis; Jeffrey Jones uses the analogy of a prosecutor to describe how the program assembled footage to interrogate multiple witnesses, cross-examine, summarize the evidence, and create a closing statement.[16] Arguments both sprang from and incorporated video. For instance, images of Tea Party organizers unpacking boxes with a million bags of tea intended to be used in a protest are then questioned by Stewart: "Let me get this straight. To protest wasteful spending, you bought a million tea bags? Are you protesting taxes or irony?"[17] Unlike *NNTN*, video used in *TDS* either added to a conversation or provided a jumping-off point to deconstruct the actions or logic behind the clip.

Sound bites, as a specialized type of video, were used in similar ways. Statements from officials were analyzed and placed within a broader context. Although the show was interested in expanding political discourse, *TDS* depended on existing sound bites carried by the networks they monitored. This is an often-mentioned drawback of news parody that limits its ability to actually *create* journalism; programs use already-existing footage borrowed from television networks, so the news they cover is preselected.[18] Newscasts have become notorious for using shorter and shorter speaking clips too, which was down to an average length of 4.3 seconds in 2005, creating short utterances divorced from context.[19] *TDS* frequently engaged such clips by editing sound-bite montages and mashing up statements from one individual or a group of newsmakers. These sound-bite montages primarily fall into three common strategies, each creating the illusion of dialogue through editing. One method was to combine statements from various political actors to tease out the logic behind their political speak, which was especially useful for events like congressional hearings. Following Secretary of State Hillary Clinton's appearance in front of a House committee on the 2012 Benghazi consulate attack, the program presents a montage of Republican lawmakers asking essentially the same questions over and over, hoping to have their statement be selected for a sound bite by traditional news media covering the hearing. *TDS* also included a montage of Democratic House members commending Clinton, with Stewart following up by referring to their "questioning" as "ass-licky."[20] By isolating and unifying statements from the hours-long C-SPAN coverage, *TDS* helped to emphasize the political theater of the hearings.

A second strategy was to edit longitudinal montages of one politician's or media figure's statements over time to illuminate hypocrisy or logical fallacies. The sound-bite culture of news, along with its emphasis on immediacy and the fear of seeming partisan often discourage news organizations from connecting statements in this way. In one extended montage on *TDS*, former Fox News personality Bill O'Reilly repeatedly advocates for the privacy rights of celebrities across several years. O'Reilly's strong repudiation of paparazzi tactics is juxtaposed with a subsequent montage composed of historic *O'Reilly Factor* ambush interviews with lesser-known media personalities being questioned as they walk outside to get mail, load their children in vehicles, or board public transportation. Using the raw evidence produced across multiple years of the cable news program, Stewart damns O'Reilly with his own words and actions, summing up the segment in O'Reilly's voice with "Coming up on the *Factor*: cognitive dissonance and why I don't experience it."[21] Such segments provided a highly effective strategy for holding politicians and media personalities responsible for logical and moral inconsistency in the face of shifting political pressures.

In the third type of sound-bite edits, *TDS* would create thematic montages of prevailing wisdom or discourse about news topics to offer a deeper analysis of politics and media culture. Connecting voices from across a range of sources and outlooks, this strategy helped raise questions about conventional wisdom and sometimes even deconstructed political language. After the retirement of Supreme Court Justice David Souter, President Barack Obama presented his criteria for nominating a replacement, including "empathy." Conservative commentators latched onto the phrase, and *TDS* presented a montage of voices condemning empathy as a code word for "judicial activism." Stewart offered his own interpretation of conservative buzzwords by noting "activist judge is a code word for pro-choice. . . . They're helping us break the code with a code. Is this an episode of *Lost*?"[22] In the morass of conventional broadcast news coverage of partisan outrage and individual political drama, journalists rarely have time to synthesize information. *TDS*'s thematic montages offered a method of connecting dominant discourses in order to question and interrogate their logic and hidden motivations.

More than any preceding news-parody program, *TDS* offered a true stylistic and visual parallel with broadcast and cable news. A combination of increasing budget (due to the show's success) and the lowered costs of technology enabled an imitation of professional news spaces in the studio and elaborate incorporations of footage from a large number of sources.

THE PARTISAN PARODY OF *THE COLBERT REPORT*

While *TDS* offered a general parody of broadcast and cable newscasts, its spin-off *Colbert* structured its humor around a *specific* style of cable show and even an individual host. *Colbert* began airing in the mid-2000s, at a time when partisan cable news programs flourished in the wake of 9/11 and the wars in Afghanistan and Iraq. The divisive politics of the time increasingly convinced viewers to seek out information from their own political perspective, with Fox News and MSNBC personalities benefiting the most from partisan rancor. These personality-driven news shows set their own politically informed agendas and funneled almost all reports exclusively through the hosts, who evaluated the news and proclaimed their own interpretation of events. Modeled specifically on Fox News' *The O'Reilly Factor* and host Bill O'Reilly, *Colbert* imitated the look, style, and rhetoric of these partisan programs.

Stephen Colbert started with *TDS* in 1997 and remained after the departure of Kilborn. He adapted and thrived under the show's new direction, creating a character as a burlesque of conservative commentators, egocentric and totally secure in his own knowledge; yet in news packages and opposite Stewart, his true ignorance was apparent. As the Bush administration took the nation to war in Iraq, the Colbert persona became an ardent defender of conservative values and politicians, indicting them with the character's idiocy. In 2005, Colbert, Stewart, and Karlin spun the character off into his own program, airing nightly after *TDS* and creating a news-parody programming block.

Colbert successfully developed the host into a fully formed personality, earning positive reviews and leading to his selection to host the 2006 White House Correspondents Dinner. Colbert's speech at the event catapulted him into the broader public eye. Standing in a room with the president, first lady, national politicians, and some of the most powerful members of the press, Colbert delivered a vicious rebuke of journalism's coverage of the Bush White House and criticism of the president's policies and underlying philosophy of governance within a seemingly congenial shell of irony. Referring to Bush's giving a speech at Ground Zero after the 9/11 attacks and flying a fighter jet onto an aircraft carrier to declare the war in Iraq as "Mission Accomplished," Colbert said, "I stand by this man. I stand by this man, because he stands for things. Not only *for* things, he stands *on* things. Things like aircraft carriers and rubble and recently flooded city squares. And that sends a strong message: that no matter what happens to America, she will always rebound with the most powerfully staged photo-ops in the world."[23] At an event that often celebrates the cozy relationship between the press and those in power, Colbert's character shamed both sides.[24] The speech brought condemnation from many politicians and mainstream journalists, who considered the rhetoric rude, but Colbert's real audience of television and Internet viewers applauded his honesty and made the speech one of the most-watched clips of the year. On YouTube alone, the speech was viewed 2.7 million times in 48 hours, becoming an Internet sensation.[25] A wave of press coverage followed the speech, and viewership of *Colbert* jumped by over a third shortly after the event. With the Correspondent's Dinner, Colbert made a conscious decision to utilize his persona on the public stage, creating a kind of active, real-life satire that will be further explored in the next chapter.

Adapting Partisan News Format

The basic format of *Colbert* mimicked *TDS*, as it usually featured two blocks of news followed by an interview segment and a brief sign-off. All aspects of the news blocks revolved around Colbert, though. There were no correspondents or packages other than Colbert's occasional interview of members of Congress. The news segments still integrated footage and sound bites into news blocks, but to a much lesser extent than *TDS*. Colbert, after all, *was* the news on his program. Sound bites or footage were used to launch the host's commentary on the news item. A quick Lou Dobbs clip from Fox News, for instance, introduces concern that Secretary of Defense nominee Chuck Hagel may have received funds from a group called "Friends of Hamas," initiating Colbert's commentary revealing the group "is so sinister it doesn't even exist."[26] His interaction with sound bites and their use within the show was not drastically different from Stewart's; however, like the partisan personality cable programs being parodied, the focus was always on Colbert and what *he* thinks, resulting in less footage and more host commentary.

The program was just as graphics-rich as *TDS*; multiple layers of computer-generated images usually occupied the screen with Colbert, along with frequent over-the-shoulder graphics and other stills. In the late-2000's redesign, the left side of the screen was dominated by a row of opaque arced stars moving across a red and blue background with a rotating capital C as a graphics bed. A flag motif with undulating stars and stripes ran behind full-page graphics, such as newspaper images. Just as with *TDS*, the program's graphics accentuated the set design, credibly imitating the visual style of cable news.

Colbert's basic set layout remained mostly the same throughout its run, with the set visually divided between news space and interview space. On the news side, called "The Eagle's Nest," a partial wrap-around desk in the shape of a "C" surrounded Colbert. A 2010 redesign added a virtual rotating "C" to the front of the desk. Three large screens behind Colbert allowed changing motion graphics with video columns in between, which created even more spaces for graphics. To either side of the screens, the "Shelves of Honor" displayed items accumulated by the host over the course of the show, including books and photos. The design reinforced the Colbert persona—his unquestioning patriotism, love of capitalism, and ego. He specifically rejected using traditional video monitors displaying news feeds and sources of news on the wall, saying, "I *am* the source."[27] As Colbert was the ultimate authority on the show, all elements of the set converged towards his head at the anchor desk, much like Jesus centered in Da Vinci's *Last Supper*. Side by side with The Eagle's Nest, a separate interview area, featured a desk and two chairs with a background monitor. A hearth stands to one side, with a portrait of Colbert standing at the hearth. Over the hearth in the painting, another portrait hangs, and then yet another, creating multiple images of Colbert embedded in the one portrait. Each year the portrait was updated to include new awards and other tokens of ego-gratification; however, Colbert reminds the audience: "This isn't just a portrait of me. It's a portrait of you, in the form of me. And I have to say, you look great."[28] The set created a rich sign system that semiotically supported and extended the megalomaniacally narcissistic character created by Colbert (figure 6.2).

Regular segments hosted by the anchor replaced reporter packages and news presentations from correspondents, keeping the focus on Colbert. The recurring segments allowed Colbert to present extended rants, condemning public figures or actions and sometimes praising politicians or media personalities. Of course, his character's advocacy always carried a double voice, ironically damning with its transparently misplaced praise. His most frequent segment, "The Wørd," always began with Colbert addressing one particular issue or action, shown as text on the opposite side of the screen. As Colbert continues his argument, the text begins to question and challenge Colbert's statements, creating a dialogue between actor and graphics. Structurally similar to segments such as *O'Reilly Factor*'s "Talking Points Memo," *The Wørd*'s presentation upended a common trope of news-personality shows, where the hosts would proclaim their opinions as truths, reinforced by short graphics. After a *New York Times* article alleging that Republican

Figure 6.2 Stephen Colbert on the Set of *The Colbert Report*. *Source*: Screenshot by the author.

presidential hopeful John McCain may have had an affair, Fox News called the story "bad, bad journalism." Playing off this clip, Colbert introduces the night's word, "Good, Bad Journalism," ironically noting that the *Times* should learn about the art of character assassination from Fox, which excels at it. During the segment, a clip is played of a Fox host derisively laughing about the *Times* article's being on nine different pages of the paper. Colbert responds: "Nine pages? Look, if bad journalism is good enough, it can be done in a sonnet." The text opposite Colbert reads "Brevity Is the Soul of Libel."[29] During *The Wørd*, text on the right side of the screen constantly undercut Colbert's voice. Parodying this visual strategy highlighted the way text commonly replaces actual logic in partisan news to reinforce viewpoints.

Colbert featured a number of other recurring segments similar to those favored by the cable news personalities of the day, either valorizing or criticizing newsmakers. The "Alpha Dog of the Week" saluted, as Colbert says, "the men or lady-men who have the biggest balls in these U. S. of A.s." Colbert would ironically praise outrageous behavior by those he named "Alpha Dogs," such as Virginia State Senate Republicans, who waited until after a black lawmaker, who was attending President Obama's inauguration, left town. The GOP then passed redistricting that consolidated minority voting into one district—on Martin Luther King Jr.'s birthday.[30] Like much of the satire on *Colbert*, the seemingly celebratory segment implicitly condemned the actions of officials. Another segment, "Tip of the Hat/Wag of the Finger," presented a string of brief commentary on issues. Former Pope Benedict XVI earned a wag of the finger for allowing the installation of solar panels at the Vatican because, according to Colbert, "God does not care about the environment." The host then gives a tip of the hat to Marvel Comics for placing Colbert on the cover of Spider-Man as a presidential candidate but quickly follows with a wag of the finger because, in the Marvel Universe, Colbert won the popular vote and then lost to Obama in the Electoral College.[31] Many of the outspoken cable-news personalities of the day utilized similar segments to drift off into editorializing. *Countdown with Keith Olbermann* had "Worst Person in the World," and *O'Reilly Factor* featured "Pinheads and Patriots." The segments on Colbert, while parodying the Olbermanns and O'Reillys of cable news, also replicated their logic, passing judgment with an added layer of irony.

THE PARRHESIA OF STEWART VERSUS THE IRONY OF COLBERT

Colbert and *TDS* shared structural similarities, but their actual content diverged due to the different targets of their parody (*TDS* as cable newscast and *Colbert* as cable news opinion). The two comic strategies manifest most plainly in the different presentational styles of the two hosts at the anchor desk. As described in the previous chapter, Stewart utilized sincerity, self-effacement, and his Jewish background to craft an image of authenticity. This allowed him to operate as a type of trusted truth-teller in the media field. Colbert's character, by contrast, was defined by narcissism and irony, creating an uncertainty and textual openness to his program.

Throughout the 2000s, at the same time Stewart was being recognized for his political and media commentary, he was also accused of increasing audience cynicism, media distrust, and possibly political apathy.[32] Writers like Roderick Hart and Johanna Hartelius dismissed Stewart as damaging democracy, accusing him of being a postmodernist cynic.[33] However, *TDS* produced neither a simple nihilist critique of journalism and politics nor a partisan message. In that way, perhaps the message *was* more postmodern, refusing to dichotomize parties, politicians, and media outlets simply as good or bad, but questioning the accepted terms of evaluation in these fields. As an anchor, Stewart spoke not only to his citizen audience but also to media professionals and politicians themselves. In a series of lectures, Michel Foucault discussed the ancient Greek concept of *parrhesia* as a type of truth telling. The goal of *parrhesia* "is not to speak the truth to someone else, but has the function of *criticism*," either of the speaker or the audience.[34] On *TDS*, Stewart acted as *parrhesiastes* to the media, enunciating unpleasant truths and questioning some of the underlying logic of dominant American journalism. The *parrhesiastes* place themselves in danger when they risk speaking truth.[35] In modern society, when humorists engage in *parrhesia*, they risk removal from public discourse, such as the response to Bill Maher's statements after 9/11. As *TDS* circulated in the journalistic and political fields, Stewart's risks in speaking the truth increased. Being engaged in public debate meant that an ill-conceived statement could lead to attacks from the media, or Stewart could lose legitimation, with journalists ignoring him or refusing to appear on the show. Foucault says *parrhesiastes* are necessary because all people flatter themselves and need a truth-teller to offer critique, and this seems especially true of the media.[36]

Several years before his lectures on *parrhesia*, Foucault wrote an article also dealing with speaking truth and the function of the intellectual. Traditionally, the intellectual spoke for universal concerns; however, Foucault saw the emergence of what he called "specific intellectuals," persons who carry discursive power within their field. Specific intellectuals engage in their particular work and life, carrying the "specificity of the politics of truth in our societies."[37] This specific intellectual operates within a particular field, creating the possibility for more radical action. Stewart, through his acceptance by the media and ability to speak to traditional journalistic outlets, functioned as a specific intellectual to the media during *TDS*. It may seem odd for Foucault, who spoke of truth as being an establishment of power, to discuss truth-telling; however, he defines truth in this instance as "a system of ordered procedures for the production, regulation, distribution and circulation of statements."[38] The specific individual seeks to rupture that system, to "emancipate" truth from the situation in which it is embedded, to illuminate the process. Satire can be a highly useful tool to accomplish this goal, introducing absurdity to the normally ordered, seamless process of replicating truth.

On *TDS*, Stewart spoke as part of the media and questioned routines and representational processes, asking for *better* journalism. Following the 2008 election of President Obama, in a segment called "Baracknophobia," *TDS* presents a montage of media puns discussing increased gun sales, using phrases like "booming business," "explosive sales number," and "Americans fired up." Stewart follows, gleefully raising his hand and declaring, "I've got one! I've got one! These sales numbers could accidentally kill someone you care about." He stops, reflects, and looks down at his script quizzically before continuing dryly, "It's funny cause it's true."[39] In addition to humor, the juxtaposed comments point out the lack of serious coverage the television media gave the story and actually delves into the potentially sobering consequences. Following the shooting at an Aurora, Colorado movie theater in 2012, discussions about gun violence were quickly waved aside by politicians and conservative media pundits. After airing a montage of media personalities saying now is not the time to discuss gun control,

Stewart launches into a commentary on *why* the media must foster deeper conversations:

> So you're telling me it's too soon to even have a conversation about it? You're telling me that to discuss the epidemic of gun violence in this country, for *that*, there is a waiting period? Yeah, I guess you'd hate to go into a conversation about guns all hotheaded, say something impulsively you'll never be able to take back. Look, this is the time to talk about *all* of it. Everything should be on the table, anything that could possibly mitigate these terrible events. I'm not even saying gun control would do it. I'm just saying it's gotta be part of the conversation. I mean, is there anything we can talk about that shows this country's problem-solving mechanism is not irrevocably damaged? [*Quick Fox News clip asking if costumes should be banned from movie theaters*] All right. Didn't realize, all right, I stand corrected. Problem solved.[40]

Although playing to the audience, Stewart is also speaking to news media as a "specific intellectual" within that realm, pleading for a better journalistic practice that embraces the public sphere. His rhetoric is constructive, not destructive. Repeat viewing of *TDS* made plain that Stewart believed in the press and its ability to hold those in power responsible. His *parrhesia* attempted to remind the media of that calling.

Stewart's discourse aided his audience in reflecting on processes of truth. Jonathan Gray makes the distinction that, rather than stating truth, Stewart's mode of comedy encouraged the viewer to establish his or her own truth.[41] Stewart functioned as a facilitator who rhetorically constituted his audience as collaborators in the program's critical project. Stewart often engaged in conversational direct address with viewers, breaking out of the traditional authoritative anchor role and fostering the illusion of intimacy, by leaning in and speaking to the audience. A common transitional device to move into this mode of address was Stewart's invitation to "meet me at camera three," where he would turn to a different camera and act as if he were speaking to a particular newsmaker. In reality, his speech was directed at the audience and meant to influence their perception of the story being covered.

In 2009 *TDS* aired a clip of conversative U.S. Representative Michele Bachmann telling Fox News personality Sean Hannity the government will place young people in "re-education camps." Hannity responds that Bachmann will continue to be attacked because she fights tyranny. Stewart then asks them to meet him at camera three, saying

> I think you might be confusing tyranny with losing ... when the guy that you disagree with gets elected, he's probably going to do things you disagree with. He could cut taxes on the wealthy, remove government's oversight capability,

invade a country that you thought shouldn't be invaded. That's not tyranny—that's democracy. See, now you're in the minority. It's supposed to taste like a shit taco.[42]

His comments reject the partisan demonization of opponents purely over political disagreements, reminding viewers that elections inevitably yield political consequences. Through this process, Stewart fostered an image of sincerity and a willingness to look beyond differences in opinion to deeper structures.

Writing about the program's interview segment, Kelly Wilz argues that Stewart generated constructive discourse in line with agonistic democracy, that he "encourages responses, enters the engagement with a level of humility, and is willing to be 'changed' in his views."[43] This openness perfectly complemented Stewart's complex anchor persona, which presented him as a strong, intelligent advocate for political and media responsibility, yet with a sincere and self-effacing presentational style. As with all meaning, though, Stewart's persona was open to interpretation, and some audience members saw hypocrisy and a lack of willingness to take responsibility for his own cultural influence. The *TDS* host offered a parallel point of deviation for Stephen Colbert to develop his own on-screen character.

Stephen Colbert and Ironic Confusion

Predating Stewart on *TDS*, Colbert experienced the program's shift from entertainment to news-oriented focus as a field reporter, with Colbert's pieces moving from news of the strange to more political topics. While his original reporter persona usually played the straight man, the "Stephen Colbert" host character evolved over the first several years of Stewart's tenure to become an egocentric, idiotic prophet of conservatism. Developed as the counterpoint to Stewart's thoughtful sincerity, Colbert became the lead correspondent for *TDS*, advocating extreme conservative positions and engaging in hyperbole for Stewart to countermand.[44] With the 2005 launch of *Colbert*, the character solidified into a parody of self-important cable hosts, speaking boldly with scant information and less self-awareness: "I am a humble man—and I would shout that from the mountain top."[45]

Regular viewers of *Colbert* knew the character was an act. However, Colbert weaved aspects of his real-life biography into the mix; for instance, both Colbert and "Colbert" were raised in South Carolina and each is Catholic. As a result, there was some confusion over how much of the Colbert character was an act and how much was real.[46] When appearing on the program or at a public event, Colbert stayed in character, refusing to acknowledge the act. During media interviews, however, Colbert the person emerged and provided important context for his character. When asked in a *60 Minutes* interview whether the *Colbert* host is smart, proud, or stupid, the satirist responds, "I think of him as a well-intentioned, poorly informed, high-status idiot."[47] The "well-intentioned" part seems especially important, because it allowed the character to potentially be viewed as a subject of pity—his politics were not necessarily mean, just ill-conceived and unreflective.

Both the Colbert character and program specifically copied Fox News' host Bill O'Reilly, whom Colbert referred to as "Papa Bear." O'Reilly had one of the longest-running and most consistently popular shows on 24-hour news at the time, making it and the host an obvious target for parody. One study about the *O'Reilly Factor* describes the host's constructed persona as "honest, working class roots, the courage to speak truth to power, a commitment to truth and facts over ideology and spin."[48] Colbert claimed to actually admire O'Reilly's hosting and rhetorical abilities, even if not agreeing with his politics.[49] In an in-character interview on *O'Reilly Factor*, Colbert says he emulates the Fox host, reminding O'Reilly that emulation means no money is owed.[50] Colbert amplified O'Reilly's qualities to a ridiculous extreme. *Colbert* criticized the Fox News show specifically but Jeffrey Jones describes how the program extended its reach to become a parody of an entire genre of late-night cable yelling shows not limited to one person or even one network.[51]

From the opening of *Colbert*, American exceptionalism and patriotism are invoked. Audio of a screaming eagle kicks off the program, followed by headlines and an opening replete with patriotic imagery: an American flag-festooned bald eagle flies across the screen, as an image of Colbert, arms outstretched, is surrounded by god terms: "authority," "power," "patriot," "honorable," "strong," "originalist," "star-spangled," "self-evident," and the adapted "me pluribus unum." Colbert disappears only to run back on screen, grabbing and literally waving the American flag. Geoffrey Baym calls Colbert's antics "spectacle scripted for the stage," and his larger-than-life opening helps establish that spectacle.[52] The red, white, and blue graphics accent the color scheme of the set, screaming "U.S.A.," just as the audience occasionally did. Bill Bergeron, who created the original opening for the show, says the design team closely reviewed the graphics of both O'Reilly and MSNBC's *Scarborough Country* when deciding on the visual style.[53] Colbert's character defined his love for America with no exceptions, positioning the character as a kind of unthinking patriot. After calling America the greatest country in the world, Colbert launches into an attack on *Newsweek* for ranking the United States eleventh on the list of best countries, saying the ranking is "based on useless criteria. The criteria is education, quality of life, and health."[54] Colbert often mocked the jingoistic attitudes of other hosts by endorsing their arguments, such as when Sean Hannity called America "the greatest, best country God has ever given man on the face of the Earth." Colbert walks through an extended Venn diagram to show how Hannity could arrive at such a statement and then tells viewers Hannity must love America almost as much as he does.[55] The blind patriotism of the character went hand and hand with his political viewpoint.

Like O'Reilly and other Fox News hosts, Colbert's character advocated a brand of "common sense" conservative populism on his show, whereas the rest of the media were liberal extremists waging war against good, God-fearing Americans. In the wake of the 2012 Newtown school shooting, Colbert warned that "the media's morbid obsession with the tens of thousands of people who are killed every year with guns is just part of the media's anti-gun agenda."[56] Since the elite are positioned against "Real America," information is not to be trusted because according to Colbert "reality has a well-known liberal bias."[57] This perspective is captured in the word he now-famously introduced on his premiere episode of *Colbert*: "truthiness." Promising to speak plainly to his audience, Colbert says he is no fan of dictionaries and reference books, who might say truthiness is not a word: "they're elitist." He continues, "I don't trust books; they're all fact and no heart, and that's exactly what's pulling our country apart today. . . . We're divided between those who think with their head and those who know with their heart." Colbert talks about how President Bush doesn't need to think because "he feels the truth" and then tells his audience that although they may not trust their gut yet, "you will, with my help. . . . Anyone can *read* the news *to* you. I promise to *feel* the news *at* you." Discussing the word in an interview, Colbert points to the concept of truthiness as a major stumbling block that "is tearing apart our country" and laments the decline of facts over perceptions.[58] When no one can be swayed by facts, then there is no common ground for debate, and partisanship creates its own internal logic. Colbert the character simply refused to acknowledge facts, thereby avoiding any need for debate.[59]

The Colbert character, in creating his own reality, also made himself infallible. Not only did he refuse to acknowledge conflicting facts, he never admitted mistakes. If footage failed to roll, he would draw a picture or act as if he suddenly changed his mind and no longer wanted the video.[60] The 2008 live election special became a difficult scenario for Colbert to navigate in character, as Obama won state after state. Each McCain loss sent the Colbert character further into a state of denial, blaming plumbers for not voting and then later accusing hockey dads of not pulling their weight. As Stewart called the election for Obama, Colbert presaged Karl Rove's 2012 Fox News meltdown, saying, "Maybe, maybe," but then enthusiastically declared "McCain can still pull this thing out" before slipping on dark glasses and headphones.[61] The safety of the adoring Colbert audience offered an easier stage to stay in character and never admit defeat.

From his very first episode, Colbert cultivated a relationship of confederacy with his audience, inviting them to play along with the gag. Most nights the audience chanted "Stephen, Stephen" following the opening, creating a raucous din of approval that accentuated the character's own self-promotion. Playing the populist (and imitating Fox News hosts like Hannity), Colbert called his audience "The Colbert Nation," placing himself center stage. He repeatedly invoked populist language extolling the voice of the people, but always brought the attention back to himself. During a press conference, he said, "I am here to represent your voice, so please quiet down, so we can all hear what you have to say with my mouth."[62] Physically, he presented himself as a traditional news anchor with a serious demeanor, intense eye contact with the viewer, and less body movement than Stewart. While he occasionally broke character to kiss an over-the-shoulder graphic or engage in some physical silliness, such moments were exceptions. While playing the straight anchor to the viewers, he also engaged his studio audience and reacted to them—although in character. Just as he refused to admit mistakes, he also willingly misinterpreted audience reactions to align with the Colbert character's perceptions. During a segment of "The Wørd," Colbert says Rush Limbaugh was "praising Obama for being so conniving he makes Lex Luthor look like a candy striper." The text to the side of Colbert changes to say, "same candy striper who supplies Rush with Oxycontin," eliciting laughs and applause from the audience. Colbert, acting oblivious to the real source of humor and wanting to offer faux support to Limbaugh, comments, "I *am* making a good point, aren't I?"[63] The ignorance, the politics, the extremism, all these elements constituting the Colbert character required decoding by the audience—an ability to discern irony and reconstitute the message with that awareness. Colbert's reliance on irony created a different type of news parody than *TDS* and a multifaceted anchor persona.

The Presentational Complexity of Irony

From the headlines to the sign-off, every episode of *Colbert* trafficked in irony. His presentational mode was insincerity; even if Colbert did actually agree with one of his statements, the audience was left wondering. Stewart constituted his identity of sincerity and ethos primarily through satire. Although irony was a weapon he employed, satire was Stewart's primary mode of humor. Colbert used satire, but always within an ironic shell, saying the exact opposite of what he meant. As mentioned in the introduction, Linda Hutcheon conceives of irony, parody, and satire as overlapping circles.[64] Stewart and Colbert used all three on their Comedy Central shows, but Colbert fell more within irony and parody, while Stewart occupied a space closer to satire and parody. These separate means of presentation resulted in very different approaches and arguably greater acceptance for Stewart within the journalistic and political fields. Interacting with Colbert's character created more risk by being forced into either agreeing with or being attacked by outrageous comments, unable to shame or pin down the host. *Colbert*'s use of irony raised concerns from some media critics who suggested audiences may not see beyond the face value of the program's message.

Two studies demonstrate the complexity of audience perceptions of irony. In one, researchers found that viewing clips from *Colbert* actually increased young viewers' affinity for President George W. Bush and Republicans. The test subjects seemed unable to decode *Colbert*'s irony, suggesting that viewers might actually take away the exact opposite message than the one intended. The study only used short clips from the show and test subjects unfamiliar with *Colbert*, so the authors theorize regular viewers would likely have had fewer problems understanding the program's criticism.[65] Another study examined whether political affiliations affected viewers' interpretations of *Colbert*, finding similarly complex results. Audiences found clips humorous, regardless of political ideology; however, liberals perceived his humor as satiric, while conservatives believed Colbert was being genuinely critical of liberals.[66] These concerns about television viewer's misinterpretations of irony go back at least to the 1970s, when researchers found similar results with audiences watching *All in the Family*. Audience members who identified with Archie Bunker's bigoted views were less likely to identify statements as ironic.[67] The double-voice of irony always risks not being detected. *Colbert*'s use of parody created an even more layered text.

Both the look and content of *Colbert* mimic conservative news programs to such an extent that at least one researcher suggests they appear almost identical. Lisa Colletta compared the coverage of two stories about race from *Colbert* and *O'Reilly Factor*, and found the results troubling. Their strategies "are identical: reference to anecdote not facts, appeals to emotion rather than reason, use of 'everyman' language and syntax (including a racial slur), and the spinning of a probably racist agenda into something that appears caring and courageous."[68] She argues the parody, taken out of context, becomes indistinguishable from the original and each runs the risk of merely confirming an audience member's predisposed beliefs. Like the previous studies, Colletta raises an important note of warning: viewers unaware of personality-driven political programs or of the Colbert persona run the risk of misinterpreting the message. However, repeat viewing and increased familiarity with a genre's conventions reward audiences. A study of the Colbert online fan community found that only 11% seemed to not recognize the show's irony, and some of those respondents may, themselves, have been utilizing irony in their comments.[69] Colbert's fear of bears, for instance, would likely have left viewers mystified until it took on greater meaning through repeated viewing.

While there are legitimate concerns about irony in news parody, too little credit is given to audiences who consistently engage in ironic Internet memes and other sources of humor.

Although Colbert seemed to always be speaking the "untruth" of his beliefs on the show, the play of irony created an openness to the text. He utters a statement with insincerity that he must disagree with, so what *does* he mean? Kevin Decker suggests the Colbert persona lacks any true center, and, therefore, his irony forces viewers to examine their own ideas in comparison.[70] Rather than advocating a Habermassian-style public sphere like Stewart, Colbert seems closer to Foucault's genealogical process of questioning the very categories produced by culture. While interviewing Maryland Representative Donna Edwards, Colbert notes her district is the first majority African-American suburban congressional district. He then follows up, "I don't see race. I've evolved beyond that. I just pretend everybody's white and it's all good." Edwards then says Colbert's strategy would not work for her because she is black. Colbert stoically responds, "But I didn't know that until you told me. You see how you're the problem?"[71] Is Colbert commenting on his character's dependence on truthiness to create reality? Is the joke a commentary on Obama and post-racial utopianism? Does the sequence revisit the "colorblind" new racism of the 1980s? Is it merely absurdist? The answer to all these questions could be "yes."

Whereas Stewart's repeated appearances on *TDS* solidified the core of his utopian ideals for political and media discourse, frequent viewing of *Colbert* only left the same question—what does Colbert believe and is there an idealist vision underlying his comedy? K. A. Wisniewski suggests this very polysemy opens up the program for different types of audiences to make sense of the stories covered by the show. Viewers can applaud his patriotism while still rejecting conservative dogma.[72] This openness is a hallmark of postmodern humor and its use of irony.[73] The indeterminate stances can be reconfigured by savvy audiences while reflecting on their own desires and expectations for the public sphere. Admittedly, not every viewer would be expected to so actively engage the program, but the ironic form does open up the opportunity.

The Colbert persona represented a conflicted presence at the anchor desk. On the one hand, he brilliantly caricatured a conservative political host, shifting all aspects to their extremes: nationalist, ultraconservative, religiously dogmatic, and profoundly uninformed. Yet his ironic mode turned all of these qualities on their head. He sincerely delivered the news as he saw it to his audience, denying the statements as they were uttered. Despite their drastic difference in presentation and strategy, *Colbert* and *TDS* engaged the same subjects, often creating two voices of criticism querying each other and the audience.

PRESIDENTIAL POLITICS

While previous news parodies like *NNTN* and "Weekend Update" tackled the presidency and politics, those shows only aired weekly (or even more infrequently). Through four nights a week of coverage, *TDS* and *Colbert* created a deeper and more sustained criticism of the political process as a whole. The Comedy Central shows established comedic strategies for Presidents Bush and Obama during their two terms. Conventional wisdom and a number of commentators accused the programs of emphasizing partisanship in their coverage, favoring liberal policies and politicians; however, studies reveal a more complex dynamic.

Partisanship can, of course, be measured in a variety of ways. One content analysis looking at the time *TDS* devoted to coverage of presidential primaries leading up to the 2008 election found mostly equal airtime given to the two major parties. Once McCain became the presumptive favorite for the GOP, coverage tilted in favor of the Democrats as the battle between Obama and Hillary Clinton continued. In other words, *TDS*'s coverage roughly equaled the newsworthiness of each party's nomination process, shifting to more reporting on the Democrats after the Republicans locked in their pick. Interestingly, the study found more jokes about the Democrats and the media during the time period studied than about Republicans, although the content of the jokes were not analyzed.[74] Another study by the Pew Center found similar equity in terms of the politics of guests appearing on *TDS*; however, they reported harsher treatment of conservatives versus liberals.[75] The difference in partisan jokes is confirmed by an earlier *TDS* analysis conducted during the 2004 elections. That study found a higher number of jokes about the GOP and reported those jokes were more substantive, while humor about Democrats tended to be based on physical appearance. In addition, the study also compared attitudes of viewers, finding that watching *TDS* resulted in more negative perceptions of Bush and Cheney but no effect on opinions of the Democratic challengers.[76] With Bush running for a second term, Republicans were more likely to be criticized as the governing party; however, the results could suggest a partisan lean by the program.

Stewart and others involved in *TDS* denied charges of partisanship, claiming humor as their primary concern. In an early interview, Ben Karlin says, "We always cut to the funny." Stewart backs him up but emphasizes the critical nature of the humor, "What we go after are not actual policies, but the façade *behind* them."[77] The timing of *TDS* likely increased perceptions of partisanship. The program's rise in political content and popularity coincided with eight years of conservative governance under Bush, defining the outlook of the program in opposition to the administration. Both *TDS* and *Colbert* continued to hold politicians accountable under President Obama; however, viewers would be hard-pressed to argue the coverage is parallel. The progressive outlook of each program led to assumptions about freedom of speech, economic equality, and other ideological positions that affect coverage at every level, from gatekeeping to framing. However, the political outlook does not neatly align with Democrats and Republicans. Jeffrey Jones offers a more compelling framework by looking beyond simple partisanship to examine the guiding principles the show embodies.[78] *TDS* and *Colbert* focused more on revealing hypocrisy and illusion *across* politics than forwarding a specific political agenda. *Quality* of discourse, both from the media and politicians, took center stage and set the tone for their coverage.

W—the Punchline

Coverage of the 2000 presidential election left little doubt where *TDS* would take its comedy if Bush were to win the White House. In the same article emphasizing the show's nonpartisanship, Karlin reflected on the Republican nominee, saying "This is just a clear case of one candidate being inferior to the other. . . . It's so obvious he's wrong in every way."[79] Karlin's statement reflects the general tone of *TDS* toward Bush across the campaign and even into his presidency. The night the Supreme Court settled the election by awarding Florida's votes to Bush, *TDS* led first with the Court's action, then covered Al Gore's concession with extended sound bites, and finally got to Bush. Supposedly introducing a video of Bush's reaction to Gore's speech, the show then rolls a video of the cartoon character Yosemite Sam shooting himself into the air with two guns pointed at the ground. Part of Bush's actual speech then rolls, discussing how the election of Thomas Jefferson took multiple ballots. Stewart, speaking for Bush and with an image of Sherman Hemsley over his shoulder, continues, "Me, I'm not even *George* Jefferson." The dialogue with Bush's video continues:

BUSH: I was not elected to serve one party.
STEWART: You were not elected.
BUSH: I have something else to ask you, to ask every American. I ask for you to pray for this great nation.
STEWART: [speaking softly] We're way ahead of ya'. [80]

Tapping into the dominant comedic mode at the time, *TDS* presented Bush as unintelligent, unsophisticated, and childlike. In future years, this portrayal would continue to resonate, but with the invasion of Iraq, the so-called war on terror, and attacks on civil liberties, the show's coverage of Bush became more heated, treating him less like a man-child and more like a dangerously ignorant and potentially devious leader.

Following 9/11, Bush experienced overwhelming support from both the public and traditional media. *TDS* continued to question certain policy decisions, but coverage of Bush was less aggressive than before the attacks. Bush's first State of the Union address only garnered a couple of easy jokes. The program played Bush's opening statement, "As we gather here tonight, our nation is at war, our economy is in recession, and the civilized world faces unprecedented dangers." Stewart followed with, "and that's just my first year."[81] Foreign policy, such as Bush's reference to the Axis of Evil, barely ranked a mention. Stewart and Colbert did engage in a dialogue warning that Bush's economic plans would lead to large deficits; however, the focus was on policy, not the president himself. During America's steady march to war in Iraq from 2002 to 2003, *TDS* devoted increased coverage to international apprehension over the nation's military plans and the lack of any proof of weapons of mass destruction.

After the invasion of Iraq, Stewart expressed concern over the tone of public discourse and the administration attacking any dissent as unpatriotic. In what became a classic segment of *TDS*, Stewart announces, "Tonight, we're going to have an honest, open debate between the president of the United States and the one man we believe has the insight and cojones to stand up to him." Stewart then, in a masterfully edited sequence, moderates a debate between 2002 President Bush and Governor Bush from two years earlier when he was running for president, with Governor Bush disagreeing with statements from the president. The debate sometimes uses split screen to make it seem as if the two Bushes are reacting to each other. In one example, the president states, "We will tear down the apparatus of terror and we will help you to build a new Iraq that is prosperous and free." Governor Bush responds, "I don't think our troops ought to be used for what's called nation-building." The segment reportedly took two weeks to create, using multiple VHS cassettes.[82] In the absence of public dialogue and the hesitancy of television journalists to ask hard questions leading up to Iraq, the segment stands out for holding Bush accountable for his policy shifts.

Over the remainder of Bush's presidency, both *TDS* and *Colbert* continued to cover the wars in Iraq and Afghanistan at a time when many mainstream television news sources were no longer devoting as much space to the conflicts. Stewart regularly covered the wars using the graphic "Mess O'Potamia," and leaned into criticism of the administration. Looking back, he says, "The war was something incredibly visceral, and it was the first time where I had a sense of we, as a nation, had turned down an incredibly dangerous and wrong path and had committed fully to it."[83] However, the shows were able to show support for American troops, while continuing to critique the administration's handling of the war.[84] *TDS* correspondents Rob Riggle and Colbert even visited troops in Iraq.

True to his character, Colbert supported Bush with irony from the very beginning of his television show, tying his admiration for truthiness directly to the president. Standing up for Bush amidst concern over policies toward torturing detainees, Colbert points to Bush's statement that his administration is acting within the law. Colbert then argues, "If we're doing it, it's legal, okay? Torture is illegal, ergo—and that's Latin for bite me—we do not torture. So, Senator McCain, stop trying to take our right away to do it, because it doesn't exist."[85] Colbert generally ran with Bush's logic, making it all the more absurd. Throughout Bush's second term, Colbert advocated the conservative policies of the administration and took their rationales to illogical extremes. In a later controversy over the firing of United States attorneys, the administration stipulated former counsel Harriet Miers and political advisor Karl Rove could only be questioned in private interviews without oaths or transcripts. Colbert praised Bush for compromising and noted, "See, the president's just trying to save the country from another painful perjury trial!"[86]

Colbert's appearance at the 2006 White House Correspondents Dinner proved to be his ultimate commentary on the Bush presidency. The host unleashed a scathingly ironic speech on the president, leaving everyone looking uncomfortable: "The greatest thing about this man is he's steady. You know where he stands. He believes the same thing Wednesday that he believed on Monday, no matter what happened Tuesday. Events can change; this man's beliefs never will."[87] Colbert presented the president as out of touch and inflexible, an image already constructed nightly on the Comedy Central shows.[88]

In the waning days of Bush's second term, *TDS* coverage continued to focus on the administration's actions and policies, especially in the president's "reflective" comments on his legacy. *World News Tonight*'s Charles Gibson asked the president if there was an "uh-oh moment" in his presidency. Stewart, in outrage, responds, "An uh-oh moment? Why do we have to talk to this jackass like he's four? When did foolhardy war and an economic collapse become uh-oh moments?"[89] In these end-of-term interviews, Stewart expressed outrage both at the tepid questions and Bush's responses. Covering Bush's farewell address, *TDS* played a clip of the president: "You may not agree with some of the tough decisions I had made, but I hope you can agree that I was willing to make the tough decisions." Stewart, imitating Bush, responds, "The things that I did may have been catastrophically wrong, but I think we can all agree I *did* do them."[90]

TDS and *Colbert* were overwhelmingly negative in coverage of Bush, but whether partisanship was the primary reason is open to interpretation. Satire always targets those in control, and not only was Bush president, but the expansion of powers given to and taken by him after 9/11 only increased the potential for criticism and satire. The Bush administration's repeated inventions of facts and incorporation of the logic of truthiness also created plenty of opportunities for playing conflicting sound bites.[91] Due to their increased influence, both programs helped to define Bush in the American consciousness. Unsurprisingly, Bush never accepted repeated invitations to be a guest on either show.

Yes, but Can We? Coverage of Obama

Unlike his predecessor, Barack Obama appeared as a guest on *TDS* multiple times both before and after becoming president. Less than two weeks before the 2008 election, Stewart hosted Obama via satellite. Following the cheers of the audience, the host noted, "Our audience, very excited sir. Clearly our show, not a swing show." Like the *TDS* interview of John Kerry four years earlier, Stewart asked easy questions of the candidate about campaign activities and strategy, even inviting Obama to respond to conservative fears about an Obama presidency.[92] The program offered a friendly venue for a Democratic nominee to excite young viewers already likely to lean progressive. Initial *TDS* coverage of Obama as both candidate and president tended to be accommodating, giving him the benefit of the doubt, and presenting him as a welcome alternative to the John McCain/Sarah Palin GOP ticket.

Leading up to the election and in the early days of the administration, most of *TDS*'s Obama humor revolved around inflated rhetoric labeling him the candidate of change and the fact that Obama was something of a blank slate, not yet defined in the political imagination. While covering the Democratic National Convention, *TDS* presented a fake nominating film supposedly leaked to the program called "Barack Obama: He Completes Us." The feature distills varies discourses about Obama into a condensed code of signifiers. Opening with black-and-white images of conflict, partisanship, and a burning US flag, a narrator introduces America as a country torn apart, but "a hero will come." Shifting to the full-color opening sunrise from Disney's *The Lion King*, complete with instantly recognizable chants and music, the film interweaves enthusiastic comments about Obama with the Disney scene of Simba's introduction on top of Pride Rock. The music builds, and the monkey Rafiki lifts the lion cub to reveal an animated Barack Obama face on Simba's body. The film ties Obama to an American fairy tale of success through hard work but introduced through a Disneyfied African story, invoking the candidate's mixed cultural heritage and also ascribing a mythic quality to Obama's success. The first scene could be interpreted in multiple ways, invoking an almost messianic framework and presenting the candidate's success as a "too good to be true" type of fairy tale. The film continues, borrowing heavily from the presentational style of historical documentaries, using animations, Ken Burns-style photo effects, and fake archival footage (showing Raj from *What's Happening!!* as a teenage Obama, for instance). The candidate's history is presented as the reconciliation of conflicts: white and black, Christian and Muslim, land mammal and sea creature, with the narrative ultimately suggesting Obama will help the nation overcome all its divisions. "Now, at the precipice of a new age, one man seems ready-enough-ish to lead. One man who will once more unite the world." As the film ends, the continents on a spinning globe come together to form Obama's face.[93] While not a negative piece, the film satirically exaggerates discourses about hope, change, post-racialism, and the hype surrounding a largely untested political candidate. Humor about Obama on *TDS* commonly wove in this sense of caution and disbelief—not rejecting these discourses but approaching the nominee as an open text that voters were filling with their own hopes and desires.

Exaggerations about Obama continued after his election, with the *TDS* post-election special adding a new segment, "Greatness Watch: Road to Rushmore" with a graphic of the president-elect's face added to the monument. A montage of cable news' in-depth coverage of Obama's meeting with President Bush sets up the story, with pundits interpreting the body language of the two men in absurd detail. Stewart and correspondents Samantha Bee, Jason Jones, and Aasif Mandvi discuss the "twenty-second" clip of the meeting. Bee says she was struck by "the grandeur of the man in the moment making history [*with slow motion video running*]. Just look at the way the president-elect grasped his predecessor's hand—swift, precise, breathtaking, thumb over fingers, interlocking. If he continues to greet world leaders with this kind of handshake, history may well judge him to be the greatest president of all time." Mandvi disagrees and dismisses the handshake but points to Obama's portico walk with Bush, "a healthy, young black man striding beside a decrepit, barely-ambulatory white man. A historical tableau that I've entitled 'Driving Mr. Daisy.'"[94] The segment criticizes the media's overanalysis of insignificant detail, but also continues to play on the over-hyping of Obama, with the media and American people as the actual target of the humor.

Subsequent years brought tougher coverage of Obama from *TDS* and more bipartisan reproach for Congress. The politics of the show continued to lean progressive, and as a result their criticisms of Obama never reached the kind of sustained, vehement objections leveled at Bush. One of the *TDS*'s main lines of satire against Obama was his continuation of Bush-era policies, opening a gap between campaign rhetoric and presidential actions. The program pointedly criticized the administration's secrecy after Obama promised increased government transparency. Stewart dives into a spirited condemnation of the president's policies after Obama refused to release images of prisoner abuse in Iraq. A clip of Obama plays, with the president saying such photos would "flame anti-American opinion and put our troops in greater danger." Stewart points out the irony of Obama's statement that torturing prisoners to keep America safe creates pictures that would make the nation unsafe and then asks, "Is there any line we still will not cross?" The program cuts to coverage about a soldier who translates Arabic being dismissed from the military because he is gay. Stewart responds in outrage, "So it was okay to waterboard a guy over eighty times, but God forbid the guy who can understand what that prick was saying has a boyfriend!" More media coverage follows, explaining that despite supporting the rights of gay soldiers, the president will not intervene in any cases. Stewart then reminds viewers to always "check the fine print," as they cut to an image of Obama giving a speech with a "Yes We Can" sign on the podium and then shows a close up of the sign, with a tiny phrase underneath: "But that doesn't necessarily mean we're going to."[95] Moments of condemnation like this are much fewer than in the Bush era, but they reveal the show's alignment with the progressive disappointment of Obama failing to live up to desires for a more active and transparent government.

Response to Obama's election from *Colbert* was predictable, given the show's ironic conservative mode. After the election, the program described how Kenya declared a state holiday and showed other nations celebrating Obama's election. Colbert, in character, condemns the international response, minimizing the election and saying America already honors all presidents on President's Day under the founder's original plans, "with a half-off sale at J.C. Penney."[96] Tapping into his previously established "color-blindness," Colbert condemned any mention of the historic nature of Obama's election, accusing Democrats of being secret racists and only voting for Obama to get him out of the Senate: "Notice how they give him his own separate, but equal branch of government."[97] The show parallels some of *TDS*'s criticisms—for instance, Obama's failure to adopt policies he campaigned on; however, Colbert's mode of imitating O'Reilly and other cable-news personalities also linked his humor to prevailing conservative rhetoric.

Following Obama's election, in an out-of-character interview on *Fresh Air*, Colbert says he saw new trends in the messaging of right-wing pundits. Presaging the rise of Trump, conservatives claimed America was ripped away by liberals and has to be restored: "There's been this sense that you mustn't criticize America because it's perfect. But then again, America is in the toilet and we have to fix it. This strange paradox: America is perfect, and we must fix it."[98] Adopting this position from conservatives and taking it to extremes, Colbert's character argued "real Americans" must take back the nation, but the show highlighted the most divisive personalities engaged in this rhetoric, like Glenn Beck and Michele Bachmann, undercutting the argument.

Criticism of Obama on *Colbert* often functioned both to challenge conservative claims and to defend the president. Following the killing of Osama bin Laden in 2010 and GOP complaints of Obama's taking credit, Colbert condemned the president for being in office at the time of the raid and thus politicizing it: "This president is so desperate for a bump in the polls to push his agenda, that he took the easy road of killing the world's most wanted man."[99] By limiting the program to the replication and parody of conservative cable programs that relentlessly attacked Obama, *Colbert* actually created more consistently supportive coverage of Obama than *TDS*, although encased within its ironic framework.

In examining the coverage of the last two presidents by *TDS* and *Colbert*, conclusions could be drawn about the programs' partisanship. Bush certainly received harsher treatment from both shows. Early *TDS* coverage of Bush's presidency focused criticism on his policies rather than his character and dismissively presented the president as being out-of-his-league. By his second term, though, stories increasingly ascribed more agency and responsibility to the president, directing their satire at his motives as well as his agenda. *Colbert* took the latter route with its ironic blessings of Bush, presenting him as ideological and inflexible. Coverage of Obama mostly stayed away from character attacks. Rather than impugning his motives, the programs called attention to the disconnect between his rhetoric and actions. The political reporting on both programs defies easy categorizations, though. More than presidents or even political parties, the two news-parody programs targeted a lack of humility and public integrity from the powerful, broadening their focus to include a vast array of elected and unelected officials: staffers, lobbyists, business leaders, and so on. *TDS* and *Colbert* attempted to expose the broken aspects of America's political, economic, and social systems.

KILLING THE MESSENGERS: NEWS PARODY AS MEDIA CORRECTIVE

A 2012 report from the Pew Center outlined the state of the media after the first decade of the new millennium, describing how deep cuts in personnel and funding over the previous decade severely reduced reporting across traditional media. The study warned, "This adds up to a news industry that is more undermanned and unprepared to uncover stories, dig deep into emerging ones or to question information put into its hands."[100] Since the 1990s, television news, especially cable, had increasingly turned its back on traditional public policy coverage and investigative stories, opting for ratings-driven tragedies and scandals, inexpensive pundit roundtables, infotainment, and public relations. Audience trust had fallen to an all-time low in 2012, with 56% of the public believing the information from major news organizations, down from 71% ten years earlier (although trust has plummeted even further since then).[101] *TDS* and *Colbert* developed during these shifts, fashioning themselves as both critics of the state of the media and correctives.

One of the most frequently identified problems with modern journalism is a constrained view of objectivity. There are still high-quality journalism outlets that incorporate objectivity, while still producing truth and holding the powerful to account. However, many organizations, especially on television and online, utilize a vulgar objectivity that reduces any issue into dichotomous viewpoints and becomes a routine to insulate reporters from claims of bias. This type of objectivity encourages journalists to shy away from asking hard questions about political framing and conflicting information and allows politicians to set the news agenda. Without the support of a publication dedicated to protecting and supporting quality journalism, a reporter's fear of seeming subjective can prevent them from functioning as a watchdog.

A critique of journalistic objectivity was one of the major themes of both *TDS* and *Colbert*. By trying to focus on facts to the exclusion of analysis and perspective, some journalists inevitably fall prey to the rhetoric and machinations of politicians and power structures in society. Writing in the 1920s, Walter Lippmann argued that news and truth could overlap at times but only for brief moments; otherwise, reporting is about uncertainty and personal perspective.[102] News-parody programs in the 2000s and 2010s have embraced this uncertainty as a mode of inquiry. Their coverage seeks to produce more discussion of a given event rather than cutoff discussion by proclaiming the truth. In interviews, Stewart seemed to commiserate with the plight of journalists: "If they feel like they express any moral authority or judgment, which is what you would imagine is editorial control, that they will be vilified."[103] However, at the same time, Stewart held the press accountable for their craft and demanded more courage from the media. Colbert's concept of truthiness operates as the flipside of extreme objectivity, setting up absolute truth against unproven belief. More partisan media, like Fox News and MSNBC, actually share a commonality with news parody: each feature more stories *about* the press than the networks.[104] *Columbia Review of Journalism*'s Michael Hoyt suggests both Fox News and *TDS* (and, by extension, *Colbert*) can be viewed as "reactions to distorted objectivity."[105] The Comedy Central programs advocated an idealist view of journalism and satirically pointed out the areas where the press falls short.

Critiquing News Routine

The humor of *TDS* and *Colbert* expanded beyond a parody of visual news style to include satire of the highly routinized newsgathering and reporting process. News continually replicates itself, leading to pre-created stories to be filled with current information. The presidential campaign as a horse race story, for instance, is a kind of simulacra, using Jean Baudrillard's designation for a copy without an original.[106] Beyond simply its presentational mode, the entire process of newsgathering operates under its own logic and routines. Discussing the 2006 White House Correspondents Dinner, Robert Tally, Jr. suggests Colbert's speech received so little coverage specifically because it revealed the assembled press as "simulacra of simulacra," journalists unaware of their own fake standing.[107] Colbert reminded the media of the way journalism now works: "The President makes decisions. He's the decider. The press secretary announces those decisions, and you people of the press type those decisions down. Make, announce, type." Since they no longer practice journalism, Colbert then suggested members of the press could use their free time to "write that novel you got kicking around in your head. You know, the one about the intrepid Washington reporter with the courage to stand up to the administration? You know, fiction!"[108] Colbert, embodying the role of the satirist, reminded the press how they sometimes fail to live up to their own calling: a call for action met with silence. Through parody, these shows delighted in stripping away the veneer from news, in revealing its own constructed nature.

As discussed in the last chapter, the move to 24-hour media and the need to fill all that time, along with the rise of infotainment and the constant fight for exclusive coverage, drove television newsworthiness into a tailspin. *TDS* and *Colbert* frequently commented on this extensive coverage of inconsequential events and speculation. After months of stories on the American embassy attack in Benghazi, Libya, in 2012, three so-called whistleblowers were expected to testify in front of a House committee. *Colbert* aired a montage of Fox News coverage anticipating the testimony and discussing potential information that might be revealed before finishing the clip with Chris Wallace admitting that journalists have no idea what the content of the testimony will be. Colbert followed with, "this is the best possible kind of political story. We have no idea what's in it and it's going to be explosive! [*making hand motions of an explosion*] It's the Taco Bell of breaking news!" Talking heads were spending hours speculating about testimony they expected to occur, but with no actual details.

The decreased emphasis on audience impact as a news value, as well as fewer filters on ethical propriety led to the kind of story *TDS* covered after Obama's first election: the presidential daughters' first day of school in the nation's capital. Stewart introduces the story, saying, "As the economy continues to struggle and the Middle East continues to burn, there was big news yesterday out of Washington." A montage of news clips follows showing Malia and Sasha Obama on their way to school, discussions about a doll hanging off their backpacks, and even a graphic with their food choices for lunch. With Sasha's face pressed up against the glass of the SUV driving them to school, a reporter says, "The first day of school is stressful." Cut back to Stewart, looking stone-faced, who responds, "I don't think that's first day of school stress. That's, 'Mommy, there are so many cameras. Am I integrating this school?'"[109] Both *Colbert* and *TDS* regularly featured such excesses from television news, advocating for a more relevant concept of newsworthiness.

The Comedy Central programs' more general critiques of the media occasionally morphed into attacks on specific news programs and individuals.[110] One of the earliest and most celebrated confrontations occurred on the former CNN program *Crossfire*. Emblematic of the "partisan yelling as talk show" genre, *Crossfire* featured conservative Tucker Carlson and liberal Paul Begala bickering about politics. In 2004, Stewart appeared on the show and immediately began questioning the very structure of *Crossfire*, challenging the hosts to foster useful discourse about politics. His complaints reinforced jokes previously made on *TDS* about *Crossfire*'s lack of journalistic integrity. Refusing to be sidetracked by questions about current politics, Stewart pressed his attack on *Crossfire*, "it's not so much that it's bad, as it's hurting America." Stewart then describes how such shows become part of political strategy, calling the hosts partisan hacks and discounting the value of the discussions they create. When Begala tries to defend their format as presenting useful discourse, Stewart responds, "But that's like saying pro wrestling is a show about athletic competition."[111] Stewart's appearance went viral and was repeatedly dissected and retransmitted by the media.[112] Joanne Morreale demonstrates, using Aristotle's deliberative and epideictic rhetoric, how Stewart, as a mix of entertainer and journalist, was challenging hosts of a show that also mixed these modes of address.[113] The criticism seemed to resonate with audiences, and several months later CNN canceled the program, partly in response to Stewart's appearance.[114] The pleas for civil discourse to enrich the public sphere regularly resurfaced from both Stewart and Colbert in their vision for a "better journalism," along with pleas for responsible coverage of politics and business.

Following the meltdown of financial markets and companies in the late 2000s, *TDS* turned its coverage to the business sector, specifically CNBC. In March 2009, *TDS* played eight minutes of footage and commentary that juxtaposed CNBC hosts' financial advice with facts about how damaging their advice actually was. For instance, a montage of CNBC personalities enthusiastically endorsing Bear Stearns is followed by a graphic stating, "Bear Stearns went under six days later." Over and over, the program shows how following the advice of the financial network would have been catastrophic. Ending the segment, Stewart shows CNBC host Karl Quintanilla interviewing Allen Stanford, a man who was later discovered to have been stealing billions of dollars from investors in a Ponzi scheme.

STEWART: Come on CNBC's Carl Quintanilla, you got one of the biggest white-collar criminals in history live on the air. Don't let him get off the hook!
QUINTANILLA: Before we let you go . . .
STEWART: Here it comes, the million-dollar question!
QUINTANILLA: Is it fun being a billionaire?
STANFORD: Well . . . yes, yes, I have to say it is fun being a billionaire.
STEWART: Fuck you! You know, between the two of 'em, I can't decide which one of those guys I'd rather see in jail![115]

Stewart's withering attack on the journalistic malfeasance of CNBC quickly became a hot topic in the media.

CNBC *Mad Money* host Jim Cramer took to the airwaves across several NBC platforms to dismiss *TDS* and Stewart and argue clips were taken out of context, in a move he undoubtedly quickly regretted. Stewart responded by devoting a segment exclusively to Cramer's complaint that *TDS* took his advice to buy Bear Stearns out of context. The program combines a range of clips from the time period in question, showing that Cramer not only endorsed purchasing Bear Stearns stock but also advised holding onto it as the meltdown neared. As the feud continued, Cramer eventually appeared on *TDS* as a guest, subjecting himself to an entire episode of tough questioning.[116] Cramer acted with as much humility as he could muster. Stewart, rolling clip after clip, followed up with statements like, "I can't reconcile the brilliance and knowledge that you have of the intricacies of the market with the crazy bullshit I see you do every night." While refusing to let him off the hook, the *TDS* host acknowledged Cramer had become the face of a larger problem, but accused the media of being complicit in the inside games of the finance industry: "I understand you want to make finance entertaining, but it's not a fucking game. . . . I can't tell you how angry that makes me."[117] *TDS* tied its coverage of the finance media to lawmakers and the president with a regular feature called "Clusterf#@k to the Poor House." Jeffrey Jones points to the show's overall coverage of the economic recession, including the Cramer battle, as emblematic of the kind of journalism news parody can provide.[118] Although the financial media took the spotlight on *TDS* for a period of time during the recession, the consistent favorite target for both Stewart and Colbert was conservative icon Fox News.

Fox News and Its Parody of Journalism

In his book *Television and American Culture*, Jason Mittell details a number of similarities between *TDS* and Fox News. Both rose to prominence during roughly the same time period, each appeals to niche audiences—older suburban and rural viewers for Fox and younger, urban audiences with the Comedy Central program—and each produces a brand of news meant to entertain and appeal to emotions.[119] As discussed in the introduction, Dannagal Goldthwaite Young proposes that liberal satire and conservative political-opinion shows even serve similar functions for their political constituents and suggests that both *TDS* and Fox News were identifying problems with modern journalism from their own perspectives.[120] In many ways, Fox News and *TDS* existed as parallel entities, attracting audiences dissatisfied with current mainstream journalism. For *TDS* and *Colbert*, however, Fox News represented the greatest threat to media, embodying the concept of truthiness by presenting lies and blind partisanship *as* objective—"fair and balanced." Colbert says discrediting the mainstream press is essential for the right wing "because a press that has validity is a press that has authority. And as soon as there's any authority to what the press says, you question the authority of the government."[121] Geoffrey Baym and Jeffrey Jones seem to agree, accusing Fox News of participating in a broader effort on the political right to challenge existing ways of knowing and define its own truth.[122] Fox News existed at the time as an alternative, "conservative approved" media outlet, working to discount the press and challenge government from its own ideological perspective, leading *TDS* and *Colbert* to regularly criticize the network and dissect its partisan strategies.

During and after Obama's election, glaring moments of Fox partisanship appeared regularly on *TDS*. Before the 2008 election, *TDS* presented a montage of Fox personalities questioning whether Obama really was leading in polls, ending with a reporter asking people whom they planned to vote for. After each person says "Obama," the Fox reporter turns to the camera and explains, "The key is not who they like, the key is who they're going to vote for." Cut back to a smirking Stewart, who says, "Fox News: the world is unfair, and we're becoming mentally unbalanced."[123] After the election, in a "Baracknophobia" segment, Stewart outlines how gun sales are rising and details other paranoid responses to the new president, then questions, "Where's all the fear coming from?" before showing a montage of Fox personalities talking about Obama being sure to endorse socialism, encourage radicals, silence dissent, and so on.[124] The program regularly ripped away the façade of the "we report, you decide" tagline and established how the network constructed the news to manipulate reaction.

One of the most conspicuous indicators of the partisanship Fox News denies was its repeated endorsement of conservative groups through publicity and material support. Both *TDS* and *Colbert* regularly satirized Fox host Glenn Beck, especially Beck's decision to create "grassroots" staged demonstrations for conservative politics. In launching his "9-12 project," advocating conservative ideals, Beck claimed his fantasy had come true. Colbert follows a clip of Beck's announcement, asking, "The fantasy where a hysterical Glenn Beck tells his audience of desperate shut-ins through tears and spittle that vague unnamed enemies have failed them and that it's time to take angry action?" The show continues with clips of Beck, eventually cryptically saying, "Truth is, they don't surround us. We surround them." Colbert follows up, "who are *them*? *Thems* the ones we're surrounding. And *we*? *We're* the voices in Glenn's head telling him to get us to take back what is rightfully ours."[125] Colbert actually seemed to find it hard to stay in character during such extreme rhetoric, endorsing Beck on the one hand, but also going beyond irony to more openly mock him.

TDS and *Colbert* also underscored Fox News' political hypocrisy, comparing how the network would shift coverage of an event depending on the political moment. The network's switch in priorities between the 2012 Republican and Democratic national conventions presented plenty of opportunities for satire with a segment called "Last Week/This Week." *TDS* presented Fox clips from the GOP convention with correspondents downplaying the importance of party platforms, followed by repeated discussions on the channel about the absence of God in the DNC platform. Fox pundits also accused the rest of the media of playing up social issues during the Republican event, inevitably juxtaposed with the network doing the same during the Democratic convention.[126] In another *TDS* story, footage rolls of Fox News Money anchor Lou Dobbs endorsing Mitt Romney's suggestion to defund *Sesame Street* to save $8 million. The clip is edited with Dobbs's earlier dismissal of Obama's idea to cut $4 billion in tax breaks for big oil, with the commentator calling the saving "inconsequential." Responding to the *Sesame Street* controversy, Stewart says, "I see; so Fox News is upset that empty-headed puppets are trying to brainwash and indoctrinate Americans? . . . Perhaps you could sue them. The charge would be copyright infringement."[127] While political differences helped inspire the enmity *TDS* and Stewart displayed for Fox News, the network's journalistic methods were the real target. Just like their criticisms of the rest of the media, the news-parody programs focused on divisive discourse, hypocrisy, inaccuracies, the inconsequential, and the devotion to broadcast-news conventional wisdom. The conservative network simply offered low-hanging fruit for such satire.

FOX NEWS SELF-OWNS: *THE ½ HOUR NEWS HOUR*

As the two Comedy Central shows were increasing their criticism of Fox News, the conservative network decided they could do parody too. In 2007, they attempted to subvert Stewart and Colbert's criticism with their own conservative version of *TDS* dubbed *The ½ Hour News Hour*, the brainchild of *24* cocreator Joel Surnow. Rather than imitating news format, the program was more akin to *TW3*, with lots of stand-up commentary and political sketches mixed with news-style headlines and reports. In its short run, the program attracted conservative stalwarts like Rush Limbaugh, Ann Coulter, and even former "Weekend Update host Dennis Miller. Despite strong initial numbers for its premiere (1.5 million viewers), curiosity quickly turned to lack of interest, and the program was canceled that same year after just 17 episodes.[128]

The program was conservative in an overt, calculated fashion that was in sharp contrast to the more organically arising liberalism of *TDS*. Whereas Stewart and Colbert would occasionally attack Democrats and point out logical inconsistencies of those on the left, *The ½ Hour News Hour* hewed tightly to conservative dogma and Fox News editorial ideology. Talent on the show lacked the perceived sincerity of Jon Stewart. The program offered a revolving door of conservative-talk stock villains: global-warming researchers, atheists, apologists for American power, the LGBTQ+community, Muslims, and so on. On their pilot episode, an anchor reports that if Hillary Clinton wins, she plans to staff the White House with "a diverse, multi-ethnic, multi-generational group of angry lesbians."[129] In another news segment, a correspondent from Iraq depressingly relates the bad news that American military casualties are down and that forces continue to take territory, satirically suggesting the news media root against America. Young identifies that one problem with the show was a seeming misunderstanding on behalf of the writers of how comedy works: satire invites the audience to make connections and to understand the humor themselves, often through incongruence. Instead, the Fox News show hits the audience over the head with the point. Satire, as Young describes, is a mode of persuasion that appeals more to politically liberal audiences. As conservatives, Fox News viewers likely share "psychological traits that make people less comfortable with and less appreciative of political satire."[130]

Along with the potential mismatch for its audience, *The ½ Hour News Hour* producers repeatedly violated the expectation of "punching up" at those in power. They did include segments specifically making fun of politicians like Nancy Pelosi, but also made fun of the victims of sexual assault, the LGBTQ+ community, and undocumented residents. Geoffrey Baym makes clear that the network seemed to totally misunderstand the spirit of political parody: "If the power of parody lies in its ability to offer a form of resistance, a counter-weight to discourses of hegemony, ½ *Hour* instead functioned as an agent of hegemony, using comedy in support of institutional power and its political-economic agenda."[131] The failure of conservative news parody (or at least its only major attempt) definitely seems connected to a fundamental miscalculation that satiric humor and parody can serve any ideological goal, whether supporting dominant power structures or attempting to undercut them. However, beyond the strategic mismatch, the airwaves and cable systems were already flooded with conservative media mocking their enemies, dismissive of progressive values and continually setting up straw-man arguments against their opponents in a peculiar style of didactic humor. In essence, Rush Limbaugh and other conservative hosts already produced news parody, both intentionally and unintentionally.

CONCLUSIONS ON NEWS PARODY IN THE 2000S

The analysis of *TDS* and *Colbert* in this chapter approaches the programs as active participants in the journalistic and political fields, functioning both as correctives and supplements to mainstream journalism. However, the shows also replicated some of the same problems facing media. Their reliance on press outlets for much of their source material was problematic as cuts in budgets and staffing constrained what might be available for them to satirize.[132] Some research has shown that the programs replicated inaccuracies by repeating claims from other media sources without fact-checking, suggesting such programs should create their own ethical criteria.[133] Although the programs engaged in criticism of media, they also partook in the same commercialized media structure under Viacom, one of the most powerful media companies in the world (now merged into the even-larger ViacomCBS). Although the programs critiqued the journalistic media system and its practices, it would be naive to omit that those programs also supported and reconstituted the very same system grounded in ratings and commercialism.

The Comedy Central programs reshaped and redirected the news-parody genre. Rather than integrating news-style content with a sketch or topical comedy, *TDS* and *Colbert* formed blocks of news parody, closely simulating the look of broadcast and cable news through contemporary technology. These programs then filled out their half hour with news interviews that extended their critical mode. Their focus on national public-affairs news, rather than personality-driven and entertainment topics, created a formula for news parody more likely to discursively crossover into the journalistic field.

Developing during the post-network era of television, the two programs are further set apart from others in the genre by benefiting from multiplatforming and active fan communities. Distribution in the early 2000s was limited to broadcast or physical media for almost all television series. *TDS* was an early online success, with short clips that could be successfully streamed at the limited speeds of the day. Unlike narrative programming, the clips could be appreciated even when removed from the context of the episode. As Baym notes, both *TDS* and *Colbert* were perfectly positioned to be repurposed across multiple platforms.[134] Audiences could eventually access content from the two shows by viewing the cable channel, downloading via iTunes and other services, streaming online from their individual web pages, or as embedded links on social media.

The growth of Internet use in the post-network era also created new opportunities for connecting with television fans, allowing both programs to foster community and a dedicated following. John Hartley discusses how television generates a new kind of identity formation, set not in location, race, or other traditional cultural concepts but by creating a kind of "republic of television."[135] The dedicated audiences of these Comedy Central programs constituted a much more active sub-category of this larger viewing republic, with many viewers directly connecting with other fans. Colbert's carefully cultivated "The Colbert Nation" concept fed into this dedicated fan base.[136] Jeffrey Jones illustrates how Colbert's fans operated as a further parody of right-wing political hosts and their rabid fan communities.[137] Both *Colbert* and *TDS* fostered a kind of insider mentality through repeat jokes. Writers would flatter the audiences of the two shows by incorporating high culture or Internet culture, making the audience "in on the joke." Colbert invited his audience to participate online, such as through different "Green Screen Challenges," where viewers could download video, replace the background, and then upload their video to the Colbert Nation site. One video featured Colbert fighting with a lightsaber; another included John McCain and invited the audience to make the politician more exciting. All these various activities were invitations for viewers to participate in fan activities beyond their nightly viewing, harnessing digital, two-way technologies and new channels of communication (including social media) to foster an audience of savvy, politically engaged viewers aware of both the shortcomings of traditional journalism and the potential for its reconstitution.

NOTES

1. *The Daily Show with Jon Stewart*, November 9, 2006.
2. Chris Smith, *The Daily Show (The Book)* (New York: Grand Central Publishing, 2016), 73.
3. *The Daily Show with Jon Stewart*, September 20, 2001.
4. Ari Fleischer, "Press Briefing," White House, updated September 26, 2001, https://georgewbush-whitehouse.archives.gov/news/releases/2001/09/20010926-5

.html#BillMaher-Comments. Some have claimed Fleischer's comments were meant in a broader context, not only referring to Maher, but also racist characterizations in the wake of the attacks.

5. Jeffrey P. Jones, *Entertaining Politics: New Political Television and Civic Culture* (Lanham, MD: Rowman & Littlefield Publishers, Inc., 2005), 80–84.

6. "The Daily Show," *Rolling Stone*, 2001.

7. Paul Achter, "Comedy in Unfunny Times: News Parody and Carnival after 9/11," *Critical Studies in Media Communication* 25, no. 3 (2008).

8. Smith, *The Daily Show (The Book)*, 84.

9. "News Audiences Increasingly Politicized," Pew Research Center, updated June 8, 2004, https://www.pewresearch.org/politics/2004/06/08/news-audiences-increasingly-politicized/.

10. "Public Knowledge of Current Affairs Little Changed by News and Information Revolutions," Pew Research Center, updated April 15, 2007, http://people-press.org/report/319/public-knowledge-of-current-affairs-little-changed-by-news-and-information-revolutions.

11. Marian Sandberg, "Daily Dose," *Live Design*, updated July 1, 2007, https://www.livedesignonline.com/venues/daily-dose.

12. Jim Hanas, "And That's the Way It Isn't," *Print Magazine*, October, 2008, 52.

13. For more detail about the mimicking of visual news style on *TDS*, see Lawrence J. Mullen, "Visual Aspects of *The Daily Show with Jon Stewart*," in *The Daily Show and Rhetoric: Arguments, Issues, and Strategies*, ed. Trischa Goodnow (Lanham, MD: Lexington Books, 2011).

14. Amber Day, "And Now...The News? Mimesis and the Real in *The Daily Show*," in *Satire TV: Politics and Comedy in the Post-Network Era*, ed. Jonathan Gray, Jeffrey Jones, and Ethan Thompson (New York: New York University Press, 2009), 85; Amber Day, *Satire and Dissent: Interventions in Contemporary Political Debate* (Bloomington, IN: Indiana University Press, 2011), 54.

15. Smith, *The Daily Show (The Book)*, 259–60.

16. Jeffrey P. Jones, *Entertaining Politics: Satiric Television and Political Engagement*, 2nd ed. (Lanham, MD: Rowman & Littlefield Publishers, Inc., 2010), 116–28.

17. *The Daily Show with Jon Stewart*, April 15, 2009.

18. Aaron McKain. "Not Necessarily Not the News: Gatekeeping, Remediation, and *The Daily Show*." *Journal of American Culture* 28, no. 4 (2005).

19. By comparison, the average television news soundbite lasted 31 seconds in 1969. Richard J. Schaefer and Tony J. Martinez III, "Trends in Network News Editing Strategies from 1969 through 2005," *Journal of Broadcasting & Electronic Media* 53, no. 3 (2009).

20. *The Daily Show with Jon Stewart*, January 24, 2013.

21. *The Daily Show with Jon Stewart*, February 10, 2009.

22. *The Daily Show with Jon Stewart*, May 4, 2009.

23. *White House Correspondents' Association Dinner*, April 29, 2006.

24. For an extended analysis of the speech and reactions, see Sophia A. McClennen, *Colbert's America: Satire and Democracy* (New York: Palgrave Macmillan, 2011), 13–40.

25. Noam Cohen, "A Comedian's Riff on Bush Prompts an E-Spat," *New York Times*, May 6, 2006, C, 6.
26. *The Colbert Report*, February 21, 2013.
27. Nathan Rabin, "Stephen Colbert," *The Onion A.V. Club*, updated January 25, 2006, http://www.avclub.com/articles/stephen-colbert,13970/.
28. *The Colbert Report*, November 15, 2012.
29. *The Colbert Report*, February 26, 2008.
30. *The Colbert Report*, January 23, 2013.
31. *The Colbert Report*, November 13, 2008.
32. Jody C. Baumgartner and Jonathan S. Morris, "*The Daily Show* Effect: Candidate Evaluations, Efficacy, and the American Youth," *American Politics Research* 34 (2006); Jody C. Baumgartner and Jonathan S. Morris, "Stoned Slackers or Super Citizens? *The Daily Show* Viewing and Political Engagement of Young Adults," in *The Stewart/Colbert Effect: Essays on the Real Impact of Fake News*, ed. Amarnath Amarasingam (Jefferson, NC: McFarland & Company, Inc., 2011); Julia R. Fox and Edo Steinberg, "News You Can't Use: Jon Stewart's *Daily Show* Media Critiques," *Journalism & Mass Communication Quarterly* 97, no. 1 (2020); R. Lance Holbert et al., "Primacy Effects of *The Daily Show* and National TV News Viewing: Young Viewers, Political Gratification, and Internal Political Self-Efficacy," *Journal of Broadcasting & Electronic Media* 51 (2007).
33. Roderick P. Hart and Johanna Hartelius, "The Political Sins of Jon Stewart," *Critical Studies in Media Communication* 24, no. 3 (2007).
34. Michel Foucault, *Fearless Speech*, ed. Joseph Pearson (Los Angeles, CA: Semiotext(e), 2001.
35. Ibid., 13–15.
36. Ibid., 135.
37. Michel Foucault, "The Political Function of the Intellectual," *Radical Philosophy*, no. 17 (1977): 13.
38. Ibid., 14.
39. *The Daily Show with Jon Stewart*, November 13, 2008.
40. *The Daily Show with Jon Stewart*, July 23, 2012.
41. Jonathan Gray, *Television Entertainment* (New York: Routledge, 2008), 150–51.
42. *The Daily Show with Jon Stewart*, April 7, 2009.
43. Kelly Wilz, "Models of Democratic Deliberation: Pharmacodynamic Agonism in *The Daily Show*," in *The Daily Show and Rhetoric: Arguments, Issues, and Strategies*, ed. Trischa Goodnow (Lanham, MD: Lexington Books, 2011), 84.
44. After the launch of *The Colbert Report*, Stewart would essentially "toss to" Colbert at the end of *The Daily Show*, further intermingling the two programs and hosts.
45. *The Colbert Report*, September 27, 2012.
46. K. A. Wisniewski, "It's All About the Meme: The Art of the Interview and the Insatiable Ego of the Colbert Bump," in *The Stewart/Colbert Effect: Essays on the Real Impact of Fake News*, ed. Amarnath Amarasingam (Jefferson, NC: McFarland & Company, Inc., 2011), 170.
47. *60 Minutes*, April 30, 2006.

48. Matthew Norton, "A Structural Hermeneutics of *The O'Reilly Factor*," *Theory & Society* 40, no. 3 (2011): 325.
49. Maureen Dowd, "America's Anchors," *Rolling Stone*, November 16, 2006.
50. *The O'Reilly Factor*, January 18, 2007.
51. Jones, *Entertaining Politics: Satiric Television and Political Engagement*, 186.
52. Geoffrey Baym, *From Cronkite to Colbert: The Evolution of Broadcast News* (Boulder, CO: Paradigm Publishers, 2010), 130.
53. Hanas, "And That's the Way It Isn't."
54. *The Colbert Report*, August 17, 2010.
55. *The Colbert Report*, June 19, 2008.
56. *The Colbert Report*, February 25, 2013.
57. *White House Correspondents' Association Dinner*, April 29, 2006.
58. Rabin, "Stephen Colbert."
59. Geoffrey Baym, "Stephen Colbert's Parody of the Postmodern," in *Satire TV: Politics and Comedy in the Post-Network Era*, ed. Jonathan Gray, Jeffrey Jones, and Ethan Thompson (New York: New York University Press, 2009), 137.
60. Rabin, "Stephen Colbert."
61. Indecision 2008 – America's Choice Live Election Special, November 4, 2008.
62. "Colbert: 'Re-Becoming' the Nation We Always Were," *Fresh Air*, October 4, 2012.
63. *The Colbert Report*, December 3, 2008.
64. Linda Hutcheon, *A Theory of Parody: The Teachings of Twentieth-Century Art Forms* (Urbana: University of Illinois Press, 2000), 55–56.
65. Jody C. Baumgartner and Jonathan S. Morris, "One "Nation" under Stephen? The Effects of *The Colbert Report* on American Youth," *Journal of Broadcasting & Electronic Media* 52, no. 4 (2008).
66. Heather L. LaMarre, Kristen D. Landreville, and Michael A. Beam, "The Irony of Satire: Political Ideology and the Motivation to See What You Want to See in *The Colbert Report*," *International Journal of Press/Politics* 14, no. 2 (2009).
67. Neil Vidmar and Milton Rokeach, "Archie Bunker's Bigotry: A Study in Selective Perception and Exposure," *Journal of Communication* 24, no. 1 (1974).
68. Lisa Colletta, "Political Satire and Postmodern Irony in the Age of Stephen Colbert and Jon Stewart," *Journal of Popular Culture* 42, no. 5 (2009): 862.
69. Shaheed Nick Mohammed, "'It-Getting' in the Colbert Nation Online Forum," *Mass Communication and Society* 17 (2014).
70. Kevin S. Decker, "Stephen Colbert, Irony, and Speaking Truthiness to Power," in *The Daily Show and Philosophy*, ed. Jason Holt (Malden, MA: Blackwell Publishing, 2007), 242–43.
71. *The Colbert Report*, May 7, 2013.
72. Wisniewski, "It's All About the Meme: The Art of the Interview and the Insatiable Ego of the Colbert Bump."
73. Lance Olsen, *Circus of the Mind in Motion: Postmodernism and the Comic Vision* (Detroit, MI: Wayne State University Press, 1990), 18.

74. Ryan Lee Teten, "Mouthpiece of the Liberal Left? Jon Stewart and *The Daily Show*'s "Real" Coverage of Election 2008," *Public Integrity* 14, no. 1 (2011).

75. "Journalism, Satire or Just Laughs? "The Daily Show with Jon Stewart," Examined," Pew Research Center, updated May 8, 2008, https://www.pewresearch.org/journalism/2008/05/08/journalism-satire-or-just-laughs-the-daily-show-with-jon-stewart-examined/.

76. Jonathan Morris, "*The Daily Show with Jon Stewart* and Audience Attitude Change During the 2004 Party Conventions," *Political Behavior* 31 (2009).

77. Marshall Sella, "The Stiff Guy Vs. The Dumb Guy," *New York Times Magazine*, September 24, 2000, 77.

78. Jones, *Entertaining Politics: Satiric Television and Political Engagement*, 111.

79. Sella, "The Stiff Guy Vs. The Dumb Guy," 77.

80. *The Daily Show with Jon Stewart*, December 13, 2000.

81. *The Daily Show with Jon Stewart*, January 30, 2002.

82. Smith, *The Daily Show (The Book)*, 106.

83. Ibid., 116.

84. Bruce A. Williams and Michael X. Delli Carpini, *After Broadcast News: Media Regimes, Democracy, and the New Information Environment* (New York: Cambridge University Press, 2011), 275.

85. *The Colbert Report*, November 8, 2005.

86. *The Colbert Report*, March 21, 2007.

87. *White House Correspondents' Association Dinner*, April 29, 2006. It is an interesting inconsistency that *TDS*'s Bush v. Bush segment criticized the president for changing his stances, while Colbert's speech accused Bush of not evolving with new information.

88. For analysis of Colbert's speech, see Jones, *Entertaining Politics: Satiric Television and Political Engagement*, 80–83; Day, *Satire and Dissent: Interventions in Contemporary Political Debate*, 80–81.

89. *The Daily Show with Jon Stewart*, December 3, 2008.

90. *The Daily Show with Jon Stewart*, January 19, 2009.

91. For more on Bush and truthiness, see Frank Rich, *The Greatest Story Ever Sold: The Decline and Fall of Truth in Bush's America* (New York: The Penguin Press, 2006).

92. *The Daily Show with Jon Stewart*, October 29, 2008.

93. *The Daily Show with Jon Stewart*, August 28, 2008.

94. *The Daily Show with Jon Stewart*, November 11, 2008.

95. *The Daily Show with Jon Stewart*, May 14, 2009.

96. *The Colbert Report*, November 6, 2008.

97. *The Colbert Report*, January 5, 2009.

98. *Colbert: 'Re-Becoming' the Nation We Always Were, Fresh Air*, October 4, 2012.

99. *The Colbert Report*, May 5, 2010.

100. "The State of the News Media 2012," Pew Research Center, updated March 19, 2012, https://www.pewresearch.org/2012/03/19/state-of-the-news-media-2012/.

101. "Further Decline in Credibility Ratings for Most News Organizations," Pew Research Center, updated August 16, 2012, http://www.people-press.org/2012/08/16/further-decline-in-credibility-ratings-for-most-news-organizations/1/.

102. Walter Lippmann, *Public Opinion* (Toronto, Canada: Collier-Macmillian Canada, Ltd., 1965), 226.

103. *Jon Stewart: The Most Trusted Name in Fake News*, Fresh Air, October 4, 2010.

104. David Wise and Paul R. Brewer, "News About News in a Presidential Primary Campaign: Press Metacoverage on Evening News, Political Talk, and Political Comedy Programs," *Atlantic Journal of Communication* 18, no. 3 (2010).

105. Warren St. John, "The Week That Wasn't," *New York Times*, October 3, 2004, 9, 1.

106. Jean Baudrillard, *Simulacra and Simulation*, trans. Sheila Faria Glaser (Ann Arbor, MI: University of Michigan Press, 1994), 21–22.

107. Robert T. Tally, Jr., "I Am the Mainstream Media (and So Can You!)," in *The Stewart/Colbert Effect: Essays on the Real Impact of Fake News*, ed. Amarnath Amarasingam (Jefferson, NC: McFarland & Company, Inc., 2011), 160.

108. *White House Correspondents' Association Dinner*, April 29, 2006.

109. *The Daily Show with Jon Stewart*, January 7, 2009.

110. Hess examines the relationship between *TDS* and cable news using several case studies. Aaron Hess, "Purifying Laughter: Carnivalesque Self-Parody as Argument Scheme in *The Daily Show with Jon Stewart*," in *The Daily Show and Rhetoric: Arguments, Issues, and Strategies*, ed. Trischa Goodnow (Lanham, MD: Lexington Books, 2011).

111. *Crossfire*, October 15, 2004.

112. For a full analysis of the *Crossfire* appearance, see Megan Boler and Stephen Turpin, "*The Daily Show* and *Crossfire*: Satire and Sincerity as Truth to Power," in *Digital Media and Democracy: Tactics in Hard Times*, ed. Megan Boler (Cambridge, MA: The MIT Press, 2008).

113. Joanne Morreale, "Jon Stewart and *The Daily Show*: I Thought You Were Going to Be Funny!," in *Satire TV: Politics and Comedy in the Post-Network Era*, ed. Jonathan Gray, Jeffrey Jones, and Ethan Thompson (New York: New York University Press, 2009).

114. Bill Carter, "CNN Will Cancel 'Crossfire' and Cut Ties to Commentator," *New York Times*, October 16, 2005, 5. Carlson would become more extreme in his conservativism and find new life on Fox News with his show, *Tucker Carlson Tonight*, appearing the week after Trump's election in 2016.

115. *The Daily Show with Jon Stewart*, March 4, 2009.

116. For discussion of Jim Cramer's attempts to repair his image during and after *TDS* coverage, see Nicholas Browning, "'Mad Money' Madness: Jim Cramer's Image Restoration Effort," *Public Relations Review* 37, no. 2 (2011); Josh Compton, "Cramer Vs. (Jon Stewart's Characterization of) Cramer: Image Repair Rhetoric, Late Night Political Humor, and *The Daily Show*," in *The Daily Show and Rhetoric: Arguments, Issues, and Strategies*, ed. Trischa Goodnow (Lanham, MD: Lexington Books, 2011).

117. *The Daily Show with Jon Stewart*, March 12, 2009.

118. Jeffrey P. Jones, "More Than "Fart Noises and Funny Faces": *The Daily Show*'s Coverage of the US Recession," *Popular Communication* 8, no. 3 (2010).

119. Jason Mittell, *Television and American Culture* (New York: Oxford University Press, 2010), 144–46.

120. Dannagal Goldthwaite Young, *Irony and Outrage: The Polarized Landscape of Rage, Fear, and Laughter in the United States* (New York: Oxford University Press, 2020), 61.

121. Rabin, "Stephen Colbert."

122. Jeffrey P. Jones and Geoffrey Baym, "A Dialogue on Satire News and the Crises of Truth in Postmodern Political Television," *Journal of Communication Inquiry* 34, no. 3 (2010): 285.

123. *The Daily Show with Jon Stewart*, October 9, 2008.

124. *The Daily Show with Jon Stewart*, November 13, 2008.

125. *The Colbert Report*, March 31, 2009.

126. *The Daily Show with Jon Stewart*, September 7, 2012.

127. *The Daily Show with Jon Stewart*, October 8, 2012.

128. Michael Learmonth, "Satire Scores for Fox News Net," *Variety*, updated February 21, 2007, http://variety.com/2007/scene/news/satire-scores-for-fox-news-net-1117959928/.

129. *The 1/2 Hour News Hour*, February 18, 2007.

130. Young, *Irony and Outrage: The Polarized Landscape of Rage, Fear, and Laughter in the United States*, 196.

131. Geoffrey Baym, "Rush Limbaugh with a Laugh-Track: The (Thankfully) Short Life of the *1/2 Hour News Hour*," *Cinema Journal* 51, no. 4 (2012): 177.

132. Robert W. McChesney, "Introduction," in *The Stewart/Colbert Effect: Essays on the Real Impact of Fake News*, ed. Amarnath Amarasingam (Jefferson, NC: McFarland & Company, Inc., 2011), 2.

133. Bruce A. Williams and Michael X. Delli Carpini, "Real Ethical Concerns and Fake News: *The Daily Show* and the Challenge of the New Media Environment," in *The Stewart/Colbert Effect: Essays on the Real Impact of Fake News*, ed. Amarnath Amarasingam (Jefferson, NC: McFarland & Company, Inc., 2011).

134. Baym, *From Cronkite to Colbert: The Evolution of Broadcast News*, 148.

135. John Hartley, *Television Truths* (Malden, MA: Blackwell Publishing, 2008), 96–125.

136. Dan Schill, "Understanding the 'Heroes' and 'It Getters': Fandom and the Colbert Nation," *Mass Communication and Society* 17 (2014).

137. Jones, *Entertaining Politics: Satiric Television and Political Engagement*, 226–27.

Chapter 7

Passing the Torch in the 2010s
A New Generation of News Parody Anchors

"Bullshit is everywhere." Jon Stewart could not have made a more prophetic statement as he signed off from *The Daily Show with Jon Stewart* (*TDS*) for the last time in 2015. Presaging an era dominated by accusations of "fake news" and the invocation of "alternative facts," Stewart passed the torch to a new generation of news-parody hosts who would wrestle with the question of "what does humor mean during a time of national absurdity and outright lies?" *TDS* and *The Colbert Report* (*Colbert*) entered the 2010s with continued cultural relevance and high ratings for night-time cable. Political coverage and commentary mixed with criticism of the contemporary news media as they continued to cover President Barack Obama's administration and his eventual reelection, along with national tragedies and outrages.

By the time the 2016 elections rolled around, and the two major parties had chosen their nominees, both hosts had signed off. Colbert finished his show in December of 2014 and made the shift from cable to broadcast network. He joined the highly competitive ranks of late-night talk-show hosts, replacing the retiring David Letterman on CBS's *Late Show*. The move signaled Colbert's departure from news parody and the retirement of his ironic *Colbert* persona. Like other late-night hosts, he shifted to the venerable model of presenting news headlines as stand-up comedy, along with skits and interviews, no longer specifically employing news parody.

Stewart's departure was much more unexpected, at least to fans and the press. He had taken the summer off in 2013 to direct the film *Rosewater*. During Stewart's absence, correspondent John Oliver filled in as host of the program. The directing experience and time away from the show seemed to be the catalyst for Stewart's 2015 retirement, which he announced at the end of his February 10 show: "Seventeen years is the longest in my life I've ever held a job . . . in my heart I know it's time for someone else to have that opportunity." He said he didn't have any specific plans, but "this show doesn't deserve an even slightly restless host, and neither do you."[1] His final appearance on the anchor desk was August 6.

The departures of Stewart and Colbert inaugurated a new generation of news-parody hosts with ties to the *TDS* "mothership." The 2010s increased diversity within the genre, both on the anchor desk and behind the scenes. Trevor Noah, who hosted a late-night talk show in his native South Africa, began appearing on *TDS* as a correspondent in 2014. Noah became the first person of color to solo-host a news-parody show with *The Daily Show with Trevor Noah* (*TDSWTN*) when he took over the anchor desk in 2015. Two years earlier, John Oliver, who had proved his abilities in filling in for Stewart, launched *Last Week Tonight with John Oliver* (*Last Week*) on HBO. Both Noah and Oliver bring an international perspective to their comedy. Another former *TDS* correspondent, Samantha Bee, took an anchor spot in 2016 on TBS's *Full Frontal with Samantha Bee* (*Full Frontal*), becoming the first woman to solo-anchor a news-parody program. All three shows continued into the 2020s.

Beyond the *TDS* "expanded universe," the "Weekend Update" segment of *Saturday Night Live* (*SNL*) remains the longest-running news-parody feature on American television. In the first two decades of the twenty-first century, the segment regained cultural influence and helped launch the careers of multiple breakout stars from the show. The segment also offered more diversity on the anchor desk and the writers' room, featuring the first female head writer, the first dual-female anchor team, and the first Black anchor.

Yet another television news-parody program launched in the 2010s from an unlikely source. At a time when traditional media outlets were falling over themselves to establish digital, online footprints with streaming content, a well-known online site decided to make the jump "backward" to traditional television. The satirical newspaper and website *The Onion* is an essential part of the larger news parody ecosystem beyond television, focusing on print and digital journalism styles. *The Onion* began as a print paper in 1988 and launched its own website in 1996, quickly gaining popularity online. Imitating the peculiar structure and syntax of print journalism, writers skewer the press, politicians, and the American public, mixing irony, satire, and parody. Unlike *TDS* and subsequent programs, *The Onion* mostly creates fake stories with satirical implications rather than focusing on existing news. *The Onion* writers research their topics in order to mix reality with absurdity.[2] In 2007, the website extended its brand by launching the *Onion News Network* (*ONN*), creating video clips originally streamed from its website and available as vodcasts. The company hired 15 employees and invested $1 million, creating a virtual newsroom environment for anchors.[3] The IFC cable network picked up *ONN* at the beginning of 2011 and renewed the program for 2011–2012, but canceled before the third season. The company then shot a pilot for a behind-the-scenes comedy about their fictitious network, *Onion News Empire*, which would have integrated fake news reports like those on *ONN*; however, Amazon declined to pick up the series after making the pilot available for audience review. Although *The Onion* still posts video package clips, the *ONN* brand and the concept of anchored news parody were abandoned. Audiences who had already watched *ONN* clips online probably found little reason to seek them out at a specific time on cable.

The short-lived *ONN* notwithstanding, news parody flourished in the 2010s. This chapter analyzes the end of both *TDS* and *Colbert*, focusing especially on how the hosts of the two programs expanded their critique of politics and the media outside the confines of their 30-minute shows through real-life interventions that intersected with their programs. This same approach of creating spectacle outside the space of the television studio was adopted by John Oliver, whose show forms the major case study for this chapter. *Last Week* adapted *TDS* format in an innovative way, using a newsmagazine-style approach that focuses on depth over breadth of coverage. The creation of both *TDSWTN* and *Full Frontal* is also discussed, along with the last two decades of "Weekend Update."

THE END OF AN ERA—STEWART AND COLBERT MOVE ON

Leading into the 2010s, one of the major stories covered by both *TDS* and *Colbert* was the rise of the conservative Tea Party movement, which was protesting the Obama administration and a government they claimed was out of control. Fox News host Glenn Beck had become the top draw on the channel and aligned himself with the Tea Party. Beck had risen through the ranks of conservative talk radio and became increasingly inflammatory and conspiracy-minded on his *Glenn Beck* television show. In August 2010, on the 47th anniversary of the civil rights March on Washington, Beck organized his "Restoring Honor" rally to celebrate American exceptionalism, condemn what he considered the liberal direction of the country, and wrap his message in a return to religion. Beck exhorted that Americans "must remember who we were, who we can be—not what we've allowed ourselves to become."[4] Naturally, the rally was covered exhaustively by Fox News, and Beck spent an entire episode of his program celebrating and recounting the event. It was an example of activism as media franchise.

In 1967, Guy Debord wrote his seminal *The Society of the Spectacle*, criticizing how life had become mediated and dominated by spectacle within consumer capitalism. Spectacle had not merely replaced real life;

the two had blended to such a degree that they were indivisible: "Reality emerges within the spectacle, and the spectacle is real."[5] The spectacle distracts and keeps us isolated from each other, unifying us only to gaze at the spectacle. Modern society is dominated by such spectacles, whether it is the news media frenetically shifting between top stories throughout the day, politicians at press conferences, or celebrities dropping their newest album or lifestyle brand. Television journalism is addicted to reporting on and creating spectacle; special election-night coverage with holograms, continual live shots of tragedies, and other methods help ensure that each report must be made to seem unique and important.

In the wake of the Tea Party protests and Beck's rally, Stewart and Colbert conspired to create their own spectacle as a commentary on the state of political discourse and media coverage. Both hosts had already engaged in public criticism beyond their respective shows, but in the 2010s, they began creating events to extend their personae and public-sphere projects outside of television. Stewart's appearance on *Crossfire* was the first major indicator he could wield broader rhetorical power. Similarly, Colbert's speech at the White House Correspondents Dinner in 2006 gave him the opportunity to deploy Colbert the character in a live media spectacle. The speech raised real issues of presidential power and media timidity. As writers have mentioned, one of the powerful functions of such an event is that audience members normally less engaged with politics in the media can be pulled into a discussion of news and policies.[6]

Colbert's subsequent political performances continued to encourage his audience to engage and learn about political processes. In 2007, Colbert claimed he was being pressured to run for president, an extension of the grandiose personality of his character. He told his audience he would need a sign in order to actually run; cue Viggo Mortensen entering the studio as his *Lord of the Rings*' character Aragorn to hand Colbert the divine sword of kings, Andúril.[7] Colbert attempted to get his name placed on the Democratic party ballot in his native South Carolina, continually updating his audience as he walked through the process. Ultimately, Colbert's application to be on the ballot was denied, with the party claiming he was not a viable national candidate.[8] Colbert revealed the political power structure was limiting election choices in a democracy through the process. His appearance on a Viacom channel and candidacy sponsorship by Doritos, called "The Hail to the Cheese Stephen Colbert Nacho Cheese Doritos 2008 Presidential Campaign," also provided the opportunity to discuss the role of press advocacy and corporate money in elections.[9] Through a little less than two months of coverage, Colbert helped his audience learn more about the process, the finances, and the barriers to running for president.

Colbert's and Stewart's flirtations with taking their satire outside of the television screen grew to full-scale political spectacle when they announced their own Beck-style rally in 2010. Originally labeled the "Rally to Restore Sanity," hosted by Stewart, and the corresponding "March to Keep Fear Alive," hosted by Colbert, they were consolidated into one mega-event to be held on October 30 of that year and billed the "Rally to Restore Sanity and/or Fear." Although many in the press drew comparisons to Beck's rally, Stewart specifically denied the event was meant to be a commentary or rejoinder to Beck; instead, it would be a satiric, live version of the humor on their shows. According to Stewart, the rally was planned to celebrate and recognize that the America conjured by partisan media did not represent most citizens: "This is for the people that are too busy, that have jobs and lives, and are tired of their reflection in the media as being a divided country and a country that's ideological and conflicted and fighting."[10]

The rally extended the persona of each host, with Stewart as the voice of moderation, handing out "Medals of Reasonableness" to real-life individuals who took moderate stances and Colbert, taking the tongue-in-cheek conservative extreme, awarding "Medals of Fear." The two hosts presented dueling visions of political speech, creating social critique on the public stage. At one point, Stewart invites Cat Stevens to sing "Peace Train," while Ozzy Osbourne is asked to perform "Crazy Train" by Colbert, with each host repeatedly interrupting the two songs. Ronald Placone and Michael Tumolo view the battle of songs as a microcosm of the event itself: "Instead of hearing the songs out and judging them on their merits, as a metaphor for deliberating in good faith, we are thrust into a cacophony of indistinguishable noise."[11] The "collision" of the two trains mirrors the political voices dominating public speech. Colbert and Stewart then put aside their differences to sing "Love Train" with the O'Jays. Rather than a message of partisan activism, the rally advocated a return to "sanity," defined through the speeches and appearances that day as a compromise on the part of politicians and responsibility on the part of journalists. Stewart closed out the event with a moment of sincerity, asking the crowd not to fall into division and reminding them, "we work together to get things done every damn day! The only place we don't is here (motioning to the Capital building) or on cable TV."[12] The rally allowed the hosts to engage their audience as fellow citizens, not simply viewers, and also gave individuals the opportunity to participate in the performance art by attending, making signs, and dressing up.[13]

Rather than using the hosts' platform to mobilize political action, the rally subverted media and political organizers' expectations by simply bringing people together to highlight a problem without a call to action. As with the comedy of the actual shows, the audience was left to decide for themselves what to do with the information, and this ultimately may have been one of the most confounding aspects of *TDS* and *Colbert* for critics. At a time when most political activists and conservative media were attempting to mobilize support against specific policies and bills, two of the most influential media programs on the left refused to join in. Ian Reilly and Megan Boler frame the rally as a "prepolitical" event, signaling the *potential* for new political relationships and practices with *possible* future action. The authors conducted interviews with attendees and found many of them discussed voting; they point out the audiences were full of active viewers of the programs willing to attend a rally with a sense of optimism.[14] However, the lack of definitive action ended up disappointing some on the political left.

While functioning as a commentary on the lack of civil discourse, the rally also highlighted conservative post-Obama obsession with Tea Party rallies and the celebration of visible political outrage. In Debord's view, spectacle is action without reason, with "all *real* activity having been forcibly channeled into the global construction of the spectacle."[15] The Tea Party existed as a commodity of political belief, marked by fears, loose concepts, and the spectacle of their gatherings, complete with costumes. One study of the event referred to the Comedy Central rally as "critique through spectacle *of spectacle*," pointing out how the rally existed purely as an excuse to have a rally, with the hosts making no direct requests for action.[16] The spectacle called attention to its own construction.

While Debord framed spectacle as utterly oppressive, Douglas Kellner, writing after Obama's first election, applies a more open, cultural-studies approach to spectacle in American society. Media rituals, the everyday routines, are peppered with media spectacle, where coverage is lifted to special emphases and treated as extraordinary; of course, the flow and economic pressures of journalism virtually guarantee that such media spectacles will appear daily if not more. Unlike Debord, though, Kellner envisions these media spectacles as contested sites. While they do reinforce societal values, they can also reveal conflicts within society.[17] Different interests can manipulate spectacle to their own agendas, which seems especially true of contemporary political satirists.

Colbert Moves beyond the Screen

Colbert continued his interventions in politics during the 2010s. The summer before the rally, he hosted the United Farm Workers (UFW) on his show to announce their "Take Our Jobs" challenge, where American citizens were invited to replace immigrant laborers. Colbert participated in the awareness-raising campaign, working in a field for a day. He was asked to testify about his experience before a Congressional subcommittee but announced he would be testifying in character as *Colbert*'s ironic, conservative host. Colbert's brief statement submitted to the committee was written in an official voice, describing his day working on a farm, statistics about farms in America, and empathy for the plight of immigrants. His live, in-person testimony, however, consisted mostly of ironic jokes. For instance, his solution to being dependent on immigrant labor: "Now, the obvious answer is for all of us to stop eating fruits and vegetables, and if you look at the recent obesity statistics, you will see that many Americans have already started." Suggesting that he is anti-immigrant, Colbert argued, "My great-grandfather did not travel across 4,000 miles of the Atlantic Ocean to see this country overrun by immigrants. He did it because he killed a man back in Ireland."[18] He attempts to persuade at some moments, although always within the double voice of his comedic mode. His brief testimony offered little insight into his experience and certainly seemed unlikely to persuade politicians; however, that was not really the point of the exercise.

By testifying at a Congressional hearing, Colbert brought his audience along for the ride. The host broke down the supposedly divided realms of the comedic and the serious through his participation and called attention to a process unfamiliar to most Americans.[19] Members of the subcommittee asked questions after his testimony, and for most of them, Colbert remained in character. In an especially odd moment, GOP Representative Steve King questioned whether Colbert had actually *packed* corn or if the footage shown on *Colbert* had been reversed and he was only *unpacking* it. Colbert stepped out of character, though, when asked by Democratic Representative Judy Chu why he was interested in immigrant labor. He paused and replied:

> I like talking about people who don't have any power. And it seems like one of the least powerful people in the United States are migrant workers who come and do our work but don't have any rights as a result. And, yet, we still invite them to come here and, at the same time, ask them to leave. And that is an interesting contradiction to me. And you know, whatsoever you do for the least of my brothers. And these seem like the least of our brothers right now. A lot of people are least brothers right now because the economy is so hard, and I don't want to take anyone's hardship away from them or diminish it or anything like that. But migrant workers suffer and have no rights.[20]

The heartfelt statement, weaving in religious quotes, seemed unexpected in the wake of his character performance. Sophia A. McClennen argues that his ending statement was incredibly effective, and more so because "it came after his in-character performance where he had satirized the commonly advanced conservative and neoliberal views about immigration and labor issues."[21] Colbert's volunteerism with and coverage of the UFW event, combined with his appearance on Capitol Hill, resulted in broader coverage of government policies and rhetoric surrounding undocumented labor than television journalism traditionally delivers. Just like his appearance at the White House Correspondents Dinner, the actual audience for his testimony was not the assembled members of Congress, but his viewing audience.

The following year (2011), Colbert embarked on another performance art/investigation after the show produced a fake political advertisement that included a website for the fictional "Colbert PAC," or political action committee.[22] The Colbert PAC was meant as a one-time joke until Comedy Central expressed concern, saying that if Colbert really was creating a PAC, "that could be trouble." His response? "Well, then I'm definitely going to do it." Colbert says he realized that in the wake of the *Citizens United* ruling, which allowed virtually unlimited money to be donated to political campaigns, starting his own PAC could be an effective way of reporting on the process.[23] Without any pre-planning, Colbert began to pursue creation of the PAC and covered it step-by-step on his show throughout 2011. He hosted Trevor Potter, former chair of the Federal Election Commission (FEC), who helped him fill out paperwork. He pivoted to making his organization a "Super PAC," which has fewer regulations, and sought out and was granted an exemption from the FEC to cover his Super PAC on the program regularly. In September, Colbert complained to Potter that corporations were not funneling money into his Super PAC, leading Potter to suggest setting up a 501(c)(4) shell corporation in Delaware that could take anonymous money and then send it to the Super PAC, with Colbert as the sole board member. Colbert asks, "So I can take secret donations of my (c)(4) and give it to my supposedly transparent Super PAC? . . . What is the difference between that and money laundering?" Potter responds, "It's hard to say."[24]

In January 2012, Colbert announced he would run for president, or at least "President of South Carolina"; however, since he could no longer administrate the Super PAC as a candidate, Colbert turned it over to Jon Stewart. The move satirized actual political practice, where Super PACs are supposedly not allowed to coordinate with candidates, but often involve friends and associates with knowledge of what a candidate would want to be done on their behalf. The Super PAC received over $1 million in donations by that month's reporting deadline. Colbert eventually created another 501(c)(4) to further mask the source of any funds, and then finally donated the money to charities.

Coverage of the Super PAC on *Colbert* functioned as a form of investigative journalism, revealing the hidden world of political finances by walking through it with the viewer. The creation of Colbert's Super PAC and his subsequent appearance in front of the FEC led to numerous news reports, both on his program and within traditional media, about the role of money in campaigns and why laws about campaign financing matter.[25] The satirist says such excursions into the real-life world of politics offer opportunities to illuminate the process: "I like playing political games to see what really happens in them."[26] Marcus Paroske calls Colbert's comedic excursions outside the studio "participatory satire," where the host moves beyond the role of journalistic observer to become an active participant.[27] This kind of activity can demystify especially complex stories, such as the role of money in politics. One study found that viewing *Colbert* led to greater knowledge of campaign finances and PACS than other types of news media.[28] Beyond educating his audience, Colbert also encouraged viewers to participate with him through either donating money to his Super PAC or actually starting their own. The *Colbert* website sold do-it-yourself Super PAC kits for $99 so viewers "actually managed to get involved and bring that involvement to media attention" as journalists covered individuals who were starting their own PACs.[29] By extending their criticisms beyond the confines of their respective television shows, Colbert and Stewart furthered their critical message. Through that process, they continued to interrogate norms of political speech, political procedure, and journalistic routines.

Two years after his presidential run, Colbert was announced as the replacement for Letterman, with his final show on December 18, 2014. The finale was a mix of news headlines, skits, and even a musical number to wrap up its nine years on the air. In the recurring "Cheating Death" segment, Colbert would open the sketch by playing chess against Grimmy, the Grim Reaper (à la *The Seventh Seal*), and usually cheated. In the final installment, though, Grimmy sees Colbert cheat and attacks him. The host shoots Grimmy dead, thereby making himself immortal. This leads to a star-studded sing-along of "We'll Meet Again," with Colbert and Stewart leading a cavalcade of roughly 100 former guests from politics and entertainment joining in. The host signs off, "from Eternity, I'm Stephen Colbert."[30] The final episode was a fitting ending for a character steeped in irony, shoving multiple, conflicting "last TV show tropes" into a send-off. From the montage of show highlights, to the celebrity guests, to the surreal final skit with Colbert riding on a sleigh with Santa Claus, an Abraham Lincoln unicorn, and Alex Trebek, the program reveled in its parody of television form and the subversion of those expectations. For a character unwilling to learn from facts or change his mind on any issue of conservative dogma, Colbert's ascension into the heavens as an eternal being who will always be in the cultural zeitgeist was apropos, especially in light of politics and media during the last half of the 2010s.

Calling Bullshit to the End—Stewart Steps Down

Stewart decided to flex his influence two months after his and Colbert's rally in 2010 by using *TDS* for pure political advocacy in his coverage of the 9/11 responders' Zadroga bill. The legislation was meant to pay for medical treatment for the many health issues suffered by Ground Zero first responders and those who worked in the aftermath to try to rescue survivors; however, it was stalled in Congress due to a Republican filibuster. Stewart became an active participant in the story rather than a commentator or critic. *TDS* highlighted inaction on Zadroga earlier in the year, but the entire December 16th show was dedicated to discussing the bill and calling out those responsible in Congress. In a five-minute headline segment dubbed "Worst Responders," Stewart says the bill has already passed the House, and "they're going to pay for it by closing a corporate tax loophole. It's a win, win, win, win, just fucking do it!" He calls out Republicans who "turned 9/11 into a catchphrase" for blocking the bill, the television networks which had not covered the Zadroga bill for several months, and especially Fox News who, despite bringing up 9/11 at every turn when it could be used as a cudgel against Democrats, had been virtually silent on the legislation.

TDS's first block was followed by a nine-minute interview with four 9/11 first responders, Chris Bowman, John Devlin, Ken George, and Kenny Specht. Each was suffering from longer-term or terminal health conditions and talked about their experiences, medical- and financial-related problems, and their reactions to the stalling of Zadroga. Stewart mentioned that Congress wants to go home before Christmas, and Devlin replied, "It was an honor to work through Christmas on that 9/11, to give that closure to those people who were on the other side of that gate every morning showing us the pictures of their loved ones."[31] Specht had said something similar to Stewart in the green room before the show, and Stewart replied, "That's how we're ending."[32] The episode was a self-conscious turn to advocacy by Stewart on a topic he has continued to support, passionately testifying in 2019 for a second reauthorization of the bill. Along with others, Stewart is credited with forcing movement by Congress. Glen Caplin, a congressional communications director at the time, said, "The important thing is Jon didn't just shame Congress, he shamed the media."[33] The next day, Fox News began covering the bill, and within a week, Congress approved Zadroga.

Taken together, the rally and his advocacy of the 9/11 responders bill signaled a shift for both Stewart and discussions about the show. Matt Carlson and Jason Peifer analyzed coverage of the two events and how, stepping outside of his role as host, Stewart was essentially claiming the cultural authority of journalists. Media reacted by noting how Stewart was beginning to mix more serious discourse with his humor and becoming a kind of political and media insider—a shift not necessarily welcomed by members of the media. As the authors describe, some journalists suggested Stewart's style of satire had negative effects on journalistic authority.[34]

Stewart announced his departure from *TDS* in February 2015 and the passing of the torch to Trevor Noah in March. In the months leading up to his final August 6 episode, Stewart covered the tragedy of the racist shooting of nine Black parishioners at a South Carolina church and the continued candidacy of Donald Trump for the Republican presidential slot. The two stories exemplify what *TDS* and Stewart had become known for in American media: passionate discussion of tragedies linked to systemic or political issues and making fun of the powerful and self-serious. The day of the Emanuel African Methodist Episcopal Church shooting in Charleston, Stewart began the show and his coverage with no prepared script, speaking from his heart. Comparing the extreme measures used to prevent foreign terrorism versus domestic, racial violence, he says, "I'm confident though, that by acknowledging it, by staring into that and seeing it for what it is, we still won't do jack shit."[35] In five impassioned minutes, he called out the media for acting as if the attack came from nowhere, politicians for failing to address racial violence, and the continued veneration of the Confederacy.

The next month, *TDS* covered Trump's doubling-down on his comments calling immigrants from Mexico rapists and criminals. Stewart and Trump had a long-standing mutual disdain for each other. In 2013, Trump tweeted that he was smarter than Stewart and used Stewart's birthname, Jonathan Leibowitz, making it seem like the comedian had suddenly been "outed" as Jewish. Stewart joked that Trump had changed his name from Fuckface Von Clownstick, leading to a barrage of tweets with that hashtag. After Trump announced his run for president, *TDS* took renewed interest. Discussing the candidate's comments about immigration, Stewart opined, "It is hard to get mad at Donald Trump for saying stupid things, in the same way you don't get mad at a monkey when he throws poop at you at the zoo. It's a monkey, it's what they do."[36] He went on to attack Fox News and conservative politicians, though, for defending Trump's racism. Coming to the show's close, the two stories showcased what *TDS* added to the journalistic field.

In the final episode of *TDS*, after the correspondents and staff said their goodbyes, Stewart moved into his last commentary as host, where he asked the audience to meet him at camera three and described the three different kinds of bullshit everyone encounters. There is the innocuous bullshit that is required of everyday life, the "what a beautiful baby" bullshit. There is "premeditated institutional bullshit" where bad things, like the Patriot Act, are made to sound good, and where loads of bullshit are used to obscure, such as end user agreements. The third kind, the bullshit of infinite possibility, describes people who refuse to act on problems because they never finish studying them, such as finding solutions to climate change. Stewart closes with, "I say to you tonight friends the best defense against bullshit is vigilance. So, if you smell something, say something."[37] That detecting bullshit was both the essence of Stewart's project on *TDS* and, ideally, of journalism writ large.

JOHN OLIVER BRINGS NEWS PARODY BACK TO HBO—*LAST WEEK TONIGHT*

As Colbert and Stewart departed from the late-night news-parody milieu, fresh shows emerged with concrete connections to *TDS* and the potential for tapping its audience. John Oliver's summer hosting stint on the show received rave reviews. Afterward Oliver went to Afghanistan for two weeks as part of a USO entertainment tour and said his phone blew up when he got back home and checked his messages. Multiple networks expressed interest in recruiting him, including the president of programming for HBO, Michael Lombardo: "I was dazzled by this guy who came in and pulled it off."[38] Comedy Central was still reportedly in talks for Oliver to spend summers on the anchor desk of *TDS*, but HBO offered double the money.[39] Oliver took the deal.

The show format of *Last Week* was always going to be a challenge. Expectations and fears were that Oliver would simply be doing his own version of *TDS*, resulting in inevitable disappointment. The challenge was to utilize audience expectations of Oliver's comedic persona and innovate the format of news parody. HBO even seemed a little unsure what the show would end up being, saying they chose Oliver because of his "singular perspective and distinct voice," but that the network had not originally been "searching for another weekly *talk show* [emphasis added]."[40] Producing topical satire once a week after audiences were used to watching shows four nights a week also added to the challenge. The strategy they hit on harkened back to television news from the network era. In 1968, looking to develop a news-oriented program distinct from the network and local newscasts, CBS launched *60 Minutes*, becoming one of the earliest and most successful examples of the "news magazine" style television report. This genre covered fewer stories, often not necessarily the most topical but that required extended reporting to convey the information to the audience. *Last Week* followed the same logic, starting with a handful of headlines and then transitioning into a single in-depth segment, frequently 15 to 20 minutes in length, on one particular topic. The program also decided to shy away from news that could be found in the headlines of the networks or even *TDS* and select issues that may be more systemic or have simply eluded American broadcasts.

HBO seemed to offer an ideal match for Oliver's comedic sensibilities. The pay network's looser policies and different economic imperatives from regular cable and broadcast allowed for a more acerbic style, with few subjects off the table. As Oliver described it, HBO "seemed to offer the kind of freedom that does not exist anywhere else. Not just the classic blood and boobs, which they're very good at, but in terms of content, no restrictions on anything."[41] That included not having to worry about angering advertisers due to the network's subscriber model. *Last Week* also benefited from HBO's forays into alternative distribution in the post-network era. The show had a YouTube channel from its launch, at a time when many networks were attempting to keep their content off of social media or at least severely limit what could be accessed. Even before the first episode was released, two fake political ads were posted on YouTube, making fun of current Republican outreach efforts to young voters. "GOP—Hashtag Awesomesauce" and "GOP-Whatevs" feature a parody of a hipster conservative with receding hairline and glasses presenting policy: "I don't like it when people tell me what to do, like 'you should buy healthcare' or 'don't carry a concealed weapon into this park' or 'hey, that leather jacket is way too small for you.' I can make my own decisions."[42] In addition to priming audiences for a type of ironic humor, the fake ads also augured the importance of social media and internet culture to the show's success.

The first episode of *Last Week* launched on April 27, 2014, after Colbert and Stewart departed Comedy Central. That night's show featured coverage of the upcoming elections in India, questions about the health claims of POM Wonderful juice, and a prerecorded interview with former National Security Administration director Keith Alexander. Press response was mostly positive, although some reviews pointed out that politically engaged Americans were likely already aware of Indian politics and that the flow of the show, with the ending interview, seemed too similar to *TDS*. The interview with Alexander, who had retired earlier that year, did differ in at least one significant way from most interviews that took place on *TDS* and *Colbert*, which was that the interviewee had no "product" to advertise. The discussion was a look back at the three-star general's time leading the agency, and Oliver leaned into questions about domestic surveillance.[43] In the first year of the program, Oliver and executive producer Tim Carvell, a former head writer and coproducer on *TDS*, continued to develop the format and garnered critical praise and steady viewership.

Visual Style and Structure of *Last Week*

The HBO program breaks with a number of the stylistic norms established by *TDS* and *Colbert*. From its visual language, to its segmentation and rundown, to the types of stories chosen, *Last Week* was differentiated enough from its predecessors to be accepted as an addition to the genre rather than a simple spin-off or reconfiguration.

Instead of starting with a host cold open, the show launches into its preproduced intro. *TDS* revealed news space during its opening, while *Colbert* dealt in patriotic imagery, but *Last Week*'s intro is visually simple yet semiotically complex. Starting with an hourglass against a shaded white background, the image spins upward and seemingly pulls a set of three new images from below, neatly divided into three rectangles: the Statue of Liberty, the Earth, and an "On the Air" sign. The Statue's torch flickers, and the Earth rotates, continuing a sense of motion within the static screen. Each of these images is labeled with text, "Time," "New York City," "Earth," and "TV Show," becoming symbolic (or in the case of earth, iconic) images for their referents. The images take on additional connotations through individually attached, seemingly Latin phrases. For instance, the hourglass with the word "time" includes the phrase "tempus fugit," meaning "time flies." In addition to creating second-level connotations, Latin takes on the official air of the sciences, which uses Latin to categorize. Subsequent images, though, introduce absurdity by creating pseudo-Latin and purely fake phrases for images: Statue of Liberty—"Frenchium Garbagum," Earth—"America Et. Al.," and the On the Air sign—"Carpe Weekem." These then rotate away to reveal additional images, always weaving in an image directly related to the primary topic of the evening, as well as those linked to previous episodes. The pictures are cleanly arranged against a white backdrop with identifying English names and fake Latin identifiers, including a rotating image of Oliver, labeled "John" and "Hostus Mostus." The opening was created by Trollbäck+Company, who were specifically instructed not to make it a parody of news openings. Their idea was to create a structure that could be continually reused but filled with new images: "The dense visual language keeps the open fresh."[44] The intro immediately separates the program from a parody of traditional network and cable news by refusing the trite visual language of on-location video, behind-the-scenes studio shots, and common journalistic iconography.

After the opening, a camera swings along Oliver's set and isolates him at a desk with a skyline background, which becomes the primary space for the rest of the episode. Guests and special in-studio segments, such as musical performances, the dedication of statues, and dancing furry mascots, make use of the broader, extended studio space; however, the viewing frame is mostly locked on the small area around Oliver. Unlike most news desks, the desk is modern, with a glass top, seemingly metallic front, and singular wood accent. It recalls as much a late-night host as a journalist. The lower third of the background is dark wood cutouts with insert lights that give a boardroom feel, with a city skyline in the top third. While it suggests a familiar crowded cityscape, the image is an amalgam of different city skylines, such as Chicago, Hong Kong, Los Angeles, and New York, as well as various iconic buildings from across the world inserted throughout the image, including the

Dome of the Rock, the Royal Albert Hall, the Taj Mahal, the Brandenburg Gate, the Jefferson Memorial, the Leaning Tower of Pisa, and even *Game of Thrones'* Castle Dragonstone. Taken together, the images evoke a kind of officiousness, a journalistic claim to authority. Literally, the world exists behind Oliver's desk and is being covered. At the same time that the backdrop creates a kind of legitimacy, there is also an aspect of absurdist humor since viewers can recognize the landmarks and understand their illogical placement.

The format and rundown of *Last Week* differentiate it from other news parody programs, past and present. One major difference is its distribution on a pay-cable channel with no advertising. In discussing *NNTN* in Chapter 4, I pointed out that the earlier program's frenetic format created breaks, but not the kind of traditional television *flow* that Raymond Williams had said defined the televisual format in the heyday of the network era.[45] Instead of the familiar sequence of show intro, ad, first segment, ad, second segment, ad, third segment, ad, preview of next program, and so on, *NNTN* included fake ads and other kinds of content interspersed to break up bits. *Last Week* is formatted more like a traditional broadcast program, though breaks are not needed on pay cable.

The first block following the intro originally covered a small number of topical headline stories for around 5–10 minutes; however, that evolved into usually focusing on one particular story during the first block with interrelated topics. For instance, Oliver begins one show talking about how the state of Texas has three mascots before focusing on the armadillo as being the perfect mascot, complete with a video of a screaming armadillo, beginning the show with observational humor. He then pivots into topical news with clips about a Texas law banning abortion after six weeks of pregnancy before highlighting how the law creates a system that allows private individuals to sue people for aiding in an abortion and follows with the Supreme Court's declining to stay the law. The show cuts to a clip of *TMZ's* oddly cogent discussion of the legislation and the Texas governor's response to a lack of exceptions for pregnancy caused by rape or incest, which was simply to say they would arrest rapists. Oliver's response? "Oh, fuck off. Just fuck right off. Set aside you're announcing 'we'll arrest rapists' like it's a brand-new idea and you're Tim Cook unveiling a new iPhone." He then describes how most rapists are not strangers, the many reasons someone may choose abortion, and how internet users quickly flooded a reporting website set up by a pro-life group with fake tips and pornography. Oliver ends by calling out the silence of corporations who do business in Texas and those, like his own parent company AT&T, who donate to Texas politicians who voted for the abortion ban while tying the story to national efforts to ban abortion and upcoming cases at the Supreme Court.[46] The report is presented in typical broadcast-news style, with a continual over-the-shoulder graphic to the left of Oliver, changing based upon the course of the report. As the host discusses how an Uber driver might be sued for transporting someone for an abortion, a picture of a forlorn man with a car and an "Uber" sign is displayed. The eight-minute opening segment is packed with information about this one important story, going beyond the most immediate developments, such as the governor's speech or the Supreme Court's decision not to intervene. *Last Night* provided synthesis and framing of the story from different angles, approaching the law from a newsmagazine style.

After the headline block, Oliver creates an ad break by transitioning with the phrase "And now, this." Video then switches to a title slate read by an announcer, breaking away both from Oliver and his news space to create a transition. The break segment includes either video montages or single clips, usually making fun of television news personalities. Example segments include: "The Inevitable Sad Consequences of Morning Show Anchors Celebrating Halloween," "Wolf Blitzer States the Obvious," and "Newscasters Misidentifying Photographs as Selfies." Politicians are also frequent targets, with montages of "John McCain Tells the Same Joke 6 Different Times in 6 Places" and "The Dismal Prop Comedy of the United States Congress." The montages are brief, usually one to two minutes, and reinforce how repetitive and silly journalists, politicians, and celebrities can be, a standard presentational strategy of news parody since the days of *That Was the Week That Was* (*TW3*). The program then transitions out of the segment to a much lengthier second block comprising the bulk of the show.

The second block has become the signature content of *Last Week*, the segment that receives the most attention from other news outlets and the majority of social media views and interactions. The segments are usually 15 to 20 minutes, or sometimes even longer. On HBO, there is no need for the show to neatly fit into a 30-minute time slot, especially when much of the viewing is on their streaming service. During the second block, the show creates a deep dive into a single story that network and cable news has mostly ignored. Since the program airs weekly on Sunday nights, the showrunners decided to treat stories in depth and call attention to underreported stories, rejecting the conventional wisdom that contemporary audiences of YouTube and social media would never invest 20 minutes in one story. The show assumed that viewers would appreciate longer reports that, as Oliver says, contain "actual information they might not have known. . . . I think we underestimate people when we think they only care about a two-minute video where someone gets kicked in the nuts."[47] The show produces the depth that classic newsmagazine shows would devote to issues but often addresses more systemic or obscure topics. *New York Times* critic David Carr expected the show to be a failure given its host, weekly schedule, and competitors, but at the end of the first season had to admit *Last Week* was a major success:

What he and his co-creators came up with was counterintuitive to the prevailing conventions of television, not to mention journalism. Each half-hour episode contained a big explainer of a complicated issue. The list of topics sounds like the arcane scraps from the cutting-room floor of most newsrooms—the amount of sugar in food, civil forfeiture, the false hopes of lotteries, the failure of the American government to safeguard people who served as interpreters in Iraq and Afghanistan.[48]

Carr points out that both the live audience and online interactions with clips proved the show was accumulating a sizable and dedicated audience after just one season. The stories in this block are also a primary reason the program is often credited with actually generating its own journalism, as discussed later in this section.

There is no standard ending to the second block, sometimes transitioning to another "And Now, This" segment, or more frequently, seamlessly shifting into a different presentational mode as an extension of the second block story. One way is through a call to action with Oliver pleading, through his continual first-person address to the audience, to get involved by calling a company, voting, or participating with him in a kind of *interactive journalism*, where viewers walk through a process facilitated by the program. No crossfade or new segment sections off the call to action from the in-depth news report; they are as inseparable visually as journalism and advocacy are thematically. To raise an issue is usually to offer a solution on *Last Week*.

Another way of ending the second block is through what might be termed a *pop-culture intervention* into the subject of the report. In this approach, Oliver ends the official coverage and then tosses to an either prerecorded or live performance by an actor, musician, or other type of media figure that brings humor and can often dramatize the issue as well. In the first season, Oliver reports on the leaked emails of Syrian dictator Bashar al-Assad, including more banal reveals such as his iTunes music purchase of a song by the 1990's band Right Said Fred. Oliver then questions whether the show should fly the group from London to perform a re-written slam song against Assad: "Would it really be worth all that time and expense just for the momentary catharsis of mildly irritating one of the worst people on the planet?" Of course, it would, and Oliver then brings the band out to perform a live song about Assad called "You're Too Awful for this Earth," to the tune of their hit "I'm Too Sexy."[49] In another example, after coverage of the plight of Puerto Rico and the lack of Congressional action to help the island, Oliver introduces Puerto Rican native and *Hamilton* creator Lin-Manuel Miranda, who performs a rap about the economic state of the island and calls out Congress.[50] Sometimes these popular culture moments are sprinkled in during reports, such as having actress Helen Mirren read sections of the Senate Torture Report in her very comforting voice and then combining descriptions of torture with parts of the children's book *Peter Rabbit*.[51] These popular-culture interventions create comedy by intertwining the serious (news topic) with the unserious (popular cultural figure or trend) and creating commentary furthering discussion of the story. In the torture report, the horrifying descriptions are reframed from the "official" voice of the report and even that of the television host by using the clashing presentational mode of Mirren's gentle, sing-song voice.

Like other aspects of the show, the pop-culture interventions are tailor-made for contemporary internet audiences. The juxtaposition of celebrities presenting humorous takes on serious topics is exactly the kind of content that is easy to share on social media without context and aligns with the ironic comic sensibilities of online culture. Anne Ulrich has written about *Last Week*'s modalities and analyzes how the show is a mix of traditional television flow (such as the self-created breaks) and newer modes of address that mix post-network television and online style, allowing for a broader audience. The show engages "new audiences that are moving away from broadcast television or have already left it."[52] One example of *Last Week* embracing this online style is Oliver's constant creation or use of hashtags during his reports, such as #NotMyChristian, to complain about the casting of *50 Shades of Grey* character Christian Grey, and the much-beloved #WeUnderstandThatAsCorporateEntitiesOurPresenceInCertainDiscussionsIsNotAlwaysRequiredSoWeWillStriveToLimitOurActivitiesToJustSellingYouShit, after DiGiorno Pizza posted in a hashtag conversation about domestic violence. The recurring #feminism is reserved for stories or statements where gender inequality is used in odd ways. For instance, after Donald Trump called Hillary Clinton the cofounder of the terrorist group ISIS, Oliver ironically congratulates Trump for giving her credit, then points down to a graphic with #Feminism #IsisWithHer.

The viral aspect of the show, where clips are shared on social media, and Oliver's encouragement of action by the audience are further aspects of this online mode. The aforementioned skyline backdrop, for instance, functions as an "Easter egg" in which the audience can find the hidden buildings. In fact, shortly after the premiere, the show's official Facebook page encouraged viewers to name all the landmarks they could find. All of these aspects help to blend online media norms with the more traditional television structure of *Last Week*.

When the show first launched, interviews seemed to be a recurring feature. The premiere featured Keith Alexander, and subsequent episodes included on-set interviews with journalists Fareed Zakaria and Simon Ostrovsky, as well as pretaped segments with Stephen Hawking and Jane Goodall. By the second season, though, interviews were sporadic and quickly disappeared as a regular segment. Even though interview segments have been the traditional bread and butter of television news magazine programs, the decision to cut the segment allowed *Last Week* to develop a tighter, more focused structure.

John Oliver—From Outsider to Assimilation

After Oliver joined *TDS* as "senior British correspondent" in 2006, most of his bits either revolved around news from Britain, where he would play the immigrant outsider covering American news, or straight-up playing British stereotypes, even wearing a monocle sometimes. Oliver was born in England and went to Cambridge. While in Britain, he performed stand-up comedy and appeared in the early seasons of the BBC news-satire program *Mock the Week*. His interview for *TDS* was his first time coming to America. In interviews, Oliver talks about having the immigrant "crush" on the United States and how feeling like an outsider was not a new experience: "If you've never felt like you fit in anywhere in your life, as you grow up, it's almost reassuring to go somewhere you definitely don't fit in. Like America."[53] During his early days, first with *TDS* and then behind the anchor desk at *Last Week*, this outsider status defined his presentational style and celebrity image within the broader culture.

The idea of a British host making fun of America each week *to Americans* was a bold and unlikely casting decision. On *TDS*, Oliver was able to play the befuddled outsider to Stewart, but on *Last Week* he had to decide whether he was still a British comic observing America or whether he was now an insider commenting on his adopted home. He started working on *TDS* with a temporary visa that required him to fly back to London periodically, but in 2009 received a green card. He was also dating Iraq War veteran Kate Norley; they married in 2011 and now have two children. After getting his green card, Oliver says he was flying back from London and, upon landing in New York, thought, "Oh, great to be home. And then realizing, that is a dangerous thought when there is someone behind a glass panel deciding whether this is your home or not."[54] By the time *Last Week* launched, Oliver had shifted the presentation of his national identity. He began to refer to himself as American, incorporating himself with the "we" when discussing American politics and events. In an interview at the end of *Last Week*'s first season, Oliver says, "I think I'm entitled to say 'we' now . . . I love living here, I love this country, I've married an American, I want to stay regardless of what happens. I've been here 10 years and I'm not going anywhere. This is my home."[55] Oliver told one reporter that after he "arrived here as an imposter," his views changed as he felt more connected so that he can now feel both outraged as an American and also see how strange American viewpoints can be.[56] The same reporter calls Oliver "refreshing" and says that the host has an outsider's perspective, but without seeming mean or accusatory.

Oliver's identity as an immigrant makes him impassioned when he discusses the country's immigration policies, especially the vilification of immigrants during the Trump presidency and its xenophobic policies. Oliver expressed concern about radical shifts in the treatment of immigrants, saying, "I have an American wife and an American son now, but who knows what's enough? Having a green card used to be enough."[57] This rhetorical and identity shift from "you Americans" to "we Americans" allows Oliver, despite his prominent accent, to frame criticism of the country as regenerative.

International coverage is an important aspect of *Last Week*'s reportage, and even though Oliver identifies himself as American, he also plays off his British heritage. In covering the United Kingdom (UK), Oliver consistently uses "they" to refer to UK citizens, firmly separating himself off. However, subtle references to his Britishness are incorporated into the show's comedy in two specific ways. When covering UK politics or policies, he reminds audiences that he is British to establish credibility. For instance, when voters were choosing whether to stay or leave the European Union (EU), Oliver outlined why it would be disastrous for the UK to leave the EU and then noted, "but still, polls suggest my homeland is on the edge of doing something absolutely insane."[58] Here Oliver addresses the audience as an expatriate living across the Atlantic, commenting on the complex British relationship with Europe as someone who grew up in the UK, negotiating his identity as both American and British.

Self-deprecation is a defining aspect of Oliver's outsider persona, and he often incorporates his UK roots into jokes. Where most hosts are framed as attractive and masculine, Oliver plays up being small, frail, unathletic, unattractive, and socially awkward. When describing himself to someone who has never seen his show, he called himself "a near-sighted parrot that works at a bank." Advertisements for *Last Week*'s 2020 season featured his pimply-faced secondary-school photo with massive glasses and poofy mane, both too large for his thin head. The accompanying tagline reads, "If there's hope for him, there's hope for all of us." Throughout his career, Oliver has made fun of his appearance. After his show's launch, several interviewers commented on his looks as a way of driving home the unlikeliness of his success. *The New York Times's* David Carr described him as "a boyish, rangy fellow whose narrow face and shaggy mop are set off by fashionably unfashionable dark-framed glasses."[59] Just as Jon Stewart invoked his Jewish identity as a source of self-deprecating humor, Oliver does the same with his Britishness, playing on stereotypes of the "proper" English and the colonial English empire. Transitioning to a story about UK Parliament insults, Oliver says, "For now, let's move on to the UK, where 2000 years of civilization led to this face (*pointing at his own*)." The audience starts applauding for an extended time, to which he responds, "It's hurtful when you clap that."

He then makes fun of the quintessentially British way that members of Parliament mock each other and ends with the ironic, "I'm so proud."[60]

On the anchor desk, Oliver shares similarities to Stewart. His reporting becomes constitutive rhetoric toward the end of stories, with a call to action and an empathetic style that attempts to bind the audience together. He is also emotional, yelling, cursing, and acting as a surrogate for audience outrage as he introduces stories. Four-letter profanities are a regular feature of the pay-cable show, providing catharsis by condemning politicians and businesses. Like Stewart, Oliver has earned the respect and attention of traditional media companies and broader culture by functioning as a *parrhesiastes* within the journalistic field. Marc-Olivier Castagner and David Grondin characterize Oliver's approach as a kind of "silly citizenship," where he speaks truth and calls out falsehoods, encouraging his audience to do the same.[61] In addition to creating original research and reporting on stories, *Last Week* helps facilitate this method by creating real-world interventions into public issues and encouraging the audience to take action.

Satiric Activism on *Last Week Tonight*

While Stewart and Colbert extended their satire into the real world through their rally and Colbert's SuperPAC and presidential aspirations, Oliver goes a step further and consistently integrates *satiric activism* into his news parody. The term satiric activism describes two types of actions that often follow coverage of the episode's main issue. One is when Oliver takes demonstrative action to walk through a process and reveal counterintuitive information to the audience. The second type of satiric activism is when the audience is given a facilitated call to action, where the show provides some kind of assistance to help harness the activism of the viewer. These are not mutually exclusive, either; sometimes, a demonstrative action will then be followed by a call to action. In this section, I focus on three examples of this satiric activism on the show: its coverage of net neutrality, the creation of its church, and its purchase of medical debt.

In *Last Week*'s inaugural season, the show produced several in-depth reports that went viral; however, the story that brought the most attention and praise to Oliver and his crew was their coverage of the Federal Communication Commission's (FCC) plan to drop rules for net neutrality, which requires companies to treat all data the same, rather than favoring their content or charging sites to throttle speeds. In the 13-minute report, Oliver points out net neutrality's importance in allowing new companies to start up and compete with established internet behemoths and calls "bullshit" on telecommunication companies' efforts to reframe the argument to make it seem as if net neutrality is bad for consumers. He then explains how cable companies are cozy with politicians, showing a CEO golfing with Obama, and discusses how Obama picked a former cable lobbyist to chair the FCC. As Oliver says, "That is the equivalent of needing a babysitter and hiring a dingo." Using an interview with the CEO of Comcast, he then demonstrates how cable companies have decreased competition and act as monopolies, shows charts of America's poor internet speeds, and discusses how cable companies rate incredibly low for consumer satisfaction. However, Americans have taken little notice of the threat of doing away with net neutrality, according to Oliver, "because cable companies have figured out the great truth of America—if you want to do something evil, put it inside something boring." FCC policy is meant to be impenetrable to normal citizens, so it was a prime candidate for *Last Week*'s coverage. The report then reveals that the FCC is currently taking public comment on the proposed change in policy. Oliver puts up the website's address on-screen and unleashes the Internet trolls: "We need you to get out there and for once in your lives focus your indiscriminate rage in a useful direction."[62]

Oliver's viewers rallied to the cause as the comment section of the FCC's website crashed due to heavy traffic. After the segment aired on HBO Sunday night, problems with the site were confirmed and made worse after the clip was posted online Monday. By the following Tuesday, the YouTube video from *Last Week* had almost 800,000 views.[63] Two days after the clip aired, the FCC reported they had received 45,000 comments specifically on net neutrality since it opened the comments two and a half weeks before and another 300,000 messages to a box for comments about the open Internet. Previously, the highest number of comments the FCC had received on any proposal was under 2,000.[64] Comments continued to roll in, with many in the press crediting the unprecedented public interest in Oliver's story. A Pew Center study suggested the same.[65] The actual reporting on the episode also proved effective based on a study by Amy B. Becker and Leticia Bode, who had participants watch both *Last Week*'s and ABC News' net-neutrality coverage. They found that both programs increased knowledge about net neutrality at a similar level, although those who watched ABC found net neutrality more important overall.[66] Internal FCC communications reveal the agency was aware of and discussed the program's coverage. FCC Chair Tom Wheeler, after being asked by a reporter about *Last Week*, noted, "I would like to state for the record that I am not a dingo," which Oliver naturally covered on his show.[67] The FCC upheld net neutrality in a vote the following year.

The program revisited net neutrality in 2017 when the Trump FCC proposed and eventually approved overturning net neutrality. This time the show set up a special URL, GoFCCYourself.com, to facilitate viewer comments, again crashing the FCC servers. The net-neutrality story is emblematic of Oliver's use of trolling, which Amber Davisson and Mackenzie Donovan have identified as a way the host engages digital audiences through memes, creating raids, and other activities to encourage transgressive behavior.[68] Through its reporting on net neutrality and satiric activism, *Last Week* showed the power of an engaged, active audience in the post-network era.

In the second season of the show, Oliver channeled Colbert and decided to directly walk through a process as part of the show's coverage. The subject of the 20-minute extended report was the so-called "prosperity gospel," preachers and churches who instruct their audience to send in "seed money" with promises that those donors will then get their own financial "blessing" somewhere down the road—essentially an evangelical multilevel marketing scheme. Oliver introduces the story of Bonnie Parker, who gave money to a church instead of seeking cancer treatment because she was sure her seed money would bring healing. Parker died from cancer. After rolling a clip of evangelist Gloria Copeland asking her audience whether they would rather get cancer treatment that will make them sicker or sit in church and hear the word of God, Oliver responds, "It's pretty clear that women cannot hear the word of God, because if she could I'm pretty sure he'd be shouting 'Fuck you, Gloria!' right in her ear!" Oliver then shifts to the legalities of church donations, how all these activities are allowed, and how the donations are even tax-free, calling IRS regulations on churches so vague they are "close to meaningless." Preachers can live in a $6.3-million home and pay no taxes because it is considered a "parsonage." He reveals the show has been corresponding with Robert Tilton's church for seven months, producing a huge stack of mail to demonstrate how people are convinced to donate. Oliver donated $20 and then was asked for more money in the second letter from Tilton's church; this continued with the church sending items to Oliver and then asking they be sent back with donations, culminating in $319 in donations to the church and 26 letters from the church.

This first part of the satiric activism walked through how preachers convince people to give using encouragement, persuasion, and even veiled threats from God. The second part went much further. After showing a clip where Tilton says a viewer will receive the purpose they were looking for, Oliver announces, "and that is when I realized the message Robert Tilton was sending me was that I should set up my own church to test the legal and financial limits of what religious entities are able to do." The week before airing, the show filed paperwork to create "Our Lady of Perpetual Exemption" as a legal, religious, nonprofit entity, saying "it was disturbingly easy." After having the audience profess belief in the made-up, but legal church, the show cuts to a pretaped segment with reverend and CEO of the church, Oliver, and *SNL* alum Rachel Dratch as Wanda Joe Oliver, his evangelical wife, seated in a faux living-room style set. They hype www.ourladyofperpetualexemption.com, a mailing address, and a toll-free phone number, asking viewers to send in their seed money: "because if Robert Tilton, Kenneth Copeland, and all these bastards can get away with it and we get stopped, truly we have witnessed a fucking miracle tonight. Give us money."[69]

The invitation for viewers to participate created a satiric analog to televangelists. Callers would hear demands for money, and those who sent in money received additional letters telling them to send more. Oliver describes how he wanted to *show* viewers, not just *tell* them, and that "the point of it was to show that the barriers of entry to this is too low. And when it's this low, you can have bad actors enter."[70] Oliver officially shut the church down a month later, having received $70,000 from viewers and donated the money to Doctors Without Borders. As in the net-neutrality episode, Oliver encouraged the audience to take action, creating a shared goal as both an educational exercise and further solidifying fan identity. This time the program also added its own sense of spectacle by walking through the legal process, reporting on those actions, and performing its church identity.

In 2016, the show presented a report on American debt and the companies that purchase that debt. One debt-buying company reported that one in five Americans either owe them money or has in the past. The report includes discussion of the lack of oversight of the debt-buying industry, the unscrupulous and illegal methods used by the companies, and the human cost of their threats and policies. *Last Week* sent staff to the Las Vegas conference for DBA International, the trade group for debt buyers, and recorded footage of glib statements about consumers. Oliver begins to wrap up the segment with, "Any idiot can get into it, and I can prove that to you because I'm an idiot, and we started a debt-buying company. And it was disturbingly easy." The show spent $50 to incorporate "Central Asset Recovery Professionals," created a website, and was quickly offered $15 million in Texas medical debt representing 9,000 people, at the cost of around $60,000. The show bought the debt and forgave it, claiming they had now outdone Oprah Winfrey in giving away money. Oliver walks over to a huge red button surrounded by rotating dollar signs, creating a physical spectacle for the boring paperwork to actually forgive the debt. With "Fuck you Oprah!" he presses the button, and money falls from the sky. Each season brought multiple examples of satiric activism meant to involve the show and audience in political and cultural processes. One study found Oliver's calls to action increased a subject's likelihood to participate in some way.[71]

In each of these examples, satiric activism is precipitated by genuine reporting from the show's staff. Like *TDS* and *Colbert*, researchers and editors pour through footage and interviews from other media sources to gather raw materials; but while the Comedy Central shows assembled the equivalent of a news package, *Last Week* is synthesizing multiple aspects of an issue. In the report on prosperity gospel, they examine persuasive methods of churches, the effects on donors, tax laws surrounding donations, how much is spent, and so on. The fusion of information provides a powerful overview of the topic. *Last Week* also does its own reporting and generates new information, which previous shows have not done. The show sent the reporter to the debt-buying conference, for instance, to gather first-person accounts of how the industry talks about and to itself. *Last Week*'s satiric activism is an essential element of its mission to inform and entertain.

When They Call You a Journalist, Maybe You Should Listen?

Much like Stewart and Colbert, Oliver has been asked since the earliest days of his show whether *Last Week* is producing journalism, and just like his predecessors, he denies it. That has not stopped the media from pointing to the show as a kind of journalism, though, suggesting both Oliver and *Last Week* circulate within the journalistic field and wield cultural power.

Discussing the process of writing for the show, Oliver always emphasizes that stories start with research. Leading into the second season, the show hired three additional researchers. The staff makes sure older facts are still accurate and will even call primary sources cited in other media to fact-check.[72] However, if those facts are not easily available, researchers will find them, and this is where the show is often cited as adding its own brand of journalism distinct from Oliver's *TDS* roots. In their first season, *Last Week* carried a story about the Miss America pageant. The researchers could not verify the organization's claim that it awards $45 million in scholarships. At the same time, Oliver says the show is not producing journalism, he notes,

> But you sometimes want to find things that—yeah, the random acts of journalism would come in if you're looking for something, and you realize it isn't there. Even when we did something as silly as the Miss America thing. It's just annoying when you're trying to find what their charity has actually done, and no one has found it because it's Miss America.[73]

His staff spent a week pulling the organization's tax forms and found that although there may be $45 million in scholarships *available*, they actually *awarded* under $500,000. In an interview about the show, the Poynter Institute's Andrew Beaujon referred to the Miss America story, saying, "I don't know what else you'd call that kind of digging through public documents except journalism . . . I think it's inarguably legit."[74]

After the research, *Last Week* writers begin to figure out the narrative for the report. The writing room is staffed by several former journalists from publications like *The New York Times Magazine*, *Al Jazeera*, and *ProPublica*. Oliver says that once the foundation of the story is set, "Then we can kind of bring comedic writing to that process and work out how we'll tell the story, what elements we want to use, what kind of story arc we want to employ. And then we write jokes, so jokes come late."[75] Anyone who has worked in a newsroom will recognize that Oliver is describing the same process that most journalists use to tell their stories. Rick Edmonds, the media business analyst for the Poynter Institute, was a source for a *Last Week* report about local newspapers and wrote about how impressed he was with the interview and the quality of the final story, calling it "a distinguished piece of journalism about journalism."[76] Due to its dependence on other media sources, *Last Week*'s coverage may be more derivative than the best news outlets; however, in an age of reblogging, news aggregating, and opinions masquerading as reporting, Oliver and his staff produce information better than many organizations calling themselves news media. In a 2017 analysis of *Last Week*, one study found there were as many facts as jokes on the average episode.[77]

As an immigrant, Oliver brings an international perspective to his show reflected in the stories covered on *Last Week*, regularly introducing important global stories without the need to always tie them directly back to America. As mentioned earlier, the premiere included a story about Indian elections that specifically called out American media for not discussing such a consequential event for one of the largest countries in the world. The show's critical coverage of international regimes comes at a time when media outlets are owned by multinational organizations and seem less inclined to upset countries where parent companies might be trying to cultivate favor. *Last Week*'s coverage has resulted in censorship within some countries by distributors for HBO. China blocked access to HBO outright for both the channel's website and subscription service after a segment making fun of President Xi Jinping. The Disney-owned Hotstar, which licenses HBO for Indian distribution, censored the show after critical stories about Indian Prime Minister Narendra Modi. Episodes about Brexit were blacked out by Sky Atlantic in the UK. Surprisingly, though, HBO seems to have continued to take a hands-off policy with the program regarding editorial control.

Last Week often functions as journalism, but not the objective framework that dominated the American press in the latter half of the twentieth century. Don J. Waisanen uses the term *advocacy satire* to describe the actions of Oliver and other political humorists, saying, "comedians are now engaging in actions in the public interest."[78] According to Waisanen, the increase in advocacy satire is partially linked to the growth of alternative forms of media advocacy in society, as well as the historic use of satire in activism. *Last Week*, like previous news-parody shows, presents its stories with a clear expectation of the right and wrong pathways for politics and culture, expectations built on a critique of neoliberalism. As Nickie Michaud Wild describes, Oliver condemns powerful interests that extend inequality and institutions that fail to protect the vulnerable. While media tend to reduce stories to an easily identifiable villain, Wild argues that Oliver focuses on stories that are more structural and endemic.[79] The creators of the show challenge viewers with stories that have multiple sides without a clear, unproblematic solution. Like many high-quality media outlets, *Last Week* also continues to follow new developments and update viewers on previously covered stories, such as the earlier net-neutrality example.[80]

Another aspect of journalism practiced by *Last Week* is its critique of the media industry, calling out shallow coverage, corporate interests, and some journalists' coziness with those in power. At its most simplistic level, the short "And Now This" segment highlights the silly, infotainment aspects of journalism through repetitive montage; however, Oliver also consistently provides a deeper examination of contemporary media issues for his viewers. In the very first season of the show, *Last Week* produced a segment on "native advertising" in print and online media, advertisements meant to look like actual news reports mixed with legitimate reporting. The story highlights the ethical concerns and examples of companies like Chevron producing an article about energy needs—blatant conflicts likely to manipulate the content of the article.[81] Seven years later, the show created a companion piece about local television sponsored content, showing how stations incorporate paid segments and even provide interview platforms for paid guests to discuss dubious medical products and treatments.[82]

Last Week has also covered the quality of reporting about specialized fields. In 2019, Oliver discussed how private weather-reporting media companies, such as AccuWeather and The Weather Channel, hype weather events and both depend on and attempt to compete with the National Weather Service. Some media organizations even supported a bill to limit the amount of data the Weather Service provides to the American public so that the companies could provide exclusive information through their services.[83] In a report on the problems of scientific reporting by the media, *Last Week* describes how outlets consistently misunderstand and oversimplify scientific studies. Oliver also gives examples of journalists uncritically using error-ridden studies with obvious red flags as the foundation for news stories, such as one that claimed underhydrated drivers were just as dangerous as drunk drivers—based on a report paid for by an organization with partial funding from Coca-Cola.[84] While critical of journalistic failures, the show's coverage is not nihilistic. Oliver regularly touts the importance of journalism, especially local media, in creating a regenerative critique that journalists can do better and often succeed in that goal.

That optimism does not extend to newer conservative media outlets, however. While many issues covered by the show are apolitical, Oliver is unapologetic in his liberal outlook.[85] As a result, *Last Week* has produced multiple segments specifically calling out newer far-right media, as well as more stalwart conservative media organizations like Fox News. The show has produced critical reports about Fox personality Tucker Carlson, NRA TV (an online channel of the National Rifle Association), One America News (which became Trump's favorite news source while he was in office), and InfoWars, the website known for conspiracy theories and other false information. In these segments, Oliver examines the quality of reporting and the worldview behind each news source, measuring them against traditional standards of journalism and finding them lacking.

Despite Oliver's continual denials of being a journalist, the show replicates many of the same processes and goals as traditional news outlets. One study, for instance, showed that viewers interested in political humor acquired more information from *Last Week*'s style of in-depth reporting than viewers of other late-night comedy.[86] In an interview, Oliver makes the comparison that musicians do not create music for workouts in the gym, but some listeners will perceive it as perfect for that use. Similarly, his show is a comedy, and "we can't really control how people receive it."[87] To extend the metaphor, though, just because the music was not designed for exercise does not mean it may not be perfectly suitable and effective for that use. *Last Week*'s acceptance within the journalistic field as a legitimate information source and insider critic of media clarifies that intent is not the deciding factor in what functions as news.

Playing the Drumpf Card

In its first three seasons, *Last Week* rarely directly addressed Obama. They produced no segment specifically about him, and only a handful on particular policies or actions. There were jokes about Obama, especially regarding his inaction on issues like the closure of the Guantanamo Bay prison and the use of military drone strikes; however, he was a relatively minor character in the larger world of unexplored news stories. The candidacy and then election of Donald Trump in 2016 motivated the show to be more active in its inquiry and discussion of the presidency. Throughout Trump's four years, Oliver addressed the audience in a mode of assumed mutual disgust, criticizing everything from the president's looks to specific policies such as separating families at the border and banning transgender soldiers from serving in the military.

As the 2016 election geared up, the show ignored the pregame jockeying for party nominations until February of that year, after Trump won the GOP primaries in three states and was polling high moving into Super Tuesday. Oliver, almost in disbelief, announced the unthinkable—having to pay attention to Trump. In the episode, he refers to the candidate as "America's back mole," saying Trump "seemed harmless a year ago, but now that it's gotten frighteningly bigger, it's no longer wise to ignore it." The segment examines reasons GOP voters say they like Trump and counters those rationales with additional facts and context. For those who like that, he "tells it like it is," Oliver points out how dramatically Trump lies with no regard (a now-naive sounding criticism). The main part of the segment focuses on Trump's claims of business acumen, his failed businesses, and questions about the actual value of his companies and personal wealth. Oliver describes how Trump has become a brand, a character that he plays, and is even entertaining in a buffoonish way—"there's a part of me who even likes this guy. It's a part of me I hate." He then reveals that one of the candidate's ancestors changed the family name from Drumpf, a much less-appealing sounding name, and asks America to "make Donald Drumpf again," complete with hashtag.[88] To assist, the show created a web browser extension for viewers to download that changed all mentions of Trump to Drumpf, began selling caps similar to Trump's MAGA caps, and trademarked the name Drumpf. The story quickly became the most-viewed segment of the show on social media. It garnered 19 million YouTube views within eight days, and within six weeks, its combined Facebook and YouTube views were 85 million, dwarfing any previous *Last Week* clips (figure 7.1).

While *Last Week* continued to cover stories about Trump throughout 2016, it only produced three more second-block segments focused on him: one in March on Trump's border-wall proposal, a September look at controversies surrounding both Hillary Clinton and Trump, and the season finale, immediately following the election, in which the entire program was devoted to

Figure 7.1 John Oliver Introducing "Make Donald Drumpf Again" on *Last Week Tonight*. *Source: Screenshot by the author.*

coverage of President-elect Trump. Season Four launched with the main story about Trump's tenuous relationship with the truth, with Oliver saying the show could not move on to its normal type of important stories that season without addressing what seemed like a seismic shift in America. Unlike *TDS* or late-night talk shows, *Last Week* tends not to focus on the political intrigue and day-to-day events within the White House. As a result, the show limited the number of in-depth stories about Trump, with Oliver saying writers were "very anxious to not make it 'all Trump all the time,' both on a level of interest and a level of what the human soul can sustain."[89] Trump would often end up in the top block with discussions of his responses to national tragedies or international trips, but only a handful of second-block stories each season.

In 2017, the show launched a recurring extratextual intervention connected to Trump. The media quickly noticed that Trump religiously watched several Fox News programs, based on both his public statements and frequent calls to those shows. In the segment on Trump versus Truth, Oliver provides an overview of the frequency and range of lies the president tells and how he sometimes seems to be directly spreading mistruths heard from conservative media, such as Fox News and InfoWars. To try to educate Trump, *Last Week* announced it would be placing ads on morning news programs to "sneak some useful facts into his media diet." Parodying a real advertisement with a cowboy selling painless catheters, the advertisement starts off with actor Thomas Kopache portraying a cowboy talking about hating pain when he "caths." The ad then takes a different direction as Kopache makes clear the importance of the nuclear triad of land-based missiles, submarine-launched missiles, and aerial bombers, "In case you're the kind of person who might really need to know that."[90] The ads continued to run periodically on various conservative shows into 2018, providing facts on such topics as the Iran nuclear deal, the American Health Care Act, and sexual harassment, for the education—and ridicule—of Trump."

Oliver discussed the show's coverage of Trump in a 2021 *Washington Post* article after he was beaten in the election by Joe Biden. Like many in the media, the host says he recognized Trump simply wanted coverage, so he had to decide "'when is it irresponsible to give him that attention' and 'when is it actively irresponsible to ignore him.'" *Last Week* writers recognized that Trump was often simply a character and "the systemic problems underneath were there before him and will remain after him," so they tried to look beyond Trump in their reports. By the end of 2020, Oliver says he was thrilled to be able to move back to covering the show's regular "wonky stories."[91]

Last Week was far from the only news-parody program openly hostile to the Trump administration during his time in office, as I discuss later in this chapter. However, the HBO program seemed more cautious in not letting the president dominate its weekly coverage, unlike other shows. From its beginning, *Last Week* established its prioritization of factual information and truth-telling about important, underreported events. Trump's obsession with personal vendettas, ego, trivialities, and lying seemed to outrage Oliver and the other writers on the program, colliding against the very goals of the program. Trump's ideas, policies, and rhetoric simply added to the mismatch of ideological worldviews. Beyond the obvious disdain for Trump, though, *Last Week* produced solid reporting discussing policy details, such as the feasibility and cost of his proposed border wall, rather than just focusing on personality.

The show has continued to thrive post-Trump in the 2020s. Despite launching on a pay-cable channel near the implosion of the cable industry, as subscribers fled for streaming and internet content, the show continues to draw consistent viewership both on the HBOMax streaming platform and through YouTube and social media shares. Oliver was signed for an additional three-year contract with HBO in 2020, so the show will continue until at least the end of 2023.

Last Week created a new iteration of news parody unique on American television. While retaining the tone and satire of earlier shows like *TDS*, the program broke with parodying traditional newscasts. *Last Week*'s incorporation of the style and structure of newsmagazine television led to the program's addressing fewer stories but with greater context and more factual information. Its weekly schedule also shaped that approach and encouraged the show's creators to seek out less high-profile news left unaddressed by other news outlets. The result is reportage that synthesizes information from other outlets but that also includes facts uncovered by the show's researchers within a framework that advocates for its progressive point of view and often encourages audiences to join the show in its satiric activism.

"WEEKEND UPDATE" IN THE TWENTY-FIRST CENTURY

"Weekend Update" mostly stumbled through the 1990s, with some bright spots but no defining, consistent anchor like Jane Curtin or Dennis Miller. However, a new century launched influential and enduring comic personalities from the anchor desk that revitalized "Weekend Update," brought back a period of relevance, and also expanded diversity within the news-parody genre. *SNL*'s signature segment contended with a changing television landscape; no longer was broadcast king. By the end of the 2010s, cord-cutting— the cancellation of pay-cable service—had become mainstream, which meant smaller potential audiences for the live *SNL*. "Weekend Update" defined news parody for its first several decades through longevity, but the success of *TDS* and then *Colbert* suddenly created, if not competition, comparison. Audiences were unlikely to abandon one show for the other since *SNL* mostly provided topical sketch comedy; however, "Weekend Update" increasingly was framed by the media and audiences as a clunky prototype, a short-form, simpler version of full-length news-parody programs. As one writer put it in 2006, "[Weekend] Update can often come off as a Daily Show for people with lower SAT scores."[92] The segment remained well-known but had lost its luster.

The 2000–2001 season launched with the first duo on the anchor desk since the Jean Doumanian-helmed days. Tina Fey and Jimmy Fallon brought vitality and offered a different take on anchoring than then-newcomer Jon Stewart. The two wore their anchor roles loosely, often breaking the fourth wall, and seemed more light-hearted than serious about their political satire. The more at-ease style proved an effective balance to the increased political content Fey, the show's first female head writer, brought to the segment. Unlike "Weekend Update's" anchoring teams from the 1970s, where Aykroyd and Curtin were iterations of the same solemn news personality, Fey and Fallon developed conflicting personae. Fey presented herself as smart and informed, while Fallon seemed shallow—an entertainer riding on his good looks.[93] After jokes Fallon would often pause with a slightly vapid look, and at the end of the segment, would throw his pencil at the camera. Critic Ken Tucker suggested Fallon would do better to stick to *SNL* sketches rather than "Weekend Update," but praised Fey's writing and delivery of politically savvy "long, precisely parsed sentences unprecedented" on the segment.[94]

George W. Bush's personality and policies became a favorite punching bag for the segment under Fey. During the disputed 2000 election results, Fey reported that Bush called the idea of a hand recount "arbitrary and chaotic. Bush then looked down and crossed two words off his vocabulary word sheet."[95] *SNL*'s coverage of the 2000 election helped reinforce unfavorable public ideas about the candidates' traits: Gore as stiff and too verbose and Bush as clueless.[96] In a 2003 report about a taped speech by Bush, Fey describes that "when addressing the Iraqis, the president spoke slowly and chose simple words because he always does."[97] Even though Fey was more political than other cast members, only a small number of jokes could be included in the segment, and those would be interspersed with celebrity and lifestyle-oriented jokes. Amber Day and Ethan Thompson describe how Fey was especially assertive in her comic voice on the anchor desk regarding issues she cared about, such as social justice.[98] By their second year anchoring together, reports suggested Fallon might take the Chevy Chase route to pursue a career outside of the show. He departed in 2004 and acted in several forgettable films before returning to NBC to host *Late Night with Jimmy Fallon* in 2009, eventually taking over Jay Leno's role on *The Tonight Show* in 2014.

With the departure of Fallon, Fey was joined by Amy Poehler on "Weekend Update" from 2004 to 2006, the only time two women anchored the segment. The pair continued the more playful presentational style begun by Fey and Fallon. Whereas Fallon's anchor was portrayed as dim, Fey and Poehler established themselves as equals (frequent jokes about Poehler's supposed drug and alcohol use notwithstanding), unified by gender. For instance, the two announced they will be mentoring young women and then brought guest Lindsay Lohan onto "Weekend Update" to question her about her revealing clothes and life decisions. The bit humorously plays on second- versus third-wave feminist expectations, which Fey would continue to work with on her later sitcom *30 Rock*. Fey departed the anchor desk for her writing and acting career in 2006 but returned to "Weekend Update" with Poehler two years later for a special "women's news" segment. In discussing Hillary Clinton's run for the Democratic presidential nomination in 2008, Fey called out conservatives for focusing on the candidate's looks and for saying Clinton is "a bitch." Fey tells the audience that both she and Poehler are also bitches, "But bitches get stuff done!" The segment was a stunning outright endorsement of Clinton for *SNL* and a reflection of the anchor duo's incorporation of their own style of feminism.

The popular press wrote several articles celebrating what seemed to be a breakthrough moment for women in the early 2000s on *SNL*, a show well-known for being a "boys' club." Fey's head-writer position, the female anchor duo, and the increased number of women in the cast were held up as signifying a new era for the program. However, Caryn Murphy claims that the reports tended to be exaggerated and overstated Fey's control of *SNL*; she also observes that women never accounted for more than a third of the entire cast.[99]

Seth Meyers appeared opposite Poehler during "Weekend Update" from 2006 to 2008. During this time, the segment moved away from politics and cultural issues and more toward jokes about celebrities and entertainment media. The dominance of *TDS* and *Colbert* may be one reason, as those two hosts had become known for their political coverage, but the absence of the more political Fey as head writer likely played a role as well. During 2007 and 2008, *SNL* suddenly vaulted back into cultural relevance with the unexpected nomination of Alaska governor Sarah Palin for the GOP vice presidential slot. Fey physically resembled Palin and returned to portray her in skits on multiple occasions, with Poehler appearing during the same time as Clinton. Fey's folksy imitation of Palin drew applause and online views to a show that had struggled to provide many breakout moments for YouTube. Newspapers wrote with delight about *SNL*'s political satire during the election, and the show's ratings increased by 50% from 2007 to 2008.[100] A number of studies have analyzed Fey's portrayal and its effects on voter's perceptions; findings indicate decreased support for Palin among viewers, and that *SNL* influenced press coverage of the governor.[101] Fey's line in her first Palin sketch, "I can see Russia from my house!" was re-aired so many times by broadcast outlets and online that voters even started to wrongly attribute the quote to the real

Palin. Although "Weekend Update" benefited from the more increased attention given to *SNL*, the most widely shared and discussed clips tended to be from other parts of the show.

When Poehler left *SNL* in 2008, Meyers began a long run as solo anchor until 2014, when he moved to *Late Night* to replace Fallon. In Meyers's last year, he was joined on the desk by Cecily Strong. Head writer Colin Jost finished out the season with Strong after Meyers' departure. Later the same year, Jost and Michael Che took over anchoring "Weekend Update" and have continued as of this writing into 2022, making them the longest-serving anchor team on the segment. Che is the first Black cast member to take on the anchor role, beginning in the show's 40th season.

Che started at *SNL* as a writer in 2013, but departed the following year to become a correspondent for *TDS*. During his brief stint with Stewart, Che reported on the shooting of Michael Brown by a white police officer in Ferguson, Missouri, in August 2014. The shooting resulted in multiple protests and renewed attention to racism and social justice. Throughout his report, Che moves around to different locations via chromakey, looking for a safe place for a Black reporter to file a report. With each new setting, Stewart has to tell Che that police have killed a Black man in that location also. At the end, Che appears to be floating in outer space, where he can be safe, until blue lights suddenly start flashing.[102] The "Live from Somewhere" segment was one of only nine Che produced for *TDS*. It was widely speculated that discussions around racial inequality in the wake of Ferguson may have prompted *SNL* to make the long-overdue decision to finally diversify the anchor desk, and in September, it was announced that Che would rejoin the program. Earlier in the year, producers were specifically looking to add Black women to the show, an historically underrepresented group at *SNL*, and hired LaKendra Tookes and Leslie Jones as writers, as well as Sasheer Zamata as a featured cast member.

On the anchor desk, Che and Jost developed a different approach to anchoring "Weekend Update" than their predecessors. They break the fourth wall, but not in ways that call attention to themselves, like Norm MacDonald or Fallon. They reject the dispassionate newsreader approach, laughing and offering asides; however, the duo remains reserved without much variation in tone and body movements. Their delivery is conversational and informal, where one will begin to read a story with set up and punchline and then extend the story to talk about his personal reactions or thoughts about the topic, segueing into a kind of commentary. This might then be followed by the other anchors also commenting or asking a question. The flow combines traditional newscast with commentary and late-night talk style in an effective combination of contemporary delivery modes. Combined with the retro-feeling set that includes a grid map of the world expanding across the entirety of the background and a large wooden desk, Che and Jost's "Weekend Update" harkens back to the segment's past while grounding it in modern sensibilities (figure 7.2).

Che's presence on the anchor desk and in the "Weekend Update" writer's room coincided with a period of increased attention to racial inequality in the nation, resulting in more jokes about race in American politics and society. Previous anchors would sometimes discuss race but from an outsider's perspective. Che weaves himself directly into jokes, such as his comments during the hearings on Brett Kavanaugh's Supreme Court nomination: "These hearings have taught me a lot about what happens at white prep schools, and I never thought I'd say this, but I'm sending my kids to a Black school where it's safe."[103] The election of Donald Trump, in addition to providing a huge bump in viewership for the show, also continued to bring race into the national discussion. In an interview, Che called Trump "the poster child of ignoring people that may not have it as good as him."[104] After Trump called Haiti and African nations "shithole countries," Che reflection, "Can I be honest? When someone asks me, 'Did you hear what Donald Trump called Haiti and Africa,' I'm like, 'oh boy, did it start with an n?'" He continued, "Here's the thing, my job is to make jokes about the news, but Trump saying something racist isn't exactly news anymore."[105] Although Jost has claimed that the show is not partisan and simply covered Trump so much because the president was obsessed with media, on the final episode before the 2020 election, Jost told viewers America could not afford four more years of Trump and that he wakes up at night and Googles "America still democracy?"[106]

Figure 7.2 Colin Jost and Michael Che Are the Longest-Running Hosts of *Saturday Night Live*'s "Weekend Update." *Source: Screenshot by the author.*

Throughout the 2000s, in the face of massive upheaval in the television industry, the most surprising aspect of "Weekend Update" has been how little the segment has changed since its launch in the 1970s. There have been moments when content became more politically engaged or more focused on entertainment, but the basic structure and format continue. On the one hand, the show knows its brand and delivers what audiences expect. However, that audience has shrunk as consumers continue to reject live television and even time-shifting. The brief 10–15 minute format was perfect for the network era when the bottleneck of distribution made it difficult to sustain an entire program built around news parody. However, the segment has struggled to shift to shareable, online clips. In the late 2000s, *SNL* not only created viral moments with its Palin sketches, but also short films that were tailor-made for social media. The film "Lazy Sunday," from the comedy troop Lonely Island, aired on *SNL* in 2005 and went viral just as YouTube was launching. The format of "Weekend Update" makes it an unlikely candidate for dispersion through social media, though. Most of the actual news-parody headlines from the segment consist of a brief setup and punchline. Che and Jost tend to add additional commentary, but stories are neither long nor focused enough to create the kind of "stickiness" that makes for successful shareable media. Stories are usually tied to the specific moment of a politician saying something outrageous or an event, so there is a shorter shelf life to the jokes. Clips from full news-parody programs, whether they are a 20-minute deep dive from *Last Week* or a three-minute segment from *Full Frontal*, provide more time for a viewer to appreciate the topical context of the discussion and embed multiple jokes about that particular topic throughout the clip, with greater potential for gaining traction on social media.

TREVOR NOAH BRINGS THE ONLINE AUDIENCE

After Jon Stewart announced he would be departing *TDS*, a number of high-profile comedians were considered for the hosting job, including Chris Rock and Amy Schumer. Trevor Noah was an unexpected pick. Noah had been introduced to *TDS* audience just the year before when he appeared a handful of times in 2014 as a correspondent. Noah had hosted multiple television shows in his native South Africa, including his own late-night show, before coming to America in 2011. Although little known in America, Noah was huge internationally and had to decide whether it was worth it to take the desk at Comedy Central since it would be a pay cut from his touring income.[107]

TDSWTN launched in September of 2015 and struggled at first. Noah contended with expectations from an audience resistant to change. He knew he wanted to carry on the spirit of the *TDS*, but he was not interested in being a

Stewart clone. Noah grew up in apartheid-era South Africa, the son of a white father and Black mother when interracial relationships were illegal. In interviews, he discusses learning to fit in with various groups in different situations without necessarily belonging and how taking over the Comedy Central program was difficult because he was automatically challenging the ideas of certain viewers. He was surprised by the negative reaction from some fans of the show: "I knew liberal hatred existed, but I didn't think it would come for me."[108] Viewership in the first year declined almost 40% from Stewart's last season; however, those numbers only account for television views. Digital engagement, representing the younger demographics Noah was meant to target, increased with the new host.[109]

In 2016, the sudden surge in popularity of Donald Trump became an unwelcome moment of clarity that honed Noah's perspective and the direction of the show. Obama was president when he started hosting, and Hillary Clinton was expected to succeed him: "I was in a space where essentially everything seemed like it was on track . . . from a progressive point of view."[110] Trump's nomination and election made Noah realize he had a unique perspective to bring, and this is when he stopped simply feeling like Stewart's replacement, "I know what it's like to live in a country extremely divided by race—where people feel like it's crashing every day and they don't trust that their president has their best interest at heart."[111] Noah began to speak his experience as part of *TDSWTN* coverage, his perspective as international and biracial, his life growing up poor with an alcoholic stepfather who abused his mother, and his own struggles with depression. He spoke to his audience with knowledge and understanding in a personal way. It took the writing room some time to adjust to a new host. Showrunner Jen Flanz described how "we were now writing for a Black host and we needed to make sure that we were writing for his point of view."[112] The program developed more of an international perspective than when Stewart hosted, and Noah made clear he wanted to increase diversity—especially female voices—and intellectual diversity, including hiring writers with conservative points of view. In the first year, the show added two writers from Africa, a Malaysian correspondent, a female correspondent, and Baratunde Thurston, who is Black, as supervising producer.

As the emphasis of the show shifted under the new creative team, Trump provided a target for its satire. Rather than focus on the president, though, Noah viewed Trump as a catalyst for deeper conversations with his audience: "I don't think of Donald Trump as the story. I see this as America's story, and Donald Trump is the antagonist. . . . That character offers up the opportunity to have conversations about things that people may not have otherwise been interested in."[113] Trump's hostility against immigrants and seeming ignorance about global issues became perfect openings for Noah to delve into issues where he could bring a unique international perspective that stood out from other late-night or news-parody hosts (figure 7.3).

TDSWTN became the defining late-night program to address issues of race during the Trump era. While "Weekend Update's" Che added commentary on race to *SNL*, Noah brought an outsider's perspective of trying to understand America's history of racial violence and white supremacy, its unwillingness to address continued racial inequality directly, and the outright hostility of Trump and his voters. Unlike South Africa, which had to confront its apartheid past partially through truth and reconciliation commissions, Americans are locked in conflict over willingness to even open a dialogue.

One of the most powerful moments on *TDSWTN* happened when it was off the air. On May 25, 2020, George Floyd, a Black man in Minneapolis, was murdered by white police officer Derek Chauvin. Protests erupted around the nation. *TDSWTN* happened to be on break between May 21 and June 8, but a week after the killing, Noah sent his producers a video he shot at home on his iPhone of his thoughts and reactions to Floyd's death—no suit, no set, just a vertical video of Noah's upper torso in a green shirt. Editors trimmed it to 18 minutes and posted the clip online, drawing 48 million views in less than two weeks.[114] Noah describes how everyone is facing the lockdown and coronavirus, but Black Americans are still facing racism. "There was a Black man on the ground in handcuffs and you could take his life, so you did. Almost knowing that there would be no ramifications." Noah discusses conservative outrage over some looting that occurred during protests and uses his own experience in South Africa to talk about how there is no right way to protest

Figure 7.3 Trevor Noah on the Set of *The Daily Show with Trevor Noah*. *Source*: Screenshot by the author.

because of its very nature. But rather than condemning potential audience members, he tries to connect: "Maybe it would help you if you think about that unease that you felt watching that Target [store] being looted, try to imagine how it must feel for Black Americans when they watch themselves being looted every single day because that's fundamentally what's happening in America. Police in America are looting Black bodies."[115] There was no attempt to insert jokes or irony, the monologue was raw, direct, and seemed to connect with online audiences.

TDSWTN has only increased its online presence. Where Stewart's show shared clips and would extend interviews for internet consumption, online engagement and stickiness are central to Noah's show and appeal to a millennial audience. YouTube views averaged 8 million when he took over from Stewart but climbed to an average of 74 million in 2019.[116] Under Stewart, social media was another distribution method for content created by the show, but Noah is a digital native, and the program leverages various platforms both to hype the television show, and to create content specifically for social media audiences. The show became the perfect foil for a president obsessed with his online image. Christina M. Blankenship chronicles how *TDSWTN* treated Trump like a "reality television president," reframing Trump's fame and supposed accomplishments to diminish him, such as through the segment "The Celebrity Appresident," which uses his background of firing people on reality television to make fun of his difficulties keeping subordinates in his administration.[117] Noah's success with reaching younger, online audiences prompted Anthony Fauci to make *TDSWTN* his first stop for a late-night interview to discuss the coronavirus.[118] Noah has carved out his own niche both in late night and news parody. His life story and experiences allow him to directly address topics with credibility that white hosts cannot, appealing to the traditional Comedy Central audience but expanding to younger audiences and digital natives.

THE VOICE OF FEMINIST NEWS PARODY – SAMANTHA BEE

After Stewart announced his planned departure from *TDS*, there was speculation that correspondent Samantha Bee might be tapped for the anchor chair. Bee left her native Canada, where she had done sketch comedy, and started with the Comedy Central program in 2003. At the time, she was the only female correspondent on the show and became known for her field pieces and her fearlessly ironic interviews. Her point of view and humor stood out on the program, resulting in frequent packages. Her husband, Jason Jones, also worked on *TDS* from 2005 to 2015. Bee and Jones began developing the sitcom *The Detour*, which was picked up by TBS at the beginning of 2015. After Noah's selection to replace Stewart, TBS offered Bee her own late-night show, and she left *TDS* in April 2015 to develop the new program, hiring *TDS* alumni Jo Miller and Miles Kahn as coexecutive producers.

Press coverage of the announcement focused on late night as an almost exclusive "boys' club," and how Bee would be the first woman to front a news-satire show. The public would not have to wait until the launch of the program, though, to find out how Bee was going to shake up late night with her own brand of humor. In September of 2015, *Vanity Fair* featured an article about late-night comedy with a picture of ten men, including past and present *TDS* talent Stephen Colbert, John Oliver, Larry Wilmore, and Trevor Noah. Bee was not asked to participate in the story or photo. In response, she tweeted the picture @*Vanity Fair*, saying "Good . . ." Then followed with another tweet of her head on a centaur's body, shooting lasers out of her eyes in front of the group of men, with the text "BETTER." The tweet blew up on social media and gave a preview of the defiantly feminist attitude and brand *Full Frontal* would adopt.

TBS gave Bee and her cocreators freedom in developing the show format and approach. The network wanted to connect more with current events and culture through the program.[119] For Bee, the idea was to make a show she would want to watch, one that tackles issues important to women and places social justice front and center. "We wanted a show that was visceral, that came from a really gut place, that tapped into our fury."[120] She knew the program would be groundbreaking and in your face, so she expected to get only six episodes before it was canceled, but wanted to know she created a show that was true to herself. Six years later, *Full Frontal* is still on the air.[121] Bee wanted the writing room to be diverse and instituted a blind submission process, so there would be no indication about identity. They also created a sample application packet to help inexperienced writers apply. The process yielded an even split between male and female writers.[122]

Promos before the show's debut further played off Bee as a feminist host. One released in May of 2015 showed her at an art museum with framed pictures of male late-night hosts. A waiter offers up a tray of sausages, to which she responds, "Actually, you know what? I think I'm kind of done with sausage." She then shoves the male waiter's head out of the frame.

In designing *Full Frontal*, Bee broke with tradition by rejecting an on-set desk. She stands throughout the show, creating a sense of urgency and allowing for more movement and physical comedy. In an interview, Bee talked about having a lot of body energy and recognizing that a desk would be confining. She also decided there would be no interview segment. She admits to turning off shows when interviews start, "pitter-patter is not super interesting to me."[123] These two choices helped to structurally and stylistically set *Full Frontal* off from other news parody programs.

Full Frontal debuted on February 8, 2016, to positive reviews. In a show premier skit, Bee sits in front of a press conference as reporters keep asking her questions about being a woman doing a late-night show. One reporter asks, "What did you have to do differently to make this show a reality . . . as a woman?" She pauses and answers, "Hard work, a great team, maybe just a little bit of magic [*wink*]." Cut to Bee in the middle of a circle of candles, moving around like a possessed Linda Blair and yelling. Cut back to the press conference: "It's true, we're all witches."[124] The skit satirizes the prevalence of press stories about her new show that only wanted to dwell on a woman breaking into the fraternity of late night. *The New York Times* described Bee as "fiery and fierce—the acid delivery, cut with a touch of Canadian syrup," and claimed that her age puts her between millennials and second-wave feminists.[125] During the presidential campaign, this often played out with Bee's supporting Hillary Clinton, but still critiquing her through more of a third-wave lens.

Throughout its run, *Full Frontal* has crafted a proud, aggressive feminist voice that sets it apart from other news-parody programs. One magazine called it the most feminist show to ever appear on television.[126] The show launched as Trump was beginning to dominate the Republican presidential field, positioning Bee as one of his most prominent female critics. She regularly called Trump out on issues related to women and inequality and highlighted the sexism of press coverage of Clinton. After MSNBC's Joe Scarborough tweeted that Clinton should "smile" after she won primaries in March, a common sexist male suggestion, Bee launched the hashtag #SmileForJoe, where women tweeted themselves not smiling. TBS's social-media account retweeted a video comparing Clinton to a hyena, prompting Bee to respond, "Delete your account." TBS took it down and apologized, saying they would leave political satire to Bee. Before the presidential debate, the show ran a montage of media personalities giving Clinton conflicting, micromanaging advice, followed by Bee summarizing, "So, be perfect, but not too perfect. Save us from fascism, but like don't be a bitch about it. No one was suggesting superficial changes for Trump, like try wearing a suit that actually fits, or embrace your baldness proudly."[127] The month before the election, the *Boston Globe*'s Matthew Gilbert wrote, Bee "has been providing the vicarious catharsis that so many disgusted Americans need in the middle of such a relentlessly personal, petty, and fact-impaired race. She has become the torchbearer for sanity and common sense, like Stewart before her."[128] Previous news-parody hosts had kept some semblance of nonpartisanship, even if their content seemed lopsided; Bee told her viewers to get out and vote for Clinton (figure 7.4).

Figure 7.4 Samantha Bee Discusses Press Coverage of Hillary Clinton on *Full Frontal with Samantha Bee. Source: Screenshot by the author.*

While mainstream journalists tried to treat Trump like any other candidate, Bee highlighted his racism, sexism, and lies. John Oliver saw his weekly schedule as a reason not to follow each development in the Trump campaign too closely, but Bee took it as a challenge, packing stories and criticism into her show. Stephen J. Farnsworth and S. Robert Lichter, in their book on late-night comedy's treatment of Trump, describe how *Full Frontal* "considered the human impact of Trump's incendiary rhetoric throughout 2016" and how Bee treated Trump as a danger to the nation, merging "political humor with political commentary perhaps more than any other" host.[129]

Bee has discussed her passion for issues like reproductive rights, immigration and migration, and women's health, and how the program is a reflection of her concerns.[130] The show has produced several stories about rape and rape culture, including a 2017 story about a backlog in rape kits that was credited with shaming the Georgia legislature into passing a new law to test past kits. Bee discusses women's issues with sincere exasperation and calls out politicians and public figures for misogyny. The show was the first late-night program to seriously address the sexual abuse allegations against producer Harvey Weinstein, press reports that instigated the #MeToo campaign. In response, Weinstein told the press he knows he has to change and that "a lot of people would like me to go into a facility." Bee reacts, "Oh my God, I'm so behind on the slang. Is a facility what people call hell?" After reporting that Weinstein attempted to excuse his behavior because he came of age in the 1960s, Bee points out, "It's serial sexual harassment, not a Monkees tattoo." The report aired only days before #MeToo blew up on Twitter, but the host seemed to already be channeling the spirit of the movement when she commented, "The extent of [men's] creepiness seems to be a surprise to everyone, except women."[131] In an analysis of *Full Frontal* stories about rape culture, Viveca S. Greene and Amber Day explain how women in the public sphere have to be careful not to seem angry in order to avoid sexist criticism, but that Bee rejects that strategy. Instead, she "reclaims feminism and feminist anger, and in so doing educates her audience about feminist issues."[132] Coexecutive producer Alison Camillo said they instantly knew they were going to cover the Weinstein story and that they went around the writers' room and talked about their own experiences with harassment, becoming more and more angry: "This is the type of stuff that gets us really upset. This is what we're built to respond to."[133]

A breakdown of show topics created by TBS showed that immigration and migrant issues were frequent subjects on *Full Frontal*.[134] In a study of the show's coverage of the plight of displaced Syrians, results showed that audiences who watched *Full Frontal*'s reporting increased their support for the refugees.[135] However, Bee's concern about immigration ended up unintentionally embroiling her in the show's biggest controversy to date when she attacked the Trump administration in 2018 for their policy of separating undocumented children from families. After describing the outrageous living conditions in which children were kept, Bee pivoted to a picture recently posted by Ivanka Trump of the first daughter hugging her son. Juxtaposing children being removed from undocumented parents versus the serene picture of the presidential daughter and grandson, Bee comments, "You know Ivanka, that's a beautiful photo of you and your child, but let me say, one mother to another [*here shifting from speaking to yelling*], do something about your dad's immigration practices, you feckless cunt!"[136] It was the final invocation of the dreaded "c-word" that landed Bee at the top of seemingly every news show and website the next day. Although bleeped on TBS, the segment was originally posted on social media with the curse word intact. Response was immediate and harsh, with even politically friendly media outlets like CNN saying Bee had hurt her cause by using the word. The day before the *Full Frontal* show ABC had canceled its program *Roseanne* following a tweet from star Roseanne Barr that was widely interpreted as racist. Conservative media, who were outraged at the Barr firing, gleefully equated the two situations and called for TBS to cancel the show and prove the media industry did not have different standards based on politics. White House Press Secretary Sarah Huckabee Sanders also insisted the network should take action, calling the Ivanka comment "vile and vicious." Several advertisers pulled out of the show, and TBS issued an apology denouncing the use of the word. Bee tweeted her own apology the next day, saying the use of the word "was inappropriate and inexcusable. I crossed a line, and I deeply regret it."[137] In later discussions of the controversy, Bee says she learned how strong a person she is from the attacks; however, she regretted how the use of the one word became the focus for the media: "But the thing that really, really enraged me that I will never forget and absolutely never forgive is the number of valid news outlets that made the whole thing about my civility. What a shame that a conversation about family separation had to be consumed by conversations about this naughty word."[138] TBS seems to have attempted to bury the situation in the past; the entire season is available for purchase on platforms such as YouTube and Apple TV, except for that one episode.

Although the Ivanka Trump story created controversy, it seemed to have no effect on *Full Frontal*'s audience. The cursing and the aggressive presentation perfectly align with Bee's persona, even if the use of such a forbidden word shocked the media. Despite TBS regularly bleeping curse words, Bee sprinkles them throughout her show. The decidedly nonjournalistic descriptions she uses, such as calling Senator Ted Cruz a "fist-faced horseshit salesman" is part of her larger rejection of traditional femininity. She curses, swings her arms, yells, and gets angry. Standing on the set, rather than sitting at a desk, allows her to constantly be in motion. The camera even accentuates Bee's kinetic energy as the operator shoots off the shoulder, rather than locking it down on a tripod, allowing the frame to move with the host. In an analysis of Bee's critique of Ivanka Trump, Leopold Lippert compares Ivanka's image of traditional "modest femininity," presenting herself as restrained and composed, with Bee's more feminist "unruly aggressiveness."[139] Another study found Bee averaged a curse word about every one and a half minute on *Full Frontal*. After she apologized for the Ivanka segment, Bee's frequency of cursing remained about the same, although she temporarily used profanity less to attack individuals for several months before returning to form.[140]

Full Frontal has created a needed feminist voice within news parody. Although "Weekend Update" hosts Fey and Poehler started off the decade with more of a focus on gender politics, the short format of the segment only allowed for a limited number of jokes and much briefer discussion of any one story. Bee and her writers have placed inequality and injustice front and center in the show's coverage, especially as it relates to issues of gender. TBS, which signs shorter extensions for its shows, renewed the program again for 2022.

A DECADE OF CHANGE

The popularity and development of *TDS* and *Colbert* forced cultural critics and the media to finally take news parody seriously, but it was the launch of additional shows in the 2010s that brought diversity and new ideas into the genre. Since its inception in the 1960s, news parody had overwhelmingly been the domain of white, male writers and hosts. Women did play important roles in earlier programs, including Nancy Ames, Jane Curtin, Lucy Webb, Anne Bloom, and of course the original *Daily Show* creators Madeleine Smithberg and Lizz Winstead; however, they were often viewed more as the exception to the rule. At the same time *TDS* was lauded for its incisive satire, articles also discussed the shocking lack of diversity behind the scenes. Although it took the better part of the decade, the 2010s were a reckoning for the media industry and its refusal to make meaningful changes to open the door to underrepresented groups. News-parody anchor desks represent only a small sliver of the television industry; however, the genre expanded behind the scenes as well, with increased diversity of writers, producers, and technical staff. From #OscarSoWhite to #MeToo to increased social justice movements in the wake of racial and police violence, film and television were forced to recognize exclusionary policies in hiring, wages, and talent development during the decade—a process still ongoing and that must be extended.

In addition to new voices, the shows of the 2010s also innovated news-parody formats, expanded types of coverage, and incorporated their hosts' own experiences into reporting. John Oliver and Trevor Noah brought international perspectives, consistently covering stories outside of America for the first time within the genre and providing a global perspective to understand events within the United States. Oliver challenged the traditional format by proving that viewers were willing to invest time in longer reports about stories outside the headlines. Noah and Michael Che spoke plainly and with authority on racial issues from their anchor desks, weaving their identities into their coverage and commentary when white hosts had traditionally mediated those topics. Noah targeted millennial viewers through his selection of stories and use of social media. Samantha Bee created a show with a feminist voice on issues of inequality. Each program has built on the success of the shows that have come before, but without being beholden to them.

NOTES

1. *The Daily Show with Jon Stewart*, February 10, 2015.
2. Kathryn S. Wenner, "Peeling *The Onion*," *American Journalism Review* (September 2002): 53.
3. "Press 'Play' for Satire," *Wall Street Journal*, March 23, 2007, W, 3.
4. Andrea Seabrook, "On the National Mall, Divisions Kept in Check," August 28, 2010, https://www.npr.org/templates/story/story.php?storyId=129500025.
5. Guy Debord, *Society of the Spectacle*, trans. Ken Knabb (London: Rebel Press, 2006), 3.

6. Jonathan Gray, Jeffrey P. Jones, and Ethan Thompson, "The State of Satire, the Satire of State," in *Satire TV: Politics and Comedy in the Post-Network Era*, ed. Jonathan Gray, Jeffrey P. Jones, and Ethan Thompson (New York: New York University Press, 2009).

7. *The Colbert Report*, September 13, 2007.

8. Katharine Q. Seelye, "Colbert's Presidential Bid Ends after a 'No' in South Carolina," *The New York Times*, November 2, 2007, A, 18.

9. For an examination of these legal questions, see Clifford Jones, "The Stephen Colbert Problem: The Media Exemption for Corporate Political Advocacy and the 'Hall to the Cheese Stephen Colbert Nacho Cheese Doritos 2008 Presidential Campaign Coverage'," *University of Florida Journal of Law & Public Policy* 19, no. 2 (2008).

10. *Larry King Live*, October 20, 2010.

11. Ronald A. Placone and Michael Tumolo, "Interrupting the Machine: Cynic Comedy in the 'Rally for Sanity and/or Fear'," *Journal of Contemporary Rhetoric* 1, no. 1 (2011).

12. Russell Berman, "'Sanity' Rally Pleads for Tolerance, but Stars Don't Plead for Dem Voters," *The Hill*, October 30, 2010, https://thehill.com/blogs/blog-briefing-room/news/126661-sanity-rally-pleads-for-tolerance-but-stars-dont-plead-for-dems-to-vote.

13. Jeffrey P. Jones, Geoffrey Baym, and Amber Day, "Mr. Stewart and Mr. Colbert Go to Washington: Television Satirists Outside the Box," *Social Research* 79, no. 1 (2012): 41.

14. Ian Reilly and Megan Boler, "*The Rally to Restore Sanity*, Prepoliticization, and the Future of Politics," *Communication, Culture & Critique* 7 (2014).

15. Debord, *Society of the Spectacle*, 27.

16. Art Herbig and Aaron Hess, "Convergent Critical Rhetoric at the 'Rally to Restore Sanity': Exploring the Intersection of Rhetoric, Ethnography, and Documentary Production," *Communication Studies* 63, no. 3 (2012): 282.

17. Douglas Kellner, "The Media, Democracy, and Spectacle: Some Critical Reflections," *Cultural Politics* 11, no. 1 (2015).

18. U.S. Congress, House of Representatives, Subcommittee on Immigration, Citizenship, Refugees, Border Security, and International Law, *Protecting America's Harvest, before the Subcommittee on Immigration, Citizenship, Refugees, Border Security, and International Law*, 111th Cong., Serial No. 111-150 (September 24, 2010), 32.

19. Sarah Bishop, "'I'm Only Going to Do It If I Can Do It in Character': Unpacking Comedy and Advocacy in Stephen Colbert's 2010 Congressional Testimony," *The Journal of Popular Culture* 48, no. 3 (2015).

20. U.S. Congress, *Protecting America's Harvest*, 56.

21. Sophia A. McClennen, *Colbert's America: Satire and Democracy* (New York: Palgrave Macmillan, 2011), 146–47.

22. *The Colbert Report*, March 10, 2011.

23. *Fresh Air*, October 4, 2012.

24. *The Colbert Report*, September 29, 2011.

25. R. Sam Garrett, "Seriously Funny: Understanding Campaign Finance Policy through the Colbert Super PAC," *St. Louis University Law Journal* 56, no. 3 (2012).

26. *Meet the Press*, October 14, 2012.

27. Marcus Paroske, "Pious Policymaking: The Participatory Satires of Stephen Colbert," *Studies in American Humor* 2, no. 2 (2016).

28. Bruce W. Hardy et al., "Stephen Colbert's Civics Lesson: How Colbert Super PAC Taught Viewers About Campaign Finance," *Mass Communication and Society* 17 (2014).

29. Sophia A. McClennen and Remy M. Maisel, *Is Satire Saving Our Nation? Mockery and American Politics* (New York: Palgrave Macmillan, 2014), 44.

30. *The Colbert Report*, December 18, 2014.

31. *The Daily Show with Jon Stewart*, December 16, 2010.

32. Chris Smith, *The Daily Show (The Book)* (New York: Grand Central Publishing, 2016), 277.

33. Ibid., 278.

34. Matt Carlson and Jason T. Peifer, "The Impudence of Being Ernest: Jon Stewart and the Boundaries of Discursive Responsibility," *Journal of Communication* 63 (2013).

35. *The Daily Show with Jon Stewart*, June 19, 2015.

36. *The Daily Show with Jon Stewart*, July 2, 2015.

37. *The Daily Show with Jon Stewart*, August 6, 2015.

38. Gary Levin, "John Oliver Is Ready to Talk," *Gannett News Service*, April 23, 2014, https://www.proquest.com/wire-feeds/john-oliver-is-ready-talk/docview/1518734603/se-2?accountid=8577.

39. Smith, *The Daily Show (The Book)*, 342–43.

40. Adam Sherwin, "British Comic John Oliver Gains His Own Show on HBO," *The Independent*, November 16, 2013, 12, 13.

41. Gary Levin, "'Last Week' Is a First for Host and HBO," *Gannett News Service*, April 23, 2014, https://www.proquest.com/wire-feeds/last-week-is-first-host-hbo/docview/1518734659/se-2?accountid=8577.

42. Last Week Tonight with John Oliver, "GOP - Hashtag Awesomesauce," (YouTube, 2014). https://www.youtube.com/watch?v=gdQCtWlhx90.

43. *Last Week Tonight with John Oliver*, April 27, 2014.

44. "Trollbäck Crafts Last Week Tonight Open," *Digital Video* 22, no. 6 (2014).

45. Raymond Williams, *Television: Technology and Cultural Form* (London: Routledge, 1974), 86–96.

46. *Last Week Tonight with John Oliver*, September 12, 2021.

47. David Hinckley, "'Last Week Tonight' Returns with More Ammo Than Fish," *New York Daily News*, February 4, 2015, 62.

48. David Carr, "British Comic's Offbeat News Show Connects with U.S. Viewers," *International New York Times*, November 18, 2014, 19.

49. *Last Week Tonight with John Oliver*, June 8, 2014.

50. *Last Week Tonight with John Oliver*, April 24, 2016.

51. *Last Week Tonight with John Oliver*, June 14, 2015.

52. Anne Ulrich, "Attention through Distraction: Basic Modalities and Rhetorical Medialities of *Last Week Tonight*," *Poetics Today* 40, no. 2 (2019): 312.

53. David Marchese, "In Conversation: John Oliver: The Last Week Tonight Host Swears He's Only Kidding," *New York*, February 22, 2016, https://www.proquest.com/magazines/conversation-john-oliver/docview/1847915068/se-2?accountid=8577.

54. Dave Itzkoff, "John Oliver Returns: 'I'm Not a Complete Nihilist'," *The New York Times*, February 8, 2017, C, 1.

55. Carr, "British Comic's Offbeat News Show Connects with U.S. Viewers."

56. Melissa Hank, "Brit Wit John Oliver Dances His Way to HBO; Comic Brings His Own Spin to American Politics," *Calgary Herald*, April 26, 2014, C, 13.

57. *The Late Show with Stephen Colbert*, February 7, 2017.

58. *Last Week Tonight with John Oliver*, June 19, 2016.

59. Carr, "British Comic's Offbeat News Show Connects with U.S. Viewers."

60. *Last Week Tonight with John Oliver*, April 17, 2016.

61. Marc-Olivier Castagner and David Grondin, "From Irritated Hostages to Silly Citizens: Infotainment Satire as Ludic Surveillance," in *The Joke Is on Us: Political Comedy in (Late) Neoliberal Times*, ed. Julie A. Webber (Lanham, MD: Lexington Books, 2019).

62. *Last Week Tonight with John Oliver*, June 1, 2014.

63. Amanda Holpuch, "John Oliver's Cheeky Net Neutrality Plea Crashes FCC Website," *The Guardian*, June 3, 2014, https://www.theguardian.com/technology/2014/jun/03/john-oliver-fcc-website-net-neutrality.

64. Elise Hu, "John Oliver Helps Rally 45,000 Net Neutrality Comments to FCC," *NPR*, June 3, 2014, https://www.npr.org/sections/alltechconsidered/2014/06/03/318458496/john-oliver-helps-rally-45-000-net-neutrality-comments-to-fcc.

65. Alex T. Williams and Martin Shelton, "What Drove Spike in Public Comments on Net Neutrality? Likely, a Comedian.," The Pew Research Center, updated September 5, 2014, https://www.pewresearch.org/fact-tank/2014/09/05/what-drove-spike-in-public-comments-on-net-neutrality-likely-a-comedian/.

66. Amy B. Becker and Leticia Bode, "Satire as a Source for Learning? The Differential Impact of News Versus Satire Exposure on Net Neutrality Knowledge Gain," *Information, Communication & Society* 21, no. 4 (2018).

67. *Last Week Tonight with John Oliver*, June 15, 2014.

68. Amber Davisson and Mackenzie Donovan, "'Breaking the News . . . on a Weekly Basis': Trolling as Rhetorical Style on *Last Week Tonight*," *Critical Studies in Media Communication* 36, no. 5 (2019).

69. *Last Week Tonight with John Oliver*, August 16, 2015.

70. *Fresh Air*, March 7, 2018.

71. Leticia Bode and Amy B. Becker, "Go Fix It: Comedy as an Agent of Political Activation," *Social Science Quarterly* 99, no. 5 (2018).

72. Alex Weprin, "HBO's John Oliver on How to Avoid the 'All Trump All the Time' Comedy Trap," *Politico*, February 6, 2017, https://www.politico.com/blogs/on-media/2017/02/john-oliver-on-how-to-avoid-the-all-trump-all-the-time-comedy-trap-234698.

73. Rose Miller, "John Oliver Talks Net Neutrality, Salmon Cannons, and the Future of Last Week Tonight," *The Verge*, February 4, 2015, https://www.theverge.com/2015/2/4/7976983/john-oliver-interview-best-of-last-week-tonight.

74. Asawin Suebsaeng, "'Last Week Tonight' Does Real Journalism, No Matter What John Oliver Says," *Daily Beast*, April 14, 2017, https://www.thedailybeast.com/last-week-tonight-does-real-journalism-no-matter-what-john-oliver-says.

75. *Fresh Air*, March 7, 2018.

76. Rick Edmonds, "I Was Interviewed by 'Last Week Tonight.' Here's Why the Show Is Journalism," The Poynter Institute, August 8, 2016, https://www.poynter.org/newsletters/2016/i-was-interviewed-by-last-week-tonight-heres-why-the-show-is-journalism/.

77. Julia R. Fox, "Journalist or Jokester? An Analysis of *Last Week Tonight with John Oliver*," in *Political Humor in a Changing Media Landscape: A New Generation of Research*, ed. Jody C. Baumgartner and Amy B. Becker (Lanham, MD: Lexington Books, 2018).

78. Don J. Waisanen, "The Rise of Advocacy Satire," in *Political Humor in a Changing Media Landscape: A New Generation of Research*, ed. Jody C. Baumgartner and Amy B. Becker (Lanham, MD: Lexington Books, 2018), 11.

79. Nickie Michaud Wild, "'The Mittens of Disapproval Are On': John Oliver's *Last Week Tonight* as Neoliberal Critique," *Communication Culture & Critique* 12 (2019).

80. Paul Alonso, *Satiric TV in the Americas: Critical Metatainment as Negotiated Dissent* (New York: Oxford University Press, 2018), 38.

81. *Last Week Tonight with John Oliver*, August 3, 2014.

82. *Last Week Tonight with John Oliver*, May 23, 2021.

83. *Last Week Tonight with John Oliver*, October 13, 2019.

84. *Last Week Tonight with John Oliver*, May 8, 2016.

85. Paul Farhi, "John Oliver of 'The Daily Show' Gets His Own Fake-News Program on HBO," *The Washington Post*, Posted April 3, 2014.

86. Freddie J. Jennings, Josh C. Bramlett, and Benjamin R. Warner, "Comedic Cognition: The Impact of Elaboration on Political Comedy Effects," *Western Journal of Communication* 83, no. 3 (2019).

87. Marchese, "In Conversation: John Oliver."

88. *Last Week Tonight with John Oliver*, February 28, 2016.

89. Weprin, "HBO's John Oliver on How to Avoid the 'All Trump All the Time' Comedy Trap."

90. *Last Week Tonight with John Oliver*, February 12, 2017.

91. Steven Zeitchik, "HBO's John Oliver Says Trump Was Not Good for Late-Night Comedy," *The Washington Post*, February 11, 2021, https://www.proquest.com/blogs-podcasts-websites/hbo-s-john-oliver-says-trump-was-not-good-late/docview/2488438136/se-2?accountid=8577.

92. Scott Collins, "Saturday Night Live Updates Weekend Update," *The Ottawa Citizen*, September 30, 2006, K, 15.

93. Tom Shales and James Andrew Miller, *Live from New York: An Uncensored History of Saturday Night Live* (Boston, MA: Little, Brown and Company, 2002), 441.

94. Ken Tucker, "Saturday Night Live," *Entertainment Weekly*, March 2, 2001, https://ew.com/article/2001/03/02/saturday-night-live/.

95. *Saturday Night Live*, November 18, 2000.

96. Chris Smith and Ben Voth, "The Role of Humor in Political Argument: How 'Strategery' and 'Lockboxes' Changed a Political Campaign," *Argumentation and Advocacy* 39 (2002).

97. *Saturday Night Live*, April 21, 2003.

98. Amber Day and Ethan Thompson, "Live from New York, It's the Fake News! *Saturday Night Live* and the (Non)Politics of Parody," *Popular Communication* 10, no. 1–2 (2012): 178.

99. Caryn Murphy, "'Is This the Era of the Woman?': *SNL*'s Gender Politics in the New Millennium," in *Saturday Night Live and American TV*, ed. Nick Marx, Matt Sienkiewicz, and Ron Becker (Bloomington, IN: Indiana University Press, 2013).

100. Rebecca Dana, "SNL Rides High on Campaign Satire," *Wall Street Journal* (New York), October 6, 2008, B.

101. Angela D. Abel and Michael Barthel, "Appropriation of Mainstream News: How *Saturday Night Live* Changed the Political Discussion," *Critical Studies in Media Communication* 30, no. 1 (2013); Jody C. Baumgartner, Jonathan S. Morris, and Natasha L. Walth, "The Fey Effect: Young Adults, Political Humor, and Perceptions of Sarah Palin in the 2008 Presidential Election Campaign," *Public Opinion Quarterly* 76, no. 1 (2012); Margaret E. Duffy and Janis Teruggi Page, "Does Political Humor Matter? You Betcha! Comedy TV's Performance of the 2008 Vice Presidential Debate," *The Journal of Popular Culture* 46, no. 3 (2013); Jason T. Peifer, "Palin, Saturday Night Live, and Framing: Examining the Dynamics of Political Parody," *The Communication Review* 16, no. 3 (2013); Nickie Michaud Wild, "Dumb Vs. Fake: Representations of Bush and Palin on *Saturday Night Live* and Their Effect on the Journalistic Public Sphere," *Journal of Broadcasting & Electronic Media* 59, no. 3 (2015).

102. *The Daily Show with Jon Stewart*, August 26, 2014.

103. *Saturday Night Live*, September 29, 2018.

104. *Fresh Air*, November 10, 2015.

105. *Saturday Night Live*, January 13, 2018.

106. Jonathan Capehart, "A Conversation with SNL's Colin Jost," *Washington Post Live*, July 20, 2020, https://www.washingtonpost.com/video/washington-post-live/a-conversation-with-snls-colin-jost/2020/07/20/f7794df0-f0c1-48dc-9aa6-dfe6b5c9c089_video.html; *Saturday Night Live*, Season 46, Episode 5, October 31, 2020.

107. Lacey Rose, "From Pain and Tragedy to Global Empire: How Trevor Noah Became the Busiest Man in Comedy," *The Hollywood Reporter*, June 19, 2019, https://www.hollywoodreporter.com/tv/tv-features/how-trevor-noah-became-busiest-man-comedy-1219141/.

108. Ann Marie Cox, "Trevor Noah Wasn't Expecting Liberal Hatred," *The New York Times Magazine*, November 6, 2016, 58.

109. Tony Maglio, "How Trevor Noah's 'The Daily Show' Is Beating Jon Stewart's," *The Wrap*, November 1, 2015, https://www.thewrap.com/trevor-noah-first-month-daily-show-comedy-central-michele-ganeless-digital-tv-ratings-twitter/.

110. *Fresh Air*, November 22, 2016.

111. Rose, "From Pain and Tragedy."

112. Bill Bradley, "Trevor Noah Is Taking 'The Daily Show' Places It's 'Never Been Before'," *Huffpost*, July 9, 2020, https://www.huffpost.com/entry/trevor-noah-taking-the-daily-show-places-its-never-been-before_n_5f036140c5b6acab28541764?ncid=txtlnkusaolp00000616.

113. Greg Braxton, "Trevor Noah Strikes a Nerve - and Ratings Gold - as He Steers 'The Dailyshow' into the Trump Era," *Los Angeles Times*, June 8, 2017, https://www.latimes.com/entertainment/tv/la-ca-st-sunday-conversation-trevor-noah-20170608-htmlstory.html.

114. Bradley, "Trevor Noah Is Taking."

115. *The Daily Show with Trevor Noah*, "Trevor Speaks Out About the Murder of George Floyd," June 21 2020,18:05, https://www.cc.com/video/9fd8dt/the-daily-show-with-trevor-noah-trevor-speaks-out-about-the-murder-of-george-floyd.

116. Rose, "From Pain and Tragedy."

117. Christina M. Blankenship, "President, Wrestler, Spectacle: An Examination of Donald Trump's Firing Tweets and *The Celebrity Appresident* as Response to Trump's Media Landscape," *Journal of Communication Inquiry* 44, no. 2 (2020).

118. Bradley, "Trevor Noah Is Taking."

119. Dave Itzkoff, "Samantha Bee Prepares to Debut 'Full Frontal'," *The New York Times*, January 10, 2016, AR, 1.

120. Alex Morris, "Who's Afraid of Samantha Bee," *Rolling Stone*, July 14, 2016.

121. Television Academy Foundation, *Samantha Bee Interview* (October 3, 2019), https://interviews.televisionacademy.com/interviews/samantha-bee?clip=112516#interview-clips.

122. Itzkoff, "Samantha Bee Prepares."

123. Television Academy Foundation, *Samantha Bee Interview*.

124. *Full Frontal with Samantha Bee*, February 8, 2016.

125. James Poniewozik, "Samantha Bee's Fierce, Fiery Feminism Anchors 'Full Frontal'," *The New York Times*, February 10, 2016, C, 1.

126. Virginia Heffernan, "Samantha Bee's Full-Frontal Assault on the Trump Regime," *Wired*, March 28, 2017, https://www.wired.com/2017/03/full-frontal-assault/.

127. *Full Frontal with Samantha Bee*, September 28, 2016.

128. Matthew Gilbert, "Without Samantha Bee, This Election Would Be So Much Worse," *The Boston Globe*, October 6, 2016, N, 1.

129. Stephen J. Farnsworth and S. Robert Lichter, *Late Night with Trump: Political Humor and the American Presidency* (New York: Routledge, 2020), 71–73.

130. Television Academy Foundation, *Samantha Bee Interview*.

131. *Full Frontal with Samantha Bee*, October 11, 2017.

132. Viveca S. Greene and Amber Day, "Asking for It: Rape Myths, Satire, and Feminist Lacunae," *Signs: Journal of Women in Culture and Society* 45, no. 2 (2019).

133. Hilary Lewis, "Samantha Bee on Tackling Harvey Weinstein Claims: 'It's in Our Wheelhouse'," *The Hollywood Reporter*, October 14, 2017, https://www.hollywoodreporter.com/news/general-news/samantha-bee-full-frontal-team-harvey-weinstein-penis-psa-jo-miller-trump-news-cycle-paleyfest-ny-20-1048920/.

134. Television Academy Foundation, *Samantha Bee Interview*.

135. Lauren Feldman and Caty Borum Chattoo, "Comedy as a Route to Social Change: The Effects of Satire and News on Persuasion About Syrian Refugees," *Mass Communication and Society* 22 (2019).

136. *Full Frontal with Samantha Bee*, May 30, 2018.

137. Rebecca Morin, "Comedian Samantha Bee Apologizes to Ivanka Trump," *Politico*, May 31, 2018, https://www.politico.com/story/2018/05/31/samantha-bee-ivanka-trump-apology-615588.

138. James West, "Samantha Bee on What That C-Word Controversy Taught Her About Trump-Era Comedy," *Mother Jones*, July 29, 2020, https://www.motherjones.com/media/2020/07/samantha-bee-david-corn-podcast-full-frontal-trump-c-word/.

139. Leopold Lippert, "Neoliberal Feminisms, Late-Night Comedy, and the Public Sphere, Or: Samantha Bee Takes on Ivanka Trump," *Feminist Media Studies* (2021), https://www.tandfonline.com/doi/full/10.1080/14680777.2021.1998182.

140. Barbara K. Kaye, "A Feckless Punt: Cursing on *Full Frontal with Samantha Bee*," *Comedy Studies* 11, no. 2 (2020).

Chapter 8

News Parody Moving Forward

After a decade of reporting for NPR, Andrea Seabrook left the network and traditional journalism in 2012, saying she was sick of being lied to by politicians and covering political theater instead of real news. Seabrook began to see the relationship between politics and media as part of the problem: "As a journalist, when you walk into that and pretend that it's a functioning system, or at least decide you're going to cover it as such, it plays right in. It allows those lawmakers to use manipulative language, stretched truth, untruths to communicate through you."[1] Seabrook's comments highlight the increasing difficulty for journalists operating in a field whose norms are still tied to an era where a few media gatekeepers set the agenda, the public was more trusting of institutions like the press, and politicians were still capable of being shamed. Over the decades, news parody has evolved from just humorously observing the media and politics to becoming legitimate participants within journalism. The genre does not replace objectivity-based reporting but helps provide additional information and points of view and offer critiques of press outlets, especially television.

Since the early 2000s, news parody hosts have increasingly been sought out by other media to provide commentary, accepting roles as cultural critics of the journalistic and political fields. Amber Day notes, "It seems clear that their work functions as political speech in and of itself, affecting the direction of public discourse while elevating the parodists to the level of legitimate political experts."[2] Even their satire weaves itself into traditional news, with journalists regularly including news parody reports, providing what Pierre Bourdieu calls functional capital. Established institutions already wielding power within a field can convey this functional capital to others by treating them as valid contributors. Each time media outlets invite news parody shows to participate in the journalistic and political field, the comedy shows accumulate more cultural capital. The hosts themselves also continue to legitimate their participation in these fields by accruing both personal and professional capital.[3] There is a cross-pollination, too, with traditional journalists having regularly appeared with Jon Stewart, Stephen Colbert, Trevor Noah, and John Oliver as guests or sometimes even acting in comedy sketches on their shows. The hosts' status as both outsiders and participants within the journalistic field allows them to expand on and rearticulate news through such functions as contextualizing news stories, demystifying government and business processes, challenging official voices, and linking news events to larger cultural and social issues.

One of the most frequent criticisms of the American press today is its presentation of information without adequate context. Mitchell Stephens, writing about journalism in the Internet age, discusses the glut of online news outlets but argues that audiences need "thoughtful, incisive attempts to divine the significance of events."[4] News parody frequently adds information to stories reported by other media that, once considered, can either make the story less sensational or even negate the dominant narrative frame or source for the story. Following the 2008 election of President Barack Obama, *The Colbert Report* (*Colbert*) aired a montage of news clips with lawmakers (mostly Republicans) and media commentators insisting that Obama's election was no liberal landslide or mandate. Colbert's character ironically agrees with the montage, stating, "That is right. The largest majority in 20 years, 349 electoral votes—that is not a mandate." With just one quick sentence, Colbert reminds viewers that despite claims to the contrary, contemporary politics rarely get any closer to a mandate than the numbers generated in Obama's win. *Last Week Tonight with John Oliver* (*Last Week*) evaluated a 2015 news story circulating about Obama commuting life sentences for 46 people convicted of drug charges. The press played up how the event was the largest number of sentences commuted since the 1960s. While pleased the president took the action, Oliver used the story as a springboard for a 15-minute report to question the underlying logic of the judiciary giving mandatory minimum sentences and provided the history of drug sentencing in America.[5] In both instances, shows provided context that either corrected or recontextualized the original news item.

Public institutions and private businesses increasingly emphasize their own complexity, inflating their importance within the bureaucratic and economic systems and creating a screen of technical jargon that obscures their inner workings from everyday citizens. During his days on *The Daily Show with Jon Stewart* (*TDS*), the host once explained, "I think that very clearly government and corporations have set up a system that is purposefully obtuse, that is very hard to penetrate."[6] *TDS* and subsequent programs actively engaged this problem by creating meaningful coverage meant to demystify structures and educate viewers. Stewart's showdown with Jim Cramer and CNBC provides an excellent example of this type of activity. Ryan McGeough describes how Stewart continually forced Cramer into speaking in everyday language during his interview. Cramer, attempting to dismiss concerns, continually tried to find cover in the impenetrable discourse of the financial sector, but Stewart successfully engaged him both in that technical field and in broader public-sphere discourse.[7] In 2020, President Donald Trump announced further restrictions on immigration to "protect our great American workers." Broadcast headlines focused on the announcement, but *Full Frontal with Samantha Bee* (*Full Frontal*) presents a more nuanced breakdown of the issue (as did many print media outlets). Bee discussed exactly who immigrants are, the types of programs allowing people from other nations into the country, and how dependent some industries are on these individuals. The report took the singular category of "immigrant" and the legalistic language persistently used by the Trump administration and walked through the complexity of those policies.[8]

Despite the prevalence of soundbites on television news, broadcast journalism tends to be hesitant to hold public officials accountable when contradicting themselves; this became especially problematic during the Trump administration. When reporters pointed out falsehoods, they were shouted down with cries of being "fake news," despite having evidence. After the January 6, 2021 insurrection, when Trump supporters stormed the capital as Congress was formalizing the election of Joe Biden as president, *The Daily Show with Trevor Noah* (*TDSWTN*) called out the hypocrisy of politicians and Fox News hosts who were defending the attackers as "solid Americans." The conservative media and officials who normally demonize anyone who questions police authority were suddenly defending rioters attacking law enforcement. Noah responded, "The point is, you guys clearly don't care about cops. You only care about the idea of using cops to keep Black people in their place. So please, miss me with that bullshit."[9]

In a similar example, *TDS* covered conservative reactions to the revelation that the Obama White House held morning phone calls with liberal groups. After showing clips of former vice president Dick Cheney and Bush Chief of Staff Karl Rove making the rounds of morning talk shows criticizing Obama, Stewart reveals that while in the White House Rove regularly spoke with conservative groups like Grover Norquist's anti-tax organization and Focus on the Family. Stewart suddenly gasps with false concern, covering his mouth, before proclaiming, "Oh my God, I know what's happening here. Dick Cheney and Karl Rove, once two of the most powerful men in this country, are now suffering from Balzheimers Disease. [*Shaking his head and acting as if holding back tears*] Why didn't I see it before? Balzheimers is a terrible illness that attacks the memory and gives its victims *the balls* to attack others for things they themselves made a career of."[10] Traditional news outlets can and sometimes do report on such contradictions, but the point can easily be lost in the need for journalistic decorum. News parody dispenses with such restraint and reminds viewers of the inconsistency of political players, calling bullshit on hypocritical officials in the best journalistic sense.

Rather than taking soundbites or public statements at face value, these programs also deconstruct the language of officials and question their logic, evaluating their truth claims. Politicians and others in the political field utilize linguistic shorthand, political "common sense," and euphemisms to obscure their stances and convey ideological concepts without explicitly stating them. Don Waisanen identifies the rhetorical strategy of satirical specificity in *TDS* and *Colbert*'s demystification of language, where grand concepts, or "ideographs," become linked with specific everyday concepts to "expose abstractions that public actors employ to gloss over the important details of policies and political actions."[11] During the 2008 presidential campaign, GOP nominee John McCain attempted to defuse a politically thorny problem after a woman at a town-hall meeting called Obama an "Arab." While attempting to shut down the woman's false claim, McCain's response was perhaps equally telling: "No ma'am, he's a decent family man." In response, *TDS* correspondent Aasif Mandvi, who was often identified as the show's "Muslim Correspondent," points out, as if educating the public on a little-known fact, that the identifiers "Arab" and "decent family man" are not mutually exclusive: "There's no mathematical reason why someone of Arab descent could not, somehow, also love his family." However, Mandvi ironically admits the unison of the two terms is purely theoretical, "I don't know of any cases. Not in the America I live in."[12] The commentary reveals the assumptions behind McCain's response: No ma'am, Obama is not Arab equals he is a decent family man and, therefore, not Arab.

In questioning the language and assumptions of newsmakers, news parody calls into doubt the logic of their statements. In 2010, plans to build a Muslim community center several blocks from ground zero in New York City brought swift outrage from politicians and community organizations, claiming a "mosque" would be built "at ground zero." *TDS* coverage pointed out those inaccuracies and also showed a clip with former Speaker of the House Newt Gingrich rejecting appeals to allow the center based on religious liberty, saying that Saudi Arabia has no churches or synagogues. Stewart, decoding Gingrich's logic, responds, "Exactly! Why should we as Americans have higher standards of religious liberty than Saudi Arabia! It makes no sense!"[13] The report moves from the complaints about the building to laying bare the bigotry behind the outrage. Ultimately, Gingrich's argument hinges on a worldview: Islam is a *foreign* religion associated with the Middle East in the American imagination and, thus, America has no reason to treat Muslims any better than Christians and Jews are treated by certain Arab nations. Rather than adopting the prevalent practice of reporting two sides of an issue with equal emphasis, the program exposed the ideological assumptions underlying the story itself.

In his book on the press and the Vietnam War, Daniel Hallin introduced his concept of the spheres of journalistic discourse to describe how objectivity is incorporated into press coverage. Hallin describes three concentric circles, with the "sphere of consensus" in the middle, describing the issues on which society seemingly agrees and, therefore, remain unquestioned, such as democracy and private-property rights. Around that circle is the "sphere of legitimate controversy," encapsulating topics normally discussed by politicians and the press, where diverging opinions are considered worthy of debate. Surrounding that is the "sphere of deviance," which includes issues outside the normal bounds of debate.[14] As societal viewpoints change issues can shift between these spheres. For example, questioning rigid divisions between male and female gender categories has moved from the sphere of deviance into legitimate controversy, with news outlets including transgender perspectives in their coverage. Like most journalism, news parody programs usually address topics within legitimate controversy, but their coverage does sometimes interrogate the sphere of consensus by questioning "common-sense" viewpoints and underlying ideology.

In covering the 2014 shooting of Michael Brown in Ferguson, Missouri, on *Last Week*, Oliver shifts to a discussion of the increased militarization of local police as photos from protests in the city show officers in camouflage and body armor. The United States military, since the 1990s, has transferred a massive amount of military hardware to law enforcement, from clothing and weapons to armored vehicles and literal tanks. Much of that equipment ended up being used by local SWAT teams, primarily for executing drug investigation warrants. Oliver argues that giving equipment designed for military engagement to local police creates both the potential for escalation and the possible use of those weapons against protesters and nonviolent offenders. The sphere of consensus has traditionally included the unquestioned funding and outfitting of local police, but *Last Week*'s coverage, taking place at a time of social reckoning, interrogates the assumption that all weapons are appropriate for law enforcement.[15]

Full Frontal has embraced discussing a number of issues news programs tend to consider as being on the fringe of too controversial. Coverage of abortion and transgender issues is often restricted to the latest legal developments or a provocative statement from a politician on national newscasts. Bee, however, devoted an entire segment to abortion education for senators, focusing on women's health and reproduction. Discussions of women's bodies and biological processes are rarely brought up and explored in media, instead of being relegated outside the bounds of acceptable discourse. However, Bee highlighted statements made by male politicians on the political right *and* left and corrected them through explanations and illustrations of miscarriage, ectopic pregnancy, birth control, and so-called late-term abortions. Bee divides actual facts from the opinions of lawmakers, declaring, "I don't give a shit about your personal opinions."[16] The segment rejects discussing abortion and women's health merely as a political stance, instead it provides medical information outside the frame of political policy.

Each news parody program that continued on into the 2020s has found its own particular niche to appeal to viewers and to provide commentary and critique. "Weekend Update's" longevity offers an easily accessible format, where the audience is not expected to have deep political knowledge to interpret stories. Reports are brief, focused on timely events, and usually include celebrity news, actually making the segment harder to follow for viewers not steeped in the latest popular culture, like music and fashion. *TDSWTN* targets more knowledgeable viewers, as did Stewart when he was on the show. Noah specifically discusses race and international news and reaches out to millennials through social media and online platforms in addition to his regular program. *Last Week* delves into complex issues likely unfamiliar to many viewers but adopts a pedagogical reporting style where Oliver provides context and draws parallels to clarify stories. Audiences of *Full Frontal* expect reporting through a very specific ideological lens, concerned with progressive values and a focus on human rights, inequality, and gender politics. Each program provides its audience with a different approach to the genre.

COVID-19 AND NEWS PARODY: STAYING ON THE AIR DURING A PANDEMIC

As the 2010s came to a close, the next presidential election was ramping up. 2020 would be a reelection year for Trump. News parody programs were united in their disdain for the man and his policies. Everyone assumed the story would dominate 2020, but of course no one could have predicted a global pandemic that would shut down television production just as primary voters were preparing to head to the polls. In the middle of March 2020, every news parody program went on hiatus, some for a week and others longer. Each show responded in its own unique way based on its specific production situation, audience, and creative personnel. All of the hosts took to producing content from home, temporarily becoming vloggers.

Full Frontal was the first to announce a break on their March 11 episode, saying they would be off the air the following week. Due to concerns about the virus, there was no live audience for the March 11 show, instead, a smattering of staff watched the taping. The staff tried to make up for the lack of live laughs and energy by including jokes that Bee had not previously seen. When *Full Frontal* returned on March 25, it had moved outside, shooting in the woods near Bee's home with husband Jason Jones directing and running camera and their children helping out in other production roles. Staff were able to work from home to submit material. During the outside production, the show was subtitled "Little Show in the Big Woods" (figure 8.1).

The first episode begins with pastoral music and slow, sweeping shots of trees and a stream. Bee begins to walk towards the camera as the lens flares: "This too shall pass. The seasons are changing, the brook is babbling, the birds are chirping. Guys, I think we're gonna be alright." A slate then reads "20 Minutes Later," thunder sounds, and cut to a frantic Bee surrounded by snow: "What the fuck is happening? Why are you doing this to us? I'm sorry I called the president's daughter a c-." Cut to the show open before the offending word can be re-uttered.[17] Shooting in the woods created a very different aesthetic from other news parody programs during the pandemic. The setting allowed Bee to continue standing when she anchored and to incorporate her physical reactions into stories. Over-the-shoulder graphics and other visual elements were edited in post to continue the general look of the show. The program moved out of the woods to a brand-new studio at the end of October 2020.

Perhaps not surprisingly, given his online emphasis, Noah started producing content even before his show went back to Comedy Central. On March

Figure 8.1 Samantha Bee Anchors "Little Show in the Big Woods." *Source: Screenshot by the author.*

18, he began posting webisodes online called *The Daily Social Distancing Show*, shot in his living room. The decision was a savvy move, connecting to his millennial audience and getting ahead of every other host. The following week the show continued to shoot from Noah's apartment but moved on air to its regular Comedy Central timeslot. Noah declined the network's offer to have a set built at his place, instead using some iPhones and the existing corner backdrop with shelves and a monitor.[18] The show expanded from 30 to 45 minutes the following month, despite the craziness of producing a show during the pandemic. After a 2021 summer break, Noah temporarily moved to studio space at the ViacomCBS offices near Times Square in September. The program was the last to add back a live audience, waiting until April of 2022, when it moved back to its original production space in Hell's Kitchen.

Saturday Night Live (*SNL*) announced in mid-March of 2020 that they would be canceling their next three episodes, instead airing reruns. They finished out their season with three virtual shows on April 11 and 25, and May 9 called *SNL at Home*. Cast members and guests shot bits in their own homes or local locations. Content ranged from skits performed by cast to sketches composed of talent arranged in a conference-style zoom configuration. Each episode featured a "Weekend Update" segment with Michael Che and Colin Jost in regular street clothes, hosting from their own homes with over-the-shoulder and other graphics. In the first episode back they even included audio from friends on teleconference in order to provide laughs, though the reactions proved distracting and were abandoned in the next two episodes. "Weekend Update" provided the most consistent material for *SNL at Home*, since the skits were negatively affected by the need for social distancing. This limitation was likely what motivated the show to be the first to return to a regular studio in October 2020 to kick off season 46 of the program.

As the COVID-19 outbreak began forcing productions to close, *Last Week* had to abandon its regular studio due to an infection at the location and move production to another space without an audience for a shortened March 15 episode. The show then took a week's break and produced its March 29 and subsequent shows from Oliver's home. Unlike other late-night hosts who showed parts of their living area (or went outside in the case of Bee), Oliver shot in front of a whitish-blue background with a desk, simulating a minimized news setting. He explained, "My home is, and this is true, a blank white void full of sad facts. Where else did you think I lived?"[19] *Last Week* retained the same format, although the lack of an audience, as with other shows, created awkward pauses. Given his self-deprecating persona, Oliver was able to successfully mitigate those moments. He was the last host to return to studio space, a year and a half later, in August 2021.

Most television programs scrambled to figure out ways of coping with the pandemic, and many remained off the air for the better part of 2020. News parody shows were able to quickly pivot to alternative means of workflow, production, and distribution. The work of writers, although perhaps most dynamic when together as a group, could be completed from home and through digital conferencing. Editing and graphics creation and insertion were done with software and computers that were quickly made accessible to crew members wherever they were social distancing. The programs benefited from having only one or two hosts and learned that the audience would accept any kind of backdrop, from apartments to trees to a blank wall, as long as the host continued their presentational style and the visuals remained consistent.

The genre has proven to be highly adaptable across decades, weathering changes in production methods, the growth of cable and the Internet, a pandemic, and even frequent changes in corporate ownership. *Last Week* has been through no less than three parent companies, starting with Oliver working for Time-Warner in 2014. HBO was then purchased by AT&T in 2018, followed by a 2022 merger between Warner Media and Discovery that formed the imaginatively-named Warner Bros. Discovery. Shortly before the merger became official, Warner Bros. Discovery unveiled a revised logo incorporating a line from the film *The Maltese Falcon*: "The stuff that dreams are made of." On his show, Oliver responded that the actual film quote is "about how the thing that seemed like a priceless treasure was actually worthless garbage that brought chaos and despair to everyone around it. Anyway, good luck with the merger! I'm sure everything's gonna go great!"[20]

The changes in HBO's ownership mirror the overall direction of the industry, moving away from legacy companies with traditional, live television channels in favor of streaming services. The programming on streaming tends to be geared toward evergreen content that will keep its appeal and can be accessed at any time in the future. Like journalism, however, news parody has a shorter shelf life. Events, controversies, personalities—even jokes—are all "of the moment." Whether news parody will need to adapt to the industry's continual shift towards streaming, and how, remains to be seen, but, unlike Oliver's doubts about media mergers, news parody's longevity and flexibility give cause for optimism.

NOTES

1. *On the Media*, August 24, 2012.
2. Amber Day, *Satire and Dissent: Interventions in Contemporary Political Debate* (Bloomington, IN: Indiana University Press, 2011), 81.
3. Pierre Bourdieu, *Language and Symbolic Power*, trans. Gino Raymond and Matthew Adamson (Cambridge, MA: Harvard University Press, 1991), 194–96.

4. Mitchell Stephens, "Beyond News," *Columbia Journalism Review* (January/February 2007): 35.

5. *Last Week Tonight with John Oliver*, July 26, 2015.

6. Eric Schlosser, "The Kids Are All Right," *Columbia Journalism Review* 41, no. 5 (2003): 29.

7. Ryan McGeough, "The Voice of the People: Jon Sewart, Public Argument, and Political Satire," in *The Daily Show and Rhetoric: Arguments, Issues, and Strategies*, ed. Trischa Goodnow (Lanham, MD: Lexington Books, 2011).

8. *Full Frontal with Samantha Bee*, November 11, 2020.

9. *The Daily Show with Trevor Noah*, January 19, 2021.

10. *The Daily Show with Jon Stewart*, April 22, 2009.

11. Don J. Waisanen, "A Citizen's Guides to Democracy Inaction: Jon Stewart and Stephen Colbert's Comic Rhetorical Criticism," *Southern Communication Journal* 74, no. 2 (2009).

12. *The Daily Show with Jon Stewart*, October 14, 2008.

13. *The Daily Show with Jon Stewart*, August 10, 2010.

14. Daniel C. Hallin, *The Uncensored War* (Berkeley, CA: University of California Press, Ltd., 1989), 116-18.

15. *Last Week Tonight with John Oliver*, August 17, 2014.

16. *Full Frontal with Samantha Bee*, May 15, 2019.

17. *Full Frontal with Samantha Bee*, March 25, 2020.

18. Glenn Whipp, "Trevor Noah Is Ready to Come Back to Life. But What Will That Look Like?," *Los Angeles Times*, June 15, 2021, https://www.latimes.com/entertainment-arts/awards/story/2021-06-15/trevor-noah-daily-show.

19. *Last Week Tonight with John Oliver*, March 29, 2020.

20. *Last Week Tonight with John Oliver*, June 6, 2021.

Bibliography

Abel, Angela D., and Michael Barthel. "Appropriation of Mainstream News: How *Saturday Night Live* Changed the Political Discussion." *Critical Studies in Media Communication* 30, no. 1 (2013): 1–16.
Achter, Paul. "Comedy in Unfunny Times: News Parody and Carnival after 9/11." *Critical Studies in Media Communication* 25, no. 3 (2008): 274–303.
Alan, Jeff, and James M. Lane. *Anchoring America: The Changing Face of Network News*. Chicago, IL: Bonus Books, 2003.
Allan, Stuart. *News Culture*. 3rd ed. Berkshire, UK: Open University Press, 2010.
Alonso, Paul. *Satiric TV in the Americas: Critical Metatainment as Negotiated Dissent*. New York: Oxford University Press, 2018.
Altman, Rick. *The American Film Musical*. Bloomington, IN: Indiana University Press, 1987.
Amernick, Dan. "The 'Not Ready for Archive Players': The Lost Seasons of *Saturday Night Live*." *Journal of Popular Film and Television* 46, no. 2 (2018): 70–81.
Anderson, Christopher. "Producing an Aristocracy of Culture in American Television." In *The Essential HBO Reader*, edited by Gary R. Edgerton and Jeffrey P. Jones, 23–41. Lexington, KY: The University Press of Kentucky, 2008.
Ashby, LeRoy. *With Amusement for All: A History of American Popular Culture since 1830*. Lexington, KY: The University Press of Kentucky, 2006.
Bakhtin, Mikhail. *The Dialogic Imagination: Four Essays*. Translated by Caryl Emerson & Michael Holquist. Austin, TX: University of Texas Press, 1981.
———. *Problems of Dostoevsky's Poetics*. Translated by Carl Emerson. Minneapolis, MN: University of Minnesota Press, 1985. 1929.
———. *Rabelais and His World*. Translated by Helene Iswolsky. Bloomington, IN: Indiana University Press, 1984. 1965.
Barbur, Jonathan E., and Trischa Goodnow. "The *Arete* of Amusement: An Aristotelian Perspective on the Ethos of *The Daily Show*." In *The Daily Show and Rhetoric: Arguments, Issues, and Strategies*, edited by Trischa Goodnow, 3–18. Lanham, MD: Lexington Books, 2011.

Baudrillard, Jean. *Simulacra and Simulation*. Translated by Sheila Faria Glaser. Ann Arbor, MI: University of Michigan Press, 1994.

Baum, Matthew. "Talking the Vote: Why Presidential Candidates Hit the Talk Show Circuit." *American Journal of Political Science* 49, no. 2 (2005): 213–34.

Baumgartner, Jody. "Humor on the Next Frontier: Youth, Online Political Humor, and the 'Jib-Jab' Effect." *Social Science Computer Review* 25 (2007): 319–38.

Baumgartner, Jody C., and Brad Lockerbie. "Maybe It *Is* More Than a Joke: Satire, Mobilization, and Political Participation." *Social Science Quarterly* 99, no. 3 (2018): 1060–74.

Baumgartner, Jody C., and Jonathan S. Morris. "*The Daily Show* Effect: Candidate Evaluations, Efficacy, and the American Youth." *American Politics Research* 34 (2006): 341–67.

———. "One "Nation" under Stephen? The Effects of *The Colbert Report* on American Youth." *Journal of Broadcasting & Electronic Media* 52, no. 4 (2008): 622–43.

———. "Stoned Slackers or Super Citizens? *The Daily Show* Viewing and Political Engagement of Young Adults." In *The Stewart/Colbert Effect: Essays on the Real Impact of Fake News*, edited by Amarnath Amarasingam, 63–78. Jefferson, NC: McFarland & Company, Inc., 2011.

Baumgartner, Jody C., Jonathan S. Morris, and Natasha L. Walth. "The Fey Effect: Young Adults, Political Humor, and Perceptions of Sarah Palin in the 2008 Presidential Election Campaign." *Public Opinion Quarterly* 76, no. 1 (2012): 95–104.

Baym, Geoffrey. *From Cronkite to Colbert: The Evolution of Broadcast News*. Boulder, CO: Paradigm Publishers, 2010.

———. "*The Daily Show*: Discursive Integration and the Reinvention of Political Journalism." *Political Communication* 22, no. 3 (2005): 259–76.

———. "Rush Limbaugh with a Laugh-Track: The (Thankfully) Short Life of the *1/2 Hour News Hour*." *Cinema Journal* 51, no. 4 (2012): 172–78.

———. "Stephen Colbert's Parody of the Postmodern." In *Satire TV: Politics and Comedy in the Post-Network Era*, edited by Jonathan Gray, Jeffrey Jones and Ethan Thompson, 124–44. New York: New York University Press, 2009.

Becker, Amy B. "Riding the Wave of the New Jew Revolution: Watching The Daily Show with Jews for Jon Stewart." International Communications Association, Chicago, IL, May 20, 2009.

———. "What About Those Interviews? The Impact of Exposure to Political Comedy and Cable News on Factual Recall and Anticipated Political Expression," *International Journal of Public Opinion Research* 25, no. 3 (2013): 344–56.

Becker, Amy B., and Leticia Bode. "Satire as a Source for Learning? The Differential Impact of News Versus Satire Exposure on Net Neutrality Knowledge Gain." *Information, Communication & Society* 21, no. 4 (2018): 612–25.

Bianculli, David. *Dangerously Funny: The Uncensored Story of The Smothers Brothers Comedy Hour*. New York: Touchstone, 2009.

Bishop, Sarah. "'I'm Only Going to Do It If I Can Do It in Character': Unpacking Comedy and Advocacy in Stephen Colbert's 2010 Congressional Testimony." *The Journal of Popular Culture* 48, no. 3 (2015): 548–57.

Blankenship, Christina M. "President, Wrestler, Spectacle: An Examination of Donald Trump's Firing Tweets and *The Celebrity Appresident* as Response to Trump's Media Landscape." *Journal of Communication Inquiry* 44, no. 2 (2020): 117–38.

Bodroghkozy, Aniko. *Groove Tube: Sixties Television and the Youth Rebellion.* Durham, NC: Duke University Press, 2001.

———. "Political Satire, *That Was The Week That Was*, and the Assassination of John F.Kennedy." *Television & New Media* 22, no. 8 (2021): 859–77.

Bode, Leticia, and Amy B. Becker. "Go Fix It: Comedy as an Agent of Political Activation." *Social Science Quarterly* 99, no. 5 (2018): 1572–84.

Boler, Megan, and Stephen Turpin. "*The Daily Show* and *Crossfire*: Satire and Sincerity as Truth to Power." In *Digital Media and Democracy: Tactics in Hard Times*, edited by Megan Boler, 381–403. Cambridge, MA: The MIT Press, 2008.

Boskin, Joseph. "American Political Humor: Touchables and Taboos." *International Political Science Review* 11, no. 4 (1990): 473–82.

Bourdieu, Pierre. *Language and Symbolic Power.* Translated by Gino Raymond and Matthew Adamson. Cambridge, MA: Harvard University Press, 1991.

———. "The Political Field, the Social Science Field, and the Journalistic Field." In *Bourdieu and the Journalistic Field*, edited by Rodney Benson and Erik Neveu, 29–47. Cambridge, UK: Polity Press, 2005.

Brownell, Kathryn Cramer. "The Historical Presidency: Gerald Ford, *Saturday Night Live*, and the Development of the Entertainer in Chief." *Presidential Studies Quarterly* 46, no. 4 (2016): 925–42.

Butler, Jeremy. *Television Style.* New York: Routledge, 2010.

Cao, Xiaoxia. "Political Comedy Shows and Knowledge About Primary Campaigns: The Moderating Effects of Age and Education." *Mass Communication and Society* 11 (2008): 43–61.

Carlson, Matt, and Jason T. Peifer. "The Impudence of Being Ernest: Jon Stewart and the Boundaries of Discursive Responsibility." *Journal of Communication* 63 (2013): 333–50.

Carpenter, Humphrey. *A Great Big Silly Grin: The British Satire Boom of the 1960s.* New York: Public Affairs, 2002.

Castagner, Marc-Olivier, and David Grondin. "From Irritated Hostages to Silly Citizens: Infotainment Satire as Ludic Surveillance." In *The Joke Is on Us: Political Comedy in (Late) Neoliberal Times*, edited by Julie A. Webber, 133–58. Lanham, MD: Lexington Books, 2019.

Colletta, Lisa. "Political Satire and Postmodern Irony in the Age of Stephen Colbert and Jon Stewart." *Journal of Popular Culture* 42, no. 5 (2009): 856–74.

Compton, Josh. "Cramer Vs. (Jon Stewart's Characterization of) Cramer: Image Repair Rhetoric, Late Night Political Humor, and *The Daily Show*." In *The Daily Show and Rhetoric: Arguments, Issues, and Strategies*, edited by Trischa Goodnow, 43–56. Lanham, MD: Lexington Books, 2011.

Crowder, Matt. "A Space and Time for Entertainment: *That Was The Week That Was* and Viewers' Utopian Expectations." *Historical Journal of Film, Radio and Television* 34, no. 3 (2014): 420–33.

Davies, David R. "The Challenges of Civil Rights and Joseph Mccarthy." In *Fair & Balanced: A History of Journalistic Objectivity*, edited by Steven R. Knowlton and Karen L. Freeman, 206–20. Northport, AL: Vision Press, 2005.

Davis, Murray. *What's So Funny?: The Comic Conception of Culture and Society*. Chicago, IL: The University of Chicago Press, 1993.

Davis, Tom. *Thirty-Nine Years of Short-Term Memory Loss*. New York: Grove Press, 2009.

Davisson, Amber, and Mackenzie Donovan. "Breaking the News...on a Weekly Basis": Trolling as Rhetorical Style on *Last Week Tonight*." *Critical Studies in Media Communication* 36, no. 5 (2019): 513–27.

Day, Amber. "And Now...The News? Mimesis and the Real in *The Daily Show*." In *Satire TV: Politics and Comedy in the Post-Network Era*, edited by Jonathan Gray, Jeffrey Jones and Ethan Thompson, 85–103. New York: New York University Press, 2009.

———. *Satire and Dissent: Interventions in Contemporary Political Debate*. Bloomington, IN: Indiana University Press, 2011.

Day, Amber, and Ethan Thompson. "Live from New York, It's the Fake News! *Saturday Night Live* and the (Non)Politics of Parody." *Popular Communication* 10, no. 1–2 (2012): 170–82.

Debord, Guy. *Society of the Spectacle*. Translated by Ken Knabb. London: Rebel Press, 2006. 1967.

Decker, Kevin S. "Stephen Colbert, Irony, and Speaking Truthiness to Power." In *The Daily Show and Philosophy*, edited by Jason Holt, 240–51. Malden, MA: Blackwell Publishing, 2007.

Denton, Robert E., Jr. *The Primetime Presidency of Ronald Reagan: The Era of the Television Presidency*. New York: Praeger Publishers, 1988.

Duffy, Margaret E., and Janis Teruggi Page. "Does Political Humor Matter? You Betcha! Comedy TV's Performance of the 2008 Vice Presidential Debate." *The Journal of Popular Culture* 46, no. 3 (2013): 545–65.

Epstein, Lawrence J. *The Haunted Smile: The Story of Jewish Comedians in America*. New York: Public Affairs, 2001.

Erickson, Hal. *"From Beautiful Downtown Burbank": A Critical History of Rowan and Martin's Laugh in, 1968–1973*. Jefferson, NC: McFarland & Company, Inc., 2000.

Farnsworth, Stephen J., and S. Robert Lichter. *Late Night with Trump: Political Humor and the American Presidency*. New York: Routledge, 2020.

Feibleman, James Kern. *In Praise of Comedy (Reissue)*. New York: Russell & Russell, 1962. 1939.

Feldman, Lauren, and Caty Borum Chattoo. "Comedy as a Route to Social Change: The Effects of Satire and News on Persuasion About Syrian Refugees." *Mass Communication and Society* 22 (2019): 277–300.

Feuer, Jane. *Seeing through the Eighties*. Durham, NC: Duke University Press, 1995.

Fiske, John. *Television Culture*. 2nd ed. New York: Routledge, 2011. 1987.

Fiske, John, and John Hartley. *Reading Television*. 2nd ed. New York: Routledge, 2005. 1978.

Fotis, Matt. *Satire & the State: Sketch Comedy and the Presidency*. New York: Routledge, 2020.
Foucault, Michel. *Fearless Speech*. Edited by Joseph Pearson. Los Angeles, CA: Semiotext(e), 2001.
———. "The Political Function of the Intellectual." *Radical Philosophy*, no. 17 (1977): 12–14.
Fox, Julia R. "Journalist or Jokester? An Analysis of *Last Week Tonight with John Oliver*." In *Political Humor in a Changing Media Landscape: A New Generation of Research*, edited by Jody C. Baumgartner and Amy B. Becker, 22–44. Lanham, MD: Lexington Books, 2018.
Fox, Julia R., and Edo Steinberg. "News You Can't Use: Jon Stewart's *Daily Show* Media Critiques." *Journalism & Mass Communication Quarterly* 97, no. 1 (2020): 235–56.
Garrett, R. Sam. "Seriously Funny: Understanding Campaign Finance Policy through the Colbert Super PAC." *St. Louis University Law Journal* 56, no. 3 (2012): 711–23.
Gettings, Michael. "The Fake, the False, and the Fictional: *The Daily Show* as News Source." In *The Daily Show and Philosophy*, edited by Jason Holt, 16–27. Malden, MA: Blackwell Publishing, 2007.
Gitlin, Todd. *Inside Prime Time*. Berkeley, CA: University of California Press, 2000.
Gray, Jonathan. *Television Entertainment*. New York: Routledge, 2008.
Gray, Jonathan, Jeffrey P. Jones, and Ethan Thompson. "The State of Satire, the Satire of State." In *Satire TV: Politics and Comedy in the Post-Network Era*, edited by Jonathan Gray, Jeffrey P. Jones and Ethan Thompson, 3–36. New York: New York University Press, 2009.
Greene, Viveca S., and Amber Day. "Asking for It: Rape Myths, Satire, and Feminist Lacunae." *Signs: Journal of Women in Culture and Society* 45, no. 2 (2019): 449–72.
Gunning, Tom. "The Cinema of Attraction: Early Film, Its Spectator and the Avant-Garde." *Wide Angle* 6, no. 2 (1986): 63–70.
Haggins, Bambi, and Amanda D. Lotz. "At Home on the Cutting Edge." In *The Essential HBO Reader*, edited by Gary R. Edgerton and Jeffrey P. Jones, 151–71. Lexington, KY: The University Press of Kentucky, 2008.
Hallin, Daniel C. *The Uncensored War*. Berkeley, CA: University of California Press, Ltd., 1989.
Hardy, Bruce W., Jeffrey A. Gottfried, Kenneth M. Winneg, and Kathleen Hall Jamieson. "Stephen Colbert's Civics Lesson: How Colbert Super PAC Taught Viewers About Campaign Finance." *Mass Communication and Society* 17 (2014): 329–53.
Hart, Roderick P., and Johanna Hartelius. "The Political Sins of Jon Stewart." *Critical Studies in Media Communication* 24, no. 3 (2007): 263–72.
Hartley, John. *Television Truths*. Malden, MA: Blackwell Publishing, 2008.
Hendra, Tony. *Going Too Far*. New York: Dolphin Book, 1987.
Herbig, Art, and Aaron Hess. "Convergent Critical Rhetoric at the 'Rally to Restore Sanity': Exploring the Intersection of Rhetoric, Ethnography, and Documentary Production." *Communication Studies* 63, no. 3 (2012): 269–89.

Hess, Aaron. "Purifying Laughter: Carnivalesque Self-Parody as Argument Scheme in *The Daily Show with Jon Stewart.*" In *The Daily Show and Rhetoric: Arguments, Issues, and Strategies*, edited by Trischa Goodnow, 93–111. Lanham, MD: Lexington Books, 2011.

Hill, Doug, and Jeff Weingrad. *Saturday Night: A Backstage History of Saturday Night Live.* New York: Vintage Books, 1987.

Hilmes, Michele. "The Evolution of Saturday Night." In *Saturday Night Live and American TV*, edited by Nick Marx, Matt Sienkiewicz and Ron Becker, 25–39. Bloomington, IN: Indiana University Press, 2013.

Hokenson, Jan. *The Idea of Comedy: History, Theory, Critique.* Cranbury, NJ: Associated University Presses, 2006.

Holbert, R. Lance, Jennifer L. Lambe, Anthony D. Dudo, and Kristin A. Carlton. "Primacy Effects of *The Daily Show* and National TV News Viewing: Young Viewers, Political Gratification, and Internal Political Self-Efficacy." *Journal of Broadcasting & Electronic Media* 51 (2007): 20–38.

Horner, William T., and M. Heather Carver. *Saturday Night Live and the 1976 Presidential Election: A New Voice Enters Campaign Politics.* Jefferson, NC: McFarland & Company, 2018.

Hutcheon, Linda. *A Theory of Parody: The Teachings of Twentieth-Century Art Forms.* Urbana: University of Illinois Press, 2000. 1985.

Jameson, Fredric. *Postmodernism, or, the Cultural Logic of Late Capitalism.* 9th ed. Durham, NC: Duke University Press, 2001. 1991.

Jeffords, Susan. *Hard Bodies: Hollywood Masculinity in the Reagan Era.* New Brunswick, NJ: Rutgers University Press, 1993.

Jennings, Freddie J., Josh C. Bramlett, and Benjamin R. Warner. "Comedic Cognition: The Impact of Elaboration on Political Comedy Effects." *Western Journal of Communication* 83, no. 3 (2019): 365–82.

Jones, Clifford. "The Stephen Colbert Problem: The Media Exemption for Corporate Political Advocacy and the 'Hall to the Cheese Stephen Colbert Nacho Cheese Doritos 2008 Presidential Campaign Coverage'." *University of Florida Journal of Law & Public Policy* 19, no. 2 (2008): 295–323.

Jones, Jeffrey P. *Entertaining Politics: New Political Television and Civic Culture.* Lanham, MD: Rowman & Littlefield Publishers, Inc., 2005.

———. *Entertaining Politics: Satiric Television and Political Engagement.* 2nd ed. Lanham, MD: Rowman & Littlefield Publishers, Inc., 2010.

———. "More Than 'Fart Noises and Funny Faces': *The Daily Show*'s Coverage of the US Recession." *Popular Communication* 8, no. 3 (2010): 165–69.

———. "Politics and the Brand: *Saturday Night Live*'s Campaign Season Humor." In *Saturday Night Live and American TV*, edited by Nick Marx, Matt Sienkiewicz and Ron Becker, 77–92. Bloomington, IN: Indiana University Press, 2013.

Jones, Jeffrey P., and Geoffrey Baym. "A Dialogue on Satire News and the Crises of Truth in Postmodern Political Television." *Journal of Communication Inquiry* 34, no. 3 (2010): 278–94.

Jones, Jeffrey P., Geoffrey Baym, and Amber Day. "Mr. Stewart and Mr. Colbert Go to Washington: Television Satirists Outside the Box." *Social Research* 79, no. 1 (2012): 33–60.

Kaye, Barbara K. "A Feckless Punt: Cursing on *Full Frontal with Samantha Bee*." *Comedy Studies* 11, no. 2 (2020): 275–88.

Kelso, Tony. "And Now No Word from Our Sponsor." In *It's Not TV: Watching HBO in the Post-Television Era*, edited by Marc Leverette, Brian L. Ott and Cara Louise Buckley, 46–64. New York: Routledge, 2008.

Kellner, Douglas. "The Media, Democracy, and Spectacle: Some Critical Reflections." *Cultural Politics* 11, no. 1 (2015): 53–69.

Kercher, Stephen. *Revel with a Cause: Liberal Satire in Postwar America*. Chicago, IL: The University of Chicago Press, 2006.

Kerr, Paul. "Drama at MTM: *Lou Grant* and *Hill Street Blues*." In *MTM 'Quality Television'*, edited by Jane Feuer, Paul Kerr and Tise Vahimagi, 132–65. London: BFI Publishing, 1984.

Kim, Young Mie, and John Vishak. "Just Laugh! You Don't Need to Remember: The Effects of Entertainment Media on Political Information Acquisition and Information Processing in Political Judgement." *Journal of Communication* 58 (2008): 338–60.

Kreuz, Roger J., and Richard M. Roberts. "On Satire and Parody: The Importance of Being Ironic." *Metaphor and Symbolic Activity* 8, no. 2 (1993): 97–109.

LaMarre, Heather L., Kristen D. Landreville, and Michael A. Beam. "The Irony of Satire: Political Ideology and the Motivation to See What You Want to See in *The Colbert Report*." *International Journal of Press/Politics* 14, no. 2 (2009): 212–31.

Lee, Hoon, and Nojin Kwak. "The Affect Effect of Political Satire: Sarcastic Humor, Negative Emotions, and Political Participation." *Mass Communication and Society* 17 (2014): 307–28.

Lippert, Leopold. "Neoliberal Feminisms, Late-Night Comedy, and the Public Sphere, Or: Samantha Bee Takes on Ivanka Trump." *Feminist Media Studies* (2021). https://www.tandfonline.com/doi/full/10.1080/14680777.2021.1998182.

Lippmann, Walter. *Public Opinion*. Toronto, Canada: Collier-Macmillian Canada, Ltd., 1965. 1922.

Lotz, Amanda. *The Television Will Be Revolutionized*. New York: New York University, 2007.

Mair, George. *Inside HBO*. New York: Dodd, Mead & Company, 1988.

Marciniak, Vwadek P. *Politics, Humor and the Counterculture: Laughter in the Age of Decay*. New York: Peter Lang, 2008.

Marx, Nick. *Sketch Comedy: Identity, Reflexivity, and American Television*. Bloomington, IN: Indiana University Press, 2019.

Matviko, John. "Television Satire and the Presidency: The Case of *Saturday Night Live*." In *Hollywood's White House: The American Presidency in Film and History*, edited by Peter Rollins and John O'Connor, 333–49. Lexington: The University Press of Kentucky, 2003.

McChesney, Robert W. "Introduction." In *The Stewart/Colbert Effect: Essays on the Real Impact of Fake News*, edited by Amarnath Amarasingam, 1–2. Jefferson, NC: McFarland & Company, Inc., 2011.

McClennen, Sophia A. *Colbert's America: Satire and Democracy*. New York: Palgrave Macmillan, 2011.

McClennen, Sophia A., and Remy M. Maisel. *Is Satire Saving Our Nation? Mockery and American Politics*. New York: Palgrave Macmillan, 2014.

McGeough, Ryan. "The Voice of the People: Jon Sewart, Public Argument, and Political Satire." In *The Daily Show and Rhetoric: Arguments, Issues, and Strategies*, edited by Trischa Goodnow, 113–27. Lanham, MD: Lexington Books, 2011.

McKain, Aaron. "Not Necessarily Not the News: Gatekeeping, Remediation, and *The Daily Show*." *Journal of American Culture* 28 (2005): 415–30.

Meltzer, Kimberly. *TV News Anchors and Journalistic Traditions: How Journalists Adapt to Technology*. New York: Peter Lang, 2010.

Mieczkowski, Yanek. *Gerald Ford and the Challenges of the 1970s*. Lexington, KY: The University Press of Kentucky 2005.

Miller, James Andrew. *Tinderbox: HBO's Ruthless Pursuit of New Frontiers*. New York: Henry Holt and Company, 2021.

Miller, Jeffrey S. *Something Completely Different: British Television and American Culture*. Minneapolis, MN: University of Minnesota Press, 2000.

———. "What Closes on Saturday Night." In *NBC: America's Network*, edited by Michele Hilmes, 192–208. Berkeley, CA: University of California Press, 2007.

Mittell, Jason. *Genre and Television: From Cop Shows to Cartoons in American Culture*. New York: Routledge, 2004.

———. *Television and American Culture*. New York: Oxford University Press, 2010.

Mohammed, Shaheed Nick. "'It-Getting' in the Colbert Nation Online Forum." *Mass Communication and Society* 17 (2014): 173–94.

Morse, Margaret. "News as Performance: The Image as an Event." In *The Television Studies Reader*, edited by Robert C. Allen and Annette Hill, 209–25. London: Routledge, 2004.

Morreale, Joanne. "Jon Stewart and *The Daily Show*: I Thought You Were Going to Be Funny!". In *Satire TV: Politics and Comedy in the Post-Network Era*, edited by Jonathan Gray, Jeffrey Jones and Ethan Thompson, 104–23. New York: New York University Press, 2009.

Morris, Jonathan. "*The Daily Show with Jon Stewart* and Audience Attitude Change During the 2004 Party Conventions." *Political Behavior* 31 (2009): 79–102.

Moy, Patricia, Michael Xenos, and Verena Hess. "Priming Effects of Late-Night Comedy." Annual Meeting of the International Communication Association, New Orleans, LA, May 2004.

Mullen, Lawrence J. "Visual Aspects of *The Daily Show with Jon Stewart*." In *The Daily Show and Rhetoric: Arguments, Issues, and Strategies*, edited by Trischa Goodnow, 171–85. Lanham, MD: Lexington Books, 2011.

Mullen, Megan. *The Rise of Cable Programming in the United States: Revolution or Evolution?* Austin, TX: University of Texas Press, 2003.

———. *Television in the Multichannel Age: A Brief History of Cable Television*. Malden, MA: Blackwell Publishing, 2008.

Murphy, Caryn. "'Is This the Era of the Woman?': *SNL*'s Gender Politics in the New Millennium." In *Saturday Night Live and American TV*, edited by Nick Marx, Matt Sienkiewicz and Ron Becker, 173–90. Bloomington, IN: Indiana University Press, 2013.

Nessen, Ron. *Making the News, Taking the News: From NBC to the Ford White House.* Middletown, CT: Wesleyan University Press, 2011.
Norton, Matthew. "A Structural Hermeneutics of *The O'Reilly Factor*." *Theory & Society* 40, no. 3 (2011): 315–46.
Olsen, Lance. *Circus of the Mind in Motion: Postmodernism and the Comic Vision.* Detroit, MI: Wayne State University Press, 1990.
Palmer, Jerry. *The Logic of the Absurd: On Film and Television.* London: British Film Institute, 1987.
Paroske, Marcus. "Pious Policymaking: The Participatory Satires of Stephen Colbert." *Studies in American Humor* 2, no. 2 (2016): 208–35.
Parsons, Patrick R. *Blue Skies: A History of Cable Television.* Philadelphia, PA: Temple University Press, 2008.
Peifer, Jason T. "Palin, Saturday Night Live, and Framing: Examining the Dynamics of Political Parody." *The Communication Review* 16, no. 3 (2013): 155–77.
Placone, Ronald A., and Michael Tumolo. "Interrupting the Machine: Cynic Comedy in the 'Rally for Sanity and/or Fear'." *Journal of Contemporary Rhetoric* 1, no. 1 (2011): 10–21.
Poniewozik, James. "Samantha Bee's Fierce, Fiery Feminism Anchors 'Full Frontal'." *The New York Times*, February 10, 2016, C, 1.
Postman, Neil. *Amusing Ourselves to Death: Public Discourse in the Age of Show Business.* New York: Penguin Books, 1985.
Powers, Ron. *The Newscasters.* New York: St. Martin's Press, 1977.
Reilly, Ian, and Megan Boler. "*The Rally to Restore Sanity*, Prepoliticization, and the Future of Politics." *Communication, Culture & Critique* 7 (2014): 435–52.
Reincheld, Aaron. "'Saturday Night Live' and Weekend Update: The Formative Years of Comedy News Dissemination." *Journalism History* 31, no. 4 (2006): 190–97.
Rich, Frank. *The Greatest Story Ever Sold: The Decline and Fall of Truth in Bush's America.* New York: The Penguin Press, 2006.
Ritchie, Donald A. *Reporting from Washington: The History of the Washington Press Corps.* New York: Oxford University Press, Inc., 2005.
Robinson, Peter M. *The Dance of the Comedians: The People, the President, and the Performance of Political Standup Comedy in America.* Amherst, MA: University of Massachusetts Press, 2010.
Rose, Margaret. *Parody: Ancient, Modern, and Post-Modern.* New York: Cambridge University Press, 1993.
Schaefer, Richard J., and Tony J. Martinez III. "Trends in Network News Editing Strategies from 1969 through 2005." *Journal of Broadcasting & Electronic Media* 53, no. 3 (2009): 347–64.
Schaller, Michael. *Reckoning with Reagan: America and Its President in the 1980s.* New York: Oxford University Press, 1992.
Schill, Dan. "Understanding the 'Heroes' and 'It Getters': Fandom and the Colbert Nation." *Mass Communication and Society* 17 (2014): 754–75.
Schudson, Michael. "Autonomy from What?." In *Bourdieu and the Journalistic Field*, edited by Rodney Benson and Erik Neveu, 214–23. Cambridge, UK: Polity Press, 2005.

Shales, Tom, and James Andrew Miller. *Live from New York: An Uncensored History of Saturday Night Live.* Boston, MA: Little, Brown and Company, 2002.
Simpson, Paul. *On the Discourse of Satire: Toward a Stylistic Model of Satirical Humor.* Philadelphia, PN: John Benjamins Publishing Co., 2003.
Smith, Chris. *The Daily Show (The Book).* New York: Grand Central Publishing, 2016.
Smith, Chris, and Ben Voth. "The Role of Humor in Political Argument: How 'Strategery' and 'Lockboxes' Changed a Political Campaign." *Argumentation and Advocacy* 39 (2002): 110–29.
Smith, Hedrick. *The Power Game: How Washington Works.* New York: Random House, 1988.
Suter, Keith. "The British Satirical Revolution." *Contemporary Review* 285, no. 1664 (2004): 161–66.
Tally, Robert T., Jr. "I Am the Mainstream Media (and So Can You!)." In *The Stewart/Colbert Effect: Essays on the Real Impact of Fake News*, edited by Amarnath Amarasingam, 149–63. Jefferson, NC: McFarland & Company, Inc., 2011.
Teten, Ryan Lee. "Mouthpiece of the Liberal Left? Jon Stewart and *The Daily Show*'s 'Real' Coverage of Election 2008." *Public Integrity* 14, no. 1 (2011): 67–84.
Thompson, Ethan. *Parody and Taste in Postwar American Television Culture.* New York: Routledge, 2011.
Thussu, Daya Kishan. *News as Entertainment: The Rise of Global Infotainment.* London: Sage, 2007.
Turner, Graeme. *Understanding Celebrity.* London: Sage Publications, 2004.
Ulrich, Anne. "Attention through Distraction: Basic Modalities and Rhetorical Medialities of *Last Week Tonight*." *Poetics Today* 40, no. 2 (2019): 299–318.
Vidmar, Neil, and Milton Rokeach. "Archie Bunker's Bigotry: A Study in Selective Perception and Exposure." *Journal of Communication* 24, no. 1 (1974): 36–47.
Wagg, Stephen. "Comedy, Politics and Permissiveness: The 'Satire Boom' and Its Inheritance." *Contemporary Politics* 8, no. 4 (2002): 319–34.
Waisanen, Don J. "A Citizen's Guides to Democracy Inaction: Jon Stewart and Stephen Colbert's Comic Rhetorical Criticism." *Southern Communication Journal* 74, no. 2 (2009): 119–40.
———. "The Rise of Advocacy Satire." In *Political Humor in a Changing Media Landscape: A New Generation of Research*, edited by Jody C. Baumgartner and Amy B. Becker, 11–27. Lanham, MD: Lexington Books, 2018.
Weinstein, Simcha. *Shtick Shift: Jewish Humor in the 21st Century.* Fort Lee, NJ: Barricade Books, 2008.
Wild, Nickie Michaud. "Dumb Vs. Fake: Representations of Bush and Palin on *Saturday Night Live* and Their Effect on the Journalistic Public Sphere." *Journal of Broadcasting & Electronic Media* 59, no. 3 (2015): 494–508.
———. "'The Mittens of Disapproval Are On': John Oliver's *Last Week Tonight* as Neoliberal Critique." *Communication Culture & Critique* 12 (2019): 340–58.
Williams, Bruce A., and Michael X. Delli Carpini. *After Broadcast News: Media Regimes, Democracy, and the New Information Environment.* New York: Cambridge University Press, 2011.

———. "Real Ethical Concerns and Fake News: *The Daily Show* and the Challenge of the New Media Environment." In *The Stewart/Colbert Effect: Essays on the Real Impact of Fake News*, edited by Amarnath Amarasingam, 181–92. Jefferson, NC: McFarland & Company, Inc., 2011.
Williams, Raymond. *Television: Technology and Cultural Form*. London: Routledge, 1974.
Wilz, Kelly. "Models of Democratic Deliberation: Pharmacodynamic Agonism in *The Daily Show*." In *The Daily Show and Rhetoric: Arguments, Issues, and Strategies*, edited by Trischa Goodnow, 77–92. Lanham, MD: Lexington Books, 2011.
Winstead, Lizz. *Lizz Free or Die: Essays*. New York: Riverhead Books, 2012.
Wise, David, and Paul R. Brewer. "News About News in a Presidential Primary Campaign: Press Metacoverage on Evening News, Political Talk, and Political Comedy Programs." *Atlantic Journal of Communication* 18, no. 3 (2010): 127–43.
Wisniewski, K. A. "It's All About the Meme: The Art of the Interview and the Insatiable Ego of the Colbert Bump." In *The Stewart/Colbert Effect: Essays on the Real Impact of Fake News*, edited by Amarnath Amarasingam, 164–80. Jefferson, NC: McFarland & Company, Inc., 2011.
Young, Dannagal Goldthwaite. *Irony and Outrage: The Polarized Landscape of Rage, Fear, and Laughter in the United States*. New York: Oxford University Press, 2020.

Index

Page references for figures are italicized

The ½ Hour News Hour, 190–91
9/11 terrorist attacks, 28, 114, 146, 149, 152, 158, 163, 164, 168, 178, 179; first responders' healthcare bill (Zadroga), 207–8
60 Minutes, 171, 210
1964 presidential election, 29–30, 36
1976 presidential election, 65–68, 70, 84n71
1980 presidential election, 56, 81, 116
1996 presidential election, 136
2000 presidential election, 140–44, 157, 177, 230
2004 presidential election, 176, 180
2008 presidential election, 145, 172, 176, 180, 190, 231, 252
2012 presidential election, 189
2016 presidential election, 199, 209, 226–28, 239–40
2020 presidential election, 228, 256

ABC (American Broadcasting Company), 16, 20, 35, 79, 80, 82n6, 92–93, 114, 118–19, 158, 241; news division, 60, 76, 102–3, 117, 157, 159, 220
abortion, 72, 213–14, 255–56

ACE awards, 90, 93
Adams, Val, 16
advertising, 5, 8, 16, 63, 78, 90, 92, 96, 97, 114, 125, 211, 213, 218, 228, 241; critiques of, 78, 117; native advertising, 225; political advertising, 7, 30, 206; power of, 15, 16, 27, 35–36, 38, 79–80
Afghanistan: Afghanistan War, 163, 178, 210, 215; Soviet invasion of, 69, 99–100
Agnew, Spiro, 55–56
al-Assad, Bashar, 215
Alda, Alan, 33, 36
Alexander, Keith, 211, 216
All in the Family, 47, 174
Altman, Rick, 104
Ames, Nancy, 17–20, *21*, 22, 27, 37, 243
Anderson, Christopher, 92
Aristotle, 147, 154, 186
AT&T, 213, 259
audiences. *See* news parody; names of individual television shows
Aurora, Colorado theater shooting, 168

Bachmann, Michele, 149, 169, 183
Bahktin, Mikhail, 7–8, 105

273

Bancroft, Anne, 39, 118
Barbur, Jonathan E., 147
Baron, Sandy, 33
Baudrillard, Jean, 185
Baumgartner, Jody C., 2
Baym, Geoffrey, 25, 171, 188, 190, 192
BBC (British Broadcasting Corporation), 14, 217
Bear Stearns, 187
Beaujon, Andrew, 223
Beck, Glenn, 183, 189, 201–3
Becker, Amy B., 148, 220
Bee, Samantha, 4, 10, 181, 200, 237–38, *240*, 242, 243, *257*. See also *Full Frontal with Samantha Bee*
Begala, Paul, 186
Belushi, John, 48, 52, 53, 76
Benghazi embassy attack, 162, 185
Benny, Jack, 149
Bergeron, Bill, 171
Berle, Milton, 149
Biden, Joe, 228, 253
Biko, Steven, 71
bin Laden, Osama, 183
Blankenship, Christina M., 237
Bloom, Anne, 95, *98*, 99, *103*, 106, 107, 109, 111, 243
Bode, Leticia, 220
Boler, Megan, 204
Boskin, Joseph, 64
The Boston Globe, 239
Bourdieu, Pierre, 3, 77, 251
Breen, Danny, *98*, 100, 101, *103*, 106
Brexit, 224
Brinkley, David, 24, 132
Brokaw, Tom, 144
Brown, A. Whitney, 128, 133, 135, 136, 139
Brown, Michael, 232, 255
Brown, Roscoe Lee, 33
Bruce, Lenny, 14, 31, 148
Bush, George H. W., 112–13
Bush, George W., 143, 145, 157, 163–64, 172, 174, 176–81, 196n87, 196n91, 230

Bush, George W. administration, 146–47, 149, 182, 253; and 9/11, 178, 179, 192n4; policies of, 179, 209
Butler, Jeremy, 50
Butz, Earl, 73

cable television, 3, 5, 8, 9, 35, 79, 81, 89–91, 93–95, 118, 119n3, 119n4, 125–27, 129, 133, 201, 219–20, 229, 259
Camillo, Alison, 241
campaign finance, 202, 206–7, 244n9
Caplin, Glen, 208
Carell, Steve, 141, 158
Carlin, George, 48
Carlson, Matt, 208
Carlson, Tucker, 186, 197n114, 226
carnivalesque humor, 7–8, 105
Carr, David, 214–15, 218
Carson, Johnny, 63, 67
Carter, Jimmy, 8, 65–71, 80, 81; family members of, 55, 68–69; *Playboy* interview, 68
Carvell, Tim, 211
Carver, M. Heather, 67, 70
Castagner, Marc-Olivier, 219
CBS (Columbia Broadcasting System), 13, 16–18, 35–36, 48, 79, 82n2, 109, 118, 120n10, 138, 199; news division, 19, 24–26, 39, 41n30, 42n34, 54, 75, 97, 128, 157, 210
celebrity culture, 127, 130, 134–35, 145
censorship, 36, 37, 59, 80, 114, 136, 224
Chase, Chevy, 50–51, *51*, 56–61, 63, 65–68, 82n16, 145, 230
Che, Michael, 10, 232–34, *233*, 236, 243, 258
Cheney, Dick, 146, 176, 253
The Chicago Sun-Times, 144
chromakey use, 52, 56, 142, 143, 192, 232
Chu, Judy, 205
class, 71, 72, 101, 106
Clinton, Bill, 136–37, 141, 160

Clinton, Hillary, 160, 162, 176, 190, 216, 227, 231, 235, 239, *240*
CNBC, 186–87, 253
CNN (Cable News Network), 91, 99, 100, 103, 106, 126, 137, 157, 158, 160, 186, 241
Colbert, Stephen, 6, 9–10, 60, 62, 139, 142, *166*, 190, 199, 223, 238, 252; Congressional appearances, 204–6; persona, 163–65, 170–73, 203; presidential run and Super PAC, 202, 206–7, 219, 244n9; White House Correspondents Dinner speech, 163–64, 179, 185, 193n24, 202. *See also The Colbert Report*; Rally to Restore Sanity/Fear
The Colbert Report, 9–10, 47, 79, 110, 117, 163–67, *166*, 171–80, 182–86, 188–89, 191–92, 199–202, 204–7, 242; audience, 164, 173–75, 192, 206, 207; comparison with other programs, 211, 229, 231; critique of journalism, 166, 182–89; irony and understanding, 174–75; learning from, 159, 207; presidential coverage, 176–80, 182–83; set design, 164–65; structure of, 164, 166; The Wørd segment, 165–66, 173
Colletta, Lisa, 174
The Columbia Review of Journalism, 184
Comcast, 220
Comedy Central, 9, 126–27, 129, 133, 135, 136, 138, 152. *See also The Colbert Report*; *The Daily Show* (original), *The Daily Show with Jon Stewart*; *The Daily Show with Trevor Noah*
Congress, 30, 31, 76, 94, 106, 109, 137, 162, 164, 175, 181, 185, 204–5, 208, 214
consensus culture, 14–15
conservative media, 2, 146, 148, 162, 168, 174, 175, 182–83, 188, 190, 225–26, 228, 252. *See also* Fox News
Cooper, Anderson, 144
Copeland, Gloria, 221
Corrin, George, 20
Cosell, Howard, 82n6
Coulter, Ann, 190
COVID, 256–59
Cramer, Jim, 187, 197n116, 253
Cronkite, Walter, 24, 25, 41n30, 60, 75
Crossfire, 141, 186, 197n112, 202
Cruz, Ted, 242
Curtin, Jane, 50–52, *53*, 55–57, 60–63, 68, 71–73, 75–78, 80, 84n56, 102, 106–7, 112, 145, 229, 230, 243

The Daily Show (original), 5, 9, 104, 125–38, *131*, 150, 151; correspondents, 128, 134–36; creation of, 126–28; critical reception, 132, 133; critique of journalism, 127–28, 134–37; interview segment, 130–31; presidential coverage, 136–38; research staff, 133–34; set design, 130; structure of, 129–30, 137; use of video and images, 131, 134, 137
The Daily Show with Jon Stewart, 2, 9, 18, 28, 34, 47, 79, 101, 104, 110, 138–49, *142*, 157–63, *160*, 167–70, 173, 176–89, 191–92, 197n110, 199–202, 207–10, 238, 242, 243, 254; and 9/11, 9, 158; audience, 144, 158, 159, 169, 180, 188, 192, 210; comparison with other news parody programs, 200, 211, 230, 231; correspondents, 142, 147–48, 181, 217, 232; critical reception, 144, 157–58; critique of journalism, 141, 169, 179, 181, 185–89, 209, 252–53; deconstruction of politics, 142–43, 162–63, 176, 253–54; graphics, 14, 160, 178; Indecision 2000, 141–44, *142*, 149; Jim Cramer, 187, 253; last episode, 209–10; partisanship,

accusations of, 143, 176, 179; presidential coverage, 157, 176–83; set design, 141, 159–60, 193n13; video footage, 160–63, 178, 180–81. *See also* Stewart, Jon

The Daily Show with Trevor Noah, 10, 234–37, *236*, 253, 256; audience, 234–37; COVID response, 257–58

Dateline, 127, 128

Davis, Murray S., 6, 31, 72, 105

Davis, Tom, 80

Davisson, Amber, 220

Day, Amber, 58, 71, 117, 160, 230, 241, 251

Debord, Guy, 201, 204

Decker, Kevin, 175

Democrats, 19, 30, 34, 36, 43n72, 176, 182, 190; national convention, 143, 180, 189

discourse, 3, 4, 6, 7, 16, 47, 64, 70, 71, 104, 105, 109, 112, 114, 134, 146, 147, 161, 163, 168, 177, 181, 186, 191, 202, 208, 251, 255

Dishy, Bob, 30

Dobbs, Lou, 164, 189

Dole, Bob, 140–43

Donovan, Mackenzie, 220

Doritos, 202

Doumanian, Jean, 115–16, 230

Downey, Jim, 150

Doyle-Murray, Brian, 58, 116

Dratch, Rachel, 221

drugs, 49, 64, 76, 151, 231, 252, 255

Du Brow, Rick, 16

Durst, Will, 113

Ebersol, Dick, 48–49, 80, 116

economic crisis, 146, 147, 186–87

Edmonds, Rick, 224

Edwards, Donna, 175

Edwards, Douglas, 24

Eisenhower, Dwight D., 23

El Salvador, 100, 106

Emanuel African Methodist Episcopal Church shooting, 209

Emmy awards, 133, 157

Englund, Pat, 31, *32*

Entertainment Tonight, 106

Esquire, 133, 138

The Esso Newsreel, 19

The Establishment, 41n12

European Union, 218

Fairness Doctrine, 37, 44n87

fake news, accusations of, 199, 253

Fallon, Jimmy, 230–32

Farnsworth, Stephen J., 240

Fauci, Anthony, 237

Federal Communication Commission (FCC), 15, 37, 79, 80, 219–21

Federal Election Commission (FEC), 206

Feibleman, James K., 5

feminism, 10, 111, 216, 231, 238, 239, 241–43. *See also* sexism

Feuer, Jane, 108

Fey, Tina, 230–31, 242

Financial Interest and Syndication Rules, 79

financial issues, 67, 72, 110, 132, 222

Fiske, John, 49, 104–5

Flanz, Jen, 235

Fleischer, Ari, 158, 192n4

Floyd, George, 236–37

Focus on the Family, 1, 253

Fonda, Henry, 25–26, 28, 31

Ford, Gerald, 6–8, 39, 47, 50, 65–70, 84n65, 109; appearance on *Saturday Night Live*, 66; pardon of Nixon, 65, 67

Foucault, Michel, 167–68, 175

Fox News, 129, 144, 157, 163, 164, 166, 169, 172, 184, 185, 188–89, 201, 208, 209, 226, 228, 253. *See also The O'Reilly Factor*; *The ½ Hour News Hour*

France, 117

Franco, Francisco, 64, 66, 71

Franken, Al, 53, 81, 148, 150

Fridays, 89, 92, 93, 95, 99, 114

Friedman, David, 94, 104
Friendly, Ed, 37
Frost, David, 14, 17, *21*, 23, 27, 29, 30, 33, 34, 39, 43n72, 112, 118–19
Fuchs, Michael, 92, 94, 107, 114
Full Frontal with Samantha Bee, 10, 234, 238–42, *240*, 253, 255–56, *257*; COVID response, 256–57; Ivanka Trump, 241–42; structure, 238–39

Gardner, Gerald, 18
gender issues, 1, 71, 231, 239, 243. *See also* sexism
genre, 3, 4, 6, 23, 49, 104, 171, 174, 210
Gettings, Michael, 147
Gibson, Charles, 179
Gilbert, Matthew, 239
Gingrich, Newt, 254
global warming, 167, 190
Goldwater, Barry, 18, 22, 28, 30, 37
Good Morning America, 76, 106, 130, 139, 141, 159
Goodnow, Trischa, 147
Gordon, Ruth, 69
Gore, Al, 140, 143, 177, 230
Gould, Jack, 16–18
Gray, Jonathan, 146, 169
Greene, Viveca S., 241
Grondin, David, 219
Gross, Mary, 116
Grover, Stanley, 33
Guest, Christopher, 116
Gulf War, 126, 127, 151
gun control, 146, 168–69
gun violence, 168–69, 172, 209
Guppy, Joe, 106
Gurwitch, Annabelle, 103–4, 108

Habermas, Jürgen, 147, 175
Hagel, Chuck, 164
Haiti, 233
Hall, Brad, 116
Hallin, Daniel, 255
Hannity, Sean, 169, 171–73
Hart, Roderick, 167

Hartelius, Johanna, 167
Hartley, John, 49, 192
Hartman, Phil, 112
hashtags, 209, 211, 216, 227, 239
Havlan, J. R., 139
Hayakawa, S. I., 72
Hayward, Leland, 16, 18, 24–25, 28, 29, 33, 35–38
HBO (Home Box Office), 5, 8–10, 89–90, 93–95, 102, 107, 113, 114, 120n10, 126, 210–11, 214, 224, 229, 259; branding, 92, 114; creation of, 91–92. *See also Last Week Tonight with John Oliver*; *Not Necessarily the News*
healthcare, 110, 135, 142, 208, 228, 240
Hendra, Tony, 69
Henry, Buck, 27, 31, 39
Henry, E. William, 15
Herzog, Doug, 126–28, 138
Hill, Doug, 59, 115
Hilmes, Michele, 56
Hokenson, Jan, 5
homophobia, 1, 55, 73–74, 116, 182, 190, 255
Hope, Bob, 67, 81
Hopper, Hedda, 44n81
Horner, William T., 67, 70, 84n71
Hoyt, Michael, 184
humor, as critique of culture, 5–6, 31–34, 48, 64, 105, 203
Huntley, Chet, 24
Hussein, Saddam, 146
Hutcheon, Linda, 7, 173

ideology, 14, 47, 108, 171, 177, 191
IFC (Independent Film Channel), 200
immigration, 27, 111, 190, 205–6, 209, 217–18, 235–36, 240–42, 253
infotainment, 63, 76, 105–6, 117, 127–28, 130, 133–34, 138, 151, 185, 225
InfoWars, 226, 228
insurrection, January 6, 253
Internet, 129, 133, 151, 161, 164, 192, 213, 216, 219–20, 235, 237, 252,

259; streaming video, 116, 126, 192, 200, 214, 229, 259; viral videos, 164, 186, 216, 219, 234
Iran, 69, 77, 112, 228
Iraq, 132, 137. *See also* Gulf War; Iraq War
Iraq War, 146, 152, 159, 163, 164, 177, 178, 182, 190, 215, 230
irony, 2, 6, 7, 9, 27, 31, 62, 77, 104, 107, 117, 128, 145, 147–49, 151, 164–67, 173–75, 179, 182, 183, 189, 200, 205, 207, 211, 216, 219, 237, 252, 254

Jameson, Fredric, 105
Jamison, Marshall, 17, 37
Javerbaum, David, 159
Jeffords, Susan, 109, 122n73
Jennings, Peter, 102–3
Jewish humor, 148–49
John, Elton, 74
Johnson, Lyndon B., 19, 28–30, 32
Jones, Jason, 181, 237–38, 257
Jones, Jeffrey P., 64, 161, 171, 177, 187, 188, 192
Jones, Leslie, 232
The Jon Stewart Show, 126, 139, 145
Jost, Colin, 10, 232–34, 258
journalism. *See* news media; newscasts
journalistic field, 3, 9, 47–48, 70, 77, 95, 125, 149, 174, 191, 209, 219, 223, 226, 251–52

Kahn, Miles, 238
Karlin, Ben, 140, 143, 159, 163, 176, 177
Katz, Eileen, 126, 127
Kavanaugh, Brett, 233
Kellner, Douglas, 204
Kelso, Tony, 92
Kennedy, John F., 22, 28, 32, 39, 42n38, 71, 100
Kennedy, Ted, 55, 56
Kenya, 182
Kercher, Stephen E., 14

Kerry, John, 180
Kilborn, Craig, 9, 128–33, 137–39, 145, 163. *See also The Daily Show* (original)
King, Steve, 205
Klepper, Jordan, 3
Kopache, Thomas, 228
Koppel, Ted, 116, 117
Kutner, Rob, 149

labor unions, 44n90, 143
Lafferty, Perry, 13
Last Week Tonight with John Oliver, 1, 10, 18, 34, 201, 210–29, *227*, 234, 252, 255, 256; AT&T, 213, 259; audience, 211, 215, 216, 219, 220; calls to action, 1, 215, 219; COVID response, 258; creation, 210–11; critical reception, 211, 214–15, 223, 224; critique of journalism, 225–26; international coverage, 218, 224; as journalism, 215, 223–25, 227, 229; net neutrality coverage, 219–21; And Now This segment, 214, 215, 225; Our Lady of Perpetual Exemption, 221–22; presidential coverage, 226–29; satiric activism, 219–23; set design, 212–13; structure of, 210, 212–16; use of video and graphics, 212–14
The Late, Late Show, 138
Late Night, 230, 232
The Late Show, 199
Lee, Pat Tourk, 93, 105, 107
Lehrer, Jim, 146
Lehrer, Tom, 14
Lewinsky, Monica, 136–38
LGBTQ+ issues. *See* homophobia
liberal humor, 2, 8, 28, 30, 34, 64, 70, 74, 108, 109, 116, 174, 188, 190, 225–26
Libya, 177, 185
Lichter, S. Robert, 240
Limbaugh, Rush, 148, 173, 190, 191
Lincoln, Abraham, 22, 207

Lippert, Leopold, 242
Lippmann, Walter, 184
Littleford, Beth, 128, 135–36, 139
Lohan, Lindsay, 231
Lombardo, Michael, 210
Lotz, Amanda, 35, 89

Macdonald, Norm, 150–51, 232
Mad Magazine, 14–15, 34
Mad Money, 187
Maher, Bill, 114, 158, 168, 192n4
Mair, George, 91, 94
Malcolm X, 23, 26
Mandvi, Aasif, 181, 254
Matviko, John, 63
McCain, Cindy, 141
McCain, John, 141, 142, 166, 172, 176, 179, 180, 192, 214, 254
McClennen, Sophia A., 205
McCurry, Mike, 136
McGeough, Ryan, 253
Meader, Vaughn, 42n38
Meadows, Audrey, 29
media conglomeration, 89, 113, 219–21, 224, 259
#MeToo movement, 240–41, 243
Meyers, Seth, 231, 232
Michaels, Lorne, 48–50, 58, 70–71, 79–81, 116, 126
Michaud-Wild, Nickie, 224–25
Middle East, 76, 80, 81, 101, 150, 186, 254
Miers, Harriet, 179
Milk, Harvey, 74
Miller, Dennis, 104, 116–17, 150, 190, 229
Miller, Jeffrey S., 37, 45n106
Miller, Jo, 238
Milne, Alasdair, 36
Miranda, Lin-Manuel, 215
Miss America Pageant, 223
Mittell, Jason, 104, 188
Moffitt, John, 92–95, 97, 99, 102, 107, 109, 112–14, 121n44

montage, 93, 97, 98, 101, 149, 161–63, 168, 178, 181, 185, 186, 188, 207, 214, 225, 239, 252
Morgan, Henry, 19, *21*, 26, 33
Morreale, Joanne, 186
Morris, Garrett, 52, 54–55, 71, 73
Morris, Jonathan S., 2
Morse, Margaret, 24
Mortensen, Viggo, 202
MSNBC, 129, 160, 163, 184
MTV (Music Television), 98, 104–5, 126, 139, 140
Mullen, Megan, 90–91, 119n3
multi-channel era of television, 5, 81, 89, 114, 117, 119
Murphy, Caryn, 61, 231
Murphy, Eddie, 116–18
Murray, Bill, 48, 51–52, *53*, 62–63, 71–73, 75–77, 102
Muskie, Edmund, 69
Muslims, 137, 149, 190, 254
Mystery Science Theater 3000, 126–27, 129

National Lampoon, 48, 69
NBC network (National Broadcasting Company), 5, 8, 15–18, 25, 30, 35–38, 40, 49, 56, 57, 74, 79–81, 89, 118, 127, 230; news division, 19, 24, 54, 144, 157. *See also Saturday Night Live*; *That Was the Week That Was*
Nealon, Kevin, 150
Neenan, Audrie, 100
Nessen, Ron, 66–67
Netanyahu, Benjamin, 149
net neutrality, 219–21
network era of television, 35, 38, 79, 80, 89
Newhart, Bob, 24
Newman, Laraine, 50–52, 56, 66, 69, 74
Newman, Phyllis, 17
news anchors, 20, 24–25, 27, 102–3, 121n46, 146; authority of, 24, 60,

132, 145; construction of audience, 26, 43n55; critiques of, 39, 63; retirement of first wave, 63, 75; specialty reporters, 76–77
newscasts, 4, 13, 20, 56, 57, 77, 132; 24-hour news, 99, 103, 126, 127, 159, 171, 181, 185; commercialization of, 76, 78, 105–6, 117, 127, 183–84, 191, 225; eyewitness style, 51–52; norms and conventions, 19–20, 127–28, 138, 251; soundbites, use of, 161, 253; visuals and newsfilm, 20, 23, 42n40, 54, 160, 161; writing style, 57, 75. *See also* infotainment
The News is the News, 39, 118
newsmagazine television format, 130, 210, 214, 217
news media, 3, 65; audience trust, 184; critiques of, 77, 202, 204, 251, 252; economics, 183; ethics, 77; news values, 161, 185; relationship with politicians, 164, 251. *See also* news anchors; newscasts; objectivity
news parody, 19, 70; audience, 2, 175, 190; critique of journalism, 2, 3, 47, 63, 75–79, 117–18, 127–28, 185–86, 252–56; cynicism, 2, 5, 8, 167; diversity, 33, 103, 200, 230, 232, 235, 238, 243; emphasis on political personalities over policy, 64, 109–10, 112–13, 176, 230; as genre, 4, 104; as journalism, 1, 144, 157, 224, 251; learning from, 159; and media corporations, 113, 191, 202, 219–20, 224; reliance on other media, 38–39, 64, 191, 224; young viewers, 2, 144, 159. *See also* names of individual television shows
The New York Times, 16, 23, 40n4, 67, 70, 93, 144, 165–66, 214, 218, 239
Nielsen ratings, 13, 16, 17, 24, 31, 37, 38, 49, 78, 79, 105, 106, 115, 191, 199, 231

Nixon, Richard M., 19, 22, 64, 65, 67, 70, 71
Noah, Trevor, 4, 10, 200, 209, 234–38, 243, 252, 256
Not Necessarily the News, 8–9, 56, 89–115, *98*, 119, 125, 150; 1989 reformat, 94, 101–2, 107, 112–13, 122n67; anchors, 97, 101–4; audience, 93, 102, 104, 107; comparison with other programs, 116, 161, 176, 213; critical reception, 93–94, 99, 115; *Not Necessarily the Media*, 103, *103*; pastiche and, 104–8, 110, 112, 113; and politics, 94–95; presidential coverage, 107–13; set design, 96–97; structure of, 95–99; use of video, 95, 99–101, 110, 112
Not the Nine O'Clock News, 93, 96
Novello, Don, 52

O'Connor, John, 67, 93–94, 99
O'Donnell, Steve, 108–9
O'Donoghue, Michael, 48
O'Neil, Chuck, 141
O'Neill, Tip, 100
O'Reilly, Bill, 9, 162, 163, 167, 171, 172, 182
The O'Reilly Factor, 162, 163, 165, 167, 171, 174
Obama, Barack, 145, 146, 149, 162, 166–68, 172, 173, 176–77, 180–83, 188, 189, 204, 219–20, 226, 235, 252, 254; administration, 181–82, 199, 201, 253; family, 185–86; optimism surrounding election, 175, 180–81
objectivity, 4, 36, 37, 77, 107, 224; critiques of, 4, 77, 184, 251, 255
Oliver, John, 10, 60, 148, 200, 201, 210, *227*, 229, 238, 240, 243, 252; Britishness, 217–19; denials of being a journalist, 223, 226; guest hosting *The Daily Show*, 199, 210; as immigrant, 217–18, 224; persona,

218. *See also Last Week Tonight with John Oliver*
Olsen, Lance, 5–6, 105
Olympic Games, 69
The Onion, 140, 158, 200
The Onion News Network, 200–201

Palin, Sarah, 180, 231–32, 234
Pankin, Stuart, 97, *98*, 100–3, *103*, 106–7, 110, 111, 145
Pardo, Don, 59, 61, 78
Parks, Tom, 101, 103–4, 108, 113
parody, 4, 7, 13–15, 48, 118, 119, 190–91; *The Colbert Report*, 163, 166, 167, 170, 171, 173, 183, 185, 192, 207; *The Daily Show* (original), 127–28, 130, 133–36, 138, 152; *The Daily Show with Jon Stewart*, 159, 173, 185; *Last Week Tonight with John Oliver*, 211, 212, 228; *Not Necessarily the News*, 97, 99, 102, 105, 108; *That Was the Week That Was*, 19–21, 24–26, 39–40; Weekend Update, 49, 51, 52, 55–60, 63, 75, 117
Paroske, Marcus, 207
parrhesia, 167–70, 219
Parsons, Patrick R., 91
participatory culture, 192, 215
partisanship, 2, 30, 143, 149, 171, 172, 175, 177, 179, 183, 184, 188, 189, 233, 239
pastiche, 104–8, 110, 112, 113
patriotism, 27, 111, 158, 165, 171, 172, 175, 178, 182, 212
PBS (Public Broadcasting Service), 146
Peabody awards, 157
Peifer, Jason, 208
Pelosi, Nancy, 190
Pence, Mike, 1
Pew Research Center, 2, 159, 176, 183, 220
Piscopo, Joe, 115–18
Placone, Ronald, 203
Playboy Magazine, 28, 68, 132

Poehler, Amy, 230–32, 242
police violence, 232, 236–37, 243, 253, 255
Politically Incorrect with Bill Maher, 126, 127, 129, 158. *See also* Maher, Bill
polling, 19, 29, 65–66, 77–78, 183, 188, 226
Postman, Neil, 2
postmodern humor, 5–6, 175
postmodern style, 26, 42n35, 78, 98, 104–5, 114–16, 167, 230
post-network era of television, 129, 159, 191–92, 211, 216, 221
Potter, Trevor, 206
Powers, Ron, 63
presidential campaigns. *See* individual entries by year and candidate names
profanity, 73, 114, 116, 146, 199, 213, 219, 241–42
Pryor, Richard, 48
public sphere, 147, 169, 175, 186, 202, 241, 253
Puerto Rico, 215

Quayle, Dan, 101, 112–13
Quinn, Colin, 151–52
Quintanilla, Karl, 187

race, 10, 15, 31–34, 44n81, 55–56, 73, 103, 166, 181, 232, 233, 236, 243, 253; Civil Rights Act, 22; Mississippi murders, 31, 44n79
racism, 29, 30, 33, 34, 71–73, 111, 174, 175, 182, 209, 236, 254
Radio-Television News Directors Association (RTNDA), 19–20, 39
Radner, Gilda, 48, 57; Emily Latella, 50, 51, 61, 77; Roseanne Roseannadanna, 52, 62, 76
Rally to Restore Sanity/Fear, 10, 203–4, 207, 219
Reagan, Nancy, 100–1, 109
Reagan, Ronald, 64, 69, 100, 101, 107–14, 117–19, 122n73, 123n89

Reich, Robert, 142
Reid, Elliot, 19, *21*, 29
Reilly, Ian, 204
religion, 31–32, 36, 71, 72, 77, 166–67, 254; prosperity gospel, 221–22
Republicans, 22, 28–30, 34, 36, 37, 43n72, 109, 166, 174, 176, 177, 208, 211, 227, 252; national conventions, 141–43, 189
rhetoric, 1, 14, 36, 111, 147, 163, 169, 180–84, 186, 189, 202, 206, 218, 219, 229, 240, 254
Richards, Renée, 74
Riggle, Rob, 178
Rocca, Mo, 141–42
Rocket, Charles, 58, 115–16
Rolling Stone, 113, 158
Romney, Mitt, 189
Rose, Margaret, 7
Rosen, Richard, 101–2
Rosewater, 199
Rove, Karl, 172, 179, 253–54
Rowan and Martin's Laugh In, 48, 49
Rowe, Mike, 128
Rumsfeld, Donald, 157

Sahl, Mort, 14
Sanders, Sarah Huckabee, 241
Sargent, Herb, 17, 24–25, 37, 39, 49, 118, 119
satire, 2, 6–10, 13, 15, 17, 18, 24, 48, 64, 74, 77, 104, 106–8, 110, 134, 152, 168, 173, 174, 179, 181, 183, 185, 190, 219, 222, 224, 230, 231, 251
satire, British, 14, 16, 40n3
Saturday Night Live, 5, 8, 39, 47–50, 56, 63–64, 79–80, 82n6, 86n133, 89, 92, 94, 102, 112, 115–18, 119n2, 121n44, 122n69, 126, 231; advertisers, 79–80; audience, 65, 70–71, 229; Buckwheat assassination, 117–18; COVID response, 258; creation of, 48–49; critical reception, 66, 67, 70, 115; Saturday Night News segment, 116; short films, 234; SNL NewsBreak segment, 116. *See also* Michaels, Lorne; Weekend Update
Scarborough, Joe, 239
Schudson, Michael, 77
Scott, Walter, 40
Seabrook, Andrea, 251
The Second City, 42n38
Second City Television (SCTV), 89, 118, 123n109
semiotics, 31, 165, 171, 180, 212–13
Sevareid, Eric, 75
sex, 14, 49, 59, 62, 64, 73, 80, 135, 137
sexism, 60–62, 72, 84n56, 104, 106–7, 138, 228, 230, 238–40
sexual assault, 190, 240–41
Shearer, Harry, 53
Sheehan, William, 76
Sherrin, Ned, 14
Short Attention Span Theater, 139
sick humor, 14, 31, 34, 41n7, 82n4
Silverman, Fred, 80–81
Simpson, O. J., 127, 128, 150–51
Simpson, Paul, 6
simulacra, 185
sketch comedy, 18, 19, 22, 28, 30, 33, 36, 39, 44n90, 48, 49, 56, 63, 64, 69, 73, 81, 90, 93, 95–96, 117–19, 190, 231, 234
Smithberg, Madeleine, 126–28, 131–33, 135–37, 140, 143, 144, 158, 159, 243
smoking, 17, 35–36, 55
The Smothers Brothers Comedy Hour, 48, 81, 82n2
sniglets, 90, 99, 119n2
social media, 5, 192, 211, 214, 216, 227, 229, 234, 237–39, 241, 243, 256
South Africa, 71, 111, 200, 234–36
South Park, 129
Soviet Union, 32, 66, 69, 70, 99–100, 109, 111, 151
spectacle, 171, 201–4
sponsorship. *See* advertising
Sportscenter, 127, 132

State of the Union address, 18, 29, 178
Stephens, Mitchell, 252
Stewart, Jon, 9–10, 27, 60, 125, 126, 128, 139–41, *142*, 151–52, 158–59, *160*, 164, 175, 190, 206, 207, 217, 223, 230, 234, 237, 239, 252; 9/11 first responders advocacy, 207–8; audience surrogate, 142–43, 146; chosen as *The Daily Show* host, 138–39; *Crossfire* appearance, 186, 197n112, 202; cynicism, accusations of, 167; Jewish identity, 148–49, 167, 218; leaving *The Daily Show*, 199–200; media critic, 144, 158, 168, 208, 252; parrhesiastes, 167–70, 219; persona, 145–48, 170, 203; sincerity, 145, 146, 167, 170, 203. *See also The Daily Show with Jon Stewart*; Rally to Restore Sanity/Fear
Storch, Larry, 26, 29
streaming video. *See* Internet
Strong, Cecily, 232
Supreme Court of the United States, 57, 72, 109, 140, 162, 177, 213, 233
Surnow, Joel, 190
Sykes, Wanda, 148
Syria, 215, 241

talk shows, late night, 4, 63, 199
Tally Jr., Robert, 185
TBS (Turner Broadcasting System), 10, 238, 239, 241, 242. *See also Full Frontal with Samantha Bee*
tea party, 161, 201, 202, 204
television industry: 1960s, 15, 34–35, 38, 44n94; 1980s, 108. *See also* cable television
Thatcher, Margaret, 93, 118
That Was the Week That Was (*TW3*), 8, 16–40, *21*, *32*, 42n47, 47, 48, 75–76, 86n134; 1985 ABC reboot, 118–19; advertisers, 35–36, 43n72; anchors, 24–27; audience, 17, 27, 35, 37; BBC show, 14–17, 27, 28, 35, 36, 38, 40n4, 43n60, 45n106; cancellation, 13, 18, 38; comparison with other programs, 50, 55, 59, 74, 79–80, 94, 100, 102, 104, 113–15, 119, 127, 130, 190; critical reception, 16–18; NBC interference, 36–38; pilot episode, 16, 25–26, 28; presidential coverage, 27–31; second season, 26–27, 29–30, 37–38; set design, 20–21; structure of, 18–19; use of photos & video, 3, 19, 21–23; viewer mail, 17, 18, 27, 30, 31, 33, 35
That Was the Year That Was, 118
This Hour Has Seven Days, 15, 38
Thompson, Ethan, 14, 15, 58, 71, 117, 230
Thurston, Baratunde, 235
Tiananmen Square, 108, 113, 122n69
Tilton, Robert, 221, 222
Time, 144
Time-Warner, 113, 259
TMZ, 213
The Tonight Show, 49, 130, 230
Tookes, LaKendra, 232
torture, 148, 179, 182, 215–16
trolling, 220–21
Trump, Donald, 2, 4, 10, 182, 209, 216, 218, 226–29, 233, 235–37, 239–40, 256; administration, 220, 241, 253
Trump, Ivanka, 241–42
truthiness, 172, 175, 180, 184, 188, 196n91
Tucker, Ken, 230
Tumolo, Michael, 203
TV Guide, 36

Ulrich, Anne, 216
Unger, Brian, 128, 134–35, 138, 139
United Farm Workers (UFW), 204–6
United Kingdom, 218, 224
United States military, 1, 34, 71, 94, 110, 178, 182, 190, 226, 228, 255

Vanity Fair, 238
Variety, 15–17, 29, 34–35, 37, 52, 66, 115, 118

variety show format, 18, 39, 82n12, 118
Viacom, 126, 191, 202, 258
Vietnam War, 15, 29, 31, 34, 39, 47, 48, 54, 65, 71, 126, 151, 255
viral videos. *See* internet

Waisanen, Don J., 224, 254
Wallace, Chris, 185
Wallace, George, 72–73
Walls, Nancy, 141
Walters, Barbara, 60
Warfield, Marsha, 103
Warner Bros. Discovery, 259
The Washington Post, 16, 38, 228
Watergate scandal, 8, 39, 47, 49, 65, 109
Webb, Lucy, *98*, 101, 102, *103*, 110, 243
Weekend Update segment, 5, 6, 8, 10, 25, 39, 47, 49–81, *51*, *53*, 115–19, 125, 131, 150–52, 200, 229–34, *233*; anchors, 58–63, 115–17, 150, 230–33; comparisons with other programs, 95, 96, 101–4, 106, 115, 127, 130, 160, 176, 230, 256; COVID response, 258; creation of the segment, 49–50; critique of television news, 75–79; political critique, 70–73, 231; presidential coverage, 63–70, 230, 233; set design, 50–54, 232–33; social critique, 73–74; structure of, 50–52, 234; use of photos and video, 54–56, 68. *See also Saturday Night Live*
Weingrad, Jeff, 59, 115
Weinstein, Harvey. *See* #MeToo movement
Wells, Claudette, 103, *103*
Westmoreland, William, 71
What's Going On Here?, 15
Wheeler, Tom, 220
Whelan, Richard, 70
White House Correspondents Dinner, 148, 163–64, 179, 185, 193n24, 202
Williams, Brian, 25, 144
Williams, Raymond, 114, 213
Wilz, Kelly, 170
Winfrey, Oprah, 222
Winstead, Lizz, 126–28, 131, 133, 134, 137–39, 243
Winters, Jonathan, 24
wire services, 21–22, 54, 55, 99–100, 131, 133, 161
Wisniewski, K. A., 175
women's health, 240, 255, 256

Young, Dannagal Goldthwaite, 2, 188, 190
YouTube, 21, 164, 211, 214, 220, 227, 229, 231, 234, 237, 242

Zamata, Sasheer, 232
Zimbabwe, 69
Zweibel, Alan, 49

About the Author

Curt Hersey is an associate professor of Communication at Berry College in Rome, Georgia. His research interests and publications focus on television news parody and the representation of addiction in media.

www.ingramcontent.com/pod-product-compliance
Lightning Source LLC
Chambersburg PA
CBHW020111010526
44115CB00008B/785